WHAT THE *GOD-S...*
FOUND IN NIETZ...

THE RECEPTION OF NIE...
ÜBERMENSCH BY THE PHILOSOPHERS
OF THE RUSSIAN RELIGIOUS RENAISSANCE

Studies in Slavic Literature and Poetics

Volume L

Edited by

J.J. van Baak
R. Grübel
A.G.F. van Holk
W.G. Weststeijn

WHAT THE *GOD-SEEKERS* FOUND IN NIETZSCHE

THE RECEPTION OF NIETZSCHE'S *ÜBERMENSCH* BY THE PHILOSOPHERS OF THE RUSSIAN RELIGIOUS RENAISSANCE

Nel Grillaert

Amsterdam - New York, NY 2008

Cover design: Aart Jan Bergshoeff

The paper on which this book is printed meets the requirements of "ISO 9706:1994, Information and documentation - Paper for documents - Requirements for permanence".

ISBN-13: 978-90-420-2480-9
©Editions Rodopi B.V., Amsterdam - New York, NY 2008
Printed in the Netherlands

Contents

Acknowledgements   ix

Chapter 1 Introduction   1
1.   Much ado about Nietzsche   1
2.   The Nietzschean turn of the century   3
3.   Definition of the problem and approach   7
4.   General methodological framework   8
5.   Structure of the book   12
6.   Who were the God-seekers?   14
7.   Note on references, translation and transliteration   17

Chapter 2 The Russian discovery of Nietzsche   19
1.   How the German philosopher set foot on Russian soil   19
2.   The first responses   24
3.   The flexible Nietzsche   35
     3.1. The aesthetic Nietzsche   35
     3.2. The religious Nietzsche   36
     3.3. The political Nietzsche   37
4.   Looking for Nietzsche, finding Dostoevskii   37
5.   Conclusion   48

Chapter 3 Dostoevskii's philosophical anthropology   51
1.   Introduction   51
2.   An ongoing dialogue with God   51
3.   Dostoevskii's Christology   54
4.   From 'legend' to anthropological 'truth'   65
     4.1. The ontological status of the human being   66
     4.2. Being what one is   67
     4.3. Becoming what one is   69
     4.4. The anthropology of freedom   71
5.   Conclusion   76

Chapter 4 "Isn't the unfortunate Nietzsche right?":
Vladimir Solov'ëv's response to Nietzsche   79
  1.   Introduction   79
  2.   The initial response to Nietzsche: merit nor danger 82
  3.   Solov'ëv's *sverkhchelovek*: renaming Christ   85
  4.   Nietzsche's *Übermensch*: defying Christ   90
  5.   Conclusion   104

Chapter 5 "Only the word order has changed":
Bogochelovek and *chelovekobog*   107
  1.   Introduction   107
  2.   Bogochelovek   108
  3.   Prehistory of the *chelovekobog*   109
      3.1. Nikolai Speshnev's coining of the term   109
      3.2. Dostoevskii's Mephistopheles   112
      3.3. Fictionalizing the demon   114
  4.   Kirillov's "most great idea"   114
  5.   Ivan's 'anthropological' upheaval   124
  6.   The Roman "ant-hill"   129
  7.   Conclusion   136

Chapter 6 Supplementing Christ:
Dmitrii Merezhkovskii's use of Nietzsche's *Übermensch*   139
  1.   Introduction   139
  2.   A transitional figure in Russian culture   141
  3.   The versatility of Nietzsche's thought in Merezhkovskii's
      intellectual development   145
  4.   Merezhkovskii's diagnosis: the vices of historical
      Christianity   147
  5.   Merezhkovskii's cure: the identification of
      Übermensch and *chelovekobog*   150
  6.   Merezhkovskii's new religious consciousness as a
      way out   159
  7.   Merezhkovskii's quotation of Nietzsche:
      reconstructing Nietzsche's tracks   167
  8.   The vicissitudes of Dostoevskii and Nietzsche   177
      8.1. Towards an affirmative assessment of Nietzsche 178
      8.2. Towards a new reading of Dostoevskii   183
  9.   The vicissitudes of Merezhkovskii's paradigm   188

	9.1. Akim Volynskii: *Tsarstvo Karamazovykh*	188
	9.2. Sergei Bulgakov: "Ivan Karamazov kak filosofskii tip"	195
	9.3. The Nietzsche boom in Dostoevskii criticism	197
	9.4. The further functioning of *chelovekobog* and *Übermensch*	201
10.	Conclusion	203

Chapter 7 Free from God, free within God:
Nikolai Berdiaev's use of Nietzsche's *Übermensch*   207
1.	Introduction	207
2.	Berdiaev's background	208
3.	The fruitful Nietzsche	212
4.	"Idealizing" Nietzsche: the immoralist rethought	215
5.	The Antichrist remodelled: proselytizing a new Christianity	217
6.	Re-Christianizing the *Übermensch*	221
7.	What Dostoevskii knew: moral freedom *versus* moral freedom	227
8.	What Solov'ëv and Merezhkovskii failed to know: the other *Übermensch*	233
	8.1. The antidote to Solov'ëv's "Antichrist"	233
	8.2. Re-modelling Merezhkovskii's paradigm	236
9.	Berdiaev's quotation of Nietzsche: reconstructing Nietzsche's tracks	237
10.	Conclusion	247

Chapter 8 Conclusion   249

Bibliography   261

Index   279

Acknowledgements

Many people have supported this book, which is based on the dissertation for which I was awarded my PhD. I am deeply indebted to Benjamin Biebuyck, my PhD supervisor and mentor at Ghent University. He gave me a most inspirational insight in the rich thought of Friedrich Nietzsche, enthusiastically followed me in my quest for the God-seekers' assessment of the German philosopher and provided me with original perspectives in this complex matter. I feel very grateful for his constant encouragement, his eagerness to read, re-read and comment on my texts and for his active engagement in my work. Cooperating with him was, and still is, a most pleasant and unique experience. I want to acknowledge Thomas Langerak, who shared with me his expertise in Russian literature and read and commented on my dissertation. I would also like to thank Bernice Glatzer Rosenthal and Evert van der Zweerde for reading and evaluating an earlier version of this manuscript and giving very helpful comments and suggestions. I am also very grateful to Danny Praet for his active belief in my research, continuous support and thought-provoking conversations.

I want to thank the Special Research Fund of Ghent University (BOF) and the Research Foundation - Flanders (FWO) for providing me the financial support to pursue my research for this book.

I feel grateful to my colleagues of the German Department of Ghent University, who created a very congenial atmosphere to work in and whose lively interest in my research was a great support in the making of this book. A warm thanks also to the colleagues of the Department of Slavonic and East-European Studies and the Department of Philosophy at Ghent University. Special thanks are in order to Frederic Lamsens, Greet Pauwelijn, Marjolein De Wilde and Carol Richards, who put a great effort in proofreading my manuscript.

I would also like to express my deep gratitude to my parents and brother for their unconditional love and acceptance of my absorption in my work. They stand side by side with me on all the roads I take in my life and their significance for my development cannot be captured in words. I thank all my friends for being there. The final word is dedicated to Tim, whose unremitting encouragement, humour and stimulating conversations are an invaluable source of inspiration.

Earlier versions of parts of this book have appeared elsewhere in academic journals. I therefore thank the publishers of *Studies in East European Thought, Dostoevsky Studies* and *Slavica Gandensia* for granting me the permission to use this material. Full references are given in the Bibliography.

Chapter 1

Introduction

Tell me what you need, and I will supply you with a Nietzsche citation (Kurt Tucholsky, quoted in Aschheim 1992: 274).

Dostoevskii knew everything that Nietzsche knew (Berdiaev [1923] 1991: 54).

1. Much ado about Nietzsche

At the end of the nineteenth and the beginning of the twentieth century, a considerable part of the Russian intelligentsia became acquainted with the works and thoughts of Friedrich Nietzsche, which for many of them were a significant source of inspiration and an incentive for further reflection. Nietzsche's ideas appealed to writers, artists, political radicals, and philosophers alike, who all, each in their own way, found in them some answers to their respective intellectual and spiritual quests.

Nietzsche's thought permeated *fin de siècle* Russia at a time when national consciousness was suffering an impasse. Late imperial Russia experienced a process of rapid modernization, war and social turmoil which plunged the country into a state of social breakdown. Philosophically and culturally, the nihilism of the 1860s and the populism of the 1870s had lost their glitter for a new generation of intellectuals and artists. Faced with the decline of contemporary mentality, these newcomers were in search of fresh and innovative inspirations to revitalize Russia's languishing identity. Nietzsche, by then already lingering in mental darkness, became a transnational, still highly prolific, muse for Russia's cultural and philosophical rebirth in the Silver Age. To quote one of its most energetic trailblazers, "Nietzsche's influence was fundamental in the Russian renaissance of the beginning of the century" (Berdiaev [1946] 1997: 194).

From the mid-1890s onwards, Nietzsche had a substantial impact on the emergence and flowering of Russian symbolism. The populist idea that art should contribute to the moral uplifting of the people had lost its attraction for the new generation of writers and artists. In search of an aesthetics that posits pure beauty and the individual's creativity at the core of the artistic experience, they found in Nietzsche the fundament for their new aesthetic creed. The key text for these symbolists was *The Birth of Tragedy* (1872), which offered them the required discourse to spell out new aesthetic theories that reinstall both individualism and the celebration of earthly joys in artistic consciousness.

Around 1905, as a result of the failed revolution and the consequential social unrest, attention moved to social and political issues. By then, Nietzsche was appropriated by some Marxist-inspired ideologues as they aimed to create a new proletarian culture. His ideas stirred these "Nietzschean" Marxists to delineate the ideology of *Bogostroitel'stvo* (*God-building*). The *God-builders* emphasized the Dionysian principle of transcendence of the individual and assimilation into a collective whole. Prompted by the anthropology of the *Übermensch*, they aspired to construct a secular religion that would exalt the humans' strength and potential as well as call for self-sacrifice for the sake of a collective goal.[1]

---

[1] Nietzsche's impact on the Russian symbolists and the Nietzschean Marxists is a fairly well-investigated line of research. See B.G. Rosenthal (ed.), 1986, *Nietzsche in Russia*, Princeton: Princeton University Press; B.G. Rosenthal (ed.)., 1994a, *Nietzsche and Soviet Culture. Ally and Adversary*, Cambridge: Cambridge University Press; B.G. Rosenthal, 2002, *New Myth, New World. From Nietzsche to Stalinism*, Pennsylvania: The Pennsylvania State University Press; E.W. Clowes, 1988, *The Revolution of Moral Consciousness. Nietzsche in Russian Literature, 1890-1914*, Dekalb, Illinois: Northern Illinois University Press; M. Deppermann, 1998, "Nietzsche in der Sowjetunion. Den begrabenen Nietzsche ausgraben", in *Nietzsche-Studien*, Bd.27: 481-514; G. Kline, 1968 "Nietzschean Marxism in Russia", in: *Boston College Studies in Philosophy* 2: 166-183; N.V. Motroshilova & Iu. V. Sineokaia (eds.), 1999, *Fridrikh Nitsshe i filosofiia v Rossii*, Sbornik statei, Sankt-Peterburg: Izdatel'stvo Russkogo Khristianskogo Gumanitarnogo Instituta.

Intriguingly, Nietzsche, the self-christened "Antichrist," was around the turn of the last century also enthusiastically received by some religious philosophers, the so-called *Bogoiskateli* or *God-seekers*, to whom he seemed to reveal a vivid sense of religiosity. The unlocking of religious motives in Nietzsche's thought was a general characteristic of the Russian response to him. In Berdiaev's account, the Russian readers did not find in Nietzsche "what was mostly written about him in the West, not his proximity to biological philosophy, not the struggle for an aristocratic race and culture, not the will to power, but the religious theme. Nietzsche was received as a mystic and prophet" (Berdiaev [1946] 1997: 199). The mysticism and religiosity excavated in Nietzsche was typically drawn from his idea of the *Übermensch*; this concept, out of all Nietzsche's 'untimely meditations', held the most fascination for the *God-seekers* and the majority of his Russian readers. Viacheslav Ivanov, for example, uncovered in the *Übermensch* Nietzsche's intuition for the mystical; he traced the idea back to the Dionysian urge to transcend the self and merge with the godhead. The idea of the *Übermensch* was perceived as a religious-metaphysical concept, and as such, played a productive and pivotal role in the rich ferment of Russian religious philosophy at the beginning of the twentieth century. This obviously raises the question of what exactly did the *God-seekers* find in a thinker, whose philosophical motives were so different from and even antagonistic to their own, and how they managed to harmonize Nietzsche's unfamiliar thought with the Russian cultural and religious context? As it turns out, while the *God-seekers* were in the process of fathoming Nietzsche's thoughts, they drew considerably on a well-known and typically Russian source: Nietzsche was substantially read through the scope of Fëdor Mikhailovich Dostoevskii.

2. The Nietzschean turn of the century

Nietzsche struck his first Russian readers – and Russian and Western generations to come[2] – with what they experienced as an intriguing

---

[2] In Russian and Western twentieth-century criticism, Nietzsche and Dostoevskii are frequently juxtaposed. See, amongst others, Andler, 1930, "Nietzsche et Dostoievsky"; Ghuys, 1962, "Dostoievski et Nietzsche, le tragique de l'homme souterrain"; Strakosch, 1963, "Nietzsche and Dostoevsky"; de Schloezer, 1964,

similarity of his thoughts to the various philosophical and psychological ponderings in Dostoevskii's fiction. The German philosopher was primarily linked to Dostoevskii's so-called nihilistic characters, an association largely mediated by his idea of the *Übermensch*.[3] During the reception process, the juxtaposition of Nietzsche and his *Übermensch* on the one side, and of Dostoevskii and his nihilists on the other, gradually evolved, a development that went hand in hand with some significant changes in the assessment of both Nietzsche and Dostoevskii.

In the first critical articles on Nietzsche, his ideas are frequently refracted through a Dostoevskian prism. In studies on Dostoevskii in that same period, conversely, there is hardly any reference to Nietzsche, and even then only marginally. To summarize, during the first years of Nietzsche's reception in Russia, he is explained in terms of Dostoevskii. From 1900 on, however, Nietzsche is repeatedly referred to in the critical literature on Dostoevskii whenever the latter's nihilistic characters are in the spotlight. This reciprocity culminates in 1902-03 in four studies that explicitly juxtapose Dostoevskii and Nietzsche. Consequently, from 1900 on, there is a fruitful interplay between their respective intellectual legacies wherein both equally serve as exegetic models for one another. Nietzsche is no longer one-sidedly interpreted in terms of Dostoevskii, Dostoevskii is also substantially explained through a Nietzschean lens.

Furthermore, in critical literature before 1900, Nietzsche is mostly linked to the characters Raskol'nikov and Ivan Karamazov. More specifically, his concept of the *Übermensch* is equated with Raskol'nikov's anthropological category of the "extraordinary" and

---

"Nietzsche et Dostoievski"; Fridlender, 1979, "Dostoevskii i F. Nitsshe"; Davydov, 1981, "Dva ponimaniia nigilizma (Dostoevskii i Nitsshe)"; Uhl, 1981, "Leiden an Gott und Mensch: Nietzsche und Dostojewski"; Woolfolk, 1989, "The two switchmen of nihilism: Dostoevsky and Nietzsche"; Ignatov, 1993, "Chërt i sverkhchelovek. Predchuvstvie totalitarizma Dostoevskim i Nitsshe"; Dudkin, 1994, *Dostoevskii-Nitsshe (Problema cheloveka)*.

[3] Note that in this chain of association no distinction seems to be made between the narrative voice within the fictional reality displayed in the novel (the nihilists') and the concrete author's voice (Dostoevskii's). This, from a contemporary academic point of view, problematical way of reading, also applies to Nietzsche, who is systematically identified with all articulations in his highly metaphorized and allegorized oeuvre.

with Ivan Karamazov's moral creed that "all is permitted." After 1900, it are rather Kirillov and Ivan's devil that figure in the commentaries on and explanations of the *Übermensch*, based on a declared identification of the anthropological model that both put forward, i.e. the *chelovekobog* or man-god.

In turn, the established connection between *Übermensch* and *chelovekobog* marks a momentous change in Dostoevskii criticism: until 1900 this concept went unnoticed. Moreover, the approach to Ivan Karamazov slightly changes as emphasis shifts from his theory that all is permitted to the devil's speech and thereby back to the *chelovekobog*.

This effects a qualitative change in the reading of Dostoevskii and in the perception of him as an ethical authority. In critical literature before 1900, Dostoevskii is chiefly considered a social critic, whose writings champion and support Russian autocracy and Orthodoxy. Accordingly, the so-called nihilistic characters are considered to express an ideology that rivals, and perhaps even contradicts, the author's personal beliefs. After 1900, they are viewed as significant voices in Dostoevskii's own deliberation process, at least as far as religion is concerned.

Finally, and most importantly for our purposes, from 1900 onwards, there is an apparent shift of emphasis in the assessment of Nietzsche too. In the first decade of the reception process, the main tenor of the responses to the German philosopher is one of dismissal. Except for some attempts to give an unbiased overview of Nietzsche's ideas, most papers offer an unfavorable evaluation of Nietzsche. The main point of critique is that Nietzsche promotes subversive views on traditional morality and Christianity; therefore he must be banned from the Russian public. Moreover, by the end of the 1890s, partly due to Vladimir Solov'ëv's response, Nietzsche, and more particularly his anthropology of the *Übermensch*, become increasingly identified with the figure of the Antichrist.[4] This epithet obviously contributes to his reputation as a rigid atheist and fosters anxiety over the possible

---

[4] Ironically, Nietzsche is partly responsible himself for this mythological self-characterization. He had given his last philosophical work the provocative title *The Antichrist* (1888, not published until 1895) and from December 1888 onwards, signed some letters with "the Antichrist" (KSB 8: 504; 544; 551). Furthermore, the first book he sent to a Russian intellectual, Princess Anna Dmitrievna Tenisheva, was signed as "the Antichrist".

threat he might pose *vis-à-vis* Russian religious consciousness. After 1900, however, the responses to Nietzsche are decisively more positive. Remarkably, the sympathetic evaluation of the previously labeled "Antichrist" comes about where Christianity is concerned. In 1902, for example, Semën Frank claims that Nietzsche, in his analysis of contemporary ethics, is in fact a brilliant moral philosopher, and that "the moral teaching of Zarathustra [...] is the first gospel written for creative people" (Frank [1902] 2001: 596). Half a century later, he still values Nietzsche for "positing the problem of religion anew" (Frank 1956: 28). Similarly, Andrei Belyi asserts that Nietzsche "opened up a new era" and that "one can compare Nietzsche with Christ" (Belyi [1908] 2001: 879; 886). For Viacheslav Ivanov, Nietzsche's highlighting of the Dionysian is an incentive to return to the religious roots of Dionysus and to draw up a new Dionysian-Christian mythopoem (Biebuyck & Grillaert 2003). From then on, these thinkers all attributed a Christian ethos to Nietzsche's thoughts; however, each did this in his own particular way and to different degrees. Despite this lack of uniformity in the ways they used Nietzsche's ideas, one thing was consistent: during this time, Nietzsche was experienced as a constructive stimulus to supplement and even amend contemporary Christian consciousness.

The shift to an affirmative understanding of Nietzsche is chiefly initiated through a new interpretation of his anthropology of the *Übermensch*. Whereas the religious intellectuals in the first years of the reception process observed in this concept the incarnate rejection of Christian values, the new generation of religious thinkers received this anthropological model as a catalyst for religious renewal. After 1900, a fruitful religious debate on the *Übermensch* starts. Berdiaev, for example, highlights it as an archetypal "religious-metaphysical idea" (Berdiaev 1902: 124). For Frank, the appearance of the *Übermensch* on earth is the moral goal of humanity (Frank [1902] 2001: 627). Evgenii Trubetskoi finds in it the hallmark of human self-deification: "the One God should be replaced by a multitude of human gods." This is the new goal for humanity:

> The new goal for the human can only be a new human, in more precise wording, a new trans-human type. The *Übermensch* becomes for us the highest goal, he fills for us not only the human world, yet "the whole earth" with meaning [...] our whole life should be accommodated to this goal (Trubetskoi [1903] 2001: 775).

Viacheslav Ivanov avows that the *Übermensch* is "possessed by the [Dionysian] god" (Ivanov 1971-1987 I: 723). He sees in this concept a being whose qualities are primarily "universal and even religious," and integrates it in his neo-Christian interpretation of the "trans-personal" (*sverkhlichnoe*) experience through which the individual human re-emerges with God and collective humanity (id.: 837). Znamenskii defines Nietzsche's concept as a "moral ideal":

> The personality, which is full of inner spiritual strength, and raised on the path of self-determination, thirsts for a positive good. Much more life, movement, intensive creation in the field of practical moral activity, this is what Nietzsche calls for in his teaching of the *Übermensch* (Znamenskii [1909] 2001: 936f.).

Belyi identifies in the *Übermensch* "the icon of the New Human" (*obraz Novogo Cheloveka*), an observation that directs him towards a juxtaposition of Christ's and Nietzsche's teachings (Belyi [1908] 2001: 902).

3. Definition of the problem and approach

The goal of this study is to describe and explain the *God-seekers'* fascination for Nietzsche in general and for his anthropology of the *Übermensch* in particular. In what way is their favorable appropriation of Nietzsche different from the assessment by the previous generation of religious thinkers, whose response to the German philosopher was utterly dismissive? And how can we understand that Nietzsche, who is traditionally received as an atheist thinker, is such a prolific source of inspiration for these philosophers' reconsideration of Christianity and formulation of their "new religious consciousness" (*novoe religioznoe soznanie*)? For them, Nietzsche's body of thought does not merely serve as a philosophical counter-model against which they antagonistically pose and defend their own views. Rather, in their case, the question is: what have they drawn from Nietzsche? Or, what did the *God-Seekers* find in Nietzsche?

The anomaly of the *God-seekers'* enthusiastic reading of Nietzsche will be dissected and explained by means of the assumed dialectics between Dostoevskii and Nietzsche. Elsewhere I have argued that if one digs into a close and contemporary scientific reading of Dostoevskii's and Nietzsche's texts, the recurrent association between them is at least a problematical one.[5] In this study, I depart from this *perceived* connection, yet not with the purpose to advance any claim with regards to the correctness or falsity of it. Rather, the established connection between them functions as one of the anomalies to be solved. So, instead of taking a 'top-down' approach, in which I would firstly develop and defend specific interpretations of Nietzsche's *Übermensch* and Dostoevskii's nihilists and subsequently investigate to what extent these interpretations can or cannot warrant a match, I adopt here a 'bottom-up' approach, in which I restrict myself to finding out *why* this match was suggested, and refrain, as much as possible, from judging on its legitimacy. The various and altering juxtapositions of Dostoevskii and Nietzsche fulfill an important heuristic function: by capturing the dynamics of the reception process of Nietzsche's *Übermensch* in relation to Dostoevskii's nihilists, we can trace the historical trajectory of Nietzsche's, and as a bonus, of Dostoevskii's thought, as it figured among the religious thinkers of the Silver Age.

In this study, I identify and examine three seminal figures in the Russian process of reading Nietzsche religiously: Vladimir Solov'ëv (1853-1900), Dmitrii Merezhkovskii (1865-1941) and Nikolai Berdiaev (1874-1948). These prominent thinkers in Russian history of ideas did not a priori brush aside Nietzsche's thought, as did many others, but rather chose to struggle with it in order to attach, each in his own way, a positive meaning to it. As I will argue, all three of them are 'landmarks' in the religious appropriation of Nietzsche's *Übermensch*, and in the related connection with Dostoevskii's nihilists.

4. General methodological framework

Methodologically, this study builds on *history of ideas* and *reception aesthetics*. In spite of several tensions between both approaches (Thompson 1993), I take them to be complementary and use them

---

[5] In my MA-thesis (Grillaert 1998) I used as my starting point the frequent link in twentieth-century criticism between the character Raskol'nikov and Nietzsche's *Übermensch*. On the basis of an in depth analysis of Raskol'nikov's discourse and Nietzsche's *Thus spoke Zarathustra*, I disclaimed the alleged identification of them.

simultaneously for an in-depth coverage of the dynamics of the reception process.

Anglo-Saxon literary critics tend to associate the very idea of the *history of ideas* with Arthur Lovejoy (1873-1962). Lovejoy famously developed, defended and exemplified his approach in *The Great Chain of Being: a Study in the History of an Idea*, delivered in 1933 as the William James Lectures at Harvard University. His preferred analogy to the natural sciences is that of an analytical chemist: the Lovejovian historian should describe how "the great ideas" developed, mutated, combined, recombined and coursed from century to century. Here, the fundamental methodological assumption is that the historian can break all the larger systems and -isms into its constitutive elements, the so-called *unit-ideas*. Whereas more complex conceptions and doctrines are typically unstable, Lovejoy clearly implies that the unit-ideas are finite in number and persistent through time. Since these unit-ideas, as Louis O. Mink (1968, quoted in Macksey 1994: 391) notes, "cannot be said to have a history at all", Lovejoy refrains from calling them "original"; instead, "most philosophical systems are original or distinctive rather in their patterns than in their components" (Lovejoy 1933: 3).

Lovejoy's "ideas" were quite influential in the United States and in Britain. However, in the francophone world and in Germany, intellectual or conceptual history developed along quite different tracks, ranging from Gaston Bachelard's "elemental" studies of literary imagery to Meinecke's *Ideengeschichte*. Although Michel Foucault was tireless in his attacks on the history of ideas, culminating in *The Archaeology of Knowledge* (1969),[6] Macksey argues that there remain certain similarities between the methodologies of Foucault and Lovejoy, such as their commitment to a cross-disciplinary approach and their anti-formalist approach to texts (1994: 391-392).

However, for my purposes, the internal criticism and, more specifically, the objections raised against Lovejoy's anatomizing

---

[6] In *The Archaeology of Knowledge* (*L'archéologie du savoir*), Foucault argues that his approach is superior to Lovejovian history of ideas in three respects. Firstly, "archaeology" does not make a distinction between old and new, or between banality and originality (1969: 184-188). Secondly, it "respects" the contradictions within a "discursive formation" and documents its effects, rather than aiming to remove and dissolve such contradictions by means of rational reconstruction (1969: 197). And thirdly, it doesn't restrict itself to a particular theory, ideology or discipline, but is always comparative (1969: 205).

procedures are more instructive. An intriguing example is Leo Spitzer's "synthetic" version of *Geistesgeschichte*, which allows the historian to comprehend the *Begriffsfeld*, i.e. the "totality of features of a given period or movement" seen "as a unity" (1944, quoted in Macksey 1994: 391). Spitzer rigorously argued against Lovejoy's conception of a unit-idea, which is mistakenly assumed to be detachable from "the spiritual climate" in which it was embedded. Maurice Mandelbaum (1965), who saw a distinction between *continuing ideas* on the one hand and *recurrent ideas* on the other, has also proposed a useful modification or rather refinement of Lovejoy's unit-ideas.

I agree with the criticisms on Lovejoy's conception of "unit-ideas" and the associated analytical procedures. However, I should at least credit Lovejoy for provoking fruitful objections, because in what follows I simply turn his methodology upside down. Whereas Lovejoy tends to foreground continuity over discontinuity by reducing "the seeming novelty of many a system" to "the novelty of the application or arrangement of the old elements which enter into it" (1933: 4), I will attend primarily to the patterning.[7] My aim is to describe and explain a quite specific and seemingly anomalous episode in the history of one particular "great idea", Nietzsche's *Übermensch*. I am not concerned with the concept's *prehistory*, e.g. by analysing it further into its "constituents" and retracing them as far as I can. Nor am I going to make any claims as to the "correct" interpretation of Nietzsche's seminal conception. What I am after is the way in which Nietzsche's *Übermensch* itself became a constituent of or was integrated within the "compounds" or "aggregates" of the *God-seekers* during the Silver Age. To put it in terms of Lovejoy's preferred analogy: Nietzsche's *Übermensch* is the atom of the present investigation and I will describe certain "compounds," or what I call "constellations," in which it took part. As a consequence, I will not foreground continuity over discontinuity; rather, I will highlight the discontinuities in the narrative. The very idea of the *Übermensch* is Nietzsche's, yet as it figures in subsequent interpretations, it is no longer Nietzsche's, because even within the constellations

---

[7] The mere conceivability of this alternative to Lovejovian history of ideas is mentioned by Macksey (1994) in passing. He doesn't claim it is desirable, though, nor does he refer to any work in which this alternative methodology is developed, defended or exemplified.

accommodating it, put forward by thinkers with roughly the same cultural background and comparable philosophical aims, its meaning changes significantly. It is precisely at this point that I draw on *reception aesthetics*.

Reception theory or *Rezeptionsästhetik* comes primarily from the work of the literary theorist Hans-Robert Jauss (1922-1997), whose basic ideas were sketched out in his inaugural address at the University of Constance in 1967. Challenging the idea that texts have but one objective and fixed meaning, Jauss developed a methodological framework to describe how and explain why the meaning of a text changes in function of the specific way in which it is received by different readers. In his *Literaturgeschichte als Provokation der Literaturwissenschaft* (*Literary History as a Challenge to Literary Theory*, 1967), he claims that literary texts are primarily communicative phenomena: a text encompasses possible meanings, but it is ultimately the reader who actualizes the potential and construes the meaning of the text. In short, meaning is the result of "reception" (*Rezeption*). In Jauss's terminology - derived from Husserl's phenomenology of perception - the reader appropriates the text from a specific "horizon of expectations" (*Erwartungshorizont*), which is, broadly speaking, the set of expectations against which a reader perceives the text. The various actualizations or concretizations (*Konkretisation*) of the text that come into being by a multitude of readers from different backgrounds effect a "change of horizon" (*Horizontwandel*) within the text. In like manner, if a text is sufficiently provocative and challenges or surpasses the reader's expectations, and if, in Jauss's terminology, the "aesthetic distance" between text and horizon of expectations is experienced as an alienating perspective, the text brings about a "change of horizon" within the reader's consciousness, and produces a whole new canon of expectations towards the work (Jauss [1967] 1970).

The aim of this study is to describe and explain the "change of horizon" of Nietzsche's anthropology of the *Übermensch*, in an ideological as opposed to a textual manner. In the reading practice of the religious philosophers, the *Horizontwandel* materializes through the dynamics of dialogical performativity. Each reader concretizes the *Übermensch* differently and as a result, produces a new meaning and a whole new canon of expectations towards this concept, both intra- and intersubjectively. Concurrently, Nietzsche's *Übermensch* challenges these readers' horizon of expectations, thereby provoking a transformation of their spiritual and intellectual consciousness.

Although I refrain from systematically using the specific terminology of both methodological approaches, this study proposes a case-based integration of reception aesthetics and history of ideas. By fusing Jauss's reception theory with Lovejoy's theory of unit-ideas, I arrive at the holistic perspective that the meaning of a component changes in function of the compound in which it figures. This approach allows us to turn Lovejoy's methodology, as it were, upside down and to attend to the *discontinuity* rather than to the continuity of seemingly recurrent ideas. In order to do full justice to the dynamics of the history of an idea, one should not focus on invariable unit-ideas, but rather on the specific compound, or "constellation" in which the idea is lodged. The Lovejovian unit-ideas merely serve a heuristic function, allowing the indispensable, synchronic explanations of the constellations. But the diachronic explanations this study offers clearly assume more: they not only require semantic holism, so that the meaning of an idea changes in function of the constellation in which it is accommodated, but also a theory of reception aesthetics that allows us to trace ideational change back to what Bevir has recently called "dilemmas" (1999).

5. Structure of the book

In the second chapter, I present an overall account of the Russian reading of Nietzsche between 1892 and 1899 to demonstrate the difference with Solov'ëv's, Merezhkovskii's and Berdiaev's interpretations. I will outline the first critical articles on Nietzsche and take particular notice of the connections therein between Nietzsche and Dostoevskii. Although Solov'ëv played a pivotal role in the initial phase of the reception process, a full-length discussion of his response to Nietzsche is deferred until chapter four. For one thing, Solov'ëv is only *indirectly* responsible for the recurring association between Nietzsche's *Übermensch* and Dostoevskii's nihilistic characters. For another, he paved the way for a more qualified reading of Nietzsche, which focuses on the religious dimension of his thought.

In order to grasp the differences in the Russian reading of Nietzsche, one should get a full understanding of the coinciding changes in the reading of Dostoevskii. To that end, Dostoevskii's philosophical anthropology, which is at the core of the *God-seekers'* assessment of him, deserves ample scrutiny. This is the object of analysis in the third chapter.

In chapter four, Vladimir Solov'ëv's vacillating "conversation" with Nietzsche is studied at length. Solov'ëv repeatedly alludes to a possible identification of *Übermensch* and Antichrist. As I see it, this identification prompts the opposing constellation of *Übermensch* and *Bogochelovek* (God-man), which is, in turn, constitutive for more favorable readings of Nietzsche's *Übermensch*.

To fully appreciate the ramifications of this opposition, it is necessary to examine the conception of the *Bogochelovek*, as it fascinated the religious philosophers of the Silver Age. In chapter five, this idea is explained as it figures within the Russian religious context. Moreover, a most relevant constellation is the opposition between *Bogochelovek* and *chelovekobog*. In the same chapter, I will also focus on the actual occurrences of the term *chelovekobog* in Dostoevskii's writings since much, if not all, of the commonly accepted concept of the *chelovekobog* can be traced exclusively back to Dostoevskii, even though the religious philosophers attributed meanings and connotations to the concept which went well beyond what Dostoevskii meant and intended.

In chapter six, Dmitrii Merezhkovskii's seminal contribution to the Russian reading of both Nietzsche and Dostoevskii is studied in detail. The aim of this chapter is to estimate the extent to which Merezhkovkii is responsible for the cluster of ideational changes around the turn of the last century. I will argue, more specifically, that the later enthusiastic response to Nietzsche's ideas by the *God-seekers* is simply inconceivable without Merezhkovskii's contribution.

In chapter seven, I aim to show that the process of reading Nietzsche religiously on the basis of the horizon of expectations supplied by Dostoevskii reaches its culmination with Berdiaev. Moreover, I will argue that Berdiaev's reading of Nietzsche is, at least partly, determined by the horizon of expectations generated by Solov'ëv and Merezhkovskii. However, at the same time, Berdiaev goes beyond their reception model to establish a new constellation in which to integrate and garment Nietzsche.

The final chapter offers a conclusion to this study and the answer to the basic question "what the God-seekers found in Nietzsche."

6. Who were the God-seekers?

From the 1860s onwards, Russian thought was dominated by a radical atheism which found expression in various philosophical systems, such as the nihilism of the 1860s, populism of the 1870s, and Marxist thought, emerging in the 1880s and growing more popular in the 1890s. There were, of course, some cracks in the monolith of atheism. From the 1860s until his death in 1881, Dostoevskii lashed out against growing atheism in all its manifestations in daily life Russia. Lev Tolstoi was also highly preoccupied with the problem of religion and aimed for a conversion to the religious belief as practiced by the peasantry. And one should, of course, credit Vladimir Solov'ëv's innovative contribution to Russian philosophy of religion. Still, by the end of the nineteenth century, the majority of the Russian intelligentsia was engaged in political, economic, and social themes. It was not until the turn of the century that, partly under the aegis of Dostoevskii and Solov'ëv, a considerable part of the Russian intelligentsia moved away from the atheist and materialist focus and began to show interest in questions of religion and metaphysics. A new generation of pre-eminently religious thinkers emerged, the *Bogoiskateli* or *God-seekers*. This term most likely originated from Lev Shestov's formula that "one should seek God" (*nuzhno iskat' Boga*) (Shestov [1899] 2001: 437).[8] Even if all were in search of a spiritual and religious renewal, these religious thinkers cannot be classified as a uniform school. Although they had in common their speculation on the existential status of the human being and their chief preoccupation with the problem of religion, they were, in the final outcome, philosophically highly distinct from each other.

In fact, the movement of *Bogoiskatel'stvo* was the result of a coalition of two separate groups: representatives of "the new religious

---

[8] "It is in this that the whole force and the convincing power of Nietzsche's philosophy lies [...] Nietzsche has shown us the way. One should seek that which is *higher* than compassion, *higher* than good. One should seek God" (Shestov [1899] 2001: 437).

consciousness" (*novoe religioznoe soznanie*) on the one hand and the neo-idealists on the other hand (Berdiaev [1949] 2003: 385). The first group joined around Dmitrii Merezhkovskii, who formulated his idea of "the new religious consciousness" around 1900. This group, whose primary activity was creative writing, consisted of Merezhkovskii himself, his wife Zinaida Gippius, Dmitrii Filosofov, Vasilii Rozanov, Andrei Belyi and Viacheslav Ivanov. The neo-idealists expressed their ideas through scholarly articles and had a greater interest in purely theoretical questions than the more artistically oriented writers. Among the neo-idealists were Semën Frank, Pëtr Struve, Sergei Bulgakov, Nikolai Berdiaev, Sergei and Evgenii Trubetskoi. Because both groups aspired to a reformation in religious consciousness, these writers and scholars looked to each other for support.

Merezhkovskii, one of the first disseminators of Nietzsche's ideas in Russia, delineated the "new religious consciousness" in his study *L. Tolstoi i Dostoevskii: Khristos i Antikhristos v russkoi literature* (*L. Tolstoi and Dostoevskii: Christ and Antichrist in Russian literature*, 1900-1901). Clearly inspired by Nietzsche, Merezhkovskii proceeded in a critique against traditional Christianity and set out to compose a new version of the Christian model.

The neo-idealist current in Russian thought found an outlet in the collection of essays *Problemy Idealizma* (*Problems of Idealism*, 1902). This work was the result of an alliance between former Marxists and liberals, and compiled articles by the neo-idealists Berdiaev, Bulgakov, Frank and Struve and the more liberal philosophers Evgenii and Sergei Trubetskoi.[9] Bulgakov, Frank, Struve and Berdiaev had been captivated by Marxism in their student years yet had grown dissatisfied with the ideology and its Bolshevist corollary as it gained popularity in Russian society. They were fundamentally Kantians and Fichteans who could not reconcile themselves to the materialism and lack of metaphysics in Marxist philosophy and therefore evolved from Marxism to Idealism (Berdiaev [1946] 1997: 192ff).[10] Their common goal was redefining and amending traditional idealist philosophy to counter the theoretical aspects of Marxism while simultaneously integrating the Marxist

---

[9] The neo-idealist debate was continued in the collection of essays *Vekhi* (*Landmarks*, 1909) and *Iz Glubiny* (*From the Depth*, 1918).

[10] Bulgakov's work on this change in intellectual mentality was entitled *Ot Marksizma k Idealizmu* (*From Marxism to Idealizm*, 1903).

social program into this new form of idealism. In this way, the neo-idealists differed from the former generation of idealists (Solov'ëv, Fëdorov, Lopatin and others) who waved aside any potential merit of Marxist thought.

Neo-idealists also clashed with the idealists with regard to the reception of Nietzsche. Whereas the idealists' chief response to the German philosopher was one of refutation of his ideas, for the neo-idealists, especially for Berdiaev and Frank, Nietzsche was a significant source of inspiration in the articulation of their neo-idealist thought. They found in Nietzsche an affirmation of their protest against positivist and utilitarian philosophy. Aspiring to determine the ontological status of ideas and values, the neo-idealists found in Nietzsche, the re-valuator of all values, an impulse to question established definitions of ideas such as good, evil, truth and beauty.[11] Nietzsche was thus appropriated as an idealist philosopher.[12] This emerges clearly from their earliest manifesto *Problemy Idealizma*, in which two articles dealt at length with Nietzsche: Berdiaev's "Eticheskaia problema v svete filosofskogo idealizma" ("The ethical problem in the light of philosophical idealism") and Frank's "Fr. Nitsshe i 'etika liubvi k dal'nemu'" ("Fr. Nietzsche and the ethics of 'love for the far'"). The fact that Nietzsche, who opposed the traditional notion and deployment of metaphysical systems, as largely rooted in Plato's dualism, was so omnipresent in this volume, is illustrative of the neo-idealists' reading of Nietzsche as a latent idealist and metaphysical thinker.

The contributors to *Problemy Idealizma* intended to articulate a liberal and idealist philosophy that would guarantee the freedom of

---

[11] In the present study I use the terms "ontology" and "ontological status" as they are mostly used in contemporary philosophical literature. Although contemporary usage, especially in the analytic tradition, most probably obscures more genuine and fruitful meta-philosophical conceptions of the aspirations and methods of metaphysics, such as Heidegger's, I use the broad definition of the study of "what there is." I adopt the definition as given in *Routledge Encyclopedia of Philosophy*: "The word 'ontology' is used to refer to philosophical investigation of existence, or being. Such investigation may be directed towards the concept of being, asking what 'being' means, or what it is for something to exist; it may also (or instead) be concerned with the question 'what exists?', or 'what general sorts of things are there?'. It is common to speak of a philosopher's ontology, meaning the kinds of thing they take to exist, or the ontology of a theory, meaning the things that would have to exist for that theory to be true" (Craig 1998: 117).

[12] See Berdiaev 1902: 120 "Nietzsche is above all an idealist."

the personality (*lichnost'*). Dissatisfied by the populist and Marxist focus on the collective well-being and their neglect of the individual's interests, the neo-idealists were in search of a new philosophical anthropology and related morality, the foundation of which was to be – to cite Novgorodtsev in the preface to *Problemy Idealizma* – "the absolute significance of the personality" (Novgorodtsev 1902, quoted in Poole 2003: 83). They perceived the individual as the sole source of creativity and producer of values. The individual was, for them, both creator and evaluator of the ideals and guiding principles by which he chooses to live. Due to their common Russian Orthodox background, idealism and Christianity were inextricably bound together. The common intellectual basis for the neo-idealists was ethical, religious individualism (Read 1979: 15ff). Their approaches towards neo-idealism were, however, very dissimilar.

In both camps disillusioned by Marxist philosophy and aspiring for a return to Christianity, the group of the new religious consciousness and the neo-idealists joined together at the beginning of the twentieth century. Berdiaev and Bulgakov, personally acquainted with Merezhkovskii and the other members of this group, were the mediators between both movements. Because they needed a journal that would serve as the mouthpiece for the new *God-seeking* union, they collaborated in Merezhkovskii's literary journal *Novyi Put'* (*The New Way*), as editors of the political and philosophical contributions. Yet, the members of the union were soon dissatisfied with the highly eclectic style of the journal so a new one was established, *Voprosy Zhizni* (*Questions of Life*) that only continued for a year due the 1905 revolution (Berdiaev [1946] 2003: 385). From 1901 onwards, Merezhkovskii organized the "Religious-Philosophical Gatherings" (*religiozno-filosofskie sobraniia*), attended by laity and clergy alike, to discuss the current condition and the future of Christianity.

7. Note on references, translation and transliteration

All quotes from and references to Nietzsche in this study are from the original German texts in the critical editions of Colli and Montinari (1975/1984, 1986, 1988[2]/Neuausgabe 1999). The references are constituted by the standard abbreviation KGB, KSB and KSA, and the volume number, followed by the page. All references to Dostoevskii are from the *Polnoe Sobranie Sochinenii v tridtsati tomakh* (compiled by the Instituted of Russian Literature of the Academy of Sciences of the USSR (1972-1990), cited as PSS followed by number of volume and page. And with reference to Solov'ëv, I use (except where indicated otherwise) the *Sobranie Sochinenii Vladimira Sergeevicha Solov'ëva* ([1911-1914] 1966-1970), edited by Sergei Solov'ëv and Ernst Radlov. References to this work consist of the standard abbreviation SS, volume number, and page number. References to Merezhkovskii's and Berdiaev's texts are indicated in the text itself.

All of the passages quoted in this book are my translations, except where indicated otherwise. In order not to give a distorted, connotative version of the key words in this work, i.e. *Übermensch*, *chelovekobog* and *Bogochelovek*, I prefer not to translate these concepts. However, I cannot always escape from the requirement to translate these terms. With reference to the *Übermensch*, I opt for *trans-human*, because this term is more representative for the religious thinkers' interpretation of the *Übermensch* than the frequently used *superman* and *overman*. There is a semantic difference between the German *Übermensch* and the Russian equivalent *sverkhchelovek*. The German prefix *über* both denotes 'above' and 'over, beyond', consequently the term *Übermensch* can either point to an otherworldly state, or refer to a condition *beyond* humanness, in which the human is overcome. The Russian prefix *sverkh*, however, implies a qualitative elevation; accordingly the word *sverkhchelovek* signifies an improvement, a perfected condition of the human type. I find that *trans-human* covers this connotation of a transcendent state of humanity better than *superman* or *overman*. Furthermore, I prefer to translate this term by the gender neutral *human*, for this captures both the German *Mensch* and the Russian *chelovek*. With regard to *Bogochelovek* and *chelovekobog*, I adopt the general translation God-Man and man-god.
Transliteration follows the Library of Congress system.

Chapter 2

The Russian discovery of Nietzsche

To us, Russians, Nietzsche is particularly close [...] for the whole future Russian and European culture, Nietzsche did not die. All the same, whether we are for or against him, we ought to be with him, close to him. Maybe we ought to struggle with him, maybe we ought to overcome him, but never turn him down or push him aside [...] we can only understand him and take him, as both concordant and contrary, in ourselves, into the final depth of our feeling and reason ("Nitsshe. Nekrolog", 1900).

1. How the German philosopher set foot on Russian soil

Nietzsche's thought gradually permeated the Russian cultural and intellectual scene from the beginning of the 1890s. His ideas thus entered Russia at a time of political, social, cultural and ideological flux. From 1890 onwards, Russia was marked by a boom of industrialization, leading to a radical transformation of the agrarian state. There was a large migration of peasants to the rapidly growing industrial areas and soon a new social class of workers emerged. In 1894, the reactionary Nikolai II was crowned tsar, and as we know from history, he was incapable of answering the need for political and social reformation.[1] From 1890 on, a new generation of intellectuals

---

[1] For a detailed overview of the political and social state of *fin de siècle Russia*, see Figes (1996).

appeared on the scene, who found the nihilistic ideas of the 1860s and the populist ideology of the 1870s-1880s failing to meet the demand for an ideological renewal, necessitated by the political and social turmoil. Nietzsche made his debut in Russia during what can be called a transition period in Russian history, when old institutions and values were at an ideological deadlock and a craving for new paradigms came into being.

Until 1890, the German philosopher, who had published his first work in 1872 (*The Birth of Tragedy out of the Spirit of Music*) and produced a large philosophical oeuvre till his mental breakdown in January 1889, was unknown to the Russian audience. Nietzsche's books were prohibited by Russian censorship, which had grown extremely strict under the reign of tsar Aleksandr III, whose liberal predecessor and father Aleksandr II was in 1881 murdered by revolutionary terrorists. The censorship was largely controlled by Konstantin Pobedonostsev, the ultraconservative Procurator of the Holy Synod, who was appointed advisor to Aleksandr III and in this position decisively shaped the tsarist reactionary policy. All books that touched upon and dared to challenge the pillars of Russian society, i.e. "Autocracy, Orthodoxy and National Character (*Samoderzhavie, Pravoslavie, Narodnost'*)," were blacklisted. Nietzsche's works incorporated everything the Russian officials feared: the philosopher provocatively questioned established political and social ideologies as well as vehemently criticized the Christian ethics of altruism and self-denial.[2] For that reason, his books were not allowed in Russia until 1898 and were thus deliberately held back from the Russian public for more than a quarter of a century.[3] In spite of the vast publication of his works and his gradually growing fame in Western Europe, Nietzsche's name appeared in neither the 1885 Russian edition of the *Brockhaus and Efron Encyclopedic Dictionary* (*Entsiklopedicheskii Slovar' Brokgaus i Efron*) nor in the additional volume that appeared in 1887. In an 1890 translation of an overview of new developments in German

---

[2] The Russian censors described Nietzsche variously as "a bold free thinker" and "an extreme materialist who denies free will" (quoted in Clowes 1983: 136).

[3] Georg Brandes, who frequently corresponded with some Russian intellectuals and had traveled to Russia in the spring of 1887, informed Nietzsche in October 1888 of the official ban on his works: "Everything, even 'Human, All-too-Human' is forbidden in Russia" (KGB III6: 320). In a letter to Gast (October 14, 1888), Nietzsche mentions the prohibition of his works in Russia (KSB 8: 450).

philosophy by I. Kheinze (*Istoriia novoi Filosofii*), Nietzsche's name appeared in the index under two different spellings (*Nitche* and *Niche*), showing the translator's ignorance regarding Nietzsche (Mikhailovskii 1894b: 111).[4]

However, before the official lifting of the ban in 1898, the Russian censors could not completely prevent the gradual and often coincidental permeation of Nietzsche's thoughts and works into Russian intellectual circles. The philosopher himself was personally acquainted with émigré Russians, who conducted a lively correspondence with the motherland. In the mid-1870s, he befriended Aleksandr Herzen's daughters in Malwida von Meysenbug's house in Sorrento and even briefly considered the idea of marrying the eldest, Natalie (KSB 5: 227). In April 1882, also via von Meysenbug, Nietzsche met the Russian-born Lou Salomé with whom he engaged in a deep and complex friendship. Lou was highly fascinated by Nietzsche and set out to disseminate his thought in Europe and Russia. In 1877, Marie Baumgartner sent a copy of her French translation of *Richard Wagner in Bayreuth* (1876) to Prince Aleksandr Meshcherskii in St. Petersburg (Benders, Oetterman, et al. 2000: 394).[5] At the end of 1888, on the recommendation of the Danish critic Georg Brandes, Nietzsche sent a copy of *The Case of Wagner* (1888) to Princess Anna Dmitrievna Tenisheva, who was a prominent figure in then Russian intellectual circles (KSB 8: 420, 457). It is noteworthy and significant for the reconstruction of the earliest responses to Nietzsche that the philosopher signed as "The Antichrist" (Clowes 1983: 135).[6] Tenisheva was shocked, but she did read the work and managed to

---

[4] Somewhat overconfident where it concerns his own popularity, Nietzsche describes in his autobiography *Ecce Homo* (written in the fall of 1888) his fame and the widespread reception of his works in several trend-setting cities, among which St. Petersburg: "everywhere else I have readers – nothing but exceptional intellectuals, proven characters, trained in high positions and duties; I have even real geniuses among my readers. In Vienna, in St. Petersburg, in Stockholm, in Copenhagen, in Paris and New-York – everywhere I am discovered: but *not* in Europe's lowland Germany" (KSA 6: 301). Nietzsche's commentary on his reputation in Russia by the end of the 1880s is somewhat exaggerated, probably to provoke the German public.

[5] Prince Meshcherskii spent the fall of 1876 in Malwida von Meysenbug's Sorrento estate, where Aleksandr Herzen and his daughters also resided (KSB 5: 198).

[6] From December 1888 Nietzsche started signing his letters as "The Antichrist" (Cfr. a letter to Chancellor von Bismarck (KSB 8: 504); see also KSB 8: 544, 551). Later on that month he signed as "Dionysus" or "The Crucified" (KSB 8: 572-577).

publish a reduced and censored version of it in 1894.[7] Again advised
by Brandes, Nietzsche sent the same book to Prince Aleksandr
Urusov, a Petersburg lawyer and respected intellectual (KSB 8: 450,
470, 514; KGB III 6: 320). And some weeks before his final
breakdown, he asked his editor Constantin Georg Naumann to send to
Urusov a free copy of *Twilight of the Idols*, due to be published in the
beginning of 1889 (KSB 8: 486f.). In 1889, Nietzsche's close friend
and proofreader Peter Gast (born Heinrich Köselitz) mailed copies of
Nietzsche Contra Wagner (1889) to Urusov and Tenisheva (Benders,
Oetterman, et al. 2000: 742).

Censorship was also bypassed by Russian intellectuals
traveling to Western Europe, where they became acquainted with
Nietzsche's thoughts and works. It is highly probable that Ivan
Turgenev had already heard of Nietzsche in the 1870s due to his
frequent travels to Germany and France. Turgenev's great love,
Pauline Viardot, was friends with Richard and Cosima Wagner, who
were dedicated patrons of the young Nietzsche. And in 1875,
Nietzsche's close friend Paul Rée visited Turgenev several times in
Paris; during these visits he might have talked about Nietzsche's
recently published *The Birth of Tragedy* (1872) (Pfeiffer 1970: 421).
Sergei Makovskii relates how the best-selling writer Pëtr Boborykin
"by accident brought along from Wiesbaden *The Dawn, Beyond Good
and Evil* and *Zarathustra*" (Makovskii [1955] 2000, 1: 515). The poet
Nikolai Minskii read Nietzsche while in Europe and upon his return,
infused his fellow intellectuals with his enthusiasm for the German
philosopher (Lane 1986: 58f.). In 1891, the novelist and critic Dmitrii
Merezhkovskii traveled to Paris where he learned about the French
symbolists and also read Nietzsche, who was in the background of
symbolist aesthetics. By the end of the 1880s, the poet and leading
theoretician of Russian symbolism, Viacheslav Ivanov, got in touch
with Nietzsche's writings and ideas in Berlin, where he was enrolled
as a student of classical philology and history, and brought with him
several volumes of Nietzsche's works to Russia (Ivanov 1971-1987 II:
19). Zinaida Vengerova, sister of the historian of Russian literature
Semën Vengerov, learned of Nietzsche during her several trips
through Germany and wrote the first article on him in the Russian
Brockhaus and Efron in 1897 (Azadovskii 1999: 113).

---

[7] See Tenisheva's letter to Nietzsche, December 2, 1888 (KGB III 6: 359).

The ban was vitiated further by visits of Western European intellectuals who brought Nietzsche's books with them. Georg Brandes, with whom Nietzsche conducted a lively correspondence beginning in 1887, and who was one of the first Nietzsche readers to treat his thought on an academic level, traveled in the spring of 1887 to St. Petersburg and Moscow where he delivered some lectures on French and Russian literature. On this journey, Brandes met some prominent Russian intellectuals, including Tenisheva, Urusov, Maria Kovalevskaia, Vera Spasskaia, and Friedrich Fiedler, with whom he frequently corresponded after his return to Copenhagen (Dahl & Mott 1980: 315). Through these intellectuals, Brandes might have disseminated Nietzsche's thoughts and works in Russia.[8] In 1895, Lou Salomé traveled to her native city, St. Petersburg, to promote her study of Nietzsche (*Friedrich Nietzsche in seinen Werken*, 1894), parts of which were published in 1896 in the journal *Severnyi Vestnik* (*The Northern Herald*) (Gurevich [1914] 1972: 255). These Russian

---

[8] In the spring of 1888 Brandes presented lectures on Nietzsche at Copenhagen University, which attracted a great audience and were published in *The German Review* (*Deutsche Rundschau*) in 1890 as "Friedrich Nietzsche. An Essay on Aristocratic Radicalism" (KGB III 6: 191 & Brandes 1895: 137-224). In a letter to Meta von Salis, dated December 29, 1888, Nietzsche reported that Brandes would shortly travel to St. Petersburg to deliver lectures on him: "This winter Georg Brandes goes again to St.Petersburg, to hold lectures on the beast (*das Unthier*) Nietzsche" (KSB 8: 561f.). In an 1887 letter (November 26) Brandes had informed Nietzsche on a visit to Warschau, Petersburg, and Moscow where he had given speeches in French, but he makes no mention of the content or subject of them. Along the lines, he claims: "I believe I have my best audience in the Slavic countries" (KGB III 6: 121). In a letter from October 6, 1888, Brandes recommends Nietzsche to send a copy of *The Case of Wagner* to Tenisheva ("my very close friend") and prince Urusov, and reports: "[I] am writing other French lectures for Petersburg and Moscow and go in the depths of winter to Russia to spend some time there" (KGB, III 6: 320f.). There is no hint at all that the planned lectures would be on Nietzsche. On November 23, 1888, Brandes writes (his last) letter to Nietzsche, in which he reports that his plan to travel to Russia is at stake, for one of his books (probably his *Main Currents in Nineteenth Century Literature*, 1887) is forbidden by Russian censorship: "one of my oldest books, recently translated in Russian, is labeled unreligious and condemned to be *burnt* in public (...) Moreover, almost all letters to me and from me are confiscated" (KGB III 6: 361). In the end, Brandes had to drop his plan to travel to Russia and spent the winter in Scandinavia. So, Nietzsche's claim to Meta von Salis (a month after Brandes' report that his journey was at stake) that Brandes was to go to Petersburg in Winter 1888-89 to deliver lectures on "das Unthier" Nietzsche, is a self-produced myth, which is most probably a symptomatic foreshadowing of his mental breakdown only a few days later (in the early days of January 1889).

and Western intellectuals brought with them Nietzsche's books and ideas, as well as rumors and writings about the philosopher, all of which stimulated their fellows to indulge in the works and thoughts of the German thinker. It was in this way that the strict ban of Nietzsche's works was already partly broken before its final abolishment in 1898, even though the access to his writings was limited to a select circle of the *intelligentsia*.

2.   The first responses

In 1891, the newspaper *Novosti* (*News*) printed a small introduction to Nietzsche's thought by A. Reingoldt under the title "Mysli i Paradoksy Fridrikha Nitsshe" ("Thoughts and Paradoxes of Friedrich Nietzsche") (Clowes 1988: 53). Furthermore, in the beginning of 1892 the prominent philosopher Vladimir Solov'ëv mentions Nietzsche, although only in passing, in an article on Konstantin Leont'ev (SS X: 509). Still, the actual discussion on the German philosopher on Russian soil did not start until the publication of Vasilii Preobrazhenskii's article "Fridrikh Nitsshe: Kritika Morali Al'truizma" ("Friedrich Nietzsche: A Critique of the Morality of Altruism"), which appeared in the last volume (15) of the 1892 issue of *Voprosy Filosofii i Psikhologii* (*Problems of Philosophy and Psychology*). The journal *Voprosy Filosofii i Psikhologii* was the official outlet of the Moscow Psychological Society, which had been founded in 1885 and soon became a landmark in Russian history of ideas: the Society assembled the growing resistance against positivism and materialism and initiated the renewed interest in metaphysical questions that generated Russia's religious and cultural renaissance. *Voprosy Filosofii i Psikhologii* was the first Russian journal that was specialized in philosophy and was an important channel for the dissemination of religious philosophy in the Silver Age (Poole 2002).[9] Preobrazhenskii's essay on Nietzsche aroused much controversy among the editors of the journal: in a preface to the article they stated

---

[9] The journal often introduced Western thinkers to the Russian reading public. Before publication of his essay, Preobrazhenskii had read it to the Psychological Society in Moscow. According to the minutes of the lecture, the paper "aroused a lively interest and exchange of opinions among the members" (Lane 1986: 51).

that they had only allowed it for publication to prove to the Russian readers "what strange and sick phenomena are presently being generated by a well-known trend in Western European culture" (Preobrazhenskii [1892] 2001: 1009). They immediately set the tone for further readings of Nietzsche by strongly condemning the philosopher for the immoral bias of his thought:

> Blinded by hatred towards religion, Christianity and God himself, Fr. Nietzsche cynically advocates the total indulgence in crime, in the most terrible depravity and moral degradation, all for the ideal of perfecting individual representatives of the human species, and the masses of humankind are in a blasphemous manner degraded as pedestal for the glorification of these unbridled "geniuses" – like Nietzsche himself –, who are not hindered by any legal nor moral restriction (ibid.).

In spite of the editors' preface, Preobrazhenskii's rational and rather sympathetic analysis of Nietzsche's thought reached a broad reading public and hence played an important role in the dissemination of Nietzsche's philosophy in Russia. In the 1880s, Preobrazhenskii (1864-1900), a philosopher and literary critic, had participated in the idealist movement against the materialism and positivism of the 1860s with an article on Schopenhauer and Kant (Clowes 1988: 55). His familiarity with and reading of Nietzsche's works in the beginning of the 1890s supplied him with original ideas to help formulate an alternative to the fading populist movement and its emphasis on the social ethos. As the title indicates, Preobrazhenskii focuses primarily on Nietzsche's argumentation against the established ethics of altruism. He ranks Nietzsche among moralists such as Pascal, La Rochefoucauld, Leopardi, and Schopenhauer (Preobrazhenskii [1892] 2001: 36). Until now moral philosophers had only concerned themselves with the question how to deliver a systematic argument for morality; Nietzsche, by contrast, is the first to question morality itself, to find the necessity and concept of an ethical system problematical. Nietzsche could only challenge morality by transgressing prevalent ethical standards, by going "beyond good and evil" (id.: 40). The ambition to establish a universal, unambiguous moral system is in vain because it does not take into account the diversity of cultures and historical periods and more importantly, because it assumes a universally recognized goal of humanity, which is a mere illusion (id.: 41). Most moral philosophers sanction the Christian dogma of "love of one's neighbor" and glorify virtues such as compassion, sympathy for the other, lack of self-interest, and self-renunciation. Nietzsche exposes these altruistic moralities as false and hypocritical: he reveals that pity and self-sacrifice have no other purpose than indulging in self-love. Effacing oneself for the other is purely based on narcissist motives. Nietzsche retraces the universally accepted virtue of compassion to a mere psychological phenomenon: "In the act of compassion a person first and foremost satisfies the requirement of his own feelings" (id.: 43f.). In spite of its egocentric motivation, altruism is granted a moral status and has become an institutionalized morality because of its benefit for society. Yet this kind of "herd morality" is insufficient to raise society and humanity to a higher level (id.: 54f.). The alleged 'altruistic' ethics has reduced the human to nothing more than a link in the social chain: it has deprived humans of their strong and creative instincts, it has molded them into "domestic animals" (ibid.).

> [Altruistic morality] has bent and weakened the will [of the individual], exterminated all the strong and powerful instincts, tied up and suppressed all the passions pulsating in him: it has destroyed all what is magnificent and splendid and transformed it into something simple and cheap [...] it has leveled out all humans, made mediocrity (posredstvennost') the archetype and ideal of humankind (ibid.).

Preobrazhenskii credits Nietzsche for his aspiration to reevaluate traditional values (*pereotsenka tsennostei*) and for the erection of new "tablets" (*skrizhali blag*) (id.: 56). Nietzsche grants the individual total moral freedom in the creation of his own laws and values. Each individual is free to be his "own experiment and own creator," to become a self-determined and self-valuing personality (id.: 58). This creative personality has the inner strength to innovate and uplift society. To accomplish this reformation, the creative individual must produce new values and perform actions that are defined as evil in the conventional moral outlook. In contrast with later interpretations, Preobrazhenskii understands Nietzsche's idea of evil not in the sense of satisfying egoistic and perverse needs but as referring to an act that is innovative, creating original values, opposing conventional standards (id.: 59). Humans hold a great potential for transformation which can be attained by overcoming the current self and prevalent ethics. The creative individual's drive to generate his own powers and produce his own values independently from ruling conventions, is what Preobrazhenskii identifies in Nietzsche's anthropology of the *Übermensch* (id.: 60f.). Interestingly, Preobrazhenskii's delineation of the *Übermensch* is chiefly substantiated by fragments from works other than *Thus spoke Zarathustra* (1883-1885), i.e. the only narrative in Nietzsche's published works in which the idea of the *Übermensch* is (through the voice of Zarathustra) exhaustively explained.[10] Instead of referring to Zarathustra's speech, Preobrazhenskii places the *Übermensch* in Nietzsche's discourse concerning the question of morality (as chiefly developed in *Beyond Good and Evil* (1886) and *On the Genealogy of Morals* (1887)), thereby rendering quite another understanding of the *Übermensch* than what is explained in Nietzsche's original discourse. An example of this can be found in Preobrazhenskii's association between the *Übermensch* and a quotation from *Beyond Good and Evil*, in which there is mention of an "order of rank" (*Rangordnung*): this is a hierarchic differentiation between humans and consequently between moral systems (id.: 61).[11] This representation of the *Übermensch*, as one for whom existing morality does not account, might have shaped the later, unfavorable responses to Nietzsche and his *Übermensch* as one to whom all is permitted. In spite of this assessment of Nietzsche's anthropology, Preobrazhenskii denies that it clears the way for total licentiousness. In his understanding, the *Übermensch* is completely accountable for and voluntarily corresponds his actions to his freely chosen and self-imposed ideal which is justified in itself (id.: 56f.).

Thus, confronted with the failure of Populism in the 1880s and in search for an innovative ideology that would re-establish the status of the individual in Russian society, Preobrazhenskii is chiefly moved by Nietzsche's critical analysis of altruistic and utilitarian ethical systems and by his emphasis on the creative, inventive, and self-determining individual. He sees in Nietzsche a fruitful inspiration to regenerate Russian culture. He hails him as the preacher of "the new commandment" (*novaia zapoved'*), a statement that paves the

---

[10] In the published works following *Thus spoke Zarathustra*, the term *Übermensch* is rarely mentioned and does not appear in an exclusive discourse on this concept (See KSA 5: 236 & 288; KSA 6: 136, 171, 300).

[11] Preobrazhenskii quotes "that what is right for one, *cannot* by any means therefore be right for another, that the demand for one morality for all is detrimental to precisely the higher men, in short that there exists an *order of rank* between man and man, and consequently also between morality and morality." (KSA 5: 165).

way for the religious and even messianic tenor of the God-seekers' interpretation of Nietzsche (id.: 66).

Preobrazhenskii is the first Russian critic to communicate Nietzsche's ideas in a coherent and impartial article and to propagate them to the Russian intellectual public. However, the sympathetic tone of his essay displeases the editors of *Voprosy Filosofii i Psikhologii* and provokes a polemic in the journal's following issue, in which the three main editors publish discrediting papers on Nietzsche. All three articles conclude that Nietzsche is not in the least a creator of new ideas but on the contrary, he represents the failure and falseness of his aspirations to transform current society and morality.

In "Bol'naia Iskrennost' (Zametka po povodu stat'i V. Preobrazhenskogo "Fridrikh Nitsshe: Kritika Morali Al'truizma")" ("Sick Sincerity. (Notes to the article by V. Preobrazhenskii "Friedrich Nietzsche. A Critique of the Morality of Altruism)") the philosopher and head of the Moscow Psychological Society Lev Lopatin (1855-1926) objects to Preobrazhenskii's favorable analysis of this "sick person" (Lopatin [1893] 2001: 71). In his view, Nietzsche's ideas represent the most morbid and merciless rejection "of everything that was until now the most holy for humanity." He finds them hateful to humankind "to the point of cynicism" (id.: 70). Lopatin considers Nietzsche's work to be full of contradictions and remarks ironically that the most interesting aspect of Nietzsche's thought is "the sick sincerity of his negation" which he finds to be typical for contemporary philosophy in Western Europe (id.: 72).

The next article in the 1893 issue, "Nravstvennye Idealy nashego Vremeni: Fridrikh Nitsshe i Lev Tolstoi" ("Moral Ideals of our Time: Friedrich Nietzsche and Lev Tolstoi"), was written by the founder of the journal: the philosopher and psychologist, Nikolai Grot (1852-1899). Opposing Nietzsche's individualistic outlook to Tolstoi's Christian altruistic ethics, he nonetheless discerns the same aspiration in both approaches: both aim to find the meaning of life not in the transcendental realm but in this earthly life by improving the human condition.[12] Nietzsche's ideas, reductively explained by Grot as the glorification of higher persons and the aversion to political and

---

[12] The article stimulated similar studies in which Nietzsche and Tolstoi are juxtaposed. See V.G. Shcheglov, 1898, *Graf Lev Nikolaevich Tolstoi i Fridrikh Nitsshe. Ocherk filosofsko-nravstvennogo ikh mirovozzreniia*; Lev Shestov, 1899: *Dobro v Uchenii gr. Tolstogo i Fr. Nitsshe: Filosofiia i Propoved'*.

social equality, represent for him a return to pagan culture (Grot [1893] 2001: 81). The main difference between Nietzsche's and Tolstoi's outlook is that the first endorses the formula: "The more the evil, the more also the good," while the latter proclaims: "the less the evil, the more the good" (id.: 81f.). Nietzsche – "a materialist, atheist and evolutionist of a rather fantastic mold" – is exemplary of "the Western European decadence." Tolstoi, by contrast, is a typical representative of "the Eastern European spontaneity" (id.: 84ff.). Grot concludes that the significance of both thinkers *sub specie aeternitatis* is evident by the fact that both protested against the Kantian distinction between theoretical and practical reason (id.: 94).

The philosopher and jurist, Pëtr Astaf'ev (1846-1893) contributes to the polemic on Preobrazhenskii's paper with the article "Genezis nravstvennogo Ideala Dekadenta" ("Genesis of the moral Ideal of a Decadent"). Astaf'ev criticizes Nietzsche for his ambition to found his ethics on a whole new basis which is completely independent from traditional Christian culture (Astaf'ev [1893] 2001: 96). Refuting the established morals of the common good, Nietzsche puts forward a moral system of the "self-sufficient, egoistic person," a "morality of anarchism" (id.: 97). In Astaf'ev's view, the only true morality is the Christian one, and the ultimate moral doctrine, the Kantian imperative (id.: 106).

Inspired by the polemic in *Voprosy Filosofii i Psikhologii*, the literary critic Vladimir Chuiko (1839-1899) published an article on Nietzsche in the journal *Nabliudatel'* (*The Observer*) in the spring of 1893. In "Obshchestvennye Idealy Fridrikha Nitsshe" ("The Social Ideals of Friedrich Nietzsche"), the author finds Nietzsche's ideas to be exemplary of the contemporary crisis in Western European culture, brought about by Schopenhauer's pessimism. Nietzsche provides European society with ideals that correspond to its current standards and demands but is at the same time a fervent opponent of contemporary European values (Chuiko [1893] 2001: 114f.). Despite the tendentious analysis of Nietzsche's ideas,[13] Chuiko values certain aspects of Nietzsche's thought. More particularly, he sees affinities

---

[13] "According to Nietzsche's profound conviction, nature creates a people with the sole purpose to make possible the existence of five or six individuals, being the true representatives of the human race. These are tigers and lions, born to devour the sheep" (Chuiko [1893] 2001: 124).

between Nietzsche and the Slavophiles in their criticism of Western European society (id.: 116f.).

Subsequently, the editor of the popular journal *Vestnik inostrannoi Literatury* (*The Herald of foreign Literature*), F. I. Bulgakov dedicates an article to the German philosopher, "Uchenie Nitsshe o Zhelanii Vlasti i t.d." ("Nietzsche's Teaching on the Desire for Power etc."), in an overview of social and literary trends in the West. The author describes Nietzsche's biography and focuses more specifically on the philosopher's current mental condition. He offers an extensive report of diagnoses by specialist doctors and the daily routine of the patient, information he apparently got from the journal *Zukunft*, which informed regularly on the status of Nietzsche's mental illness (Bulgakov 1893: 207f.).[14] Bulgakov's account of Nietzsche's ideas is highly distorted: Nietzsche distinguishes in humankind between "two races", i.e. firstly, "a small number of "nobles" and secondly, "an enormous sheep flock of the common people, an infinite number of pack animals," merely born to sacrifice themselves in favor of the 'higher' people (id.: 208f.). Nietzsche differentiates between two moralities: the morality of the "titans," to whom everything is permitted, and the morality of the "ant-hill of pygmy's," who only exist to be of use for the first group (id.: 211).[15]

In the same year three more articles are published on Nietzsche: "Chelovek-Lopukh i Chelovek-Zver'" by Ivan Bikhalets ("Human-Simpleton and Human-Beast") in the newspaper *Kievskoe Slovo* (*The Kievan Word*), the anonymous "Filosof Budushchego" ("Philosopher of the Future") in the journal *Sever* (*North*) and P. Skriba's "Sovremennye literaturnye Motivy: Simvolisty, Dekadenty" ("Contemporary literary motives: symbolists, decadents") in the journal *Russkaia Zhizn'* (*Russian Life*) (Davies 1986: 356 & Sineokaia 2001b: 971ff.).

---

[14] Bulgakov relates how Nietzsche "obediently undertakes long walks with his mother," that "strange faces arouse fear in him" and that he "from time to time reads some pages in Greek." Only the opera Carmen gives him some satisfaction. Bulgakov believes one of the causes of Nietzsche's mental illness to be the misuse of the chloral he took for his insomnia (Bulgakov 1893: 207f.).
[15] Bulgakov refers to *Thus spoke Zarathustra* as "the bible of the titans" (Bulgakov 1893: 212). All the expressions in Bulgakov's article, allegedly formulated by Nietzsche, do not appear at all in Nietzsche's texts and are hence the author's constructions.

In spite of the strict ban on Nietzsche, in 1893 the Russian censors allowed already the publication of the Russian translation of Max Nordau's *Degeneration* (*Entartung*, first published in Berlin in 1893), in which one chapter is devoted to Nietzsche. The Austrian critic who was to become one of the founders of the World Zionist Organization, presents a highly biased interpretation of the German philosopher. In his opinion, sadistic hedonism is the chief impulse of Nietzsche's reasoning, which is plainly the product of an "egomaniac." Nordau's book was the only European critical work on Nietzsche that was made accessible to the Russian readers in that crucial period when first – and in many cases permanent – responses to the philosopher were being formed. By allowing books such as Nordau's to slip through the ban, Russian censors could easily influence and mold the public opinion on Nietzsche (Clowes 1988: 51f.).

Except for Preobrazhenskii's study, Nietzsche's thought generally provoked negative reactions among the Russian intelligentsia. Surprisingly, the German philosopher found an adherent in the leading theoretician of the Populist movement, Nikolai Mikhailovskii (1842-1904). Mikhailovskii, at heart a social thinker and advocate of an altruistic morality, was attracted by Nietzsche's emphasis on the role of the individual. The Russian philosopher aspired for a socialism in which the individual could freely develop his own potential. In his opinion, any social change could only be justified when it contributed to the individual's striving for self-determination. Mikhailovskii devoted a series of articles to Nietzsche, the first of which was published in 1894 in his own journal *Russkoe Bogatstvo* (*Russian Wealth*).[16]

In "Literatura i Zhizn': Eshche o F. Nitsshe" ("Literature and Life: some more on F. Nietzsche") Mikhailovskii opposes the antagonistic tenor that surrounds Nietzsche in the first responses:

> We see in Nietzsche not a rationalist – that is mere nonsense -, neither a theoretician of egoism, nor the "immoralist" which he is generally perceived and which he considered himself to be. Until now we see a very noble and brave thinker, from another view a dreamer, an idealist, positing his demands on an extremely exalted conception of individualism. The human personality is for him the measure of all things; but he demands for it such a fullness of life and such an opposition towards all benefits and conditions

---

[16] In 1898 he published the article "Darvinizm i nitssheanstvo" in *Russkoe Bogatstvo*.

that belittle its dignity, that there cannot be spoken of egoism in the vulgar
sense of the word or of any kind of "immoralism" (Mikhailovskii 1894c:
94).

Mikhailovskii aims to rectify the influential vulgarizations of
Nietzsche's ideas disseminated by his fellow intellectuals. He sets out
to demonstrate that the philosopher's seemingly harsh statements on
the contemporary condition of humanity and conventional values arise
from an incentive to question and eventually transform present
actuality. Mikhailovskii understands Nietzsche primarily as a social
thinker and considers Nietzsche's major contribution to contemporary
social thought his analysis of the problematical relationship between
the individual and society, whereby he grants more importance to the
individual's aspiration for self-realization than to the utilitarian
demand for the common welfare of the collective whole. Eventually,
however, Mikhailovskii seems to realize that Nietzsche's
individualism is too extreme to fit into a social theory. More
specifically, his idea of the *Übermensch* is too elitist and aristocratic
to reconcile with a social ethics. Nevertheless, through this
anthropological paradigm, Nietzsche convinced humanity "to
acknowledge that the highest goal of its existence is the elevation of
the human type, the creation of *"Übermensch"* (Mikhailovskii 1894c:
106). As editor of one of the leading intellectual journals and
established intellectual authority, Mikhailovskii contributed largely to
Nietzsche's growing popularity among the Russian intelligentsia.

    Another seminal impact on the reception of Nietzsche in
Russia, and especially in the field of religion, came from the
prominent religious philosopher Vladimir Solov'ëv (1853-1900). His
first substantial treatment of the German philosopher appears in 1894,
in an article intended to argue against the so-called decadent artists:
"Pervyi shag k polozhitel'noi estetike" ("A first step towards a
positive Aesthetics"). Until his death in 1900, Solov'ëv strongly
participated in the debate on Nietzsche and expressed his ideas on the
German philosopher in both a very explicit as well as veiled manner.[17]

    In 1895, an anonymous article entitled "Idei Fridrikha Nitshe"
("Friedrich Nietzsche's Ideas") appeared in *Vestnik Inostrannoi
Literatury*. In this article, Nietzsche's concept of the *Übermensch* is
considered to justify war and violence (1895: 203f.). In the 1896

---

[17] For a detailed analysis of Solov'ëv's response to Nietzsche, see chapter 4.

article, "Literaturnye zametki: Apollon i Dionis" ("Literary notes: Apollo and Dionysus"), the critic and editor Akim Volynskii (pseudonym for Akim L'vovich Flekser) aimed to amend Nietzsche's unfavorable reputation. He found Nietzsche's aesthetic ideas, especially his duplicity of the Apollinian and the Dionysian, a prolific source of inspiration for the revival of Russian culture. Moreover, he observed in these aesthetic principles a metaphysical dimension (Volynskii [1896] 2001: 201).

In the later part of the 1890s, the number of critical articles that appeared on the German philosopher was relatively small, and their main tenor was one of disapproval. The responses center upon his animadversions on contemporary morality in which the critics sense a license for immoral behavior and a danger to Russian moral consciousness. Lev Tolstoi, for instance, decries Nietzsche for his exaltation of values that run counter to Christian ethics. In his 1897 essay *Chto takoe iskusstvo?* (*What is art*) he lashes out at the contemporary taste for a "lying" aesthetics, rapidly spreading in Russia under the aegis of Nietzsche (Tolstoi [1897] 1983: 188).[18]

The controversy surrounding Nietzsche was continued in the field of popular fiction, a medium that evidently reached a broader reading public. Even before the publication of Preobrazhenskii's article in 1892, some fiction writers who were familiar with Nietzsche's ideas after travels abroad began to assimilate and absorb Nietzsche's body of thought in their narratives. Confronted with the failure of the Populist tradition in which literature served primarily a social goal, these authors aspired to a re-evaluation of art as the individual expression of a unique personality, an ideal they saw fulfilled in Nietzsche's reflections on aesthetics. Already in 1890 the poet and literary theorist Nikolai Minskii (pseudonym for Nikolai Vilenkin, 1855-1937) published his book of essays *Pri Svete Sovesti* (*In the Light of Conscience*), which has an obvious Nietzschean undertone. Although there is no explicit reference to Nietzsche, the book echoes Nietzsche's criticism against altruistic morality and his

---

[18] In 1900 Tolstoi writes in his diary: "I read Nietzsche's *Zarathustra* [...] and became fully convinced , that he was completely crazy, when he wrote; crazy not in the metaphorical, but in the literal, most exact sense [...] he has an idée fixe that, by negating all the highest grounds of human life and thought, he proves his own trans-human genius. What kind of society is it, that recognizes such an evil and crazy man as its teacher?" (Tolstoi [1900] 1985: 128f.).

emphasis on individual self-realization (Lane 1986: 58). Also very influential in the further propagation of Nietzsche's thought is the novel *Pereval* (*The Pass*, 1893) by the novelist and playwright Pëtr Boborykin (1838-1921). This best-selling author supported the Populist striving to present a truthful account of social reality and produced a large number of books and plays that reflected Russian reality and were widely read. Boborykin was one of the first to bring Nietzsche's books from Germany to Russia (Makovskii [1955] 2000: 515). By his own account, the protagonist of *Pereval*, Kostritsyn, was inspired by the philosopher Preobrazhenskii and his explication of Nietzsche's ideas (Clowes 1988: 70f.). This novel was the first Russian fictional work that featured a Nietzschean hero and thereby had a greater impact on the reception of Nietzsche's ideas by a broad reading public than any critical article. By letting his protagonist preach the *Übermensch* and retell the fourth part of *Thus spoke Zarathustra* (Lane 1975: 37), which was not published until 1892, Boborykin introduced Russian audiences to Nietzsche's *Zarathustra* before the censorship ban was lifted in 1898. In a later article on Nietzscheanism, "O Nitssheanstve", Boborykin expresses his admiration for the German philosopher:

> Nobody before him understood so well all the personality of the human, the human's spiritual strength, and nobody has with such talent and inspiration dreamt about the possibility of the birth of the Übermensch. The word soon became funny, but the idea is not at all funny and will shine eternally before humankind as a guiding star (Boborykin 1900: 544).

In the following years, Nietzsche's ideas were gradually assimilated by fiction writers and poets, a process that resulted both in accurate popularizations and sensational vulgarizations.[19]

In 1900, on the occasion of his death (August 25), a flood of articles and necrologies about Nietzsche appeared in Russian journals

---

[19] Exemplary of the dissemination of Nietzsche's ideas in popular fiction that reaches a reading public other than the intellectual elite are Mikhail Artsybashev's *Sanin* (1907) and Anastasiia Verbitskaia's *Kliuchi Schast'ia* (*Keys of Happiness*, 1909-1912). The characters displayed in these novels advance a highly distorted version of Nietzsche's philosophy, which is reduced to a license for moral and sexual hedonism. For a detailed overview of Nietzschean motives in popular fiction, see Clowes (1988: 83ff.).

and newspapers.[20] His death did not go unnoticed in Russia and ironically awakened a new interest in his philosophy. Unlike the first responses, this re-evaluation occurred in a sphere of genuine curiosity and fascination for the German philosopher.

3. The flexible Nietzsche

From the turn of the last century on, Nietzsche's ideas became attractive to intellectuals operating in various fields of culture and philosophy. His works were eagerly read by artists, literary critics, philosophers and political ideologues alike, who all assimilated his ideas through their own ideological prisms and appropriated them for their own agenda. This obviously resulted in very heterogeneous and versatile interpretations of his ideas, in the process of which many intellectuals moved from one field to another in the development of their own thought and changed their focus in their reading of Nietzsche. Still, certain tendencies in the reception process can be sketched out, each of them centering upon a specific motive in Nietzsche's philosophy.

3.1. The aesthetic Nietzsche

Nietzsche was enthusiastically received and assimilated by the Russian symbolists who appeared on the Russian cultural scene in the 1890s and aspired to formulate a new concept of art that would outdo the fading populist idea that art should have a primordial social function. The key text for the symbolists was *The Birth of Tragedy* which offered them an aesthetic justification of reality and human existence. The exaltation of the Dionysian principle urged them to create a life-affirming and orgiastic art, and they re-established the importance of collective myth-making (*mifotvorchestvo*) in Russian culture. The symbolists were also captivated by the figure of Zarathustra and his teaching of the *Übermensch*, in which they observed an inclination towards an individualist aesthetics.

---

[20] See "Nitsshe v Rossii" ("Nietzsche in Russia") in *Novyi Zhurnal inostrannoi Literatury*; "Nekrolog" in *Mir Iskusstva*; "Smert' Nitsshe" ("Nietzsche's Death") in *Istoricheskii Vestnik*. For a full overview, see Davies (1986: 364f.).

Usually distinction is made between a so-called first and second generation of Russian symbolists. The first generation is the group around the critic and writer Dmitrii Merezhkovskii, who canonized Nietzsche for symbolists and other intellectuals alike. This group consists of Zinaida Gippius, Konstantin Bal'mont, Valerii Briusov, Nikolai Minskii, Fëdor Sologub and Akim Volynskii. These poets and literary critics shared the aspiration to create an innovative art and related concept of it, in which individual self-expression and worship of beauty were the highest good. They believed in a metaphysical truth beyond the phenomenal world and sought to grasp through symbols the mystical nature of reality. Nietzsche's aesthetics served as a fruitful source of inspiration in their creation of a mystical art.

From 1900 on, Merezhkovskii's emphasis shifted from a purely aesthetic outlook towards a more religious worldview. From then on, he was affected by what he perceived as the mystical and religious dimension in Nietzsche's discourse. This triggered the younger generation of symbolists, Viacheslav Ivanov, Andrei Belyi and Aleksandr Blok, to see a latent longing for Christ within Nietzsche's representation of the Dionysian. Each in their own way created a mythopoeic image of Christ as the life-affirming Dionysus (Clowes 1988: 115-172).

3.2. The religious Nietzsche

As is the focus of this book, from 1900 on Nietzsche proves to be a prolific source of inspiration in Russian religious thought. For the younger generation of symbolists, especially for Viacheslav Ivanov, Nietzsche restored the Dionysian godhead in philosophy of culture and inspired them to draw parallels between the ancient Deity and Christ (Biebuyck & Grillaert 2003).

Nietzsche also had a substantial impact on the thinkers of the Russian religious renaissance, the so-called *God-seekers* (*Bogoiskateli*). As I will outline in the case of Merezhkovskii and Berdiaev, whom I consider to be the exponents of the religious Nietzsche-reading, he provided them with a discursive arena in which they were able to formulate a new philosophy of religion.

3.3. The political Nietzsche

Around 1905, partly due to the failure of the revolution, some intellectuals moved to political and social issues. In response to the *God-seekers* who were chiefly concerned with the problem of religion, a new ideological movement emerged: *God-building* or *Bogostroitel'stvo* (Scherrer 1973: 309f.). Its chief ideologues, Maksim Gorkii, Anatolii Lunacharskii and Aleksandr Bogdanov, aimed to reinvigorate Marxism with a kind of Promethean heroism which they partly found in the imagery and thought of Nietzsche. These "Nietzschean Marxists" strove for a secular religion in which God was replaced by a socialist worship of human strength. They identified in Nietzsche's exaltation of the Dionysian a proclivity towards transcendence of the self and subsumption of the individual into a greater, collective whole. Through the Dionysian model, they were able to give a mystical and religious pathos to the Marxist ideal of collective well-being. Moreover, the image of the *Übermensch* supplied them with an ideal of human power and showed them the human potential to accomplish great and heroic tasks.[21]

4. Looking for Nietzsche, finding Dostoevskii

During the first years of the Russian acquaintanceship with Nietzsche, his ideas, provocative and puzzling to the Russian public, were refracted through a discourse that was familiar to any Russian reader: the one shaped by Dostoevskii. Nietzsche's own familiarity with and statements on Dostoevskii added fuel to the association between the German philosopher and the Russian writer.[22]

---

[21] The term "Nietzschean Marxism" is coined by Kline (1968). See chapter 1 for research on Nietzsche's influence on the Russian symbolists and studies on the Nietzschean Marxists.

[22] Nietzsche got acquainted with Dostoevskii's works by the end of 1886, beginning 1887. During this winter, he discovered in a Nice bookshop a French translation of *Notes from Underground* (1864), entitled *l'Esprit souterrain*. Dostoevskii's name appears for the first time in Nietzsche's correspondence in February 1887, i.e. in a letter to Overbeck on February 12, 1887 (KSB 8: 21). On February 23, 1887, he describes to Overbeck his first experience of the Russian writer: "I knew nothing about Dostoevskii, not even his name, until a few weeks ago – uncultivated person that I am, reading no "periodicals"! In a bookshop my hand accidentally came to rest on "L'esprit souterrain", just recently translated in French (the same kind of chance

Nietzsche's reading of Dostoevskij was already mentioned in
the first Russian article on him, Preobrazhenskii's "Fridrikh Nitsshe:

---

brought me in acquiantance with Schopenhauer when I was 21, and with Stendhal
when I was 35). The instinct of affinity (*Instinkt der Verwandtschaft*) (or what shall I
call it ?) spoke to me immediately, my joy was extraordinary" (KSB 8: 27f.). On
March 7, 1887 Nietzsche describes at large to Gast his encounter with Dostoevskii:
"Dostoevskii happened to me just as Stendhal did earlier: an accidental contact, a
book one flips open in a bookshop, a name never heard of, and the sudden instinct that
one has met a relative. Until now, I know little about his position, his calling, his
history: he died in 1881. In his youth, he was in dire straits: illness and poverty; at the
age of 27, he was sentenced to death, but pardoned at the scaffold, then four years
Siberia, chained, among hardened criminals. This period was decisive: he discovered
the power of his psychological intuition, what's more, his heart sweetened and
deepened in the process. His book of recollections from these years, "La Maison des
Morts" is one of the most human books ever written. What I got to know first,
recently published in French translation, is called "L'esprit souterrain", containing
two short novels [*The Landlady* and *Notes from Underground*]: the first a sort of
unfamiliar music, the second a true stroke of psychological genius – a frightening and
ferocious mockery of γνῶθι σαυτόν [know thyself], but tossed off with such a light
audacity and joy in his superior power that I was drunk with delight" (KSB 8: 41f.; for
other references in Nietzsche's correspondence see KSB 8, 50, 71, 74f., 106, 451,
457, 483, 494). In his published works, Nietzsche refers three times to Dostoevskii. In
The Antichrist (1888, not published until 1895) Dostoevskii is brought up in
association with the Gospel: "That strange and sick world, into which the Gospels
introduce us – a world, as in a Russian novel, in which the scum of society, nervous
disorders, and "childlike" idiocy seem to be having a rendezvous – must at all events
have *coarsened* the type […] It is regrettable that a Dostoevskii did not live near this
most interesting décadent [Jesus Christ], I mean someone who would have known
how to sense the very stirring charm of such a mixture of the sublime, the sickly and
the childlike" (KSA 6: 202). An equal link is made in *The Case of Wagner* (1888):
"the Gospels present us with precisely the same physiological types that Dostoevskii's
novels describe" (KSA 6: 50). This statement is, for some researchers, a nod to
Dostoevskii's novel *The Idiot* (1868) and a possible proof that Nietzsche based his
interpretation of Christ on the protagonist of this novel (see e.g. Kaufmann, 1988:
396f.) In *Twilight of the Idols* (1888-89), Nietzsche credits Dostoevskii for his
psychological insight in the criminal type and alludes to Dostoevskii's experience in
penal servitude, as written down in the semi-autobiographical *Notes from the House of
the Dead* (1860-62): "Dostoevskii's report is relevant to this problem – Dostoevskii,
the only psychologist, from whom I had something to learn; he belongs to the most
beautiful strokes of fortune in my life […] This *profound* human, who was ten times
right in his low estimate of the superficial Germans, lived for a long time among the
convicts in Siberia – hardened criminals for whom there was no way back to society –
and experienced them very different from what he had expected: they are carved out
of the best, hardest, and most valuable wood that grows anywhere on Russian soil"
(KSA 6: 146f.). For a more detailed overview of Nietzsche's reading of Dostoevskii
see Gesemann (1961) & Miller (1973).

Kritika Morali Al'truizma" (1892). Preobrazhenskii explains Nietzsche's critique of the "moral making morality" as leveling all powers in humanity (KSA 3: 147). For Nietzsche, this universally adopted and unquestioned moral system deliberately denies and rejects the most valuable powers and energies that are present in "the outcasts of society", the so-called "criminals, free-thinkers, immoral people and villains, who live, so to say, outside the tutelage of the law" (Preobrazhenskii [1892] 2001: 58f.). [23] In a commentary note to the text, Preobrazhenskii remarks that Nietzsche in this context "points at the types, portrayed in Dostoevskii's *Notes from the House of the Dead*, whom he considers to be the most profound of all psychologists he knows" (id.: 59). He refers to Nietzsche's controversial statements on the strong nature of the "criminal type" (*Verbrecher-Typus*) in *Twilight of the Idols* (1889), in which he extols Dostoevskii's description of and psychological insight into the criminal psyche (KSA 6: 146f.). Unlike the later canon, which supports the view that Dostoevskii had a decisive part in the formation of Nietzsche's thought, Preobrazhenskii does not make any statement concerning Dostoevskii's supposed influence on Nietzsche. [24] The legendary but incorrect claim that Nietzsche borrowed some ideas from Dostoevskii, is partly initiated by the critic D. Vergun.[25] In a 1901 article in the Austrian journal *Slavianskii Vek*, Vergun asserted

---

[23] In the third book of *The Dawn* (1881), aphorism 164, Nietzsche credits the ones who are in contemporary moral language labelled "Verbrecher, Freidenker, Unsittliche, Bösewichte". He finds these outlaws necessary and worthy, for they oppose the traditional idea of an "allein-moralisch-machende-Moral" (KSA 3: 147).

[24] Given Nietzsche's rather late reading of Dostoevskii (Winter 1886-1887) it is, in my opinion, unlikely that the Russian writer had any part in the formation of Nietzsche's ideas. Nietzsche appreciated Dostoevskii primarily as a psychologist. Note for example his statement in *Twilight of the Idols*: "Dostoevskii, the only psychologist, from whom I had something to learn; he belongs to the most beautiful strokes of fortune in my life" (KSA 6: 146ff.). While emphasizing the importance of Dostoevskii's psychological insight, Nietzsche hardly refers to the philosophical or ideological value of Dostoevskii's works.

[25] The view that Dostoevskii had a decisive part in Nietzsche's intellectual development is a pervasive one. See, amongst others, Charles Andler, who talks about "provable borrowings" ("des emprunts démontrables") (1930: 1). Karl Jaspers believes that "in his final years, Nietzsche experienced the influence of Dostoevskii" ([1935] 1981: 36). According to Wolfgang Müller-Lauter, "the image that Nietzsche had of nihilism is decisively determined by his reading of Dostoevskii's novels" (1971: 66). V. Dudkin aims to investigate "the question concerning Dostoevskii's influence on Nietzsche" (1994: 32).

that Nietzsche already learned of and read Dostoevskii in 1873 (Fridlender 1979: 232). To this purpose, he antedated Nietzsche's October 20, and November 20, 1888, letters to Brandes as published by Brandes himself in his essay "Friedrich Nietzsche. An Essay on Aristocratic Radicalism," in which Nietzsche mentions Dostoevskii, in 1873 (Brandes [1888] 1895: 222).[26]

In the 1893 article "Nravstvennye idealy nashego vremeni: Fridrikh Nitsshe i Lev Tolstoi," Grot associates Nietzsche with one of Dostoevskii's so-called 'nihilistic' characters, in particular with Ivan Karamazov. Explaining that Nietzsche does not acknowledge the existence of a god nor the notion of an immortal soul, Grot refers to Ivan Karamazov, who is generally known by the Russian public. In this manner, Grot reverts to Russian literary and cultural heritage to illustrate the German philosopher's thought:

> [...] Nietzsche is a materialist and atheist. The soul and God are superstitions. And this explains Nietzsche's leap from the human-animal to the Übermensch (*ot cheloveka-zhivotnogo k sverkhcheloveku*) passing the stage of "the human", in the true sense of this word. It is not surprising that this consistent materialist, atheist and evolutionist when it comes to morals repeats without any skepticism and false shame Ivan Karamazov's famous idea [...] that if one does not believe in God and in the immortality of the soul, he "is permitted everything" (*vsë pozvoleno*) (Grot [1893] 2001: 87).

Nietzsche and Ivan Karamazov are identified on the basis of an allegedly equal ethical formula, this is that "all is permitted." The wording "all is permitted" (*alles ist erlaubt*) indeed appears twice in Nietzsche's published works. In *Thus spoke Zarathustra* (1883-1884), Zarathustra's shadow says to himself: "Nothing is true, all is permitted" (KSA 4: 340). The shadow, which is in fact one of the voices of Zarathustra himself, appears to Zarathustra in the fourth part of the narrative in which Zarathustra is an old man and still teaching the *Übermensch*. The shadow represents Zarathustra's adventurous nature: he has followed Zarathustra in the dangers and risks that lie on the way to the *Übermensch*. Yet, where Zarathustra eventually grasped the meaning of the *Übermensch*, his shadow failed and lost

---

[26] Nietzsche writes to Brandes on October 20, 1888: "I quite believe it when you say that 'in Russia one can come to life again'; I count any Russian book, above all Dostoevskii [...] among my greatest reliefs" (KSB 8: 457) and on November 20, 1888: "I completely believe your words about Dostoevskii; I prize his work as the most valuable psychological material that I know" (KSB 8: 483).

his goal: "Have I – still a goal?" (KSA 4: 340). He is still stuck in the nihilism Zarathustra overcame a long time ago and cries desperately: "Nothing is true, all is permitted [...] nothing lives any longer, that I love" (KSA 4: 340). Within the discursive setting of *Thus spoke Zarathustra*, the line that "all is permitted" does not apply to the *Übermensch*. Rather, it points to the inability to unravel the mystery of the *Übermensch* as one who constructs his own goals. The same phrase returns in *On the Genealogy of Morals* (1887), as the succinct slogan of the ones who possess the true freedom of mind (*Freigeist*) (KSA 5: 399).[27]

Grot extracts this phrase from its original context and presents it in Ivan Karamazov's speech that all is permitted. The idea that all is permitted is used here to explicate the *Übermensch*. Nietzsche however, never formulates this idea with reference to his anthropology. By relating it to Ivan's central theory, this expression is not only ascribed a greater significance, but also, and more importantly, it is given another delineation than it actually has in Nietzsche's works. The *Übermensch* is here staged as one to whom all is permitted, a mythopoem that will foster and contribute to the later identification of the *Übermensch* with other Dostoevskian nihilistic characters.

From 1893 on, the explication of the *Übermensch* as one to whom all is permitted finds its continuation in other critical articles on Nietzsche. In "Genezis nravstvennogo ideala dekadenta," Astaf'ev explains Nietzsche's idea of the *Übermensch* as follows:

> For the sake of the complete development of this *Übermensch* [...] the mass is doomed to an incomplete existence, to a fate of slaves and instruments, towards which [...] for the sake of a high goal, all is permitted, up to inexorable cruelty [...] the mass should be made an instrument for the genius. To the latter all is permitted; for him guilt, sin, remorse do not exist (Astaf'ev [1893] 2001: 111).[28]

By defining the *Übermensch* as an elitist anthropology for the sake of which it is allowed to sacrifice the masses, the way is cleared for later associations between *Übermensch* and Dostoevskii's anti-heroes, in

---

[27] It is also to be found in the notebooks from 1884-1885 (KSA 11: 88, 95, 146, 155, 384, 403), but this is a source not available until 1897 (and this even in a reduced version) (WNB 1: 5).

[28] See also Boborykin 1900: 543.

particular Raskol'nikov.[29] In the critical literature on Nietzsche, the link with Raskol'nikov is furthermore encouraged by staging Napoleon as the exponent of Nietzsche's anthropology (Bulgakov F. 1893: 211; Mikhailovskii 1894c: 104; Tsertelev [1897] 2001: 283; Levitskii 1901: 511; Kheisin 1903: 129). In Raskol'nikov's theory, Napoleon is paradigmatic for the extraordinary human: he is "the real *sovereign* (*vlastelin*), to whom all is permitted, he destroys Toulon, creates a massacre in Paris, *forgets* an army in Egypt, *loses* half a million people in the Moscow campaign" (PSS 6: 211). Nietzsche also expresses his appreciation for Napoleon and his significant role in history. For him, Napoleon is an enemy of modern civilization, thanks to whom "man in Europe has become master again over the merchant and Philistine" (KSA 3: 610). Napoleon represents the archetype of the classic and Renaissance human. He appeared as

> the most isolated and late-born human there has ever been, and in him the problem incarnate of the noble ideal as such – one might well ponder what kind of problem it is: Napoleon, this synthesis of *Unmensch* und *Übermensch*… (KSA 5: 288).

In this context Napoleon is indeed associated with the *Übermensch*. This figure incorporates for Nietzsche both traits of *Unmensch* and *Übermensch*, yet he is not exclusively the one or the other. Napoleon does not fully embody the *Übermensch*, because a part of him is still *Unmensch*.[30] His '*Unmenschlichkeit*' reduces and detracts from his '*Übermenschlichkeit*' and vice versa. This is illustrated by a fragment in the notebooks from 1887, the same period in which Nietzsche was working on *On the Geneaology of Morals* in which the former fragment appeared.

> The human is both non-animal (*Unthier*) und animal-beyond-the-animal (*Überthier*); the higher human is both inhuman (*Unmensch*) and human-beyond-the-human (*Übermensch*): in that way both belong together. With every growth of the human in greatness and height, he grows in the depth

---

[29] See also Chuiko [1893] 2001: 124. "In Nietzsche's profound conviction, nature creates the people with only one goal: to make possible the existence of five or six individuals, appearing as the true representatives of the human race. These are the tigers and lions, born to devour the sheep."

[30] In this specific context, *Unmensch* implies inhuman, in the sense of a quality that is not human.

and dreadfulness: one cannot want the one without the other – or rather: the more thoroughly one wants the one, one reaches the other (KSA 12: 426).

In being both *Unmensch* and *Übermensch*, Napoleon is yet still "der höhere Mensch," the higher human. In the fourth part of *Thus spoke Zarathustra*, Zarathustra addresses "the higher humans," who are already aware of the death of God and are thus a step further on the road to the *Übermensch* than the people in the market. However, they have not yet completely crossed the rope "that is tied between animal and *Übermensch*" (KSA 4: 16): they have not yet learned to laugh and dance like the *Übermensch* (KSA 4: 356-368).[31] The higher human signals the advent of the *Übermensch*, is pregnant with the humor and lightheartedness of the *Übermensch*, though is still "human, all too human".

In spite of what the Russian critics assume, Napoleon is in Nietzsche's discourse not advanced as a paragon for the *Übermensch*. For one thing, in his consistent desire to break radically with all earlier normative systems of philosophy, Nietzsche never concretized his anthropology by putting forward an example.[32] For another thing, in spite of Napoleon's inclination towards this anthropological model, he is yet still merely "a higher human."[33] And in contrast to Raskol'nikov's ideal of the extraordinary, whose distinctiveness seems to lie in his permitted cruelty towards the ordinary human beings, the value of the higher human does not lie in his effect on the masses but in his 'being different' (*Anderssein*, KSA 13: 498).[34]

Nietzsche's claim that Napoleon is a synthesis of *Unmensch* and *Übermensch* apparently reminded the Russian reader of Raskol'nikov's idealization of this historical figure and resulted in the mythopoeic canon of Napoleon as an archetypal *Übermensch*.[35] The

---

[31] "You higher humans, the worst thing in you is: none of you learned to dance, as you ought to dance – to dance beyond yourself [...] you higher humans, *learn,* I pray you, to laugh" (KSA 4: 367-368).

[32] In some passages he did name some historical figures, whose personality bears certain traits of the *Übermensch*. See KSA 6: 136 & 300 (Cesare Borgia); KSA 6: 151 (Goethe).

[33] See also in the preparatory notes to *Thus spoke Zarathustra* (Summer 1883): "Higher H[umans] like Napoleon" (KSA 10: 413).

[34] For a detailed analysis of Nietzsche's representation of Napoleon, see Marti (1989).

[35] The association between Nietzsche's *Übermensch* and Napoleon might have been fostered by the mythological status of Napoleon in nineteenth century Russian culture. The figure of Napoleon decisively fascinated Russian popular and literary

Übermensch is thus re-contextualized and re-formulated within the typical Russian cultural and ideological context, deeply penetrated by Dostoevskii's fictional characters.

In the article "Literatura i Zhizn': Eshche o F. Nitsshe" from 1894, the eminent Populist philosopher Nikolai Mikhailovskii makes the first significant attempt to illustrate and concretize Nietzsche's thought by juxtaposing it with Dostoevskii's fiction. In 1882, Mikhailovskii had published a critical study on Dostoevskii, "Zhestokii talant" ("A cruel talent"), in which he interpreted the writer from a Populist point of view and labeled him as a reactionary and a cruel portrayer of the poor folk's suffering. Earlier in 1894, before the article on Nietzsche, Mikhailovskii published in a preceding volume of *Russkoe Bogatstvo* another article on Dostoevskii, at the end of which he links Raskol'nikov's theory "of the dual morals for the ordinary and the extraordinary people" (*dvoiakaia moral' dlia obyknovennych i neobyknovennych liudei*) to "the philosophy of Friedrich Nietzsche, which has rapidly gained fame in the whole of Europe" (Mikhailovskii 1894a: 101). In his essay on the German philosopher – published some months after the article on Dostoevskii – Mikhailovskii elaborates in detail the supposed resemblance between some of Nietzsche's ideas and Dostoevskii's nihilistic characters. At first Mikhailovskii relates that "Nietzsche knew and highly appreciated Dostoevskii" (Mikhailovskii 1894b: 116). As in Preobrazhenskii's article, he quotes the passage in *Twilight of the Idols* in which Nietzsche praises Dostoevskii for his psychological insight in the strong nature of the criminal (KSA 6: 146f.). However, in his reconstruction of Nietzsche's valuation of and alleged affinity with the Russian writer, there is some inconsistency with actual biographical facts. Mikhailovskii mistakenly dates the appearance of *Twilight of the Idols* (1889) in 1880, which obviously results in the claim that Nietzsche was already aware of and had read the Russian writer from that time on (Mikhailovskii 1894b: 116).

---

imagination. An example of this is Dostoevskii's *Crime and Punishment* (1866) and Tolstoi's *War and Peace* (1863-1869), in which Napoleon plays key roles. In both these narratives, Napoleon is represented in an unfavourable manner as the archetype of the Western state. He stands for the expansionism of the West. In this perspective, the link with the *Übermensch*, which the critics of the 1890s perceived as embodying the moral decline in Western Europe (see the preface to Preobrazhenskii's article) could have been circulating. For an analysis of the Russian mythology surrounding Napoleon, see Wesling (2001).

In spite of their different "spiritual physiognomy," Mikhailovskii discerns in both thinkers "something common" (*nechto obchshee*) in the sense, that

> both are with an extraordinary and particular interest concerned with the same questions. Where Nietzsche puts a plus, Dostoevskii in most cases puts a minus, and vice versa, but both know these pluses and minuses, both are to the highest degree interested in them, considering these concerned questions the most important, which can only be conceived of by the human mind (ibid.).

Mikhailovskii focuses on the "likeness of arguments" between Nietzsche's elaboration on the criminal type and Raskol'nikov's theory of the "dual morals" and "the extraordinary people" (id.: 117). This likeness even goes so far that both Nietzsche and Raskol'nikov put forward the same historical figure, Napoleon, as the typical exponent of this human "who may rightfully trespass every law" (Mikhailovskii 1894c: 104). Once again, the significance of Napoleon in Nietzsche's discourse on the *Übermensch* is magnified, obviously due to the effect of familiarity with Dostoevskii. In Mikhailovskii's view, Nietzsche and Raskol'nikov are equal in the sense that both do not recognize anything higher than themselves but wish themselves to be the highest (id.: 105). In spite of the identification between Nietzsche's and Raskol'nikov's ideas, Mikhailovskii considers it improbable that Nietzsche was in this matter influenced by the Russian writer (id.: 117).

In his explanation of Nietzsche's conviction that the human is by nature an egoist, Mikhailovskii once again turns to Dostoevskii: "to the Russian reader, these are not unknown statements. Dostoevskii knew well this range of ideas and feelings" (id.: 126). Reference is made to Dostoevskii's psychological analysis of the egoistic nature in *Notes from Underground* (1864) and *The Gambler* (1866). In his prophetic words that one day a gentleman will appear, who advocates that "we all should live again by our stupid will," the underground man anticipates Nietzsche (id.: 127).

In the 1897 article, "Kritika vyrozhdeniia i vyrozhdenie kritiki" ("Criticism of degeneration and degeneration of criticism"), D.N. Tsertelev posits that "almost all the essential [ideas] that Nietzsche considers to be his own discovery, can be found in *The Brothers Karamazov*" (Tsertelev [1897] 2001: 282). He claims that

Ivan Karamazov's theory that "all is permitted" prefigures Nietzsche's claim that if nothing is true, all is permitted. Tsertelev also observes an analogy between Ivan's opinion on the falsifying role of the Church in history – as he observes in Ivan's "Grand Inquisitor" – and Nietzsche's views on Christianity (id.: 283). In the confrontation between Christ and the Grand Inquisitor, it becomes clear that the Grand Inquisitor, in spite of what he pretends, does not believe in God. Christ has left humankind with the burden of freedom. The Grand Inquisitor has taken upon himself the task to "correct" Christ's deed and deprive humankind of this freedom to make an individual choice (PSS 14: 234). In his aim to actualize God's Kingdom on earth, the Grand Inquisitor completely neglects the divine potential in humanity and only focuses on the human's material needs. For the Grand Inquisitor, the "universal kingdom" means the realization of universal human happiness and a state of welfare for all humans.[36] Tsertelev identifies a foreshadowing of Nietzsche's atheism in the Inquisitor's rationalist and pragmatic stance towards God, in Whom he does not truly believe and Who is merely a fabricated idol to realize peace and material wellbeing on earth:

> Karamazov's Grand Inquisitor does not believe in God, and the will to power (*volia k vlasti*) in him is maybe not less strong, than [the will] in Napoleon, in whom Nietzsche sees the synthesis of the inhuman and trans-human (*sintez sverkhchelovecheskogo i beschelovechnogo*). The Grand Inquisitor is in his atheism, and in his contempt for the crowd, and in the iron strength of his will, very similar to Nietzsche's ideal (Tsertelev [1897] 2001: 283).

By drawing a parallel between the Grand Inquisitor's and Nietzsche's disbelief in God, Tsertelev overlooks the analogies between Dostoevskii's criticism on Christianity which is directed against Roman Catholicism, and Nietzsche's argumentation to renounce Christianity and the Christian Church. Dostoevskii demonstrates in the "Legend" that the Catholic Church has not evolved according to Christ's original teachings. This is akin to Nietzsche's criticism that Paul falsified Christ's true teachings (KSA 6: 215ff.).

In 1900, the year of Nietzsche's death, *Novyi Zhurnal inostrannoi Literatury* (*The new journal for foreign literature*) published a concise overview of Nietzsche's reception by the Russian

---

[36] The so-called "legend" of the Grand Inquisitor will be examined in chapter 3.

intellectuals in the 1890s, entitled "Nittsshe v Rossii" ("Nietzsche in Russia"). The anonymous author ascribes Nietzsche's popularity in Russia – which has exceeded at this point in time the impact of Marxism and Tolstoi's teachings on Russian society – to the fact that his ideas were already present in nineteenth century Russian literature.[37] From Pushkin on, Russian authors have emancipated the human individuality and in this manner paved the way for Nietzsche, the "prophet of individualism". He claims:

> One can even point at complete Nietzschean ideas that are in an embryonic phase expressed with us long before Nietzsche formulated them. The reader guesses that we hint at Dostoevskii. Listen attentively to what Raskol'nikov advocates. For, are these not Nietzsche's ideas in their full scope ("Nittsshe v Rossii", 1900: 103)?

Raskol'nikov's classification of the "ordinary and extraordinary" people *(obyknovennye i neobyknovennye)* and his conviction that the latter are granted the right to transgress every legal and moral law in order to achieve their goal, is employed to explicate Nietzsche's idea of the *Übermensch*. Raskol'nikov's statement that these extraordinary humans are permitted to "step over blood" *(pereshagnut' cherez krov')* (PSS 6: 199ff.) is transposed to the *Übermensch* and is, as it were, formulated by Nietzsche ("Nittsshe v Rossii" 1900: 103). This blended discourse obviously generates the false impression of absolute identification between the ideas put forward by Dostoevskii's protagonist and Nietzsche's more abstract and ambiguous concept. The *Übermensch* is reductively explained by Raskol'nikov's theory that a genius (such as Kepler and Newton), when confronted with practical obstacles that obstruct the realization of his genial idea, should not be hindered by any legal restriction or moral conflict to eliminate these, even if that implies the death of hundreds of people. Yet, whereas Raskol'nikov put his ideas into practice, Nietzsche remained in the mere theoretical sphere and eventually went insane. The author concludes that "Raskol'nikov is undoubtedly our Russian Nietzsche" (ibid.).

During the first decade of the reception process, Nietzsche and his thoughts are recurrently read through the horizon of expectations shaped by Dostoevskii's fictional nihilists. When examining the

---

[37] Vladimir Solov'ëv likewise observes 1890s cultural consciousness to be dominated by Marxism, Tolstoi's ethics and Nietzsche's demonism. See chapter 4.

critical literature on Dostoevskii in that same period, between 1890 and 1900, there are some marginal references to Nietzsche. In an 1893 essay on Dostoevskii, bishop Antonii Khrapovitskii – who then held a significant position in the hierarchy of the Orthodox church – relates Ivan Karamazov to Nietzsche: "[...] Ivan Karamazov with his eudaemonistic theory (in our days literally repeated by Nietzsche, whom our Muscovites eulogize)" (Khrapovitskii [1893] 1997: 159).[38] As mentioned above, Nikolai Mikhailovskii associates Raskol'nikov with Nietzsche in an 1894 essay (Mikhailovskii 1894a: 101). And in Akim Volynskii's 1897 sketch, "Raskol'nikov," composed as a dialogue between some persons in a restaurant, one of the interlocutors contends that Raskol'nikov is a "hero, in the newest sense of this word. Here, so many years in advance, Nietzsche's theories are in the air" (Volynskii 1897: 11. Quoted in Iakubovich 2000: 73). As for Mikhailovskii and Volynskii, the link between Raskol'nikov and Nietzsche in their respective studies is obviously established under the circumstance of their concurrent reading of Nietzsche. While writing the 1894 article on Dostoevskii, Mikhailovskii was at the same time preparing his article "Literatura i Zhizn': Eshche o F. Nitsshe," which was published only a few months later. In 1896, Volynskii had published his Nietzsche-essay, "Literaturnye Zametki: Apollon i Dionis." He had already substantially read Nietzsche, when he matched the philosopher to Raskol'nikov in the aforementioned essay.

5. Conclusion

In the first decade of the reception process, which roughly runs from 1890 until the turn of the century, the overall tenor of the critical studies and commentaries on Nietzsche could be characterized as unsympathetic. The chief focus was on his assailments against established morality, in which the critics at hand identified a symptom of the decline in Western European mentality. The responses were marked by the anxiety that Nietzsche's ideas would contaminate and put Russian values and moral consciousness in jeopardy. There were

---

[38] Reference is made to the series of articles that appeared in 1892-1893 on Nietzsche in the journal *Voprosy Psikhologii i Filosofii*. The journal was part of the activities of the Moscow Philosophical Society of which Khrapovitskii was member.

some notable exceptions to this negative bias. Preobrazhenskii (1892) and Mikhailovskii (1894) offered a rather favorable and systematic overview of Nietzsche's philosophy and in this way attempted to counter Nietzsche's reputation as the rigid immoralist. They were the first to find some merit in Nietzsche and to credit him for the originality of his ideas.

In the first studies, Nietzsche is frequently explained through Dostoevskii's literary discourse. More particularly, the philosopher and his anthropology of the *Übermensch* are linked to the characters Ivan Karamazov and Raskol'nikov. Nietzsche's saying that "nothing is true, all is permitted" is explained by and even identified with Ivan Karamazov's theory that if there is no God, all is permitted (*vsë pozvoleno*). Furthermore, the idea that all is permitted as elaborated in Ivan's discourse, is transposed to the *Übermensch*. This recontextualization of the *Übermensch* evidently paves the way for the further canonization of this anthropology as a human type for whom, in an existential world devoid of God, everything is legitimized. By defining the *Übermensch* as such, further association is made with another typical Dostoevskian nihilist, Raskol'nikov, who advances the idea that to the 'extraordinary' all is permitted. In identifying Raskol'nikov's and Nietzsche's anthropology, the *Übermensch* is represented as an "extraordinary" human for whom it is legally and morally permitted "to step over a dead body, to wade through blood" for the realization of his exceptional objective (PSS 6: 199f.). Furthermore, by making Raskol'nikov's extraordinary and Nietzsche's *Übermensch* analogous, Raskol'nikov's exaltation of Napoleon as the most concrete and perfect embodiment of the extraordinary in history, is transposed to the *Übermensch*.

The impact of Dostoevskii's vast legacy in Russian culture on the reading of Nietzsche is obvious. In particular the anthropology of the *Übermensch* is for the Russian reader highly reminiscent of Dostoevskii's nihilistic anti-heroes. The *Übermensch* is from the first instance identified with these nihilistic characters as if to elucidate and concretize this concept. In the Russian reception, Nietzsche's anthropology is re-conceptualized and re-formulated to make it correspond to Dostoevskii's nihilists. In this early stage of the reception process, Nietzsche is substantially explained through the lens of Dostoevskii's discourse. However, in studies on Dostoevskii, Nietzsche is hardly mentioned, and when he is, it is only in passing and without the purpose of clarifying any of Dostoevskii's views. Or, to put it differently, in this specific constellation Nietzsche is the passive recipient and Dostoevskii functions as the active agent.

Chapter 3

Dostoevskii's philosophical anthropology

So great is the worth of Dostoevskii that to have produced him is by itself sufficient justification for the existence of the Russian people in the world: and he will bear witness for his country-men at the last judgment of the nations (Berdiaev [1923] 1991: 147).

1. Introduction

In the first years of the reception process of Nietzsche in Russia, the philosopher is read through a Dostoevskian lens. And as I will demonstrate in subsequent chapters, Dostoevskii leaves an even more substantial imprint on the *God-seekers'* reading of Nietzsche. For them, Dostoevskii proves to be a fruitful source of inspiration not only in their assessment of Nietzsche but also in the formulation of their religious philosophy.

In order to fully understand the *God-seekers'* interpretation of Nietzsche, as shaped by the field of expectations emerging from Dostoevskii's discourse, Dostoevskii's religious worldview and in particular his philosophical anthropology deserve close scrutiny.

2. An ongoing dialogue with God

Dostoevskii was undoubtedly a religious writer, especially after his return from Siberian exile. Encouraged by his mother, who was a very devout woman, he was already at an early age deeply immersed in Russian Orthodox liturgy and spirituality. She inspired him to read the

Bible, particularly the New Testament (Kirillova 2001: 41). His religious education was built around a deep knowledge of the Bible as well as the doctrines, liturgy, iconography and hagiographies of the Russian Orthodox Church. Although Dostoevskii was raised in the Russian Orthodox tradition and practiced his religion as every Russian believer, he relied in his personal confession more on the Bible than on established ecclesiastical dogmas.[1]

In the 1840s Dostoevskii distanced himself from religious doctrines and indulged in socialist thought, yet without ever becoming a radical atheist. His preoccupation with Fourier and French Utopian Socialism at that time shows that he essentially looked for a social theory with a Christian bias. However, it was only after his experience of penal servitude in the 1850s that he fully regained his faith and began to explore problems of religion, specifically the relationship between humanity and God, a question that pursued him on a very personal level.

Nonetheless, his faith went through phases of actual doubt. In his own account, the question of whether God really existed was one that tormented him throughout his whole life.[2] For him, doubts and religious crises were even an essential element in the religious experience. Throughout his entire lifetime, Dostoevskii was in search of God: not in the sense that he ever actually disbelieved but rather that he was continuously aspiring to outline his idea of the Divinity and to establish a personal relationship with Him. Refusing to accept a dogmatic and abstract image of God, he searched for a personal consciousness of Him, a search that went through phases of indecisiveness. In a much-quoted letter to Nataliia Fonvizina which was written from his place of exile Omsk in 1854, Dostoevskii described his moments of religious despair:

> At such moments you thirst [...] for faith, and you find it, precisely because the truth shines through in moments of misfortune. I tell you about myself

---

[1] Dostoevskii frequently reread the Bible. During his exile, he was strongly attached to his copy of the Gospel that one of the Decembrists' wives had given him on the way to Siberia. His library contained several copies of the Gospel, which are full of markings and notes. In the Old Testament he especially liked the Book of Job (Kirillova 2001: 41ff; Kogan 1996: 147ff.).

[2] "[the idea of God's existence] is one that has tormented me consciously and unconsciously all my life" (PSS 29/I: 117). In the novel *The Devils*, Kirillov uses roughly the same words: "God has tormented me all my life" (PSS 10: 94).

that I am a child of the age, a child of disbelief and doubt till now and even (I know it) to the grave. What dreadful torments this thirst to believe has cost me and continues now to cost me, which is all the stronger in my soul the more opposing arguments there are in me. And yet, God sometimes sends me moments at which I am perfectly at peace; at these moments I love and find that I am loved by others, and at such moments I have composed within myself a creed in which everything is clear and holy to me (PSS 28/I: 176).[3]

This straightforward account of his "thirst for faith" is not an indication that Dostoevskii ever really lost his belief in God. Rather, it testifies to a temporary condition of being unsure about the nature and existence of God. Being "a child of disbelief and doubt," Dostoevskii did not settle with externally imposed arguments to accept God's existence, but was in need of a personal experience of the Deity. He yearned for an inner sensation in which God would reveal Himself to him, for some proof of His presence in the world and in humanity. And he found this evidence in the act of love between humans ("I love and find that I am loved by others"). It is through this feeling of love that Dostoevskii fully experienced the Deity. God resides in human beings' love for one another. His conviction that God is present in and reveals Himself in the feeling of loving and being loved by the other shows that he primarily focused on the human being in his experience of religion.

For Dostoevskii, God is both transcendent and immanent. This is in his experience a self-evident given which cannot be captured in a theological or philosophical formula. He finds that the existence of God is not a dogma that is rationally proven. God is in essence unintelligible: he cannot be grasped or known by human reason yet is revealed in the human's striving to love the other: "Nature, the soul, God, love... can only be known through the heart, and not through reason" (PSS 28/I: 53).

Dostoevskii's view on Christianity was clearly anthropocentric. As with all the subjects in which the writer engaged – aesthetics, politics, morality, history – his contemplations on religion were primarily concerned with the status of the human. All aspects of his thinking were directed "to find the human in the human" ("*naiti v cheloveke cheloveka*") (PSS 27: 65).

---

[3] Nataliia Fonvizina was one of the Decembrists' wives who accompanied their husbands in exile, and gave Gospels to the deportees on their way to Siberian prison.

Besides that, Dostoevskii's Christianity was decisively Christocentric: whereas the Deity remained in his outlook a kind of distant and unintelligible entity, Christ was a tangible human personality who showed humanity the right path to experience God.

3. Dostoevskii's Christology

The figure of Christ was of supreme importance in Dostoevskii's personal faith and his religious thought in general.[4] Not specialized in theology, the writer never elaborated a Christology in a systematic manner. Yet his fictional works, letters, non-fictional articles, and the voluminous *Diary of a Writer* served as a prolific forum to express his thoughts on the meaning of Christ. These all show that Dostoevskii's worldview was highly Christocentric and that his belief in God was primarily grounded in his faith in Christ. In the letter to Nataliia Fonvizina, in which he intimately confessed his "thirst for faith," he formulated his "creed" which reveals a persistent and unconditional faith in Christ:

> I have formulated my creed, wherein all is clear and holy to me. This creed is very simple, here it is: to believe that there is nothing more beautiful, deeper, more sympathetic, more rational, more brave and perfect than Christ. I say to myself with jealous love that not only is there no one else like Him, but that there also could be no one else. Even more, if someone were to prove to me that Christ is outside the truth, and it really were the case that the truth is outside of Christ, then I would prefer to remain with Christ, rather than with the truth (PSS 28/I: 176).[5]

This shows that, whatever evidence to the contrary, Dostoevskii holds on to Christ with a faith that cannot be countered in any way, not even by scientific or logical arguments. However, at the same time, he cannot escape from recognizing that there is indeed an inconsistency

---

[4] See the testimony of Baron Vrangel, for instance, who observed that, after his regaining of faith in the Omsk prison camp, Dostoevskii "did not often go to church, and disliked priests [...] But he spoke about Christ ecstatically" (quoted in Jones 2005: 8).

[5] This is almost literally repeated in *The Devils*, in a conversation between Shatov and Stavrogin: "Didn't you tell me that if it were mathematically proved to you that the truth is outside Christ, then you would prefer to stay with Christ, rather than with the truth?" (PSS 10: 198).

between Christ and truth, between the heavenly ideal and earthly reality. And this incongruity is a great source of torment for the religious writer: "It is not as a child that I believe in Christ and confess Him. My *hosanna* has passed through *a great crucible of doubts*" (PSS 27: 86).

Because he was not skilled in theology and was mostly focused on the human aspect in his experience of Christianity, Dostoevskii did not engage in theological debates concerning the degree of Christ's Divinity. As every Christian believer, he departs from the Gospel image of Christ as the Son of God: "Christ is the true God, was born of God the Father, and made incarnate of the Virgin Mary" (PSS 25: 167). His image of Christ is grounded in the Russian Orthodox teaching of Christ as the God-Man or *Bogochelovek*, uniting in his being both divine and human nature. For Dostoevskii, Christ's is a "synthetic nature," combining both a fully human (witness the writer's portrayal of Christ in the "Grand Inquisitor") and a fully divine nature: "[the nature of Christ] is the nature of God, this means that Christ is the reflection of God on earth" (PSS 20: 174). Thus Dostoevskii sees the appearance of Christ on earth not only as a revelation of God but also as a revelation of the human. Herein lies for him the unique character and essence of Christ, i.e. He is the most perfect demonstration that the mystery of the Deity cannot be known by the human being yet can still be experienced. For Dostoevskii, Christ is "the measure" up to which humanity should live (Tikhomirov 1994: 106).

In Dostoevskii's anthropocentric worldview, Christ is above all a unique paradigm for his philosophical anthropology. He puts Him in the center of his reflections on humanity. Christ represents "a conception of the human so noble that one cannot grasp it without a sense of awe, and one cannot but believe that He is an undying ideal of humankind" (PSS 28/II: 210). Christ is the ultimate embodiment of brotherly love, of altruistic love of one's neighbor; this is the moral proposition that is at the core of Dostoevskii's Christian faith. Christ is the ultimate touchstone, especially in the field of ethics, to whom the human being should turn for the motivation of his actions:

> Christ was an eternal ideal, towards which the human strives and by the law of nature should strive. After the appearance of Christ, as the ideal of humanity in the flesh, it became clear that the highest, the final development of the personality should reach this (at the very end of development, at the

very point of attaining the goal) [...] Christ is the great and final ideal of the development of all humanity, presented to us in the flesh (PSS 20: 172).[6]

In Dostoevskii's view, Christ represents the ultimate truth to which the whole of humanity should aspire. This does not contradict the antinomy he sees between Christ and truth because "truth" (*istina*) has for Dostoevskii two meanings. There is a truth that one gains through rational analysis and a Truth that reveals itself in faith. In assuming that Christ might be outside the truth, Dostoevskii is communicating that one cannot grasp Christ's being – the union of divine and human nature and the personification of active love – through rational argumentation. The essence of Christ can only be understood through the act of faith. Christ's Truth is beyond analytical truth because it represents an ideal to which earthly and material reality does not yet correspond. Christ stands as an ideal before humanity, or in *starets* Zosima's words: "we are on earth, as it were, astray, and if it were not for the precious image of Christ before us, we should perish and be completely lost, as the human sort before the Flood" (PSS 14: 290).

Dostoevskii's image of Christ is vividly expressed in the narrative "The Grand Inquisitor", included in his last and most religious novel *The Brothers Karamazov* (1879-1880). The tale, commonly referred to as the "Legend of the Grand Inquisitor" is in fact presented on a level of meta-fictionalization.[7] The author of the legend is Ivan Karamazov, who relates his unwritten poem, which is in fact about an imaginary character who may have imagined his encounter with Christ, to his brother Alësha (Jones 1976: 191).

The legend is set in Seville during the sixteenth century at the height of the Spanish Inquisition. Amidst the suffering and torture of heretics being burnt at the stake, Christ appears "in that human form in which he walked among humanity for three years fifteen centuries ago" (PSS 14: 226). His return to the earth is not as the one prophesied in the Second Coming but is meant to momentarily console and re-inspire "his children" who immediately recognize Him. Christ moves among the people, blessing them and performing

---

[6] Dostoevskii wrote this text in a notebook entry for April 1864 after the death of his first wife Mariia Dmitrievna. The text contains his reflections on the afterlife (Scanlan 2002: 21).

[7] Vasilii Rozanov was the first to call "The Grand Inquisitor" a legend, in his work *Legenda ob velikom inkvizitore* (*The Legend of the Grand Inquisitor*, 1891). I will also use this term to refer to "The Grand Inquisitor".

miracles, while he radiates with love and compassion. The Grand Inquisitor, a man of old age, witnesses these miracles and orders His arrest. At night, he visits Christ in his cell and holds a long monologue in which he confronts Christ with the burden He laid on humanity. He claims that Christ has no right whatsoever to appear on earth and "hinder us" because when He left the earth, He granted the Inquisitor's predecessors the right to teach and act according to His words in their own way (PSS 14: 229). Christ keeps silent during the course of the entire monologue: he makes no attempt to counter the Inquisitor's arguments nor to advance his own ideas.

The Inquisitor's argument is wholly centered on the problem of freedom. He reproaches Christ for teaching humanity the promise of freedom.[8] Yet according to the Inquisitor, humanity is too weak to handle this freedom, and that is why the Church has taken over control. The Inquisitor believes that happiness on earth can only be attained when humankind has handed over its freedom. He sets his argumentation within the biblical framework of Christ's temptation in the wilderness.[9] He claims that the three questions posed in the temptations are the most fundamental in entire human history because they contain the answer to what humanity really needs.[10] With the knowledge of fifteen centuries of human history behind him, the

---

[8] John 8: 31- 32: "If you continue to follow my teaching, you are really my disciples, and you will know the truth, and the truth will set you free."

[9] The text on which the Inquisitor's argument is modelled is Matthew 4 1-11 (Jones 1990: 173).

[10] In the main plot of *The Brothers Karamazov*, Dostoevskii has also interwoven references to Christ's three temptations. Christ resisted the three temptations to which each one of the Karamazov brothers yields. The first temptation to transform the stones into bread is refused by Christ with the claim that there is no use in satisfying the human's physical needs if there is no recognition and satisfaction of his spiritual needs. In the novel, this is reflected in Dmitrii Karamazov, whose physical desires are destructive in the absence of a spiritual guiding principle. The second temptation is that Christ should jump down from the temple, so that He might be caught by the angels and by this miracle prove that He is the Son of God. Christ's answer is that people should come to him freely and not driven by a miracle, and that he does not want to test God because faith should be much stronger than being merely based on miracles. This temptation is to be found in Alësha, who temporarily loses his faith when there comes no miracle after Zosima's death. In the third temptation the devil offers Christ all the kingdoms of the earth and hence the possibility to create a perfect order and do away with all the conflicts in humanity. This idea is present in Ivan who is in search for a perfect, secular harmony on earth (Leatherbarrow 1992: 68f).

Inquisitor poses these three questions again to Christ and aims to expose the disastrous consequences of Christ's answers for humanity. The Inquisitor rephrases the first temptation as follows:

> You want to go into the world, and you go with bare hands, with some promise of freedom, which they in their simplicity and born unruliness cannot even understand, which they fear and dread, for nothing has ever been more unbearable for the human and for human society than freedom. And do you see the stones in this parched and barren wilderness? Turn them into bread, and humankind will run after you like a flock of sheep, grateful and obedient, though forever trembling that you might withdraw your hand and no longer give them your bread. But you did not want to deprive humanity of freedom and rejected the offer, for you thought, what freedom is that, if obedience is bought with bread? You replied that man lives not by bread alone (PSS 14: 230).

In this temptation the Inquisitor reveals *his* truth which is that humans cannot deal with the freedom that Christ wanted them to have and presented to them. He believes that the real concern of humanity is not freedom, but the satisfaction of the most primitive and natural needs, such as hunger and cold. In his worldview, the human is a weak and almost animal like being ("the weak, ever sinful and ever ignoble race of man") whose behavior is fully determined by material desires (PSS 14: 231). The "heavenly bread" (*khleb nebesnyi*) or freedom that Christ promised humanity cannot match the "earthly bread" (*khleb zemnoi*) or material well-being that the Grand Inquisitor and his fellow religious leaders provide to humanity (PSS 14: 231). Since the human is by nature driven by purely egoistical motives, he will never be able to share his bread with others; that is why, according to the Inquisitor, humanity cannot be given both the promise of freedom and bread, of spiritual uniqueness and material welfare. Only some exceptionally strong individuals are capable of disciplining their natural needs and can be virtuous and altruistic while suffering from pain and hunger. Yet the majority of humans, "numerous as the sand of the sea," are determined by their physical condition and would eventually kill to satisfy their hunger. Thus the Inquisitor believes that for the sake of the universal well-being of humanity, it is imperative to acknowledge and satisfy their material desires first: "humanity will proclaim [...] that there is no crime and therefore no sin, that there are only starvelings. 'Feed them, and then ask virtue of them'" (PSS 14: 230). Humanity prefers a state of slavery over a fate of hunger. Seemingly out of love and compassion for suffering humanity and while pretending to act in the name of Christ, the Grand Inquisitor and the other Church officials have taken upon themselves the task of delivering humanity from this terrible and unbearable freedom and bringing material welfare on earth. For the Inquisitor, Christ's error is that He disregards the human's physical and material desires by focusing primarily on the human's spiritual needs. The Inquisitor acknowledges, however, that earthly bread alone is not sufficient for the human's well-being nor for the perfect human order he aspires to attain. Being born "a rebel" (*buntovshchik*), the human cannot accept that he is a mere product of natural laws and thus perceives himself in a more idealized way (PSS 14: 229). As the Inquisitor asserts, "the mystery of human existence is not only in living, but in knowing why one lives" (PSS 14: 232). Humans strive to transcend the limitations of their natural condition and add a moral dimension to their existence. In spite of their predetermined nature, they are not only satisfied with earthly bread but are also inclined to make up moral categories and observe the world and themselves within this framework. They make their conscience, which is the source of moral distinctions, the primary fundament of their being. The Grand Inquisitor does not ignore the human's assertion of his personal conscience. He maintains that if one is to take over human freedom, one should also come up with a solution for this troubling conscience, a solution which is supplementary to the immediate satisfaction of the human's physical needs. The mystery of human conscience is that "there is nothing more seductive for the human, than his freedom of conscience (*svoboda sovesti*)," yet simultaneously, "there is nothing more agonizing either" (PSS 14: 232). When one is fully aware of this paradox, one can relieve humans of this tormenting freedom, as the Grand Inquisitor perceives it. He faults Christ for affirming this freedom of conscience rather than taking possession of the human's freedom, thereby lightening his existence:

> I tell you that the human has no more tormenting concern, than to find the one to whom he can most quickly hand over that gift of freedom, with which the unhappy creature is born. But only the one who can appease their conscience, can take hold of their freedom [...] instead of taking the humans' freedom from them, you increased it even more [...] you burdened the kingdom of the human soul forever with the sufferings of freedom (PSS 14: 232).

Christ endowed humanity with the complete "free choice in the knowledge of good and evil" (*svobodnogo vybora v poznanie dobra i zla*) (PSS 14: 232). Yet according to the Inquisitor, the majority of humanity lacks the spiritual and moral strength to ascertain for themselves the moral value of good and evil. The Inquisitor reveals to Christ the ramifications of his message of moral freedom for humanity: the human's perpetual quest for good and evil has only resulted in mental torment and unhappiness. The human is too weak to determine his own moral standards, and that is why, as the Inquisitor maintains, the human yearns for idols, for external spiritual authorities, as an ethical example on which to model his behavior. Tormented by the burden of moral autonomy and personal conscience, humanity is eager to relinquish its existential freedom to an absolute authority.

The Grand Inquisitor poses to Christ the second temptation in which He was given the opportunity to prove his divinity by means of a miracle and by doing so, could have become the idol for which humanity longs. The temptation reveals the most effective means to lure humanity into handing over their freedom.

> There are three forces, the only three forces on earth, that are able to conquer and hold captive for ever the conscience of those weak rebels for their own happiness, these forces are: miracle, mystery and authority (*chudo, tajna i avtoritet*). You rejected all three and you yourself set the example for doing so. When the terrible and wise spirit set you on a pinnacle of the temple and said to you: "if you want to know whether you are the Son of God, then cast yourself down, for it is written, the angels will catch and carry him (PSS 14: 232f.).

Christ taught the human "to decide with a free heart for himself, what is good and what is evil" (*svobodnym serdtsem* [...] *reshat' vpred' sam, chto dobro i chto zlo*) (PSS 14: 232). In the Inquisitor's view, by contrast, the human should be taught that the question of good and evil is a mystery which must be accepted and believed, rather than a free choice to be made. It is not "the free decision of their hearts, nor the love that is important for them, but the mystery that they must blindly obey, even if against their conscience" (PSS 14: 234). Because, as the Inquisitor asserts, the knowledge of good and evil is inaccessible for humanity and therefore humans cannot but obey an external and absolute authority, which is above all confirmed by miracles: the human "seeks not so much God, but a miracle" (PSS 14:

233). It is the Inquisitor's opinion that the human is willing to relinquish his freedom to the one who provides him bread and holds the key to the three powers that can ease the human's moral yearning, i.e. "miracle, mystery, and authority."[11]

With regard to the third temptation, the Inquisitor holds that the human's happiness is not yet guaranteed by material welfare and moral authority alone. The third torment of humanity is the "need for universal unity," for a joining together in an "indisputable, common and harmonious ant-hill" (PSS 14: 235). Humans need to bow down to an idol, and they long to do so together with others. The Inquisitor holds that the unity humanity seeks is universal because the coexistence of different idols undermines the authority of each individual idol and results in moral disorder. He claims that this universal unity is not only to be accomplished in the spiritual sphere, by providing a spiritual authority, but even more importantly, in the realization of a secular order. And herein is the significance of the third temptation. The devil offered Christ all the kingdoms of the world in return for Christ's worship of him. And by recalling this last temptation to Christ, the Inquisitor reveals whom he really worships and in whom his faith is:

> We are not with you, but with him, that is our secret! For a long time we have not been with you anymore, but with him, already for eight centuries. Exactly eight centuries ago, we took from him what you rejected with indignation, that last gift he offered you, having shown you all the kingdoms of the world. We took from him Rome and Caesar's sword (*mech kesaria*) and proclaimed ourselves the kings of the earth (PSS 14: 234).

---

[11] The Inquisitor's charge against Christ that He refused to give humanity "miracle, mystery and authority" in the conviction that humanity should be totally free, cannot be reconciled with the image of Christ as presented in the Gospel where Christ *does* perform miracles (resurrection of the death, restoring sight to the blind). And, His divine nature and oneness with the Father is a mystery. The Inquisitor's formulation of "miracle, mystery, and authority" should not be read as Dostoevskii's intention to present another image of Christ. Rather, it is an allusion to the characterization of the Antichrist in 2 Thessalonians 2: 9: "the arrival of the lawless one will be by Satan's working with all kinds of miracles and signs and false wonders" For the Inquisitor, "miracle, mystery, and authority" are instruments of control over humans, a means to dominate their conscience and exert power over them. In fact, he has perverted the authentic meaning of miracle, mystery and authority and debased it into "magic, mystification and tyranny" (Frank 2002: 614).

Christ taught humanity that His kingdom is not of this world (John 18: 36-39). The Inquisitor, by contrast, aspires to compose an earthly paradise, a universal state in which humanity's material and spiritual happiness is assured. The reference to "eight centuries ago" is not arbitrary. The "Grand Inquisitor" takes place in the sixteenth century, but eight centuries earlier, there were two events in the Christian world that laid bare the ideological differences between Eastern and Western Church. In 756 the Frankish King, Pepin the Short, gave Pope Stephen III sovereignty over Ravenna, thus granting him secular power (Terras 1981: 234). For Dostoevskii, this seizure of temporal power in the Catholic Church was a betrayal of Christ's refusal of an earthly kingdom, as offered to Him by the devil. Although Christ had made it explicit that His Kingdom does not belong to this world, the Roman Church had accepted in His name the secularity of the Roman empire and had taken the sword of Caesar as an instrument of compulsion to bring Christ's message to the barbarian people. By engaging in earthly matters, the Western Church had been unfaithful to Christ's promise of heavenly paradise.[12]

Yet, it was another event, in the field of theology, that would be crucial for the final division between Western and Eastern Church. In 796, a local synod of Latin bishops added the *Filioque* clause to the Nicene creed which would become common practice in the Western Church. The clause proclaims that the Holy Spirit proceeds from the Father *and* the Son (*qui ex Patre Filioque procedit*). This clause was accepted by the Western theologians, but rejected by the Eastern Church, thus resulting in a theological dispute between West and East, which in turn revealed that both had a different conception of the Deity. Western Trinitarianism took the unity of God as its starting point and considered the Spirit to be the uniting link between Father and Son. In this theory, God is one entity with three hypostases. Eastern Trinitarianism, by contrast, departed from Father, Son, and Holy Spirit as three disjointed entities and sought to define the

---

[12] In the introduction to a public reading of "The Grand Inquisitor," Dostoevskii elaborated on this: "If you distort Christ's faith by combining it with the aims of this world, the whole meaning of Christianity is immediately lost, the mind must undoubtedly fall into disbelief, and instead of Christ's great ideal there arises only a new tower of Babylon [...] under the appearance of *social* love for mankind there appears a barely disguised contempt for it" (PSS 15: 198).

relationship between them in such a way as to assure their unity. In this theory, the Father is the source, the principle and the cause within the Trinity. The Trinity is a unity if both the Son and the Spirit emanate from one cause, the Father. The Eastern theologians compared the Trinity to a balance scale, in which the Father is the balance point in the center, upon which both the Son and the Holy Spirit depend. They thus condemned the Western *Filioque* because it made the Son equal to the Father (Pelikan 1977: 183ff.). Basically, for the Eastern Church, the *Filioque* clause betrayed the ultimate Christian principle of God's simultaneous transcendence and immanence, a truth that cannot be grasped by human reason and is to remain a mystery for humanity.

For Dostoevskii, the seeds of the official schism between Western and Eastern Church in 1054 were sown three centuries earlier when the Latin Bishops altered the doctrinal truth without consent of the whole Church. It is obvious that the Grand Inquisitor is on the side of the Roman Catholic Church. For, eight centuries after the *Filioque*, he continues the Latin Church's typical inclination to rationalize the unknowable and unintelligible principle of Christian truth: this is, in the Eastern view, the paradox of God's simultaneous transcendence and immanence. Western theologians, seeking for a more intelligible definition of the Trinitarian unity, overcame this paradox by emphasizing God's transcendence and excluding His immanence. For the Eastern believers, as for Dostoevskii, this implied the exclusion of God from the world.

Assuming that God is absent in this world, the Grand Inquisitor and the former Catholic leaders attempted to organize a human order based on an earthly authority. To that purpose, they engaged in an alliance with a secular power and took up "Caesar's sword." This is yet another allusion to the history of the Latin Church. In the eight century, Roman papacy, feeling threatened by the invasions of neighboring barbarian tribes, entered into an alliance with Charlemagne who helped them defeat and Christianize these pagan people. Although Charlemagne was not an expert in theological issues, he supported the *Filioque* and played a crucial role in the Western Church's acceptance of the creed. To seal the alliance, Pope Leo III crowned him emperor of the Holy Roman Empire in 800 (Ward 1986 :169). The Catholic Church thus integrated itself into the earthly state and conformed itself to the legal and civic institutions of the Roman empire. Succumbing to the human need for universal unity, the Roman Catholic Church sought this unity in a material and secular order and preferred the visible authority of both emperor and pope rather than the invisible ideal of Christ. The Western Church yielded to the third temptation and accepted the offer of all the kingdoms of this world. And herein lies the secret of the Grand Inquisitor: in the West the Church did not live by Christ's teaching of freedom, yet it relinquished its freedom to the one who tempted Christ in the wilderness, Satan:

> If you had taken the world and Caesar's purple, you would have founded the universal state (vsemirnoe tsarstvo) and given universal peace (vsemirnoi pokoi). For who is to be master of humanity, if not the ones who possess its conscience and in whose hands is its bread. We have taken the sword of Caesar, and in taking it of course rejected you and followed him (PSS 14: 235).[13]

Pursuing his rational conviction that the human can only attain happiness in an earthly paradise, the Inquisitor even goes so far as to reject the immortality of the soul and the idea of the Heavenly Paradise: "Peacefully they will die, peacefully they will expire in your name, and beyond the grave they will find only death." However, for the sake of humanity's peace of mind, "we will entice them with a heavenly and earthly reward" (PSS 14: 236). The Inquisitor thus abandons one of the most essential doctrines of Christianity, the doctrine of humankind's salvation and resurrection in the otherworld. He reproaches Christ for bringing humankind a vague promise of an unintelligible heavenly kingdom and leaving them in a condition of unhappiness and ignorance: he has taken upon himself the task to save unhappy humanity and proclaims himself the new savior ("we have saved everyone," PSS 14: 236). He doesn't place the ultimate salvation of humanity in the heavenly paradise, but seeks a universal human order in this world which will save humanity in this life. This again shows that the Inquisitor sides with Satan and not with Christ who proclaims resurrection in the Heavenly Kingdom.

---

[13] The Inquisitor sees this as in the prediction in *Revelation*, 13: "But then the beast will crawl to us and lick our feet and spatter them with tears of blood. And we will sit on the beast and raise the cup, in which will be written: "mystery". But then, and only then, the kingdom of peace and happiness will come for the people" (PSS 14: 235).

While Dostoevskii's fiction is generally marked by a polyphonic discourse, the figure of Christ in this specific text does not explicitly speak up. Still, he represents the most authoritative ideological voice in Dostoevskii's fictional discourse. The image of the silent Christ offers the solution to all ideological quests of the other fictional characters, or to put it in Bakhtin's terms, "this highest voice must crown the world of voices, must organize and subdue it" (Bakhtin 1984: 97). As I interpret it, Christ keeps silent because his truth is one that cannot be captured in human language. Christ's absolute silence in confrontation with the Grand Inquisitor's forceful accusations affirms the typically Orthodox apophatic dogma of the ineffability of the divine "word". In the Orthodox Christian tradition, the divine truth cannot be communicated, but can only made manifest by Christ's deeds. Or, as Dostoevskii jotted down in the notebooks for *The Devils*, with regard to Christ "there are not even any teachings, only occasional words, while the main thing is the image of Christ from which proceeds all teaching" (PSS 11: 192).[14]

4. From 'legend' to anthropological 'truth'

Dostoevskii's Christian worldview is fundamentally anthropocentric. Whether he reflects on religion, ethics or aesthetics, the human is always at the center of his thought. By his own account, written in a letter to his brother, "the human is a mystery. It must be unraveled and if you spend your whole life unraveling it, do not say that this was a waste of time; I am preoccupied with this mystery because I want to be a human being" (PSS 28/I: 63). For him, the human is an absolute value yet one that does not exist in itself but rather as a being whose quintessential nature is in his relationship with other humans and with God. It is precisely this condition of being interrelated to the greater cosmic and human whole, and, its negative corollary, the human's attempts to flee from this attachment, which is at the core of Dostoevskii's meditations on the human being.

---

[14] For Dostoevskii's 'poeticization' of apophatic theology, see Grillaert (2007).

4.1. The ontological status of the human being

Dostoevskii's idea of human nature is rooted in traditional Christian ontology, which departs from a dualism in reality between a phenomenal, material realm and an unintelligible, spiritual realm. The material realm is this earthly and temporal world, whereas the spiritual realm is the heavenly and eternal world, the world of the divine. In the Christian view, the human is delineated as both matter and spirit, uniting within himself both a material and a divine nature. The human's spiritual, divine entity is the soul, which is dependent on a material entity, i.e. the body as a sensory apparatus and the brain. The material nature makes up the physical, animal, earthly, finite and temporal aspect of humanity, whereas the spiritual is the immaterial, heavenly, infinite and eternal facet. Dostoevskii believes that the human, who is a fusion of two mutually exclusive natures, can never fully grasp the spiritual, divine realm, nor wholly understand earthly reality. Because the soul is partially materialized in this world, it has grown isolated from its divine origin and therefore cannot capture the mystery of God. Nor can it conceive of the complexity of this reality because this cognition depends on the material entity of reason, with which it is unable to form a perfect and complete unity. Human reason, which belongs to the material world, has no access to the divine realm, and as a result it can never completely know material actuality (Scanlan 2002: 14f.).[15]

    This concept of the human, as a creature whose combined, yet opposite, natures hinder him from having knowledge of both worlds he belongs to, sheds light on Dostoevskii's conception of the Deity and his image of Christ. God is for him a mystery, unknowable and inconceivable by human reason because the intellectual mind belongs to the material world. God cannot be known but can, at times, be experienced in the feeling of love (a feeling the human owes to his spiritual nature). At this point, Dostoevskii's statement that he would rather remain with Christ than with the truth can be understood in its actual context (PSS 28/I: 176): he believes that Christ's divine nature,

---

[15] This view is also formulated by *starets* Zosima: "Much on earth is hidden from us, but in return we have been given a secret, mysterious sense of our living unity with the other world, with the lofty and higher world, and indeed the roots of our thoughts and feelings are not here, but in other worlds" (PSS 14: 290).

which is crucial for a correct understanding of human nature, is not a rational nor empirical truth, but a truth that can only be grasped by the human's soul.

In Dostoevskii's view, the two natures of the human are not equal in value. Emanating from the Deity, the soul is affirmed as superior to the body, which only serves as a transitory wrapping of the soul. The spiritual realm is in Dostoevskii's metaphysics the real core of reality and that is where he focuses his reflections on humanity.

Dostoevskii believes that God is immanent in this world: as the unknowable source of the whole universe, the Deity is present in all things and creatures in this world, particularly in humanity. Although the human is 'stranded' in this world and limited by the laws of the material realm, God is living in humanity: he is mostly manifest in the love between humans. In the 1877 notes for *The Diary of a Writer*, Christianity, as a community built upon the principle of love, is taken as "the evidence that God can be seated in humanity" (PSS 25: 228).

For Dostoevskii, the essential anthropological truth is that the human's spiritual nature is evidence that he is created in the image and likeness of God. Still, due to his material nature, the human is irrevocably tied to this earthly world, thereby hindering his ability to develop his divine potentiality in full. The human naturally strives to attain the Absolute yet is nonetheless unable to succeed due to his attachment to the material realm. Dostoevskii, however, strongly believes that at some point in the future, the gap between spiritual and material nature will be overcome and that the human will be fully transfigured into divine nature: "this will happen after the realization of the goal, when the human is [...] eventually reborn into another nature" (PSS 20: 173).

4.2. Being what one is

In his present condition, the human being is still too attached to the material world to attain the ultimate ideal of transfiguration into the other world where his divine nature is realized. Still, the spiritual part of his being enables him to grasp the divine truth at moments, whereby he experiences the supreme moral good, i.e. the principle of active love. For Dostoevskii, the human's compound spiritual and material being results inevitably in the dialectics of altruistic love (what his divine nature aspires to) and egoism (what his earthly nature drives him to). He believes that the question of good and evil in humanity boils down to the struggle between what he calls "the law of love" (*zakon liubvi*) and "the law of the personality" (*zakon lichnosti*) (PSS 24: 165).[16] In earthly reality, "the law of the personality" stands in the way of "the law of love":

> To love a human being, as oneself, in accordance with Christ's commandment, is impossible. The law of the personality (*zakon lichnosti*) is binding on earth. The ego (*ia*) stands in the way. Only Christ could do it, but Christ was an eternal ideal [...] After the appearance of Christ, as the ideal of humanity in the flesh, it became clear that the highest, the final development of the personality should reach this [...] that the person should find, should recognize, should with the full force of his nature be convinced, that the highest use someone can make of his personality, of the full development of his ego, is to annihilate this ego, to give it totally to each and every one, undividedly and unselfishly. And this is the greatest happiness. In this way the law of the ego merges with the law of humanism, and in merging, the two – the ego and the all (at first sight two extreme opposites) – are mutually annihilated for each other, while at the very same time each separate person attains the highest goal of his individual development (PSS 20: 172).

"The law of love" or altruistic love of one's neighbor, as fully embodied in Christ and as divine potential present in every human, is the moral ideal to which the whole of humanity should aspire. And therein lies not only the "greatest happiness" for the whole of humanity but also for each individual. This shows that Dostoevskii does not believe in the utilitarian motive of 'the greatest happiness of the greatest number.' Rather, he maintains that each individual human being can only attain perfect happiness and moral peace if he acknowledges *for himself* that the supreme moral good is in the principle of active love for one another. The motivation for "the law of love" should thus come from within, from the divine element that resides in every human. Yet, the human, imperfect because of his material nature, is hindered by his ego while trying to accomplish this ideal. Active and unselfish love for the other requires that one deliberately abandons the primacy of the self. And paradoxically, the

---

[16] I borrow this classification from Scanlan (2002: 82ff.). The Russian *lichnost'* can be translated as "personality", "individual" or even "selfhood". The term is used when considering the relationship between the individual and a greater collective (Offord 1998: 13).

annihilation of the ego is the prerequisite and starting point "of the full development of this *ego*," this is of the divine element in the individual. According to Dostoevskii, one's happiness is not in the assertion of the self in isolation from the other but in the realization of the self in relation to the other and God. Only in the altruistic love for the other can one find the full acknowledgment and exploration of the human's divine potential and does the human correspond to his ontological essence: that the human is created in the image and likeness of God.

In spite of his faith in the human's spiritual capacity for the good, Dostoevskii maintains that the Christian ideal of altruistic love and the complete realization of the divine potential will not be attained in this earthly life. The human's material nature keeps him from wholly overcoming the egotistic self. Even the most lofty and saintly person is still a human being, whose ego stands in the way of achieving moral perfection. In earthly life, human existence is doomed to a constant struggle between the spiritual knowledge of good and the natural inclination towards evil.

4.3. Becoming what one is

Whereas in earthly life the human's egotistic nature hinders his ability to live up fully to the moral ideal of Christ, this moral goal can be attained in the other world, in the life after death: "If this is the final goal of humanity [the achievement of moral perfection] [...], in reaching this point, a human being ends his earthly existence" (PSS 20: 172). Dostoevskii believes that in this life, due to the human's spiritual nature, humanity is able to make progress towards moral perfection; yet the supreme moral good can only be realized when the soul is no longer attached to the material apparatus and meets its potential higher status when reuniting with the Deity. In this higher state, the soul is no longer human in the sense that it has cast off its material nature (Scanlan 2002: 22). The human is "eventually reborn [...] into another nature" (PSS 20: 173); only in this state of complete detachment and transfiguration from earthly existence can the human realize his divine potential and unite with God.

In Dostoevskii's Christian anthropology, the immortality of the soul is thus of supreme importance. He asserts that "without faith in the soul and its immortality, human existence would be unnatural, inconceivable and unbearable". The immortality of the soul is "the highest idea on earth," it is the source from which springs all other lofty and moral ideas by which humanity lives (PSS 24: 46). Moral consciousness is fundamentally related to the faith or absence of faith in the immortality of the soul. This idea is in its most radical ramifications expressed in Ivan Karamazov's formulation that if there is no immortality, then everything is permitted. His theory, rephrased by Miusov, is the following:

> [Ivan] solemnly declared in argument that there is nothing in the whole world that could force humans to love their fellows, that there is no law of nature that the human should love humanity, and that if there is and was until now love on earth, it was not from a natural law, but simply because humans believed in their immortality. Ivan Fëdorovich added in parenthesis that the whole natural law consists in this, and that if you were to destroy in humanity the belief in immortality, not only love but every living force for the continuation of earthly life would at once dry up. Moreover, then nothing would be immoral any more, everything would be permitted (vsë budet pozvoleno), even cannibalism (PSS 14: 64f.).

The logic in this argument stems from the human's assumed dualistic nature. In Ivan's view, the human is a mere material being, completely stripped of a spiritual nature and an immortal soul. In this materialist view, the human is believed to be driven solely by the laws of nature and physical desires, and as Ivan asserts, there is no such binding law of nature that urges humanity to altruistic love. Life on this earth is governed by the "law of the personality." Thus, by denying the Christian doctrine of the human's immortal soul, Ivan rejects the human's spiritual capacity for the "law of love." And without this spiritual inclination towards the supreme good, there is no morality, and consequently, everything is permitted.

In *The Diary of a Writer* for December 1876, Dostoevskii declares that "love for humanity is even unthinkable, incomprehensible and *impossible without a concurrent belief in the immortality of the human soul*" (PSS 24: 49). He asserts that the feeling of love, which is crucial in the consciousness of God, can only be experienced when one accepts the immortality of the human soul. Only the soul, the divine entity in humanity, is capable of altruistic love for the other. Dostoevskii holds that faith in immortality is of paramount importance for the human condition in this earthly life. One needs to be conscious of his spiritual nature and divine origin in order to grasp one's existential destiny in this life: that on earth one should strive for the supreme moral principle of active love and aspire to realize the law of love in the earthly atmosphere. If one loses contact with the "higher meaning of life," this inevitably results in suicide (PSS 24: 49). For Dostoevskii, "the idea of immortality is life itself, living life, it is the definitive formula of life and the main source of truth and correct consciousness for humanity" (PSS 24: 49f.).

4.4. The anthropology of freedom

In spite of his belief that the human is through his immortal soul (as an entity originating from God) inevitably bound up with the Deity, Dostoevskii's view on the human is not deterministic. Rather, he believes that "the nucleus" of man, "his genuine essence" is in his freedom (Zen'kovskii [1948] 1991, I/2: 232). The question of freedom is at the core of Dostoevskii's metaphysical anthropology because it is in freedom that the human's spiritual nature is most fully asserted. As a material being, the human is subject to the laws of nature and necessity and is thus in this earthly condition partially determined by his material nature; however, as a spiritual being, the human is totally free. And it is exactly in this spiritual freedom that the human's independence of the material realm is asserted. For Dostoevskii, the human's true essence consists of his metaphysical freedom.

He opposes any deterministic theory that limits this freedom. His most sustained attacks in this matter are directed against the nihilist intelligentsia of the 1860s and their most radical advocates, Nikolai Chernyshevskii and Dmitrii Pisarev. First of all, these are militant atheists who necessarily deny the divine aspect of the human being, his immortal and metaphysical soul, and consequently, they fail to conceive of the human as a creature with free will. They consider the human to be a purely material being who is driven only by material and physical needs. Chiefly preoccupied with social and utilitarian motives, the nihilists proceed in a mechanistic anthropology of "Rational Egoism," which enables them to build up a social utopia. The nihilists' social and anthropological formula is outlined in Chernyshevskii's novel, *Chto delat'* (*What is to be done*, 1863), in which egoism is hailed as the ground for harmonious social relations. The Rational Egoists proceed from a deterministic anthropology. They view humans as creatures lacking free will whose behavior is only motivated by what their material nature necessitates: this is pure self-interest.

In order to fit this conception of the human into a social utopian theory, the Rational Egoists add a normative ethics to this view on the human as a mere egoist. They contend that humans should be educated and reformed to understand that their personal interests coincide with the interests of the whole society, and that the greatest maximization of their lust is in the achievement of 'the greatest happiness of the greatest number.' They believe that this moral imperative – to act in such a way that your personal interest becomes beneficial for others – can be taught to the people on the basis of rational calculations provided by science. Personal egoism is redefined as Rational Egoism (Scanlan 1999: 556ff.). For Dostoevskii, the radical nihilists' conception of humanity is very frightening. For one thing, they endorse a mechanistic and material anthropology in which the human is deprived of any higher, immaterial nature and is fully determined by his material, egotistic nature. For another thing, on the basis of rational calculation, they formulate a normative ethics according to which humanity can be reformed, or reprogrammed, to act in such a way that their personal advantage corresponds to, and even lies in, the well-being of others.

The nihilists' idea of the human is diametrically opposed to Dostoevskii's view. Believing that the human's genuine essence is in his free will, the writer refutes any deterministic anthropology. And what is more, he does not accept the utilitarian idea that human behavior can be fit into a rational scheme according to which happiness for the greatest number is attained by mathematical formulas.

In Dostoevskii's anthropology, freedom of the will is the highest good because it elevates the human from the material realm and its laws of necessity as well as affirms the human's potential as the image and likeness of God. He assumes that the human is morally autonomous and contends that both good and evil, as alternative choices, should be available to humanity. Good is not a well-defined value that one has to accept unconditionally but is rather a moral idea that can only be fully grasped in opposition to evil. Augustine distinguished between two kinds of freedom: freedom in good, and freedom in the choice between good and evil. Dostoevskii decisively opted for the latter kind of freedom (Blumenkrantz 1996: 233).

How, then, can this ethical stance of ultimate freedom guarantee that the human will not relapse into his purely egotistic motivation, or in other words, take advantage of this freedom to fulfill "the law of the personality"? Rejecting any kind of external restraint on the human's free will, Dostoevskii does feel the need to limit this freedom through an internal motivation. He believes that the human will transcends the realm of natural necessity while still answering to its metaphysical origin, the soul. And because the soul descends from the Deity and is thus conscious of the principle of active love, Dostoevskii believes that the only possible limitation to human freedom is in the individual's free acceptance of God and His "law of love."

Where Dostoevskii considers freedom of paramount importance in the human's existence, it is not tantamount to Ivan Karamazov's formula that "all is permitted" which is negative freedom. For Dostoevskii, freedom is not a license for boundless or lawless behavior. Rather, genuine, positive freedom is in the human's spiritual capacity to consider both the values of good and evil, and after thorough deliberation, the human can freely make the choice to follow Christ's moral message. The field of human choice is a broad one yet stays within the boundaries of the Christian moral pattern which centers on the annihilation of the ego's impulses and the realization of altruistic love (Scanlan 2002: 75).

> The way the world at present conceives freedom is as license (*raznuzdannost'*), whereas real freedom consists only in overcoming the ego and the will, so as ultimately to achieve a moral condition in which one is always, at every moment, the real master of oneself. But giving license to your desires only leads to your enslavement. That is why almost the whole of present's world supposes that freedom lies in financial security [...] Yet, in essence, this is not freedom, but slavery once again, an enslavement from money. On the contrary, the very highest freedom is not laying up money and looking for security in it, but in "sharing everything you have and going off to serve everyone". If a human being is capable of that, is capable of overcoming himself to such an extent, is he then not free? This is precisely the highest manifestation of the will (PSS 25: 62).

For Dostoevskii, the ultimate manifestation of the human will lies not in the pursuit of one's own egotistic desires, but on the contrary, lies in overcoming the natural inclination to self-interest and in dedicating oneself to the other. The moral goal is to achieve a state in which one is "the real master of oneself," in the sense that one has transcended one's material nature and is no longer subject to his earthly instincts. In this condition, one is no longer restrained by materialist and egoist motives and is fully able to develop his spiritual potential and act according to the law of love. Dostoevskii contends that giving in to one's own egoist impulses issues in slavery; one becomes the slave of his most base and earthly instincts, of his material self. If one does not acknowledge the "higher" or divine half of his condition, in which the faculty of free will is seated, one inevitably falls into a state of enslavement. Dependence on material needs amounts to a betrayal of the human's genuine being. Dostoevskii asserts that the negative conception of freedom, as a permit to do whatever one feels like, is not only a license to give in to one's physical desires, but is also in the end even an affirmation of these material desires and an extra stimulus to develop them to the point of complete isolation from the other. For Dostoevskii, the human's striving to assert one's individual will, independently of the other, is not genuine freedom but amounts to self-will (*svoevolie*).[17]

Dostoevskii does not acknowledge any external restraint on the human's freedom of choice. Rather, he wants the limitation of freedom to be inwardly generated by a deliberate acceptance of the Christian law of love. His anthropological ideal is one of moral selfhood. He believes that the human is through his spiritual nature aware of the supreme moral good and is able to apprehend this as the best option for his personal development, in spite of being in part held back by his material nature. He rejects any rigid and externally imposed formula of good and evil; he believes that each human should have the freedom to consciously choose between good and evil because the ultimate moral good, i.e. active love for the other, only makes sense as an ethical imperative if it is deliberately and inwardly motivated. Good is only morally worthy when freely chosen in opposition to evil, which must therefore be an equally available option. Any external regimentation of good and evil is brushed aside. Dostoevskii defines freedom as the "mastering of oneself and one's inclinations" (*ovladet' soboi i svoimi stremleniiami*) (PSS 24: 213). He proceeds thereby from a conception of the human as a being fully capable of defining his own moral values.

---

[17] In chapter 5, I will show that the *chelovekobog* is a manifestation of this self-will.

Dostoevskii's anthropology centers upon free self-determination, upon the realization of one's spiritual self. He believes that the human can overcome his earthly nature and be transfigured "into another nature" (PSS 20: 173) in which the spiritual being is no longer restrained by material desires, and when in this condition of genuine freedom, the human can further develop his divine potentiality of the supreme moral good. In his Christian perspective, he believes that genuine "personal self-perfection" is to be realized "in the spirit of Christian love" (*lichnoe samosovershenstvovanie b dukhe khristianskoi liubvi*) (PSS 26: 161). *Starets* Zosima reverts to biblical imagery to illustrate this ideal of self-perfection: God took seeds from the spiritual, divine world and sowed them on this earth. Yet only the seeds that were still connected to the other world flowered. The seeds, whose consciousness of their otherworldly origins had faded away, did not grow and dried up. These seeds "will grow indifferent to life and even hate it" (PSS 14: 290f.).

Herein is for Dostoevskii the whole dialectics of freedom. He acknowledges and explores in his fictional 'nihilistic' characters the ramifications of what both Merezhkovskii and Berdjaev call "the final freedom" (*poslednaia svoboda*). There are two ways in which one can deal with ethical freedom and, equally, two ways to realize the self. One can choose to affirm and develop one's higher, spiritual nature; in this manner, to use Nietzschean phraseology, 'one becomes who he really is.' Freedom and perfection of the self, then, consist of being one with the Deity and the universal brotherhood. The other antithetical kind of freedom is the deliberate denial of God, and consequently, the isolation from the other. In this condition of complete self-indulgence, one strives to assert oneself independently from God and the other. Dostoevskii realizes that moral freedom carries a great temptation; one can strive to give primacy to the ego over the other and desire to be the center and sum of the whole universe. In this case, one aspires to supplant God and in the end become God. Freedom then becomes a goal in itself, instead of a means to affirm the Christian law of love. If no higher value, transcendent to the human's limited material nature, is acknowledged in freedom, then this amounts to unruly and boundless freedom, in which all is permitted. In the end, this freedom ruins the human self and results in slavery to the material world, the ego.

Genuine moral freedom is, for Dostoevskii, revealed in Christ. Christ taught: "you will know the truth, and the truth will set you free" (John 8: 32). His appearance on earth as the incarnation of God disclosed to humanity the mysterious truth of its essence: that the human is created in the image and likeness of God and is able to live up to this divine potential. Once the human is conscious of this truth, i.e. of the divine foundation of his personality, he becomes genuinely free. This freedom can never result in immorality, for it originates from the human's divine nature, which inspires to follow the law of love. True freedom is for Dostoevskii an act of faith in God and in the whole of humanity. Only Christianity fully acknowledges the human's freedom (PSS 21: 16).

Dostoevskii advances an anthropology of the morally autonomous human who is through his spiritual nature conscious of the ethical imperative of the law of love. Christ, as the supreme embodiment of altruistic love for the other, is the ultimate moral paradigm for humanity:

> It does not suffice to define morality as faithfulness to one's convictions. One should also continually raise the question, are my convictions true? There is only one test, this is Christ. But this is no longer philosophy, it is belief (PSS 27: 56).

Yet due to the human's attachment to the material realm, there is in every human a tension between Christ's Truth and earthly truth, between the law of love and the law of the personality. The human is torn between his two conflicting natures; his spiritual nature directs him towards altruistic love for the other, whereas his material nature, focused on self-interest, holds him back from realizing this moral ideal. Dostoevskii is highly sensitive to a degeneration in religious consciousness because he realizes that if one loses his faith in God and the immortality of the soul, one consequently loses any touch with the moral law of love. In a world devoid of God, humanity is doomed to moral perdition.

5. Conclusion

At the core of Dostoevskii's philosophical anthropology is the preoccupation to affirm the human's freedom as he sees fundamentally embodied in the figure of the *Bogochelovek* Christ. His conception of the human is entrenched in traditional Christian ontology, which stems from a dualism between the earthly and divine realm and identifies within the human a material nature (the body) and a spiritual nature (the soul). In Dostoevskii's view, the human's ontological status is made up by his immaterial and immortal soul, an entity emanating from and substantially one with God. However fundamentally related to the Deity, and despite the emphasis on collective human unity and connection with the other, the human is in no way determined by this interrelatedness. Rather, the human is an essentially free being, whose metaphysical make-up only comes into fruition through freely chosen self-realization. Dostoevskii brushes aside any excessively normative view on the human that puts forward a dogmatic set of values by which the individual ought to behave. He asserts that the human individual should have the moral autonomy to define for oneself the ethical categories by which to live. He believes that through the spiritual entity of the soul, any human is to some extent aware of the divine truth, the interrelationship and oneness with God and the other, and is eventually able to understand that exactly therein lies the ultimate realization of the self. The supreme moral good, the act of love for the other, is only authentic when deliberately willed.

An anthropology of moral selfhood inevitably has ethical implications that could become tantamount to an all-permissive definition of morality. If freedom is employed in this way, i.e. asserting the self independently and disregarding the unity with God and the other, then, in Dostoevskii's ideological language, this is no longer freedom, but slavery because then the human is enslaved to his material nature and ignores the most fundamental ground of his being, consciousness of God and the other.

As I will show in subsequent chapters, Dostoevskii's anthropological ideal of free self-determination is for the *God-seekers* a fruitful and recurrent anthropological motive, especially in their assessment of Nietzsche.

Chapter 4

"Isn't the unfortunate Nietzsche right?":
Vladimir Solov'ëv's response to Nietzsche

> *In any case, humanity did now lose Vladimir Solov'ëv*
> *and Friedrich Nietzsche, who managed to raise their*
> *intellectual activity in the field of philosophical ideas*
> *higher than the common level, who rose above the*
> *crowd of those small people, crawling between the*
> *yearnings of petty egoism (Obituary for Vladimir*
> *Solov'ëv and Nietzsche. Karutov 1900: 510).*

1. Introduction

Dostoevskii's ideological legacy served as a fruitful catalyst for the *Bogoiskateli* Merezhkovskii and Berdiaev to read Nietzsche in a new perspective. Their assessment of him was also determined by the horizon of expectations shaped by another seminal figure in Russian history of ideas, this is the religious philosopher Vladimir Sergeevich Solov'ëv (1853-1900).

Born in Moscow in 1853, Vladimir Solov'ëv was the second son of the renowned historian Sergei Mikhailovich Solov'ëv. Many relatives of the Solov'ëv family were members of the clergy, and Vladimir was raised in the everyday practice and liturgy of the Russian Orthodox Church. In 1869, he enrolled at Moscow University to study natural sciences (with a particular interest in biology) but later switched to philosophy. By then, he had turned away from Orthodox faith, and in search of a new creed, he indulged briefly in Western materialism and positivism. In those years, he thoroughly studied the prominent Western philosophers; he maintained and used this knowledge to the end of his days. He soon became disenchanted with Western materialist philosophy and he returned to his religious faith and reconverted in 1872 to Orthodoxy. In 1873, he entered the Moscow Theological Academy at Sergiev-Posad, which was a highly unusual undertaking for a lay person. In 1874, he brilliantly defended and published his master's thesis *Krizis Zapadnoi Filosofii: protiv pozitivistov* (*The Crisis of Western Philosophy: against the positivists*), which won him scholarly fame. He was offered a lectureship in philosophy at Moscow University but his academic career was short-lived. The murder of tsar Aleksandr II in March 1881 prompted Solov'ëv to deliver a public speech, in which he appealed to the new tsar to show clemency to his father's assassins. His address, however, was taken by Aleksandr III as an offence, and as a result, Solov'ëv voluntarily resigned from university and from that time forward devoted his time exclusively to his writing.[1] It is noteworthy that Solov'ëv was personally acquainted with Fëdor Dostoevskii during the 1870s and that their friendship grew to be a very close one which was maintained until Dostoevskii's death in 1881. In July 1878, Solov'ëv accompanied Dostoevskii to the monastery of Optina Pustyn', where the writer hoped to find consolation for the loss of his three-year-old son Alësha. As Dostoevskii's letters to his wife reveal, he discussed with Solov'ëv the main theme and ideas for his new work, *The Brothers Karamazov* (Kostalevsky 1997: 49ff.).[2] In February 1881, Solov'ëv delivered his first 'obituary' speech in memory of Dostoevskii which was followed by two more addresses, collected as *Tri Rechi v pamiat' Dostoevskogo* (*Three Speeches in memory of Dostoevskii*, 1881-1883). Solov'ëv's purpose in the speeches was neither biographical analysis nor literary criticism, but to pursue one question: "what did Dostoevskii serve, what idea inspired his whole activity?": it was through this question that Solov'ëv excavated a yet unnoticed religiosity in Dostoevskii's art (Solov'ëv, SS III: 185).

---

[1] For biographical information on Solov'ëv, see Sergei Solov'ëv's *Zhizn' i Tvorcheskaia Evoliutsiia Vladimira Solov'ëva* (*The life and creative evolution of Vladimir Solov'ëv*, 1977) and Konstantin Mochulsky's *Vladimir Solov'ëv: Zhizn' i Uchenie* (*Vladimir Solov'ëv: his Life and Teaching*, 1951).
[2] Commentators see features of Solov'ëv embodied in both Alësha and Ivan Karamazov (Kostalevsky 1997: 66).

Solov'ëv was the first thinker in Russia to work out an integral and methodical philosophical system. His approach to the problems of philosophy inaugurated a shift in Russian intellectual history from more reluctant positions to deal with ideas in a theoretical way towards a boom of systematic philosophical models beginning in the turn of the century. His fellow intellectual, Lopatin expressed Solov'ëv's significance in the history of Russian philosophy as follows: "Solov'ëv was the first truly original Russian philosopher, just as Pushkin was the first Russian national poet" (Lopatin [1901] 2002: 794). Solov'ëv's philosophy is marked by an attempt to reconcile a theoretical position with a religious outlook. His body of thought covers a broad area of philosophical problems: he wrote chiefly from a religious point of view on ethics, aesthetics, philosophy of history, politics and social questions. Various thinkers of the Silver Age found the versatility of Solov'ëv's thought appealing. Berdiaev, for example, pinpoints the significance of Solov'ëv in the cultural and religious renaissance that marks the beginning of the twentieth century (Berdiaev [1946] 1997: 198). Semën Frank credits him as "a unique phenomenon in the history of Russian thought" (Frank [1950] 2002: 953). The symbolist poet Viacheslav Ivanov wrote to his fellow symbolists Andrei Belyi and Aleksandr Blok: "We have been mysteriously baptized by Solov'ëv" (Ivanov 1971-1987 III: 10).

Nietzsche was an equally important source of inspiration in this period. His ideas dynamically operated in the same fields in which Solov'ëv's thought proved to be functional, particularly in aesthetics and the rise of religious philosophy. Taken together, Solov'ëv's and Nietzsche's ideological legacies made up a conflicting arena of congruities and incongruities in which later thinkers aspired to seek reconciliation. The interplay between Nietzsche's and Solov'ëv's ideas turned out be productive and decisively determined the revitalization of Russian culture and philosophy in the beginning of the twentieth century. The interaction between the two philosophers' ideas is exemplified in Berdiaev's statement that in the Russian renaissance "Nietzsche had an influence side by side with Solov'ëv" (Berdiaev [1946] 1997: 199). And also Merezhkovskii, who brought about a shift in the reception process of Nietzsche, was always under the influence of "either Dostoevskij, Nietzsche or Vlad. Solov'ëv" (Dolinin [1914] 1972: 307).[3]

There are indeed noteworthy similarities between Nietzsche's and Solov'ëv's line of thought. Both found the nineteenth century positivistic and materialist conception of the human to be lacking and aimed to supplant this with a new anthropological model that would revive the human's potential creative sources. Yet, both thinkers ultimately took divergent, and even opposite roads in their thoughts and ideas. For whereas Nietzsche thought out an anthropology in which the Christian pattern is overcome, Solov'ëv – in spite of the atheistic phase during his adolescence – aimed to solve the crisis in anthropological consciousness by reinvigorating the Christian ideal.

In this chapter, I will analyze Solov'ëv's reading of Nietzsche, which took place in the first decade of the reception process, in order to establish the impact of his response on the *God-seekers'* interpretation of the German philosopher at the turn of the century and beyond.

2. The initial response to Nietzsche: merit nor danger

It remains unclear whether Solov'ëv's interpretation of Nietzsche was based on an actual reading of his works or was distilled out of secondary sources. In his extensive correspondence there are no explicit recordings of his study of Nietzsche, and his writings on Nietzsche lack precise references to his texts. On the subject of Solov'ëv's assessment of Nietzsche, his biographer and nephew Sergei Solov'ëv declared: "for a philosopher brought up on Kant and Hegel, it was difficult to understand the whole significance of Nietzsche; he had hardly read him attentively and in his polemics with him he tried to limit himself to jokes and irony" (Solov'ëv S. 1977: 347). In light of Solov'ëv's serious scholarship and erudition whit regard to other thinkers, it seems nonetheless doubtful that he passed over the German philosopher so lightly. In his preface to *Opravdanie Dobra* (*The Justification of the Good*, 1898), Solov'ëv alludes to

---

[3] Andrei Belyi (1880-1934) aimed to unite in his thought Nietzsche's and Solov'ëv's philosophy: "How to reconcile [...] the struggling Solov'ëv and Nietzsche?" (Belyi [1928] 1982: 30). The other symbolist poets, Blok and Ivanov, also stood under the banner of Solov'ëv's and Nietzsche's thought.

"Nietzsche's latest works" which might suggest that he had actually read these works or was at least informed on them (SS VIII: 13).[4] Whether or not Solov'ëv really had read Nietzsche, his views on him were clearly shaped by the controversy surrounding Nietzsche's thought that was going on in the Russian journals in the 1890s and by his own polemics with the Russian decadents, such as Merezhkovskii and Minskii, whose discourse was permeated with Nietzschean motives. Deeply concerned with the condition of Russian culture and consciousness, Solov'ëv could not ignore the fact that Nietzsche's ideas were gradually being consumed by the Russian public.

It is noteworthy that Solov'ëv mentioned Nietzsche some months before the first Russian study on Nietzsche was published: Preobrazhenskijs article "Fridrikh Nitsshe: Kritika morali al'truizma," which appeared in the last issue for 1892 in *Voprosy Filosofii i Psikhologii*. In an article on Konstantin Leont'ev, published after his death in the beginning of 1892 and to be included in the *Entsiklopedicheskii Slovar' Brokgaus i Efron*, Solov'ëv compares Leont'ev at some point with Nietzsche (Sineokaia 2002: 77). He claims that "in his contempt for pure ethics and in his cult of the self-affirming strength and beauty, Leont'ev anticipated much of Nietzsche's ideas" (SS X: 509).[5]

In the 1894 article "Pervyi Shag k polozhitel'noi Estetike" ("A first Step towards a positive Aesthetics"), Nietzsche receives a similar kind of treatment. This essay is directed against the so-called decadents, who proclaimed a new concept of art as being a purely individualist expression and hence renounced the idea that art should have a social function.[6] Solov'ëv faults this idea of a "pure art"

---

[4] When discussing Nietzsche, Solov'ëv alludes, albeit rarely, to titles of Nietzsche's writings. He mentions *The Antichrist* (SS VIII: 13), *The Birth of Tragedy* (SS IX: 291) and *Thus spoke Zarathustra* (SS X, 29f.). His ironical designation of Nietzsche as a "philologist, all too philologist" (SS X: 29) suggests, furthermore, that he might have been familiar with *Human, All Too Human*. For Müller, these references are proof of Solov'ëv's actual reading of these works (Müller 1947: 516). Still, because Solov'ëv only alludes to titles of works, which were time and again quoted in the then Russian debate, I do not find this to be compelling evidence that he definitely read them.

[5] Leont'ev's reputation as the Russian Nietzsche would become a fashionable canon which is exemplified in Rozanov's claim that "Leont'ev is stronger and more original than Nietzsche. He was the real Nietzsche" (Rozanov [1891] 1991: 184).

[6] This upheaval in the arts and art theory occurred for a substantial part under the aegis of Merezhkovskii. In 1893, he published *O Prichinakh Upadka i o novykh Techeniiakh sovremmenoi Literatury* (*On the Reasons for the Decline and on new*

because it is detrimental to social consciousness (SS VII: 69). However, he asserts that this trend will eventually fade away, and he uses Nietzsche to demonstrate the ephemerality and transitoriness of such 'minor phenomena' in human history. Solov'ёv labels Nietzsche "a talented writer" who "unfortunately turned out to be mentally ill" and summarizes his ideas as follows:

> compassion is a base feeling, unworthy for a person who respects himself; morality only serves for slave natures; there is no humanity, but only masters and slaves, semi-gods and semi-cattle, for the first all is permitted, while the second are obliged to serve as an instrument for the first and so on (SS VII: 72).

Solov'ёv diminishes Nietzsche's ideas by identifying them as a mere reanimation of ancient beliefs, which recur in history in various guises from the time of the Egyptian pharaohs and the Assyrian kings. He sees the enthusiasm with which Nietzsche is currently hailed in decadent circles as a demonstration that these ancient ideas have since long been forgotten and that this will also be the fate of Nietzsche and the contemporary trend of decadent art: in the end, these ideologies will be surpassed, and they will remain in the wings of history.

In his first statements concerning Nietzsche, Solov'ёv's attitude towards him is rather neutral. He only refers to Nietzsche in passing, in association with specific ideological trends he aims to discredit. Unlike the other intellectuals of his time, who either offer an extensive and rather objective analysis of Nietzsche's ideas (Preobrazhenskii and Mikhailovskii) or proceed in a sharp criticism of him (the 1893 debate in *Voprosy Filosofii i Psikhologii*), Solov'ёv refrains from making any explicit statement about Nietzsche. Nietzsche's thought is a mere irrelevant phenomenon of secondary interest that holds neither merit nor danger for the Russian cultural and spiritual context because "the resurrection of dead ideas is not at all frightful for the living" (SS VII: 72).

Still, Solov'ёv's seemingly disinterested approach to Nietzsche masks anxious presentiments concerning the actual nature of his thought and its potential entailments for Russian consciousness. At the end of his argument, he hints at the coming of the Antichrist

---

Trends in contemporary Russian Literature), which would become the manifesto of the symbolist movement.

and claims that "this last masked reaction of the ideals of Dahomey [Nietzsche] will not last long" (SS VII: 73).[7]

From the mid-1890s Solov'ëv becomes gradually aware of Nietzsche's growing popularity among Russian thinkers and artists, and he can no longer trivialize his thought as an irrelevant phenomenon in the history of ideas. It is especially Nietzsche's concept of the *Übermensch*, which was becoming a very fashionable motive in symbolist discourse, that epitomizes for Solov'ëv how detrimental Nietzsche's philosophy is. Long before Nietzsche's thought and the specific Nietzschean notion of the *Übermensch* became widely spread in Russia, Solov'ëv had spelled out his own concept of the *sverkhchelovecheskoe* or the trans-human.[8] The confrontation with Nietzsche's *Übermensch* urges Solov'ëv to defend his own delineation of the trans-human against Nietzsche's determination of his *Übermensch*. From 1897 on, he engages in a dialogue with Nietzsche on the idea of the *Übermensch*, wherein he both offers a critical analysis of this concept and attempts to clarify and affirm his own definition of the term.

3. Solov'ëv's *sverkhchelovek*: renaming Christ

The first references to the *Übermensch* in Nietzsche's works appear in 1882, in the preparatory notes to *Thus spoke Zarathustra* (1883-1885), the only book in Nietzsche's corpus in which a detailed and coherent account of the *Übermensch* is given.[9] Solov'ëv, who wasn't aware of

---

[7] Dahomey – in the area of what is now southern Benin – was a kingdom in Western Africa that grew rich in the eighteenth and nineteenth centuries from the slave trade with Europe. It was a war state, not only with the goal to expand but also to take prisoners to sell as slaves. In 1892 French colonists defeated the Dahomeyan king and established the French colony of Dahomey (*The New Encyclopaedia Britannica,* 1995, Vol. 3: 848). For Solov'ëv, Nietzsche's ideas are a revival of the Dahomeyan practice of oppression and slavery, a practice that was generally known at the time in Europe and Russia through French sources.

[8] When referring to Nietzsche's concept, I use the German *Übermensch*. Consistent with this, I use *sverkhchelovek* in reference to Solov'ëv's use of the term. When translation is necessary, I use *trans-human* (see chapter 1).

[9] The term is, however, already present in Nietzsche's earliest writings in adjectival and adverbial form. In these early fragments the word *übermenschlich* is still associated with the traditional otherworldly meaning and refers to a transcendent, godlike being (cf. KSA 1: 26, 286; KSA 2: 113).

Nietzsche's thought until the beginning of the 1890s, had already reflected upon and formulated his definition of the trans-human some years before Nietzsche developed his specific interpretation of the term and long before the religious philosopher became acquainted with Nietzsche's idea of the *Übermensch*.

Solov'ëv refers to the *trans-human* (*sverkhchelovecheskoe*) as early as 1877 in the article "Vera, Razum i Opyt" ("Faith, Reason and Experience"). In the introduction to this paper, in which he argues that faith cannot be replaced by reason or science, he quotes David Friedrich Strauss' *The Old Faith and the New* (1872) as an example of the then popular positivistic attempts to overcome faith by science.[10] In this controversial work, Strauss critically analyzed traditional Christianity and its entrenchment in the narratives of miracles and myths (the old faith) and searched – in line with the new belief in Darwinian theories – for a new legitimization and foundation for humanity in science (the new faith): Strauss approached "every trans-human revelation, every religion" from an *a priori* negative point of view (Solov'ëv 2000-2001: 367). Further in the article, Solov'ëv claims that with the appearance of Christ, a "trans-human impulse" (*sverkhchelovecheskii impul's*) entered the world (id.: 381). This fragment indicates that for Solov'ëv the *sverkhchelovecheskoe* is a religious principle directly linked to the figure of Christ.

The next reference to the trans-human appears in the first lecture of the *Chteniia o Bogochelovechestve* (*Lectures on Divine Humanity*, 1878-1881), in which Solov'ëv develops the idea that society and the social order should rest upon a positive basis. This basis might either be the will of God, which has an "absolute, supernatural and trans-human character" (*kharakter bezuslovnyi, sverkhprirodnyi i sverkhchelovecheskii*), or the will of the people (SS III: 6). This implies that for Solov'ëv, the idea of the trans-human corresponds to God.

In the letter to tsar Aleksandr III (April 1881), in which Solov'ëv requests him to spare the lives of Aleksandr II's murderers, he employs the term trans-human to denote an extraordinary moral

---

[10] The first of Nietzsche's *Untimely Meditations*, "David Strauss: the Confessor and the Writer" (1873), is also a polemical treatise against Strauss and his work *The Old Faith and the New*. Strauss, believing to be the proclaimer of 'a new faith', is in Nietzsche's opinion, no more than a conservative advocate of traditional German culture.

strength.[11] By granting the terrorists mercy, the tsar would rise to "a trans-human height" and would by this act "prove the divine significance of the tsarist power" (Solov'ëv 1977: 74). The notion of the trans-human crops up again in the third speech in memory of Dostoevskii, delivered on February 19, 1883. Solov'ëv associates God with the idea of a "trans-human Good" (*sverkhchelovecheskoe Dobro*) (SS III: 211).

In *Istoriia i Budushchnost' Teokratii* (*The History and Future of Theocracy*, 1885), Solov'ëv treats the concept of the trans-human more extensively. In its present condition humankind has not yet reached "true humanity." To realize this ideal of human perfection, humans should transcend their specific human nature and become one with the Divine. The first "true human" who incorporated both human and divine nature in one person was the *Bogochelovek* or God-Man, Christ.[12]

> The Bogochelovek, who is the end and goal of human nature, is [...] for us the first-born or the decisive basis of the new trans-human development form, in which humanity, rising above itself, unites itself intrinsically with the Divine Being and becomes a part of the Kingdom of God (SS IV: 604).

This fragment shows the significance of the notion of the *sverkhchelovecheskoe* in Solov'ëv's philosophical framework because the term refers to the core of his religious philosophy, i.e. the idea of *Bogochelovechestvo* or *Divine Humanity*. In this future-oriented anthropological project Solov'ëv's metaphysical optimism on the ultimate salvation and elevation of humankind finds its utmost expression. In line with Byzantine tradition, Solov'ëv believes that the initial godlike nature of human beings has not been completely eradicated since the Fall but can be restored. The goal of human development is the collective apotheosis of humankind through God's

---

[11] The letter was an attempt to explain and defend the public lecture Solov'ëv had delivered after the assassination of Aleksandr II on March 28, 1881. In this speech, Solov'ëv had suggested that the new tsar, Aleksandr III, should act according to Christian ethics and grant his father's assassins mercy. The lecture, however, was interpreted as an insult to the tsar and the monarchy and provoked a lot of commotion. As an apology, Solov'ëv wrote a letter to the tsar to clarify his real motives. The letter was once again misunderstood by the government officials and in the end Solov'ëv voluntarily resigned as a lecturer in philosophy.

[12] In Russian Christian discourse, the term *Bogochelovek* or God-Man refers to Christ. I will explain the idea of the *Bogochelovek* more extensively in the following chapter.

glory. This restoration of human likeness with God is initiated by Christ, the authentic *Bogochelovek*, in whom *Logos* and flesh, divine and human nature are reconciled. Through the appearance and mediation of Christ, Divinity incarnate, the whole of humanity can be transfigured and find its ultimate realization in God. Solov'ëv's anthropology of *Bogochelovechestvo* is a calque of the Greek *theandria*, which in patristic sources refers to the union between God (*theos*, in Russian *Bog*) and humans (*anthropos*, in Russian *chelovek*).[13] In Solov'ëv's interpretation, the trans-human denotes an ideal of human perfectibility – a higher, deified level of human existence – a concept that is analogous with his anthropology of *Bogochelovechestvo*.[14]

This idea is reformulated in "Zhiznennaia Drama Platona" ("Plato's Life-Drama", 1898). Solov'ëv postulates that the process of the deification of humankind is only possible in mutual interaction between God and the human. Just as Divinity cannot regenerate the human being without the participation of the human himself, "it is likewise impossible for the human to create trans-humanity out of himself [...] the human can *become* divine only by the real power of [...] an eternally existing Divine Being" (SS IX: 234). The human cannot become trans-human "solely by force of mind, genius and moral will," it is necessary that a "genuine, substantive *Bogochelovek*" appears (SS IX: 241).

Solov'ëv's interpretation of the *sverkhchelovecheskoe* as a higher, perfected state of humanity in which the present human condition is transcended and the human is united with the Divine is entrenched in the spiritual and theological legacy of early Christian mysticism and Greek patristic thought. In the second century AD, Montanus introduced the concept of the *hyperanthropos* in Christian thought: he used the term for designating the Paraclete (Benz 1961: 32ff).[15] In the heretical Montanist movement, the concept fulfilled the

---

[13] As Valliere points out, the term *theandria* and related words rarely occur in the patristic writings and particularly originate from Origenist and Monophysite traditions (Valliere 2000: 13). For a more detailed account of Solov'ëv's theory of *Divine Humanity*, see Kochetkova (2001) and Sutton (1988: 70-72).

[14] This delineation of the trans-human is in line with the meaning it had in the German tradition (e.g. Goethe's use of the term), before Nietzsche radically altered its connotation.

[15] The Greek word *hyperanthropos* appears for the first time in one of Lucian of Samosata's (ca 120-190) *Dialogues of the dead* yet without any religious connotation.

early Christian hopes for the elevation of humankind, which was initiated by the coming of Christ and could only be fully realized through the effusion of the Holy Spirit into every human being. The *hyperanthropos* was the human of the coming era of salvation. After the denunciation of Montanism, the concept was banned from the official church but survived in Gnosticism. Through *gnosis* or esoteric knowledge concerning the essential truth of God and the world, the Gnostic would reach a higher, trans-human stage of being and come closer to God. Whereas in the Gnostic tradition trans-humanity was exclusively reserved for the initiated, the Greek theologian Origen (185-254 AD) applied the idea to all Christians and introduced it in Christian anthropology: all Christians are "Sons of God" and can, through God's glory, be elevated and deified. In the fifth century the mystical theologian, Pseudo-Dionysios the Areopagite, linked the concept of the trans-human to the controversial question of Christ's two natures. At the Council of Chalcedon (451), a creed was accepted that recognized and affirmed both Christ's divine and human nature. Pseudo-Dionysios was the first to associate the doctrine of Christ's Divinity and humanity with the idea of the *hyperanthropos*: in Christ the essence of human nature is united with Divinity and in this manner human nature is elevated to the trans-human (Benz 1961: 49). While in the following centuries the concept of the trans-human was gradually abandoned by official Western Christian theology, the term was further employed and reflected upon in Eastern Orthodox Christology, more particular with regard to Christ's divine and human nature.

In the Eastern Orthodox tradition, the *hyperanthropos* is thus highly associated with the figure of Christ, more specifically with Christ's incarnation. As Divinity incarnate, Christ is no longer merely human: He mediates between the divine and the human, He is both God and human, the *Theanthropos* or *Bogochelovek*.

Solov'ëv, raised in the Russian Orthodox tradition and educated in both philosophy and theology, was aware of the specific religious interpretation of the trans-human and its association with the *Bogochelovek* Christ. His anthropological project of *Bogochelovechestvo* and the related idea of *sverkhchelovechestvo* is a

---

For an extensive analysis and genealogy of the Christian interpretation of the trans-human, see Benz (1961: 29ff).

further elaboration of this prominent tradition in Russian Orthodox thinking.

In Solov'ëv's discourse, the idea of the trans-human has a pre-eminently religious meaning because it expresses his ideal of a final union between Divinity and humanity. The confrontation with Nietzsche's *Übermensch* then, spelled out to overcome the death of the old God, alarmed the religious philosopher and provoked him to disprove this corruption of his own ideal of the *sverkhchelovek*. The preoccupation with the *Übermensch* brings about a shift in Solov'ëv's attitude towards Nietzsche, from an apparent indifference to a genuine interest in his thought.

4. Nietzsche's *Übermensch*: defying Christ

In one of his widely read *Voskresnye Pis'ma* (*Sunday Letters*) from 1897, "Slovesnost' ili Istina" ("Literature or Truth"), Solov'ëv takes up the debate with Nietzsche's *Übermensch*.[16] Although the chief tenor in the paper is one of mockery, the change in Solov'ëv's understanding of Nietzsche is manifest. The "fashionable" theme of the *Übermensch* is by then for Solov'ëv "one of the most dangerous *temptations*" in contemporary intellectual life (SS X: 28).[17]

Still, he finds at the core of the *Übermensch* a most significant "truth" which he identifies as an urge to elevate and perfect the human being: "Isn't the unfortunate Nietzsche right, after all, when he maintains that all the virtue, all the value, of the human is in the fact that he is *more* than a human, that he is a *transition* to some kind of other, *higher being*?" (SS X: 29). What Solov'ëv values in Nietzsche's anthropology is that it does not acquiesce in the present condition of humanity yet focuses instead on what the human is still capable of becoming. Solov'ëv believes that present humanity has not yet lived up to its full potential and is able to realize a higher condition. And he sees an affiliated conception of the human in Nietzsche's *Übermensch* in which he observes an impulse to transcend the present human and

---

[16] In 1897-1898 Solov'ëv published twenty essays in the newspaper *Rus'* under the heading *Voskresnye pis'ma*. These essays gained a broad reading public.

[17] For English quotations from "Slovesnost' ili Istina," "Ideia Sverkhcheloveka," and "Kratkaia Povest' ob Antikhriste," I based my translation on Vladimir Wozniuk's (Solov'ëv: 2000). I have made some minor changes to his translations.

to realize a higher, more perfect condition of the human being. He perceives in the *Übermensch* a perfectionist and idealist striving, "the affinity to and gravitation toward the absolute," which is also at the center of his own delineation of the trans-human (SS X: 29). At the core of Nietzsche's anthropology, Solov'ëv finds the aspiration to develop the human's potential in order to realize a higher form of the human being, in which he identifies the typical religious striving to perfect the self. Fundamentally, the religious thinker is swayed by the perfectionist dimension of the *Übermensch* and observes within it a faint reflection of his own anthropological ideal.

However, in its final form, Nietzsche's *Übermensch* does not measure up to the authentic *sverkhchelokek*, i.e. the *Bogochelovek* Christ. Solov'ëv proceeds in an ironical juxtaposition of Nietzsche's *Übermensch* (which in his reading is identical to Zarathustra) and the only truthful *sverkhchelovek*, in order to discredit the *Übermensch* and undermine its growing authoritative status in Russian culture. In contrast with the authentic *sverkhchelovek*, who actually lived and acted according to His trans-human nature, Nietzsche's *Übermensch* is merely an abstract idea that only exists in the fictional character of Zarathustra. Nietzsche, no more than a "super-philologist" (*sverkhfilolog*), substituted the truthful delineation of the *sverkhchelovek* as a religious principle by a literary character (SS X: 29). Nietzsche exchanged truth for literature and fabricated the fictitious *Übermensch* as a surrogate for the real *sverkhchelovek*. Nietzsche's false *Übermensch* is "only a subject of university teaching, a newly instituted *department* of the philological faculty" (SS X: 31).[18] And he could not give his literary subject a simple name, like "Heinrich or Friedrich or Otto," but decided upon Zarathustra, which "carried the odor of linguistics." While the real *sverkhchelovek* spent forty days in the desert before the beginning of his public life, Nietzsche has his Zarathustra spend ten years in a cave (SS X: 30).[19]

---

[18] Well aware of the fact that his contemporaries did not understand his books correctly, Nietzsche sarcastically remarked in his intellectual autobiography *Ecce Homo* (1888): "Some day institutions will be needed, in which men live and teach as I understand living and teaching; it might even happen that a few chairs will be erected for the interpretation of *Zarathustra*" (KSA 6: 298). *Ecce Homo* was posthumously published in 1908, so this was a source not yet available to Solov'ëv.

[19] Solov'ëv passes over the fact that Nietzsche's intentionally alluded to the Gospel in order to hint at the intended epochal significance of the work. To show the difference in greatness between Christ and Zarathustra, Nietzsche deliberately let his character

In this connection, Solov'ëv quotes the opening line from Zarathustra's first speech on the *Übermensch*, addressed to the people on the market square: "I teach you the *Übermensch*" (*Ich lehre euch den Übermenschen*) (see KSA 4: 14), thereby mocking Zarathustra's teaching and juxtaposing it to the real trans-human credo of Christ.[20] Whereas Nietzsche's idea only exists in a fictional world, made merely of words, Christ substantiated His message by an actual deed, that is His rising from the dead (SS X: 31). Through His resurrection, Christ revealed His divine nature and became one with God. By this action, He showed humankind the authentic path to transfiguration.

Solov'ëv explicitly opposes the *Übermensch*, though in a playful manner, in relation to the *sverkhchelovek* or *Bogochelovek* Christ. In this constellation, the *Übermensch* thus figures as an inverted Christology, a determination that will turn out to be constitutive for the God-seekers' assessment of the *Übermensch*.

In this 1897 text, the approach to the *Übermensch* is not so unfavorable. For one thing, Solov'ëv finds in Nietzsche's concept a latent religious dimension: it urges to transcend present humanity. For another thing, although he finds that the *Übermensch* fails to equal the real *sverkhchelovek*, he does not proceed in a harsh critique of Nietzsche. Rather, he counters Nietzsche with humor. Yet, in spite of the light-hearted tenor, at the end of "Slovesnost' ili Istina," Nietzsche's *Übermensch* seems to distress Solov'ëv more than he is willing to admit. He insinuates that the *Übermensch* might be a premonition of the coming Antichrist: "In all his emptiness and artificiality, the *Übermensch* [...] perhaps represents the prototype of the one who will display, apart from his brilliant words, both deeds and signs of the times, even if they are false. Perhaps the literary exercises of the Basel philologist were only impotent expressions of a real premonition?" (SS X: 31f.).[21]

In an 1899 article, "Ideia Sverkhcheloveka" ("The Idea of the Trans-human"), Solov'ëv returns to the issue of the *Übermensch* and

---

outdo his historical 'predecessor.' Whereas Christ – at the age of thirty – started his public life after forty days in the desert, Zarathustra at the same age withdrew from public life and remained ten years in the mountains (KSA 4: 11). Solov'ëv's references to Zarathustra's 'biography' prove that he read at least the Preface to *Thus spoke Zarathustra*.

[20] This is the only Nietzsche-quote in Solov'ëv's writings.

[21] Solov'ëv alludes to 2 Thessalonians 2: 9: "The coming of the lawless one will be by Satan's working, with all kinds of miracles and signs and false wonders."

this time with a different attitude. Although he is still cautious in giving it too much attention, he shows a genuine interest and offers a more rational account of the *Übermensch*. Claiming the three most fashionable trends in Russian thought at the end of the nineteenth century to be Marx's economic materialism, Tolstoi's abstract moralism, and Nietzsche's *Übermensch* – frankly called a "demonology" – he gives priority to Nietzsche's doctrine. Nietzsche's *Übermensch* is so attractive to the Russian reader because it answers some spiritual questions arising in intellectual circles. Solov'ëv credits Nietzsche's idea of the *Übermensch* because it holds in itself a truth about the human being, which is that the contemporary human requires to be transcended. The *Übermensch* is, in essence, an appealing concept because "it opens out directly onto the immense expanse of all of life's roads" (SS IX: 267). Solov'ëv reformulates his point made in "Slovesnost' ili Istina": Nietzscheanism is in actuality "an error" that nonetheless holds within itself an essential truth, which can only be judged and disproved on the basis of its veracity (SS IX: 267). What he finds valuable in Nietzsche's anthropology is that it urges humans to be critical of and overcome their present condition. The past and future progression of humankind could and can only be realized by the immanent desire to rise above actual reality: "The human naturally wants to be better and more than he is in reality; he is *naturally* drawn to the idea of the trans-human" (SS IX: 268).

Yet, in the end, the truthfulness in Nietzsche's account of the *Übermensch* is a distorted one. For Solov'ëv, the flaw in the *Übermensch* is that it is conceived from a Darwinist background and entails a more perfect life form arising from biological evolution. This reading of the *Übermensch* from a Darwinist angle is associated with the general worldview in the last decades of the nineteenth century, in which Darwinian and other theories of evolution (Haeckel's and Spencer's among others) dominated both science and popular mentality.[22]

---

[22] In the Nietzsche Research, however, there is no univocal answer to Nietzsche's alleged Darwinism in his elaboration of the *Übermensch*. Zarathustra indeed explicates the *Übermensch* to the people on the market in evolutionist phrasing: "You have made your way from worm to human, and much within you is still worm. Once you were apes, and even now the human is more of an ape, than any ape" (KSA 4: 14). Yet the philosopher took at the same time a manifest anti-Darwinist stance: the *Übermensch* does not represent a new phase in the evolution of the species, but is rather "a fortunate accident" (*Glücksfall*) in the history of humankind (KSA 6: 171).

Solov'ёv, a former student of natural science (1869-1872), was well-informed on the evolutionist debate and opposed the alleged biological dimension of the *Übermensch* with his own phylogenetic thesis. In his opinion, the present human physical form is the culmination and final goal of biological evolution. In the animal kingdom mental capacities evolve proportionally and dependently based on the degree of complexity of the physical form. If, for example, the form of an oyster was the end of the physical development of organisms, then the evolution of mental life would have stopped there. The corporeal form of an oyster could not be sufficient for the mental processes of animals which came later in the evolutionary process, let alone for the specific psyche of man (SS IX: 269f.). According to Solov'ёv, this systematic correlation between psychic and physical development came to an end with the appearance of humanity on the evolutionist scale: in human physiology, corporeal transformation has reached its ultimate completion. Within the current human organism, the human can endlessly refine his inner self. The human type has no need for physical improvement or modification: the human corpus should not be transcended and evolve towards some new trans-human form, "because the human form can infinitely perfect itself – outwardly and inwardly, *remaining all the while the same*" (SS IX: 270). In his present physical condition the human being is capable of fulfilling everything, he is "capable of being the form of a perfected All-unity (*vseedinstvo*) or divine being (*bozhestvo*)" (SS IX: 270).[23]

This human "morphological stability" does not hinder the intrinsic human aspiration to transcend oneself mentally, to become trans-human "because the truth of this aspiration is related not to any forms of human existence, but only to the capacity of the human functioning in these forms" (SS IX: 270). Thus, Solov'ёv renounces in Nietzsche's *Übermensch* what he reads as the Darwinist idea of

---

Highly aware of the evolutionist theories that had pervaded the contemporary spirit of the age, Nietzsche anticipated and countered a Darwinist reading of the *Übermensch*: "Other learned cattle has suspected me of Darwinism on that account" (KSA 6: 300).

[23] I prefer the translation of *vseedinstvo* as 'All-unity' to Wozniuk's translation 'unity-of-all.' With this concept Solov'ёv attempts to overcome the seemingly irreconcilable views on the nature of God's presence in the world, which stress either the immanence or transcendence of God. By distinguishing between 'God as he is in Himself' and 'God as he is in relation to the world,' Solov'ёv succeeds in recognizing both natures in God (Sutton 1988: 62f.).

biological transformation into a kind of higher organic being, a trans-human form of life. In his view, the human organism in its present condition is the ultimate perfection of biological evolution and thereby no obstacle on the path to the trans-human. The striving to become a *sverkhchelovek* belongs not to the form of the human being, but only to the mode of functioning in this form. Every human being is by his divine nature impelled to realize perfection, and in that sense, every human is already in a way a *sverkhchelovek*.

The only obstacle, however, for the human to raise himself to the trans-human level is "the phenomenon of death" (SS IX: 271). Death is an inevitability in human existence: it is the final destiny of the whole of humankind. Precisely at this point, the authentic *sverkhchelovek* distinguishes himself from the mortal human:

> The sverkhchelovek must be first of all, and particularly, a conqueror of death – a liberated-liberator of humanity from those essential conditions which make death necessary, and consequently, the executor of those conditions by which it is possible either not to die at all, or, having died, to rise from the dead to eternal life (SS IX: 272).

The authentic trans-human transcends death as the ultimate human restriction. For Solov'ëv, the only legitimate ideal of the trans-human is the Christian one, in which immortality is attained through resurrection.[24] The first human to have risen from the dead, the "firstborn of the dead," and consequently, the first authentic trans-human was the *Bogochelovek* Jesus Christ (SS IX: 273).[25]

In contrast with Nietzsche's delineation of the *Übermensch*, which is a condition that should be attained on an individual basis, the Solov'ëvian ideal of the *sverkhchelovek* concerns the whole of humanity. In Solov'ëv's anthropological project the trans-human ideal is not merely reserved for Christ, but is the final and universal goal of

---

[24] The idea of immortality as a prerequisite to the authentic trans-human brings to mind Nikolai Fëdorovich Fëdorov's (1828-1903) reflections on the subject. This rather obscure philosopher believed in "the common task" of humankind: by means of past and future achievements in science and technology humankind would eventually be able to attain collective resurrection and realize the objective of true *sverkhchelovechestvo* (trans-humanity), i.e. the Kingdom of God on earth. Although Solov'ëv was acquainted with Fëdorov, who devoted some writings to Nietzsche's *Übermensch*, there is no hard evidence that his views on Nietzsche were actually influenced by Fëdorov (Zakydalsky 1986: 113-125).

[25] Colossians 1:18.

human evolution. However distant the objective of a collective trans-humanity, i.e. *Bogochelovechestvo* or *Divine Humanity*, might be, *"there is a trans-human path* over which man has gone, goes, and will go for the good of all" (SS IX: 273). Contemporary humankind should concentrate on and develop its trans-human potential "because a full and decisive victory over death is at its end" (SS IX: 273). The idea of the trans-human is not merely reserved for a single individual or at best for an elite, but has a universal and collectivist undertone: the whole of humanity can and should evolve towards trans-humanity.

Like some of his fellow intellectuals who read Nietzsche through the prism of Dostoevskii's discourse, Solov'ëv seeks a connection in Russian cultural history to substantiate his views on Nietzsche and in particular, on his idea of the *Übermensch*. In a lecture presented in 1899, he links the notion of the *Übermensch* to Lermontov.[26] He perceives Lermontov, whose poetry became only fully understandable and tangible in the figure and thought of Nietzsche, as "the direct ancestor" of Nietzscheanism (SS IX: 348). Lermontov was by nature endowed with the features of a real trans-human: "Lermontov was definitely a genius, i.e. a person, who is from his birth on similar to the trans-human, who received capacities for a great pursuit, who is capable, and hence, obliged to execute it" (SS IX: 352). The author was gifted with a strong personality and a feeling of sensitivity towards the world surrounding him, which enabled him to develop visionary qualities. He could see beyond the phenomenal world and grasp the full essence of being. However, in spite of the great talent he had received for preceding humanity on its way to trans-humanity, Lermontov reneged on fulfilling his duty. Instead of exerting his trans-human genius to lead humankind forward in the process to perfection, Lermontov chose to isolate himself from humankind and to concentrate solely on himself. He understood the power of his genius as a privilege and not as a commitment to God and humanity. In Lermontov's troubled *psyche*, the trans-human or the divine principle on the one hand, and the evil principle on the other hand, struggled to gain the upper hand. Eventually, the evil principle triumphed and incited the poet to its idealization (SS IX: 359-360).

---

[26] In the 1911 essay "Lermontov. Poet sverkhchelovechestva", Merezhkovskii adopts Solov'ëv's characterization of Lermontov as bearing traits of the *Übermensch*, wherein he frequently refers to Solov'ëv's article (Merezhkovskii 1911: 7).

The evil principle became Lermontov's demon.[27] Lermontov was corrupted by "the basic evil [...] the capital mortal sin," namely pride, which provoked him to consider himself "higher than common mortals" and to live by the principle that all is permitted (SS IX: 363). This extremely proud attitude prevented him from becoming a true trans-human. For one can become truly trans-human only by the virtue of humility.

> [...] pride is for the human the first condition for never becoming a trans-human, and humility is the first condition for becoming a trans-human; therefore one can say, that genius obliges one to humility, this only means, that the genius is obliged to become a trans-human (SS IX: 363).

Lermontov did not fulfill this commitment, he did not develop the genius he received as a divine gift and he certainly did not lead humanity to genuine trans-humanity, as he was called to do (SS IX: 366).

Solov'ëv's perception of Lermontov as the personification of the failed trans-human, precedes and foreshadows his last, though masked, response to Nietzsche in the apocalyptic "Kratkaia Povest' ob Antikhriste" ("A short Story about the Antichrist", 1900).[28] This eschatological tale, presented as a fictional parable, was added to Solov'ëv's last philosophical work *Tri Razgovora o Voine, Progresse, i Kontse vsemoirnoi Istorii* (*Three Conversations on War, Progress, and the End of History*, 1899-1900) and was not finished until some months before his death. The tale echoes the tone of moderate pessimism that marks the concluding period of Solov'ëv's philosophical and spiritual development. By the end of the 1890s, Solov'ëv's initial optimism on historical progress and the future of humankind had been gradually replaced by a fatalistic anticipation of what he identified as the coming Antichrist. The religious thinker, greatly concerned with Russian moral and religious consciousness, was faced by a rapidly changing social and cultural reality, a

---

[27] In Solov'ëv's opinion, Lermontov is swayed by three demons: the demon of cruelty ("greed for blood"), the demon of obscenity ("dirtiness"), and the most powerful, the demon of "pride" (SS IX: 360-363).

[28] The tale is to a high degree parallel with Dostoevskii's 'Legend' of the "Grand Inquisitor," a comparison acknowledged whenever both thinkers are studied. As Kostalevsky points out, the Grand Inquisitor aims to "corrects the deed" of Christ, whereas Solov'ëv's protagonist wants to outplace Him (1997: 109).

phenomenon occurring in both Europe and his motherland. In 1898, he traveled through Europe and was alarmed at what he saw as the decline of morality and culture (Sutton 1988: 27). And more importantly, he observed a similar phenomenon in the Russian homeland, in which he had put his messianistic hopes for the regeneration of depraved European society.

Solov'ëv finds Nietzsche to be partially responsible for the decline in Russian society and culture. By this time, he can no longer look away from the growing popularity of Nietzsche's ideas on Russian soil. By the end of the 1890s, new cultural and ideological movements emerged which were mainly preoccupied with the status of the individual personality and strove to establish the individual at the core of their general outlook. In aesthetics, the decadents found that art should be foremost an individualist experience and not so much a means to encourage a sense of collectivity. These decadent or symbolist writers and artists, and especially their spokesman Merezhkovskii, were by the traditional intelligentsia labeled the "first Russian Nietzscheans" (Solov'ëv S. 1977: 375). The tendency towards individualism was also endorsed by the self-proclaimed neo-idealists who advocated an ethics of moral individualism in the field of philosophical anthropology. As will be shown later in this book, Nietzsche indeed mediated in this process of the emancipation of the individual. From Solov'ëv's point of view, this trend threatened to contaminate Christian consciousness, which was largely construed around a common interest for the collective well-being. According to his biographer Sergei Solov'ëv, by the end of the century, Vladimir Solov'ëv could no longer ignore "what influence Nietzsche's ideas gained in Russia and that from this side was imminent a serious danger to Christian thought" (ibid.).

Solov'ëv's *Tri Razgovora* and the included "Kratkaia Povest' ob Antikhriste" contain his answers to these detrimental ideologies, which he believes to be subsiding in isolation from the collective interest. This culminating work is marked by, among other things, "a struggle with Nietzsche and Tolstoi" (id.: 26). In his *Tri Razgovora*, Solov'ëv attempted to restore his belief in the Kingdom of God on earth and to counter his unbelieving opponents in a decisive manner. And he preferred a narrative rather than a philosophical context to convey his final message. Setting out to explore the problem of evil from various perspectives, he adopted Plato's model and created three dialogues between five Russian, unnamed interlocutors (the General, the Politician, Mr. Z., the Lady and the Prince). At the end of the third conversation, Mr. Z. reads a manuscript of a monk with the name Pansofii, entitled "Kratkaia Povest' ob Antikhriste." This dystopian narrative offers a gloomy image of what might be the political and social state of twenty-first century Europe. After half a century of a Pan-Mongolian yoke on European soil, the scattered European nations have united themselves to chase away the Asian occupiers and have founded a coalition of democratic governments, "the European United States." During this period, a remarkable person, whom "many called a trans-human (*sverkhchelovek*)," appears and gains both political and spiritual power (SS X: 197). This "trans-human" is eventually chosen to become both the secular and religious leader of all European nations. The noble and religious emperor brings peace and material wealth to the world and, as a consequence, he is hailed by all nations and religions as the great benefactor of humanity: all believe that he is the Christ of the Second Coming. However, his belief in God and Christian principles is solely based on rational and pragmatic considerations, his whole being is only directed towards himself: "he *loved* only *himself alone*" (SS X: 198). He even prefers himself to God, albeit unconsciously. His extreme self-love incites him to declare himself the real Christ, the final and ultimate Savior, whereas he looks upon the first Christ as nothing more than his own precursor (SS X: 198). Christ had *reformed* humanity by preaching the Moral Good and living by it. The new, self-proclaimed Christ thinks it is his task to be the *benefactor* of humanity, to bring peace and material security to humankind (SS X: 199). Convinced that he is the new Messiah, the *sverkhchelovek* waits for a divine signal from God. However, the long-awaited for revelation, as described in the prophecy of the Second Coming, is not disclosed by God but by Satan who addresses the trans-human in the same wording that God used to reveal Christ's divine nature to the people: "My beloved son, in you is all My benevolence" (SS X: 200).[29] At this point the trans-human is transformed into the Antichrist.[30] He has reached the age of thirty

---

[29] See Matthew 3: 17, Mark 1: 11 and Luke 3: 22.

[30] Satan reveals himself to the *sverkhchelovek* when he throws himself off a cliff. This is an allusion to one of the temptations of Christ in the wilderness: the devil proposes that Christ throws himself off the temple in order to prove that he is the Son of God (Luke 4: 9-10).

three, the age Christ died at the cross. Not revealing his true nature and posing as the Second Christ, the 'trans-human Antichrist' appears to the people as the "human of the future" (*griadushchii chelovek*, SS X: 198, 201, 203). This designation parallels Nietzsche's "human of the future (*Mensch der Zukunft*)," the redeemer of humanity, who will deliver us from "the will to nothing, from nihilism," who "returns to the earth its goal and to man its hope, this Antichrist and anti-nihilist, this conqueror of God and nothing, *he should come once*" (KSA 5: 336).[31] During an "Ecumenical Council," where representatives of all Christian religions are present, the 'trans-human Antichrist' demands to be appointed as the sole religious authority for all churches. But the leaders of the three main churches (Catholicism, Protestantism and Orthodoxy) refuse and in the end expose the trans-human as the Antichrist incarnate. In line with biblical prophecy, the ultimate battle between Christian believers and the Antichrist, between good and evil, is described in an apocalyptic way: the orthodox and catholic leaders are murdered by a supernatural power, they later resurrect from the dead and unite the last true Christians. The Antichrist is in the end killed by a volcanic eruption near the Dead Sea. With the appearance of the long-anticipated Christ, the authentic trans-human or *sverkhchelovek*, the thousand-year Christian reign is installed.

What distinguishes the 'trans-human Antichrist' from other godless characters in nineteenth century Russian literature, is that this character does not put forward any philosophical argument to renounce God and Christian principles. The only reason why the trans-human cannot submit to God and Christ is due to his self-love. As is the case with Lermontov, whose pride and self-centeredness impeded him from developing his trans-human genius, the Antichrist's self-love and egotism makes it impossible for him to equal the real trans-human, Christ. By referring to both Christ and Antichrist as 'trans-human,' Solov'ëv for the first time acknowledges them to be equal opponents, respectively representing the absolute good and the ultimate evil. Both the Christian and the anti-Christian or demonical *sverkhchelovek* are provided with an equal genius and equal qualities. Both are strong personalities, highly conscious of themselves and the other; both have a visionary talent that enables them to elevate humankind to *Divine Humanity*. They differ, however,

---

[31] I owe this parallel to Wozniuk (Solov'ëv 2000: 318). See also KSA 5: 126 & KSA 11: 210.

in the way they ultimately use their genius. The Christian trans-human or Christ chooses to employ His trans-human capacities for the benefit of humanity whereas the demonical trans-human or the Antichrist alienates himself from humanity and uses his genius solely for the development of his own ego. Christ is the ultimate altruist: He sacrifices his life for humanity. The Antichrist is egoism incarnate whose apparent benevolence is nothing more than extreme pride and lust for power.

Only in this final work, finished some months before his death, did Solov'ëv explicitly associate the term *sverkhchelovek* with the Antichrist, yet it is only on a fictionalized level as if he did not wish to alarm his readers with what he perceived to be a real danger for humankind. The story of 'the trans-human Antichrist' is in fact presented through a technique of *indirect narrativity*: within the narrative setting of the *Tri Razgovora*, Mr. Z. reads to the interlocutors of the three conversations a manuscript of a certain monk Pansofii about whom the reader receives no further information. The doubly narrated composition of the story complicates a final and straightforward claim concerning Solov'ëv's position to the content of the text. The question is thus twofold: firstly, does the 'trans-human Antichrist' in this eschatological tale refer to Nietzsche's *Übermensch* (for Nietzsche is not explicitly mentioned in this fictional narrative)? And secondly, can we assume that Pansofii's or Mr. Z.'s voice is indeed Solov'ëv's voice and hence conclude that Solov'ëv in the end perceives of Nietzsche's *Übermensch* as the coming Antichrist? The answer is intertwined.

In a response to Prince Sergei Trubetskoi's review of his *Tri Razgovora*, Solov'ëv reveals that Nietzsche was, amongst others, in the background when writing his "Kratkaia Povest'":

> For, the fictitious author of my "story about the Antichrist," the monk Pansofii, is presented by me as our contemporary [...] In what way, on what basis, and on what occasion should I present a contemporary educated monk, who has completed a course at the religious academy, like he knew nothing about Nietzsche, Tolstoi, state socialism and freemasonry" (SS X: 222).

Moreover, in Pansofii's manuscript there is a direct hint to Solov'ëv's authorship: the epigraph to the text is the first stanza of Solov'ëv's poem "Panmongolizm" (1894) (SS X: 193).[32] When the Lady asks where this motto comes from, Mr. Z. responds: "I think, the author of the story composed it himself" (ibid.). This explicit reference to Solov'ëv's famous poem adds up to the perception that Solov'ëv is, via Pansofii, the authoritative voice in the tale.

The apocalyptic portrayal of the Antichrist in the "Kratkaia Povest'" appears indeed as Solov'ëv's ultimate settlement with Nietzsche's *Übermensch*. Solov'ëv already implicitly communicates the anxious foreboding that Nietzsche is in actual fact the anticipation of the coming Antichrist in the 1894 article "Pervyi Shag k polozhitel'noi Estetike" (SS VII: 73). In the later writings on Nietzsche, and in particular on the *Übermensch*, this association becomes more and more pronounced until it apparently reaches its culmination in the figure of the 'trans-human Antichrist.' Yet the Antichrist not only reflects Solov'ëv's considerations on the *Übermensch* but is also rooted in his critique on Lev Tolstoi's ethics and on Marxist philosophy.[33] The 'trans-human Antichrist' is the personification of the moral theories prevalent in Solov'ëv's time that he considers to be potentially subversive for Russian religious and moral consciousness.

Whether or not Solov'ëv really hinted at Nietzsche's *Übermensch* in his portrayal of the Antichrist, the fact is that Solov'ëv's contemporaries and later generations of readers filled in the indeterminacies in the "Kratkaia Povest'" and identified the Antichrist with the *Übermensch*. Solov'ëv's fellow intellectual and acquaintance Nikolai Fëdorov claims around 1900 that "if one wants to name the Antichrist a trans-human, like Solov'ëv does, than it is the trans-human in the Nietzschean sense" (quoted in Kantor 2002: 23). In

---

[32] See SS XII: 95: "Pan-Mongolism! The name is wild, yet it pleases my ear greatly, as if it were full of forebodings of the glorious providence of God."

[33] In "Ideia Sverkhcheloveka," Solov'ëv considers Marx's economic materialism, Tolstoi's abstract moralism, and the demonology of the *Übermensch* as the most threatening tendencies of his time (SS IX: 267). He perceives all three of them as potential competitors to his own philosophical program. Like Marx, Solov'ëv strives for social justice, but he rejects his political socialism and the atheist bias of his project. Like Tolstoi, he aims to construct a Christian politics and to realize a theocracy based on the Gospel, but he disagrees with Tolstoi' anarchism, anti-clericalism, his doctrine of "the non-resistance to evil," and the anti-metaphysical tenor of his Christianity. Sergei Solov'ëv also claims that besides the "struggle with Nietzsche," the last period in Solov'ëv's thought is in part marked by an attempt to counter Tolstoi (Solov'ëv S. 1977: 26).

his monograph on Solov'ëv, Prince Evgenii Trubetskoi also links Nietzsche's *Übermensch* to Solov'ëv's depiction of the 'trans-human Antichrist' (Trubetskoi [1913] 1995, Vol. II: 277f.).[34] As will become clear in subsequent chapters, the mythopoem of the *Übermensch*-Antichrist will be productive in the further evolution of the Nietzsche-canon and turns out to be constitutive for the later religious appropriations of the *Übermensch*.

In the end, Solov'ëv's claim in "Slovesnost' ili Istina" (1897) that the *Übermensch* is a mere literary exercise thought out by the "super-philologist" Nietzsche, seems to be replaced only some years later by a more serious and even anxious attitude towards Nietzsche. Because Solov'ëv observed in the *Übermensch*, which gradually grew popular in both intellectual and popular literature, an imminent threat for Russian Christian consciousness, he preferred another approach to the German philosopher than his contemporaries. He did not engage in sharp criticism but instead tried to outwit Nietzsche with humor ("Slovesnost' ili Istina") or took refuge in a fictional narrative to express his concerns about the ramifications of Nietzsche's thought ("Kratkaia Povest' ob Antikhriste"). He chose not to articulate his real premonitions of the potential ramifications of Nietzsche's thought but kept silent about them. Andrei Belyi's reminiscence of his last conversation with Solov'ëv, shortly before the philosopher's death, is noteworthy:

> I started a conversation with Vladimir Sergeevich on Nietzsche, on the relationship between the *Übermensch* and the idea of *Bogochelovechestvo*. He talked a little about Nietzsche, but there was a profound seriousness in his words. He said that Nietzsche's ideas are the only thing that one should nowadays consider a profound danger that threatens religious culture.

---

[34] This tendency finds continuation in recent scholarship. According to Müller, Nietzsche and the Antichrist are in Solov'ëv's perception highly linked up; he asserts that, where Solov'ëv mentions the Antichrist, Nietzsche is clearly present in the background (Müller 1947: 510). In Losev's opinion, Solov'ëv's premonition of the Antichrist is the inevitable and logical outcome of thinking through Nietzsche's conception of the Übermensch: "the Nietzschean Übermensch, from Solov'ëv's point of view, the Antichrist" (Losev 1990: 533). Wozniuk shares this view: "the story [of the Antichrist] appears as the culmination of Soloviev's efforts to refute Nietzsche [...] Soloviev adapted the [...] Nietzschean theme of the political incarnation of a superman to this preapocalyptic end-of-history scenario" (Solov'ëv 2000: XXV). See also Kantor, 2001: 21.

However much I disagreed with him in my opinions on Nietzsche, his serious attitude towards Nietzsche deeply conciliated me. I understood that in naming Nietzsche a "super-philologist," Vladimir Sergeevich was only a tactic, ignoring the danger that threatened his hopes (Belyi [1907] 1991: 281-282).

Solov'ëv's silence, however, could not prevent and might even have indirectly stimulated the growing appeal of Nietzsche's *Übermensch* from the turn of the century and later.

5. Conclusion

Solov'ëv's significance for the Russian cultural and religious renaissance that came into being around the turn of the last century is undeniable. And his contribution to the shift in the reception process of Nietzsche towards a more favorable reading, in particular among the *God-seekers*, is also of great importance.

In spite of his final refutation of the German philosopher's body of thought, Solov'ëv is the first Russian critic to identify in Nietzsche a religious dimension. He perceives in Nietzsche's anthropology of the *Übermensch* a fundamental ideal of human perfectibility. At the core of the *Übermensch*, he finds a latent religious aspiration to transcend the present human and to realize a higher human condition, a striving that is consistent with his own prospective paradigm of *Bogochelovechestvo*. By reading Nietzsche from a religious point of view, he paves the way for the religious appropriation of Nietzsche which begins around 1900.

However, in spite of his affirmative response to what he reads as an urge for infinite perfection, the religious philosopher cannot compromise with the godless tenor of Nietzsche's *Übermensch*. He believes that an anthropology entrenched in a worldview devoid of God can only result in a decline of moral consciousness. If humanity renounces God, it consequently brushes aside its divine, metaphysical make up and the whole collective consciousness of *vseedinstvo* (All-unity). Once humanity loses touch with the initial and essential relation to God and all other beings, it falls into immorality. Thus for Solov'ëv, Nietzsche's *Übermensch* is designed to overcome the idea of God and appears as an actual threat to his own Christian outlook and more importantly, to the Russian Christian tradition.

In Solov'ëv's Christian outlook, the only authentic *sverkhchelovek* is the *Bogochelovek* Christ. In his discourse, Nietzsche's *Übermensch* is explicitly put in opposition to the *Bogochelovek*. This ideological constellation of the *Übermensch* as opposed to the *Bogochelovek* will turn out to be constructive for the *God-seekers'* valuation of Nietzsche's *Übermensch*.

By contrasting *Übermensch* and *Bogochelovek* Christ, the link between *Übermensch* and Antichrist is prefigured. In his response to Nietzsche, Solov'ëv refrains from any explicit identification of *Übermensch* and Antichrist. However, his allusions to the anti-Christian make up of the *Übermensch* can hardly be neglected. Solov'ëv's masked association between *Übermensch* and Antichrist seems to have reached its height especially in the culminating "Kratkaia Povest' ob Antikhriste," in part written under the ideological banner of his "struggle with Nietzsche" (Solov'ëv S. 1977: 26). Although Nietzsche is not explicitly mentioned here, the reader is encouraged at least partially to read Nietzsche's *Übermensch* in the figure of the *sverkhchelovek* Antichrist.

Yet, regardless of what Solov'ëv's intentions were in drawing up the character of the Antichrist, the fact remains that after his death, the myth of the *Übermensch*-Antichrist grew into a significant canon in the following years of the reception process of Nietzsche. From then on, in both popular literature and critical responses to Nietzsche, the association between *Übermensch* and Antichrist is a frequently used paradigm.

The irony of Solov'ëv's response to Nietzsche lies in its eventual vicissitudes. Whereas the religious philosopher observed in Nietzsche a threat to Russian religious and moral consciousness and strove to counter Nietzsche's *Übermensch* by advancing his own affirmative ideal of the *sverkhchelovek* Christ, his reading of Nietzsche from a religious point of view brought about a shift in the reception process, whereby Nietzsche was mainly read as a religious thinker. He thus unintentionally had a hand in what Berdiaev later phrased as: "Nietzsche had an influence side by side with Solov'ëv" (Berdiaev [1946] 1997: 199).

Chapter 5

"Only the word order has changed": *Bogochelovek* and *chelovekobog*

> *Dostoevskii's dazzling dialectics is based on the opposition of Bogochelovek and chelovekobog (Berdiaev [1923] 1991: 132).*

1. Introduction

In the previous chapter I documented Vladimir Solov'ëv's reading of Nietzsche and hinted at the unquestionable impact of his discourse on the *God-seekers'* assessment of Nietzsche. In order to grasp the full significance of his interpretation of Nietzsche, in particular of the ideological constellation of the *Übermensch* as a principle in direct opposition to the *Bogochelovek* or God-Man, the latter concept should be explained as it functions in the Russian religious context. Furthermore, a most relevant contrast is the one between *Bogochelovek* and *chelovekobog*, or man-god, a keynote concept in the *God-seekers'* appropriation of Nietzsche's *Übermensch*. They – and most contemporary readers – ascribe the *chelovekobog* primarily to Dostoevskii and identify it as one of the major motives in Dostoevskii's thought. Still, if one closely scrutinizes Dostoevskii's works, the term *chelovekobog* appears, in fact, only three times. In what follows, I will pinpoint the specific discursive settings in Dostoevskii's writings in which this term occurs and explain its underlying rationale.

2. Bogochelovek

In Russian religious discourse, the term *Bogochelovek* or *God-Man* is employed to denominate Christ incarnate. The word is a compound from *Bog* (God) and *chelovek* (human), and refers to the compound nature of Jesus Christ. In the person of Christ, God became flesh. In Russian consciousness, this Christological term is formulated specifically to express the essential nature of Christ: in Jesus Christ there are two absolute natures, a genuinely divine and a genuinely human nature, and these two natures are united in one hypostasis (Leporskii 1903: 863ff.; Nikolskii 1891-1903: 118ff; *Polnyi pravoslavnyi bogoslovskii entsiklopedicheskii slovar'*, I: 374ff.). The term itself does not appear in the Gospel. The doctrine of the *Bogochelovek* is grounded in the exegesis of various fragments in the New Testament, such as Romans 8, Colossians 1-2 and Ephesians 1 (Nikolskii 1903: 864ff.).

The term *Bogochelovek* can be traced back to the Church Fathers. The word *Theanthropos* is coined by Origen (185-254).[1] The designation of Christ as a *Theanthropos* or *Theos anthropos* is to some extent continued by the later Church Fathers yet is hardly referred to in Christian liturgy, catechism, or sermons (Grillmeier 1983: 334).[2] In the fourth and fifth century, the question of Christ's divine or human nature did not find an unanimous solution amongst Christian theologians and aroused a controversial debate in the early Christian world. The Christological dispute was settled at the Council of Chalcedon (451), resulting in a creed about the Incarnation of Christ. It would be far beyond the scope of this book to attempt to explain in full how the Chalcedonian Creed renders the Incarnation of Christ and how this creed was disputed in theological circles over the centuries. It must suffice to state here that Orthodox Christology defines the Oneness of Christ as a Oneness of person, consisting in the co-

---

[1] It appears in Origen's *Peri archon* (*On First Principles*). The text is preserved in Latin translation: "Hac ergo substantia animae inter Deum carnemque mediante (non enim possibile erat dei naturam corpori sine mediatore misceri) nascitur, ut diximus, Deus-homo, illa substantia media existente, cui utique contra naturam non erat corpus assumere" (Quoted in Grillmeier 1983: 314f.).

[2] The term is also used by Pseudo-Athanasius and Gregorius of Nazianze (See Grillmeier 1983: 315).

presence of two natures, the divine and the human.[3] This definition underlies the idea of the *Bogochelovek* or God-Man.

3. Prehistory of the *chelovekobog*

In most critical literature to this day, the general assumption is that the term *chelovekobog* is coined by Dostoevskii. This is partly due to the first Russian critics who established this idea in critical literature and set up a canon concerning the *chelovekobog* that still resounds in present research. Dmitrii Merezhkovskii, for example, ascribes the idea exclusively to Dostoevskii. Nikolai Berdiaev claims that "the revelation of the idea of the *chelovekobog* belongs entirely to Dostoevskii" (Berdiaev [1923] 1991: 132). The fact is, however, that Dostoevskii adopted the word *chelovekobog* from one of his contemporaries.

3.1. Nikolai Speshnev's coining of the term

The term *chelovekobog* is originally thought up by Nikolai Aleksandrovich Speshnev (PSS 12: 221f.). Speshnev (1821-1882) was one of the first Russian representatives of Utopian Communism. From 1842 on, he lived abroad for long periods (Germany and Switzerland), where he passionately engaged in political thought. He started as a liberal, but soon evolved through Utopian Socialism to egalitarian Communism. During his stay abroad he also studied German idealist philosophy and the Left-Hegelians, in particular Ludwig Feuerbach and Max Stirner. In 1847, he returned to Russia as a confirmed materialist, atheist, and communist and started attending the secret Friday gatherings of the Petrashevskii circle, in which Dostoevskii also participated. Speshnev's long stay abroad and his knowledge of Western philosophy gave him a special aureole among the other Petrashevskii members, who looked up to him with awe. His status was even more special because of his revolutionary statements: unlike the more moderate members of the group, who followed Fourier's Utopian Socialism, Speshnev took a more revolutionary stance and propagated radical political activity. While most Petrashevskii

---

[3] For a full overview of the Christological debate see Chadwick (1993), Grillmeier (1983), Pelikan (1977).

members embraced a socialism with a strong Christian bias, Speshnev engaged in a militant communism that was theoretically based on atheism and materialism and that preached the necessity of violence. By analogy with extreme societies in Western Europe, he drew out a plan to found secret revolutionary societies in Russia that would prepare and instigate a popular uprising in order to overthrow the tsarist regime. To this purpose, Speshnev did not rule out the use of terror. From 1848 onwards, an increasing group of Petrashevskii members wanted to move beyond the mere intellectual engagement and carefulness of Petrashevskii and believed in the need for revolutionary action. They entered Speshnev's secret revolutionary organization; among them was also Dostoevskii. In 1849, the members of the Petrashevskii group and other secret societies were arrested and sentenced to hard labour in Siberia. Upon his return to central Russia in 1860, Speshnev showed an interest in the activity of the revolutionary democrats of the 1860s, who were ideologically supported by Nikolai Chernyshevskii and Dmitrii Pisarev (Saraskina, 2000: 99-184; Frank J., 1976: 258ff.; Galaktionov & Nikandrov 1970: 326-333).

During the Petrashevskii gatherings and other secret radical meetings, Speshnev presented various lectures on politics, economics, and religion. His ideological legacy is nonetheless only retained in two philosophical letters that were most probably written to the Polish journalist Karl Edmond Khoetskii in 1847. These letters contain elements of Speshnev's lectures on religion.[4]

A convinced materialist and positivist, Speshnev argues in these letters that any metaphysical system is fundamentally untenable because it is merely grounded in "unprovable and gratuitous hypotheses" (Speshnev [1847] 1953: 479). For Speshnev, there is only empirical reality and he therefore finds any attempt to make statements about an otherworldly reality unfeasible and absurd. He faults the idealist belief in a metaphysical other world because it assumes some autonomous entity beyond the thing itself. This is especially manifest in idealist anthropology, in which the human is artificially split up into mind and body, leading to a total

---

[4] The bulk of Speshnev's writings was destroyed after his arrest. There are letters to his mother preserved in the family archive, dealing with practical, daily life issues (published in Saraskina 2000: 328-524). What we know of Speshnev comes largely through accounts of others and the documents of his arrest and exile.

"immaterialization" (*immaterializatsiia*) of the human being (id.: 484). Ludwig Feuerbach's doctrine of anthropotheism, which posits that God is but a mental projection of humanity and foregrounds the human's material status, is for Speshnev the logical response to idealist anthropology:

> I now understand that all this means only that for humanity there exists no authority, no creator and no god; and as regards to the philosophical god, humankind is the highest and most genuine incarnation of this god; therefore, there can exist for the human no other god than himself: like any god, the human doesn't take orders from others; his own voluntary determination, his own will, his own desire – this is the only law (id.: 502).

Speshnev adopts Feuerbach's thesis that God is but a mere mental projection of the human in empirical reality because this enables him to abandon this metaphysical concept. Although he assents to Feuerbach's method of demonstrating the non-existence of God, he does not subscribe to Feuerbach's final anthropology, which is in his opinion still reminiscent of the idealist tradition. In Feuerbach's anthropotheistic conception of the human, God is completely ruled out; yet still, to fill this metaphysical void, the human is himself deified. Christianity is replaced by another religion:

> Anthropotheism is also a religion, only a different one. The object of deification is different and new, but the fact of deification itself is not new. Instead of the *bog-chelovek* (god-man) we now have the *chelovek-bog* (man-god) (*Vmesto boga-cheloveka my imeem teper' cheloveka-boga*). Only the word order has changed. For is the difference between the *bog-chelovek* and the *chelovek-bog* really that great? For is not the solitary Christian God entirely cut out by the image and likeness of man? (id.: 496).

Speshnev is more inclined to share Stirner's anthropology of the egotistic, self-authoritative individual. Both God-man and man-god are mental abstractions of the human individual. Every individual is a being on his own, cannot be identified with the whole of humanity, is an "alien authority," who decides for himself the value of all things (ibid.). Objective criteria do not exist: "Such categories as beauty and ugliness, good and bad, noble and base, always were and always will remain a matter of taste" (id.: 497). Speshnev does not acknowledge any authority over the individual personality and postulates an anthropology of the self-determining, autonomous individual Ego.

Speshnev is the first Russian thinker to transpose Feuerbach's anthropotheism to Russian actuality and to translate this term into Russian. He juxtaposes Feuerbach's anthropology of 'the human becoming god' to a typical Russian Orthodox Christological concept, the *Bogochelovek* or God-Man. Translating Feuerbach's term, Speshnev simply puts the parts of the word *Bogochelovek* in an inverted order and turns it into *chelovek-bog*. In this manner, the idea of God becoming human is literally opposed to the idea of the human becoming god. For Speshnev, this radical reversal in the relationship between God and human is no more than a linguistic operation: "only the word order has changed" (id.: 496).[5]

3.2. Dostoevskii's Mephistopheles

There is no hard evidence that Speshnev uttered these ideas to Dostoevskii, but it is rather likely that Dostoevskii was acquainted with Speshnev's radical ideas and his use of the term *chelovekobog* because in the years that the Russian writer participated in the Petrashevskii circle (mid-1840s), the mysterious and attractive Speshnev exerted a strange but vast influence over him. Dostoevskii met Speshnev in 1848 and from then on he attended several of Speshnev's lectures, among which were a speech on religion and the dismissal of God (Saraskina 2000: 161). Speshnev's personality must have had a great effect on the young Dostoevskii who decided to join him in a more radical, secret revolutionary group than Petrashevskii's. Speshnev was ideologically and politically of a different temperament than Petrashevskii. Both aimed for fundamental social changes in Russia, but whereas Petrashevskii believed that this was to be realized through gradual, long-term evolution, Speshnev proclaimed radical revolt. Speshnev's radicalism evidently led to some incidents in the Petrashevskii circle, and he left the group in December 1848 to start up a secret society with the purpose of instigating a revolution. In

---

[5] It is an ironical anecdote that Speshnev, who attempted to banish the *Bogochelovek*, had the looks of Christ. Count Semenov described him as follows: "He could well have served as a model for sketches of the head and type of the Savior" (quoted in Frank 1976: 258).

January 1849, Dostoevskii also became a participant in this secret revolutionary circle and actively recruited other members.[6]

In this period, Speshnev certainly had some enigmatic power over Dostoevskii who admitted to his doctor, Ianovskii, who had observed that his patient had grown irritated, that his mental state of annoyance was related to Speshnev:

> For I have taken money from Speshnev (he named a sum of about five hundred rubles). Now I am with him and his. I'll never be able to pay back such a sum, and he would not even take the money back, that is the kind of man he is. Do you understand, from now on I have a Mephistopheles of my own! (Quoted in Frank 1976: 269-270; Pokrovskaia 1970: 265).

Dostoevskii's anxious feeling that he had sold his soul to Speshnev cannot be merely explained by his financial indebtedness to him because this was not the first time he borrowed money from others; it was rather induced by his engagement in Speshnev's radical political project.

On April 23, 1849, Dostoevskii, Speshnev, and other members of the Petrashevskii group and the secret society were arrested and sentenced to death. This capital punishment was *in extremis*, as the convicts were already standing before the execution squad, commuted to hard labor.[7]

Speshnev certainly left a profound impact on Dostoevskii. This emerges from his statement in *The Diary of a Writer* for 1873 that he was himself "an old Nechaevets," referring to Sergei Nechaev, the leader of a secret society who murdered one of his members in 1869, a violent and revolutionary act that inspired him for his novel *The Devils*. Dostoevskii relates: "I could probably never have become like Nechaev, but as for becoming a Nechaevets, I cannot guarantee, perhaps, possibly ... in the days of my youth," this obviously under the sway of the revolutionary Speshnev (PSS 21: 129).

---

[6] Evidence for this is a letter from the poet Apollon Nikolaevich Maikov, not published until 1922. Maikov relates how Dostoevskii came to his house one night and tried to convince him to join him in this secret society. Dostoevskii supposedly said of Petrashevskii that he was "a fool, an actor and a chatterer; nothing ever sensible came out of him" (Quoted in Frank 1976: 267; Pokrovskaia 1970: 268).

[7] During the staged execution, Dostoevskii said to Speshnev: "Nous serons avec le Christ," whereupon Speshnev replied: "Un peu poussière" (Quoted in Belov 2001, Vol. 2: 242).

3.3. Fictionalizing the demon

Speshnev's personality and radical ideas thus had a great impact on the young Dostoevskii who at the time struggled with Christianity and flirted with atheist and socialist theories. Speshnev's effect on Dostoevskii was so enduring that more than twenty years later, the writer expunged his past friendship by fictionalizing Speshnev in the protagonist of *The Devils* (1870-1872). Though his name is not found in the notebooks for *The Devils*, Dostoevskii researchers are unanimous that Stavrogin is in part modelled on Speshnev (PSS 12: 221; Grossman 1996: 617f.; Frank 1991: 258; Mochulsky 1973: 132). Stavrogin is given the same forename (Nikolai) and spent, like Speshnev, some time in Switzerland, where he engaged in revolutionary circles.[8] Upon his return to Russia, he advocates atheism and installs secret revolutionary societies. With his enigmatic personality, he holds sway over the other characters and infuses them with his ideas. Stavrogin is characterized in a similar wording as Dostoevskii labeled Speshnev two decades earlier: "Sometimes silently curious and caustic, like Mephistopheles" (PSS 11: 175). Like Speshnev greatly affected the young Dostoevskii and lured him into revolutionary activity, Stavrogin makes a lasting impression on the ones surrounding him and is blindly followed by the other characters. Stavrogin's confession to Father Tikhon that the idea of good and evil is merely a prejudice is reminiscent of Speshnev's postulate that such criteria are merely subjective qualifications (PSS 12: 113). When drawing out the plan for *The Devils*, in which for the first time in Dostoevskii's works the term *chelovekobog* appears, the writer certainly recalled his former Mephistopheles and the discussions and revolutionary sphere of the secret society from his youth.

4. Kirillov's "most great idea"

In the chronology of Dostoevskii's works, the term *chelovekobog* appears for the first time in the novel *The Devils*. Dostoevskii started working on this novel at the end of 1869 and published it serially in

---

[8] Speshnev had participated in the Swiss *Sonderbund* war, where he had fought as a volunteer for the liberals (Frank 1991: 259).

the journal *Russkii Vestnik* (*The Russian Messenger*) between 1870 and 1872.

In the novel, the idea of the *chelovekobog* is spelled out by the character Kirillov. In the beginning of the narrative, Aleksei Nilych Kirillov is introduced as a young civil engineer, who had spent four years abroad and just recently returned to Russia to construct a railway bridge. He is characterized as an absent-minded, tongue-tied man: "he spoke jerkily and somehow ungrammatically, transposing words in a strange way and getting muddled when he had to compose a sentence of any length" (PSS 10: 74ff.). The lonely stay abroad alienated him from the Russian social and cultural climate, and as a result, he is now unable to communicate his thoughts to his Russian acquaintances in a fluent and sociable manner.

Dostoevskii's notebooks for *The Devils* show that the writer came up with this character rather late in the writing process. The first reference to Kirillov, at that point still called the Engineer, appears in a sketch from September 1870. It is only in the notes for the final part of the novel, written in 1872, that the character begins to take shape. At that time, the first two parts of *The Devils* were already published in *Russkii Vestnik* (Dostoevsky 1968: 303; 389f.). In these notes, there are only sketchy traces of Kirillov's argument as it appears in the final version of the text. There is already mention of Kirillov's suicide and some particular "reason" for this planned action (PSS 11: 299). Yet, the term *chelovekobog* is absent in the preparatory work. Thus, Dostoevskii drew up the whole conception of the *chelovekobog* in the very last phase of the writing process.

The notebooks do not reveal any actual source that might have been an inspiration for Dostoevskii in the creation of this fictional character and his theory of the *chelovekobog*. It is most likely, though, that the writer obtained the term *chelovekobog* and the Feuerbachian bias of Kirillov's rationale from his "Mephistopheles," Nikolai Speshnev. The mysterious and charismatic personality of Speshnev served as a model for the novel's protagonist, Nikolai Stavrogin. In this character, and especially with regard to his relationships to the other characters, there are echoes of Speshnev's personality and the enduring impact he had on the young Dostoevskii. Just like Speshnev impressed Dostoevskii with his radical ideas, Stavrogin is the ideological and intellectual authority for his fellow characters. Stavrogin's personality is so complex and full of contradictions that he infuses the different characters with the most divergent ideas. He has generated the strict Orthodox and Slavophile position of Shatov, the left revolutionary thought of Pëtr Verkhovenskii, and also Kirillov's theory of the *chelovekobog*. The fictional modeling of Kirillov as a character ideologically influenced by Stavrogin, who is in turn modeled on the historical personality of Speshnev, makes it plausible that Dostoevskii drew on Speshnev's interpretation of Feuerbach's anthropotheism when contriving Kirillov's theory of the *chelovekobog*.

The premises from which Kirillov deduces his conception of both God and humanity mirror Feuerbach's atheistic humanism. In *The Essence of Christianity* (1841), Feuerbach brushed aside the idea of a metaphysical Godhead: God does not exist in reality but is only a human projection, a product of visualizing humanity in ideal terms. Kirillov's "most great idea" is substantiated by a similar reasoning. He claims that God and the promise of eternal life in the other world are merely constructions of the human imagination. Humanity has invented the idea of God and an afterlife because the human experiences this life as painful and believes death to be the sole yet highly frightening means of escaping this tormenting and meaningless life (PSS 10: 93f..; 471). Until now, the human needed this deception of the existence of a higher divine entity and the promise of a better life in the hereafter because he could not endure the thought that this painful and useless life holds no other alternative than death. Kirillov assumes himself to be the first in the history of humankind who ventures to reveal humanity's self-produced illusion of a Godhead and a future heavenly paradise. In his logic, the only consequential act is a conscious and self-willed suicide. He plans to shoot himself in order to overcome, on the one hand, the two "prejudices" that withhold man from killing himself: the fear of pain and the other world (PSS 10: 93). On the other hand, he strives to reveal through this act that the idea of the Godhead is a deception, and that he is consequently a god himself: "If there is no god, then I am god" (*esli net boga, to ia bog*) (PSS 10: 470).

Kirillov's theory and corollary act of suicide is fundamentally motivated by anthropological concerns. He maintains that "the human now is still not that other human" (*teper' chelovek ne tot chelovek*), and proclaims the coming of "a new human, happy and proud" (*budet novyi chelovek, schastlivyi i gordyi*) (PSS 10: 93). This new human will appear when humanity overcomes the fear of death. For him, "it will be the same to live or not to live" (PSS 10: 93). Thus Kirillov takes upon himself the task to kill himself in order to prove to the rest of humanity that death should not be feared.

Kirillov's argument for committing suicide is that he aims to demonstrate that God and the heavenly afterlife are mere fabrications of the human mind, and that once this truth is exposed, the logical outcome is that the human is himself a god. His theory of self-deification centers upon the phenomenon of death. In aspiring to overcome death, Kirillov, in fact, desires to provide an alternative to one of the most fundamental doctrines in Christianity, the resurrection of Christ. In the act of resurrection, Christ's divine nature and his Oneness with the Father was revealed. Simultaneously, his rising from the dead held a promise for humanity that it would eventually attain a state of immortality in the afterlife. Christian anthropology is grounded in the belief in the immortality of the soul and the promise of resurrection in the Heavenly Kingdom. In Kirillov's anthropology of the new human who overcomes the need for a Deity and a better life in the other world, this fundamental Christian doctrine is reversed. In the conversation Kirillov has with Pëtr Verkhovenskii, just before his suicide, he gives his account of Christ's death at the cross:

> There was a day on earth, and in the middle of the earth stood three crosses. One at the cross already believed what he said to the other: "Today you will be with me in paradise." The day came to an end, they both died, departed, and found neither paradise, nor resurrection. His words did not come true (PSS 10: 471).

Kirillov does not question the historical identity of Christ but rejects that He ever resurrected. He views Christ as any mortal human being, whose death only exposes the finiteness of human life. Kirillov appreciates Christ as one of the most significant figures in the history of humanity: "that man was the highest on earth, He was what it exists for" (PSS 10: 471). However, he asserts that Christ made a crucial mistake in promising eternal life in the other world, a promise that would turn out to be pernicious for the further development of human consciousness. Because, as Kirillov maintains, in anticipating and proclaiming a perfect life in the other world, Christ disregarded life in this earthly world. Christ taught humanity to set their hopes in an eternal life beyond this life, and in this manner, He burdened future humanity with a fundamental existential problem. In anticipation of a perfect life in paradise, the human does not feel the need to seek perfection and full realization of the human potential in this earthly life. Kirillov objects to this Christian preoccupation with the otherworld and its corollary, the negation of earthly life. In the conversation with Stavrogin, he asserts that he loves this life and that this does not contradict his plans to put an end to it because "there is life, and no death." He adds that he does not believe in "a future eternal life, but in eternal life here [on earth] (*ne v budushchuiu vechnuiu, a v zdeshnuiu vechnuiu [zhizn']*) (PSS 10: 188). In the Christian pattern, resurrection and eternal life are to be attained after complete disjunction from the material, earthly world. Death is thus an absolute given because it functions as the gate to transfiguration in eternal life. By being indifferent to death, Kirillov strips it from its absoluteness. As he puts it, transfiguration becomes independent of the phenomenon of death. When death is no longer a prerequisite for attaining a higher, perfected form of life, it follows logically that eternal life, or the transition into a better life, can be realized in the human's earthly condition. Kirillov believes that paradise, or "eternal harmony," is not something awaiting us in the unknown afterlife but is to be accomplished in this earthly life:

> There are seconds, they come only five or six at a time, and suddenly you feel the presence of an eternal harmony, fully attained. It is not earthly, I don't mean in the sense that it is heavenly, but in the sense that man cannot endure it in his earthly aspect. One must change physically or die [...] if it lasted more than five seconds, the soul could not endure it and must perish. In those five seconds I live through a whole lifetime [...] To endure ten seconds, one must change physically (PSS 10: 450).

In Kirillov's theory, experience of and participation in the earthly paradise requires physical transformation. This is once again a radical reversal of the Christian anthropological model. In Christian anthropology, the ontological status of the human is exactly made up by his spiritual nature, i.e. his immortal soul. For Kirillov, by contrast, the human is primarily physical matter. The soul cannot live through the direct sensory experience of eternal harmony and "must perish"; the body though, if transformed into a new form of being, can participate in eternal life on earth. This holds the promise of physical immortality. In this new immortal condition, procreation is no longer necessary: "I think humanity should give up giving birth. Why children, why evolution, if the goal has been attained" (PSS 10: 450)?

Kirillov's concept of the new human is basically an inverted paradigm of Christian anthropology, the latter being built around the promise of eternal life in the otherworld. In the Christian doctrine, transfiguration of human life into a perfect and eternal condition is only to occur after death, after the soul is freed from its earthly attachment. In Kirillov's theory though, transfiguration takes place in earthly life and in this process, death is no longer of importance because the body becomes immortal. And the soul – the sole and crucial link between humanity and God in Christian anthropology – is depreciated as transitory and perishable.

Kirillov sees the individual will as the logical starting point to transform the relationship between God and human: "If there is a God, then all will is his, and I cannot get out of his will. If not, then all will is mine, and I am bound to proclaim self-will (*svoevolie*) [...] All will has become mine [...]" (PSS 10: 470). He rejects the Christian notion of the human will as being fundamentally tied up with God, and hence he assumes that the human is the one and only master of his individual will. God is for him the greatest restraint on the human's individual will. Thus the ultimate act of self-will, i.e. demonstrating the human independence from any will other than his own, is in overcoming the fear that preserves the illusion of God and the otherworld: death. He explains his suicide as the only means to assert his self-will: "I am bound to shoot myself because the highest point of my self-will is to kill myself" (PSS 10: 470). An actively willed suicide is for Kirillov the most explicit manifestation of his individual freedom and independence from an external godhead: "I kill myself to prove my insubordination and my new terrible freedom (*novaia strashnaia svoboda*)" (PSS 10: 472). Kirillov is very eager to kill himself because by this act, he will at the same time kill God.

Once it is established that God does not exist, the human is bound to acknowledge that he is himself a god because "to recognize that there is no God, and not to recognize at the same time that one has oneself become a god, is an absurdity" (PSS 10: 471). In Kirillov's anthropology, once one is beyond the ancient illusion of God, the way to self-deification lies within the assertion of the individual will. If one affirms that all will is his, one gains absolute power over one's own being and in this sense becomes a god. For Kirillov, "the attribute" of our divinity is "self-will" (*atribut bozhestva moego – Svoevolie*) (PSS 10: 472).

In his conversation with Stavrogin, the real significance and existential design of Kirillov's new anthropology is made clear:

- [Kirillov]: "He will come, and his name is the *chelovekobog*"

- [Stavrogin]: "*Bogochelovek?*"

- [Kirillov]: "*chelovekobog*. That is the whole difference."

(PSS 10: 189; my italics).

Kirillov drapes his anthropology in a name that is the literal inverse of the Orthodox denomination of Christ. The concept of the *Bogochelovek* or God-Man encompasses the essence of Christ, that He is God incarnate in human flesh. In the Christian tradition, the appearance of Christ on earth carried the promise of immortality and transfiguration into eternal life. Kirillov's message is the radical reversal of this. He does not want God to become human but awaits the human to become god. Because Christ was the One who brought humanity the annunciation of God and the otherworld, Kirillov – whose name is derived from the Greek word for "Lord" (Κύριος) – hopes to displace Him in the conveyance of his new anthropology. His self-willed suicide is an imitation of Christ's death at the cross. Like Christ voluntarily chose to die at the cross to redeem humanity, Kirillov considers his suicide as a sacrifice to save humanity. Through his act of willful death, Kirillov hopes to become the new Savior, the second Christ, and bring about an upheaval in anthropological consciousness: "I will begin, and end it, and open the door. And I will save. Only this one thing will save all people and in the next generation regenerate them physically" (PSS 10: 472).[9]

However, Kirillov's motivation to volunteer for his own death is from the outset an inversion of Christ's acceptance of His death at the cross. In the Gethsemane prayer Christ delivered His individual will to the will of God and accepted His death as the will of His Father

---

[9] The Grand Inquisitor also poses as the new redeemer of humanity.

("Let Thy will be done," Luke 22: 42). Kirillov's motive to kill himself is to prove the exact opposite anthropological formula, i.e. "let my will be done." Aspiring to be the new Christ, Kirillov inverts the idea of the kenotic Christ. The Greek *kenosis* means emptying; in relation to Christ it implies "the self-emptying and abasement of the Son of God [...] the renunciation of His own will in order to accomplish the will of the Father by being obedient to Him unto death and unto the cross" (Lossky [1944] 1991: 144). The notion of *kenosis* is related to Christ's divine nature and is based on a statement about the incarnation of Christ by Paul in Philippians 2: 6-8: "His state was divine, yet he did not cling to his equality with God but emptied himself to assume the condition of a slave, and became as men are; and being as all men are, he was humbler yet, even to accepting death, death on a cross" (Ziolkowski 2001: 32f.). The conception of the kenotic Christ underlies Dostoevskii's Christian anthropology. As we have seen, the writer holds that human self-perfection is in self-abandonment, in the deliverance of one's individual will to the universal will. In Kirillov's anthropology of the *chelovekobog*, self-realization is in the assertion of one's individual will against God's will. Imitating Christ's death at the cross, Kirillov hopes to establish an act that will determine the future development of humanity and the world. By his willful death he strives to demonstrate to humanity that the one who will overcome the fear of death, "will become a god himself." And from that moment on, a new epoch will begin:

> Then there will be a new life, a new human, everything will be new...then they will divide history in two parts: from the gorilla to the annihilation of God, and from the annihilation of God [...] to the transformation of the earth and of man physically. The human will be god, and will be physically transformed. And the world will be transformed, and things will be transformed, and thoughts and all feelings (PSS 10: 94).

Kirillov hopes that his suicide will bring about a turnover in the human condition, both inwardly and outwardly. The overcoming of God will naturally result in an upheaval in human consciousness. Once God is done away with, the human will direct his full attention to his earthly condition and realize that he is a god himself and that he is only to account for himself. The human will no longer await a perfect state in the other world yet will be transfigured in this earthly life. The soul will perish and humanity will be physically transformed.

In the new era, earthly life will no longer be reduced to a mere transitory condition in anticipation of a heavenly paradise and will not be passively passed by. The *chelovekobog* will glorify this life and affirm it in all its manifestations as good. He will acknowledge everything as good, "the bright green leaf" as much as "the spider crawling on the wall" (PSS 10: 188f.). The traditional moral categories of good and evil will no longer hold. Assuming himself to be the new Savior, Kirillov holds that "he who teaches that all are good, will end the world." Stavrogin replies: "He who taught it was crucified" (PSS 10: 189). The comparison with Christ is by Kirillov's "Mephistopheles" established.

Kirillov's "most great idea" is, fundamentally, Orthodox Christology turned upside down. This emerges most clearly from his denotation of the new human as the *chelovekobog*, the man-god, as radically opposed to the *Bogochelovek* or God-Man Christ. While trying to formulate his new anthropology, Kirillov time and again turns to the story of the historical Christ in an attempt to supersede Him. He undermines what is at the core of the Christian paradigm, the figure of Christ. He advances a counter paradigm of the Christian model in order to overcome this traditional pattern while at the same time using that tradition's own doctrines and values and presenting them in a disintegrated form. His whole attempt is to establish an anthropology in which the necessity for the Godhead is overcome and which provides an alternative to the consequential metaphysical void.

Kirillov's idea of the *chelovekobog* fundamentally conflicts with Dostoevskii's anthropological ideal which is entirely built around the *Bogochelovek* Christ. The anthropology of the *chelovekobog* centers upon the individual will, or "self-will" (*svoevolie*), as the means to assert oneself independently of the Godhead. The human will is for Kirillov the logical starting point to turn over the relationship between humanity and God, and generate the human's self-deification. In Dostoevskii's Christian anthropology, the human will is also the key principle in the relationship between humanity and God. Dostoevskii believes that the human is by his spiritual nature created in the image and likeness of God, and is thus essentially a self-realizing being. The human's true essence lies in his will which is entrenched in his metaphysical nature. In complete opposition to Kirillov's idea of the self-will, Dostoevskii holds that the ultimate manifestation of free will is not in the annihilation of God, but rather in the actively willed union with the divine and the other. For Dostoevskii, genuine freedom implies that one is "the real master of oneself" (PSS 25: 62). This is not in the sense that one is given the license to pursue one's individual will and manifest oneself as completely isolated from God and the other; rather, one is the real master of oneself if one attains a moral condition in which self-interest no longer counts and one lives up to one's absolute divine potential. Dostoevskii's anthropological ideal is one of the self-determining and self-perfecting individual. He pictures the realization of this ideal in a completely different manner than what is advanced in Kirillov's discourse on the human condition beyond God. Dostoevskii's anthropology is wholly grounded in his faith in God as an absolute value. He believes that the human's realization of the absolute self should concur with a free and confirmed belief in God and in his Son, Christ, as the moral paradigm for humanity. Genuine "personal self-perfection" (*lichnoe samosovershenstvovanie*) is not in the assertion of one's self-will or determination of the isolated ego, yet in the decisive choice to develop oneself in accordance to the universal will and the moral law of altruistic love for the other (PSS 26: 161). By absolutizing the human will, Kirillov touches upon the fundament of Dostoevskii's Christian anthropology: the free and self-willed union between humanity and God.

Although I wish to avoid making the naïve claim that a fictional character represents a consciousness that is either correspondent with, or antagonistic to the concrete author's point of view, I do find that within the body of the narrative there are certain phrases that hint at the inevitable failure of Kirillov's theory. Kirillov is described as a person with a peculiar manner of speech: he is unable to communicate his ideas in a correct and rational order and becomes entangled in his own sentences. It strikes the reader as odd that an engineer who is capable of building a railway bridge, is incapable of constructing systematic and coherent sentences. Moreover, when faced with his conversation partners' lack of comprehension, Kirillov rapidly becomes nervous and impatient (PSS 10: 74ff.). In my opinion, this portrayal of Kirillov is not at all arbitrary; rather, it is supposed to direct the reader towards the ethical conclusion that Kirillov's idea of the *chelovekobog* is a phantasmal construction of an alienated and eccentric person. The irrational and illogical discourse of his theory clearly affects its legitimacy. The validity of his argument is further undermined by the narrator who, after hearing Kirillov's thesis, remarks that he is "evidently mad" (PSS 10: 95) and by the horror that overwhelms Kirillov before his suicide, obviously revealing the tragedy of his alleged rational act of suicide. As I see it, the strategies that Dostoevskii uses to characterize Kirillov's personality and his relationship with the other characters impel the reader to qualify and question Kirillov's argument on self-deification. I conclude from this that Dostoevskii's motives in shaping the figure of Kirillov and his idea of the *chelovekobog* were not intended to give voice to an ideology that was his own. This is affirmed by a fragment in *The Diary of a Writer*, in which Dostoevskii claims that suicide is the only inevitable outcome when one rejects the supreme idea of immortality (PSS 24: 49).

5. Ivan's 'anthropological' upheaval

The term *chelovekobog* occurs again in Dostoevskii's fiction in 1879-1880, in his last novel *The Brothers Karamazov*. In this narrative, the concept is delineated by Ivan Karamazov's devil who appears to Ivan in a nightmare and in this role, functions as Ivan's *alter ego*. In the preparatory notes for the conversation between Ivan and his devil, at that point still called "Satan," the *chelovekobog* is not yet mentioned (PSS 15: 320ff.).

After the third conversation with Smerdiakov, who torments Ivan by suggesting that his theory that "all is permitted" (*vsë pozvoleno*) might have triggered him to murder their father and thus consciously makes Ivan responsible for the murder, Ivan falls in a state of "delirium tremens (*belaia goriachka*)" (PSS 15: 69f.). In this moment of mental breakdown, the devil makes his appearance.

If we apply the Bakhtinian model of the polyphonic novel on this character, the devil's voice is, in fact, no other than Ivan's voice because he clearly originates in Ivan's hallucinating imagination. Ivan says to the devil: "You are me, my own self, only with a different face" (PSS 15: 73). The devil is Ivan's second voice, repeating the words and ideas of Ivan himself, yet in another accent and tone, as if to confront Ivan with the absurdity of his thought. He is an exteriorization of Ivan's inner dialogue (Bakhtin 1984: 256). With regard to this scene, literary critics often compare it with Goethe's

Faust, and Ivan is frequently called "the Russian Faust."[10] Yet whereas Goethe's Mephistopheles is a character of an otherworldly nature, Ivan's devil is described as a creature with a specific earthly appearance. He has the typical looks of "a Russian gentleman," and appears as a well-mannered and amusing conversation partner (PSS 15: 70).

After the conversation with Smerdiakov, Ivan begins to realize that his idea, that all is permitted in a world devoid of God most probably induced Smerdiakov to kill their father and that consequently he himself has a part in the murder. The devil, Ivan's second voice, appears to Ivan when he is about to face the terrible and real ramifications of his theory, when he is ready to "express his own word boldly and resolutely and 'to justify himself to himself'" (PSS 15: 70). The devil thus represents the rebellion of Ivan's conscience against his reason. He does not engage in moral preaching but exposes the inconsistency between Ivan's rational arguments on the one hand and the irrationality of his conscience on the other hand. If one is rationally convinced that God and human immortality do not exist and deduces from that a legalistic immoralism, then one should never yield to the feeling of moral guilt. With ironic rhetoric, the devil presents Ivan with parodies of his own ideas, thereby arousing embarrassment in Ivan for his own theories. Ivan, no longer able to endure the shame while listening to the rephrasing of his own ideas, exclaims: "All what is stupid in my nature, what is since long outlived and hammered out in my mind, thrown away like a carrion – you present it to me like something new" (PSS 15: 82). The content of the devil's sayings is not new to Ivan, yet the form in which he presents them is. Or, to follow Bakhtin, the devil's saying does not differ from Ivan's in content but in tone, and in this "change of accent," the whole meaning of Ivan's discourse is given another purport (Bakhtin 1984: 222). By rendering Ivan's ideas in the form of a parody, the devil confronts Ivan with the ambiguity and inconsistency of his alleged rigorous immorality. Ivan, in fact, qualifies his thoughts through the other voice of the devil.

---

[10] In the text itself, the devil draws a comparison with Mephistopheles and describes himself as having another nature than Faust's devil (PSS 15: 82). In 1901, Sergei Bulgakov analyzed the Faust motif in the figure of Ivan Karamazov ([1902] 1991: 196f.). Anatolii Lunacharskii took up this theme and entitled his article about Ivan Karamazov "Russkii Faust" (1902).

At some point in the conversation, which is for the most part the devil's monologue, the devil mentions Ivan's "Grand Inquisitor." Ivan, "blushing with shame," forbids the devil to speak about his poem (PSS 15: 83). The devil then begins a parodical recapitulation of another piece of Ivan's "belles-lettres" (*poemka*), entitled "Geologicheskii Perevorot" ("The Geological Upheaval").[11] The title refers to a future era when humanity will have overcome the concept of God and as a result, a transformation in human consciousness will occur. This era is bound to come with the natural necessity of a geological change. The devil rephrases Ivan's writing on the future "new humans":

> [...] all that must be destroyed in humankind is the idea of God [...] Once humankind has one and all renounced God (and I believe that period, analogous with the geological periods, will come to pass) the whole of the old outlook on life will collapse by itself [...] and, what's more, the old morality will also fall, and everything will begin anew (PSS 15: 83).

The annihilation of God will inevitably and naturally bring about an upheaval in anthropological and moral consciousness. Like in Kirillov's vision, the devil/Ivan asserts that once the notion of God and the related promise of an eternal afterlife are cancelled out, the human will accept his mortal condition and concentrate on this earthly existence as the sole opportunity to attain happiness and perfection of the self. Inverting the Christian idea of eternal paradise in the other world into a Feuerbachian world devoid of God, Ivan's utopia of the new human is set in this world: "Humanity will unite to take from life everything that life can give, but only for joy and happiness in this world alone" (PSS 15: 83). The human will no longer exalt and worship an unknown and external authority yet will center on the self as the only possible subject of glorification because when the idea of God is overcome, humanity is bound to fall back on its earthly essence and acknowledge itself as the highest and most perfect realization in the evolution of the world. Once this is established, "the human will be glorified with a spirit of divine, titanic pride (*bozheskaia,*

---

[11] The source for this title might have been a passage in Ernest Renan's *The Life of Jesus*, which deals with Christ's promise of God's Kingdom on earth (chapter VII): "We know the history of the earth; cosmic revolutions of the kind Jesus expected do not take place for reasons other than geological or astronomical, which are in no way connected with moral good" (Terras 1981: 395 & PSS 15: 595).

titanicheskaia gordost') and the *cheloveko-bog* will appear" (PSS 15: 83).

In order to break free from the ancient need for a metaphysical world, humanity is to revert to and affirm its natural and material origin. In the old era, humanity passed over the empirical world in anticipation of "the joys of heaven." In the future anthropological age, humanity's goal is to unravel the mysteries of nature in order to conquer it eventually. The positivist knowledge of nature and empirical proof that God and the other world do not exist will evoke in humanity "so lofty a joy," that it will eagerly renounce the old hopes for eternal paradise (PSS 15: 83). As in Kirillov's logic, Ivan rejects the Christian idea of the human's immortal soul and the related promise of eternal life in the other world. He views the human as a mere material, and hence mortal, being who must accept the finite and transitory condition of human existence and even gain joy from this.

> Everyone will know that he is mortal, that there is no resurrection, and will accept death proudly and serenely like a god. Out of pride he will understand, that he needn't repine at life being a moment, and he will love his brother even without any recompense. Love will satisfy only a moment of life, but the very consciousness of its momentariness will intensify its fire, as much as it was before dissipated in dreams of eternal love beyond the grave (PSS 15: 83).

Such is Ivan's anthropological vision of the *chelovekobog*, of the future human who has freed himself from the yoke of a metaphysical other world and with "titanic pride" assumes the role of God. Yet, as the devil recounts, Ivan doubts whether this revolution in human consciousness will come with the certainty of a geological cataclysm. Because of the human's "inherent stupidity," it might take "at least a thousand years" before humanity will overcome the old notion of the Deity and realize the required revolution in human consciousness. Therefore, Ivan finds it legitimate that the elect ones "who recognize the truth [...] may order life as they please it, on the new principles" (PSS 15: 84).

The devil continues Ivan's logic:

> In that sense, to him "all is permitted" (*vsë pozvoleno*). What is more, even if this period never comes, since there is no God and no immortality all the same, then the new human is permitted to become the *chelovekobog*, even if he is the only one in the whole world, and promoted to his new position, he

may lightheartedly overstep all the barriers of the old morality of the old slave-man (*rab-chelovek*), if there is need for it (PSS 15: 84.).

Once God is overcome, the human becomes a god himself, in the sense that one's behavior or motivation is no longer restrained by moral guilt or compassion for the other. Then, one is completely free in the pursuing and satisfaction of individual desires. The *chelovekobog* distinguishes himself from "the old slave-man" who is still caught up in the binding morality of Christianity. The new human throws off any chains that might limit his freedom and lives by the principle that all is permitted: "For God, there exists no law. Where God stands, the place is holy! Where I stand will be once the foremost place... 'all is permitted'" (PSS 15: 84). In Ivan's anthropology beyond the Christian notion of God and the immortal soul, the human is granted complete moral freedom in the sense that he can organize his life as he pleases.

The devil/Ivan's idea of the *chelovekobog* represents, like Kirillov's theory, the countermyth of Dostoevskii's philosophical anthropology. At the core of the *chelovekobog* is the desire for total moral autonomy, an aspiration that is also at the center of Dostoevskii's Christian anthropology. Yet in the end, the *chelovekobog* stands for the most radical reversal of Dostoevskii's ideal because this concept is grounded in a worldview devoid of God. In Dostoevskii's outlook, moral freedom is to be consistent with faith in God and the immortality of the soul because if the metaphysical impulse towards the supreme moral good is disposed of, humanity necessarily falls into total lawlessness. For the devil/Ivan, the "old morality," based on the belief in the Deity, boils down to a restraining, enslaving morality. Ultimate freedom is identified with the ethical imperative that all is permitted.

Dostoevskii offers a completely inverted definition of freedom and slavery. For him, authentic freedom lies in the deliberate acceptance of Christ's moral law, the law of love for the other. Any other delineation of freedom that is reduced to a license for boundless behavior only leads to the human's enslavement, i.e. the slavery to one's material nature (PSS 25: 62).

Like in the case of Kirillov, I find that the narratological setting in which the *chelovekobog* is presented in this text reveals Dostoevskii's motives to discredit it. The reasoning behind the *chelovekobog* is phrased by a figure who appears in a hallucination and thus stands outside of the reality displayed in the novel. In my opinion, the fact that the theory of the *chelovekobog* is formulated in a nightmare affects the validity of the argument and directs the reader towards a qualification of it.

6. The Roman "ant-hill"

The *chelovekobog* occurs a third, and final, time in *The Diary of a Writer* for August 1880. Whereas in the previous settings the concept is embedded in a specific narrative and is formulated by voices that belong exclusively to the fictional reality in the novel, this time it is commented upon in a journalistic periodical. In his *Diary* – regularly published in *Grazhdanin* (*The Citizen*) from 1873 until his death in 1881 – Dostoevskii could freely express his opinion on recent events and the underlying problems in the social, moral, and religious sphere. The periodical reached a wide audience and contributed to the writer's status as "the most important public voice of the time" (Frank 2002: 3). Given the essayistic genre and purpose of the *Diary*, it can be definitely assumed that the voice in this work is entirely Dostoevskii's.

In the issue for August 1880, Dostoevskii unfolds his views on the history of the Church and the State in the West (the Roman Catholic West) and the East (the Orthodox East). This theological treatise is a reply to Aleksandr Gradovskii, a professor of civil law at Moscow University, who had published a critical article in response to Dostoevskii's Pushkin speech. In this speech – delivered on June 8, 1880, on the occasion of the dedication of a monument to Pushkin in Moscow – Dostoevskii had praised Pushkin as the embodiment of the Russian spirit and its striving towards a universal brotherhood, calling him a "universal man (*vsechelovek*)". He had furthermore expressed the belief that Russia should "strive to bring an ultimate reconciliation to Europe's contradictions, to indicate that the solution to Europe's anguish is to be found in the universal and all-unifying Russian soul (*v russkoi dushe, vsechelovechnoi i vsesoediniaiushei*)" (PSS 26: 148). As a result of this speech, a debate between the Slavophiles and Westernizers enflamed in the Russian press. One of the responses came from the liberal-minded Westernist Aleksandr Gradovskii, who faulted Dostoevskii's criticism on the reform movement in Russia and his focus on the Russian people as the sole bearers of true morality and the paradigmatic social formula. In reply, Gradovskii stated that the Russian people should look at enlightened Europe in the formation of their social ideals because on Russian soil, there were no sources for enlightenment. Dostoevskii chose Gradovskii's article as his target to attack the Westernist position (Frank 2002: 538).

From the outset of his essay, Dostoevskii claims that the only worthy social formula is the one that emerges from a moral ideal. In his view, people can only be united in a civic society and accomplish social goals if this union is based on a "fundamental, great moral idea." And he believes that the sole authentic moral idea, upon which civic society should be built, is the Christian law of love. The only legitimate moral idea is the one that is based on the consciousness of "personal self-perfection in the spirit of Christian love" (*lichnoe samosovershenstvovanie v dukhe khristianskoi liubvi*) (PSS 26: 161). All civic and social ideals should thus emerge from this Christian moral paradigm, for "it contains everything within it, all aspirations and all longings" (PSS 26: 164). In the course of history, civic states are time and again construed on a religious basis. In the genesis of any social organization, and even in the identification of a specific people and nationality, the moral idea has always preceded the development of national and social singularities, *"for the idea was the force that created the nationality"* (PSS 26: 165). All moral ideas hitherto originate from the human yearning to justify and affirm the experience of Oneness with a Deity and of an eternal otherworld. Dostoevskii reverts to the history of the Judaic state (inspired on Moses' Law) and Moslem social organization (grounded in the Koran) to substantiate his thesis that civic and social models organically arise out of the religious ideal. He finds an equal process in the beginnings of Christian society:

> Recall: what was the ancient Christian Church, and what it aspired to be. It came into being immediately after Christ, and was formed by only a few people; and at once, virtually in the first days after the death of Christ, it began to seek out its own "civic formula", which was wholly founded on the moral expectation of satisfying the spirit by the principles of personal self-perfection. Then Christian communities – Churches – came into being; then a new nationality, hitherto unheard of, began to be formed, a nationality of universal brotherhood and humanity, in the form of a common, ecumenical Church (*natsional'nost'* – *vsebratskaia, vsechelovecheskaia, v forme obshchei vselenskoi tserkvi*) (PSS 26: 169).

However, as he diagnoses in the further evolution of Christianity there was a flaw in the hitherto original tradition of grounding a social formula in a religious idea. The early Christian Church was persecuted by the Roman authorities and was forced to go underground; in this harsh condition of suppression and persecution, it continued to live by and shape the Christian moral ideal yet was hindered in the formation of a social and civic formula. Meanwhile, "on the surface of the earth, an enormous edifice, a massive ant-hill was being formed, the ancient Roman empire, which was the ideal and the outcome of the moral aspirations of the whole ancient world" (PSS 26: 169).[12] In the Christian Church that was hiding underground, people freely joined in a community because they all believed in and deliberately accepted the Christian moral ideal. In the Roman empire, by contrast, the community was established by means of compulsion, by means of the sword.[13] There were gods in the Roman empire, remnants of the ancient world, yet the state was not built on the ideals for which these gods stood. Rather, these gods were to serve the secular authorities in their continual expansionism as a means to subjugate and control the people. The Roman empire's reduction of the religious ideal to a civil theology and to a mere instrument in its politics of expansionism represents the total opposite of Dostoevskii's theory of the perfect social order, as evolved from a religious and moral fundament. This phenomenon in the history of Christianity is identified by Dostoevskii as the appearance of the principle of the *chelovekobog* (*iavlialsia chelovekobog*) (PSS 26: 169). In ancient Rome, the emperor as a worldly figure acquired a divine status and gained more authority and worship than the gods, who were abandoned to the second plane. For Dostoevskii, the Roman emperor's goal was to overcome the real gods

---

[12] The Grand Inquisitor's aspiration is also in the formation of an "indisputable, common and harmonious ant-hill." He believes that this is the only social order in which the whole of humanity can be united (PSS 14: 235). In Dostoevskii's discourse, the ant-hill is used to characterize a human order based on compulsion with disregard for the human's free will. He also observes this in a civic form based on socialist ideology. This "ant-hill" is typically related to the European states: "The ant-hill they have long been building in Europe without Church and without Christ (for the Church, having obscured its own ideal, has there already for a long time been incarnated in the state), with moral principles that have been shaken to their foundation" (PSS 26: 167).

[13] This is also a motive in the Grand Inquisitor's discourse: "We took from him Rome and Caesar's sword" (PSS 14: 234).

and establish the *chelovekobog* or man-god. The idea of human self-deification was the pivotal ground in the construction of the Roman social order.

Whereas the Roman state built its "ant-hill" on the ideal of self-deification, the Christian Church, hiding underground from Roman persecution, gathered around itself a community of people who lived in the promise of a final reunion with God and formed a social order in correspondence with the Heavenly Kingdom. A growing number of people joined the underground Christian community, which in the end strongly opposed the Roman empire from within and undermined its already unstable ground. Rome was confronted with an alternative religious idea and social formula as presented by the Christian Church. At this point in the history of Christianity, there occurred "a collision between the two most completely opposite ideas that were ever to exist on earth: the *chelovekobog* encountered the *Bogochelovek*, Apollo Belvedere encountered Christ (*chelovekobog vstretil bogocheloveka, Apollon Bel'vederskii Khrista*)" (PSS 26: 169).[14]

In Dostoevskii's religious Orthodox discourse, the realm of the *chelovekobog* is Roman secularity and civil theology, glorifying the worldly Caesar above the heavenly gods. The Roman empire represents for Dostoevskii an impulse and gateway to human self-deification. This is the most radical opposite of the idea of the *Bogochelovek*, which goes far beyond a mere Christological concept in Dostoevskii's discourse. The *Bogochelovek* Christ embodies the Christian moral ideal of "personal self-perfection" or self-realization in accordance with the Christian law of love.

The historical clash between *chelovekobog* and *Bogochelovek*, between Roman secularity and Christian religion, deviates from what Dostoevskii considers to be the ideal and only justified method of organizing a civic society. In his opinion – which he sees proved in the history of other nations – social ideals should be derived from the

---

[14] The statue Apollo Belvedere is one of the most famous sculptures of the Greek god Apollo. It is probably a second century Roman copy of a Greek original by the sculptor Leochares. In the late fifteenth century, it was discovered near Rome and in 1511 pope Julius II placed it in the Belvedere courtyard (hence its name) in the Vatican. The statue was a prolific inspiration for Renaissance artists, who hailed it as the most perfect embodiment of classic beauty. For Dostoevskii, the statue epitomizes both paganism and the Western Christian tendency towards rationalization and secularization.

religious ideal, and civic communities should be designed to accomplish this ideal on earth. However, in the Roman epoch, the Christian Church and the empire developed separately from each other, the former underground, the latter on the surface, and when confronted with each other, they turned out to be totally incompatible. Being two equal powers, the one in the spiritual, the other in the material realm, the initial Christian Church and the Roman state could not completely overcome each other. They succeeded in preserving themselves by means of a compromise: "the empire accepted Christianity, and the Church accepted the Roman law and state" (PSS 26: 169). Dostoevskii refers to the declaration of Christianity as the official religion of the Roman state by emperor Constantine I in 325 A.D. whereby Christianity became the new civil theology of the Roman empire. Both the empire and the Church agreed to this collaboration for pragmatic reasons. The Roman emperor hoped that the acceptance of Christianity as a civil theology would help to uplift the moral consciousness of the Roman citizens in their battle against the barbarians. The Church sought to escape from persecution, and hoped that it could more efficiently accomplish its work in its new official status (Ward 1986: 168). For Dostoevskii, the Church's integration into the Roman empire and acceptance of its function as a civil theology falsified the moral message that is at the core of the original Christian community, i.e. Christ's teaching that His Kingdom is not of this world. Being the embodiment of Christ's original teachings, the early Church should have actively transformed the earthly state into its model instead of being included in an already formed state.[15]

---

[15] In the conversation with *starets* Zosima, Ivan Karamazov advances a similar view on the active and leading role of the Church in the formation of the state. In explaining his theory about ecclesiastical and civil courts, he recalls the history of early Christianity and its final entering into the Roman, pagan empire. Ivan holds that "(with a view to the future) it is not the Church that should seek a definite position in the state [...], but on the contrary, every earthly state should in the end be completely transformed into the Church and should become nothing else but the Church, rejecting everything that is incongruous with the goals of the Church" (PSS 14: 58). Ivan's theory on the civil court is in line with his view on the encompassing role of the Church. If the Church would assume the function of government and legal court, then the criminal would not only be cut off from society (as in civil court), but more importantly, from the Church of Christ. Then, one could not commit a crime and at the same time believe that Christ is still with him. In reply, Zosima notes that only Christ's law can protect society from the criminal and regenerate him. The criminal

Still, although the early Christian Church gave up its moral ideal when integrated in the Roman empire, this does not entail the end of the Christian Church for Dostoevskii. The Church ceased to be the incarnation of the original Christian ideal only in the Western part of the Christian area, where the Church "was crushed and reincarnated once and for all in the state" (PSS 26: 169). By establishing a papacy, the secular government granted the Church an autonomous status, yet this institution was a mere continuation of the Caesar's power. According to Dostoevskii, in Roman Catholicism the Church sacrificed its essential principles and submitted to the reign of a secular power. However, Christ's legacy was continued outside the territory of Roman papacy. In the Eastern half of the Christian world, the authentic Church was saved from subjection to secularity because "the state was conquered and destroyed by the sword of Mohammed" and what remained was "Christ, detached from the state" (PSS 26: 169). Dostoevskii thus maintains that the Muslim capture of Constantinople (1453) had an indirect positive outcome for Christendom. Although the Byzantine empire was annexed into the Muslim world, the Christian community was able to preserve the Christian ideal independently of the state. The authentic Christian ideal, as preserved in Eastern Christianity, was taken over by the Russian people who became the real "bearers of Christ" (*nositel' Khrista*) (PSS 26: 170).

In Dostoevskii's Eastern Christian outlook, the Roman Catholic Church developed in such a way that it gradually deviated from the authentic Christian ideal through its integration into the Roman empire and worship of the sword of Caesar. A similar critique on the Roman religious order emerges from the "legend" of the Grand Inquisitor. In his ambition to construe a universal earthly empire, the Grand Inquisitor yields to the temptations Christ resisted and founds his church on the forces of "miracle, mystery and authority" (PSS 14: 232). For Dostoevskii, this boils down to a betrayal of Christ's teaching that His Kingdom is not of this world and of the promise of salvation in the otherworld. The Roman Catholic community is not grounded in a universal faith in the higher idea of God and the spiritual unity between one another: it is instead based on a political and compulsory human organization. In Dostoevskii's view, God is

---

can only accept his guilt before society by recognizing his sin as a sin to the Christian community (PSS 14: 59f).

completely absent in the Western Church, which is thus tantamount to atheism. In the West, the image of Christ is completely obscured by the desire for a secular, earthly order:

> The Western Church itself distorted the image of Christ by transforming itself from the Church in the Roman state and embodying that state anew in the papacy. Indeed, in the West there truly is no Christianity and Church [...] In truth, Catholicism is no longer Christianity and is transforming itself into idolatry (PSS 26: 151).

Roman Catholicism failed to organize a social order in Christ's name; on the contrary, it opted for an alliance with the one who tempted Christ in the wilderness and offered Him all the kingdoms of this world. The Grand Inquisitor and the Catholics do not worship Christ: "We are not with you, but with *him*, that is our secret! [...] we took from him Rome and Caesar's sword and proclaimed ourselves the kings of the earth" (PSS 14: 234). The Catholic Church sides with Satan, or the devil. It proclaims and glorifies a Christ who had yielded to the third temptation of the earthly kingdom and thus presents humanity with an inverted paradigm of the authentic Christ. For Dostoevskii, in the Western Church, "Christ has been sold out for earthly dominion" whereas in the Eastern Church the authentic image of Christ has been preserved (PSS 26: 85).

This idea's most radical ramifications are expressed by Dostoevskii's most Christlike fictional character, Prince Myshkin. In Dostoevskii's fictional discourse, Myshkin represents the beautiful person, who lives his life for the other and speaks and acts candidly, like a child. He expresses a consciousness that approaches the anthropological ideal of the Christian law of love. This 'holy fool' gives a trenchant critique of Roman Catholicism:

> Catholicism is as good as an unchristian religion [...] Roman Catholicism is even worse than atheism itself [...] Atheism only preaches a negation, but Catholicism goes further: it preaches a distorted Christ, a Christ calumniated and defamed by themselves, the opposite of Christ! It preaches the Antichrist [...] Roman Catholicism cannot hold its position without universal political supremacy, and cries: *Non Possumus!* To my thinking, Roman Catholicism is not even a religion, but simply the continuation of the Western Roman empire, and everything in it is subordinated to that idea, faith to begin with. The pope seized the earth, an earthly throne and grasped the sword [...] And isn't that the teaching of the Antichrist? How could atheism fail to come from them? Atheism has sprung from Roman Catholicism itself (PSS 8: 450).

In Dostoevskii's discourse there is an ideological link between the Grand Inquisitor's rationale and the phenomenon of the *chelovekobog*, as phrased in the 1880 text. In their aspirations to offer humanity an earthly kingdom, both stand for the betrayal of Christ's original teachings. In the Grand Inquisitor text, there is the explicit phrasing that the Grand Inquisitor chose to side with Satan. This impelled various interpreters to identify the Antichrist in Dostoevskii's representation of the Grand Inquisitor. Following this association, the identification of Antichrist and *chelovekobog* is imminent, a connection that will prove to be a productive one from 1900 onwards.

7. Conclusion

The idea of the *chelovekobog* occurs only three times in Dostoevskii's writing: twice in a fictional setting, and once in *The Diary of a Writer*. Basically, this concept is both literally and ideologically the complete inverse of the *Bogochelovek*. As phrased by the fictional characters Kirillov and the devil/Ivan Karamazov, the *chelovekobog* represents an anthropology that aspires to overcome and replace the Christian model by precisely touching upon and inverting its specific values and categories. Kirillov and the devil/Ivan, the spokesmen of this concept, aim to overturn the ancient theocentric worldview and establish an exclusively anthropocentric paradigm that deifies and exalts the human as the prime and sole master of himself. Their view on humanity is a purely materialist one, and in that sense, they counteract the basis of Christian anthropology, i.e. the doctrine that the human is essentially defined by his immortal soul which is an entity entrenched in the Deity. This detachment from the Godhead inevitably results in a radical upheaval of moral consciousness because if the human is no longer tied to the collective consciousness of being essentially one with God, he falls into a completely self-centered and egotistic motivation, which eventually amounts to the ethical imperative that, in Ivan Karamazov's wording, "all is permitted." In the fictional context, the *chelovekobog* is thus advanced as an anthropology that aspires to overturn all aspects of the anthropological paradigm for which the *Bogochelovek* Christ stands. In *The Diary of a Writer* for August 1880, this determination is enlarged. In this discourse, the concept is applied to characterize and refer to Roman Catholicism as distinct from the Eastern Church. The Western Church represents the *chelovekobog*, whereas the Eastern Church preserves the pure and authentic image of the *Bogochelovek*. The *chelovekobog* stands for the Roman ambition for secularization and materializiation, in which Dostoevskii finds a betrayal of Christ's original teaching that his kingdom is not of this world, and by extension, the negation of the human's divine nature and potential capacity for transfiguration in the other world. So, eventually, in Dostoevskii's fictional and non-fictional discourse, the concept of the *chelovekobog* can be summarized as a perverted ideal of what the *Bogochelovek* represents.

Chapter 6

Supplementing Christ:
Dmitrii Merezhkovskii's use of Nietzsche's *Übermensch*

The appearance of the Antichrist-Nietzsche is not only a great and significant, but also a perfect and final appearance, the "beginning of an end", a final point, after which "one cannot go further", an edge and precipice. When a man of such incredible cultural and religious power, like Nietzsche, has not solved the main contradiction in Western European culture, has not flown over the abyss, then who is more winged than he is? Who will follow him? Who will dare? (Merezhkovskii [1900-1901] 1995: 142).

1. Introduction

Although the concept of the *chelovekobog* occurs at three different occasions in Dostoevskii's oeuvre, Russian readers have not always paid much attention to it. To my knowledge, the concept is completely absent in critical literature on Dostoevskii before 1900. However, in 1901 both Volynskii and Bulgakov not only mention it but also highlight its importance for fully appreciating Dostoevskii's thought.[1] Moreover, from 1902 on, there is a flood of articles in which the

---

[1] A.L. Volynskii: *Tsarstvo Karamazovykh* (1901); S.N. Bulgakov: "Ivan Karamazov kak filosofskii tip" (1901). I will analyze these texts later in this chapter.

recurring analogies between Nietzsche and Dostoevskii are systematically mediated by the very concept of the *chelovekobog*.[2]

It turns out that 1900 marks other important shifts as well. Firstly, in the critical literature on Nietzsche before 1900, Nietzsche's ideas, in particular his concept of the *Übermensch*, are often explained in association with theories put forward by some of Dostoevskii's nihilistic characters, more specifically Ivan Karamazov and Raskol'nikov. From 1900 onwards, the characters Kirillov and Ivan's devil feature in the explanations of Nietzsche's *Übermensch*. Secondly, before 1900, Nietzsche is substantially interpreted through a Dostoevskian horizon of expectations, whereas on the other hand, there is hardly any reference to Nietzsche in interpretations of Dostoevskii. After 1900, Dostoevskii is largely read through a Nietzschean discourse, culminating in studies in which both are weighed against each other.

Related to this, there is a remarkable shift in the appraisal of Dostoevskii. Whereas before 1900, Dostoevskii is mainly read as a socio-realistic writer, after 1900 he is primarily valued for the religiosity of his works, a quality inferred mostly from his nihilistic characters.

Finally, and most importantly, 1900 also marks a salient shift in the assessment of Nietzsche. While the German philosopher was hitherto rigorously rejected for the anti-Christian bias of his thought, he is from 1900 on judged much more carefully and his ideas are considered to be potentially prolific, especially in the field of religion.

In this chapter, I aim to argue that this cluster of shifts with regard to Dostoevskii and Nietzsche, is initiated, at least to some extent, by the critic, poet, and philosopher Dmitrii Merezhkovskii and can be traced back considerably to Merezhkovskii's fascination for Nietzsche.

---

[2] Tikhomirov: "Nitsshe i Dostoevskii. Cherty iz nravstvennago mirovozzreniia togo i drugogo" (1902); Smirnov: "Dostoevskii i Nitsshe" (1903); Kheisin: "Dostoevskii i Nitsshe" (1903); Shestov: *Dostoevskii i Nitshe. Filosofiia Tragedii* (1903). All these studies will be examined later in this chapter.

2. A transitional figure in Russian culture

Dmitrii Sergeevich Merezhkovskii was born in 1865 in St. Petersburg into the family of a court official. In 1884 he enrolled at St. Petersburg University where he studied history and philology, and shortly accepted the banner of positivism, which was then a very popular philosophical trend among students; Merezhkovskii soon abjured it for its rigid materialism and began his lifelong search for an all-inclusive spiritual philosophy. In 1889 he married Zinaida Gippius (1869-1945) who was herself a prolific poet and critic. The Merezhkovskii's began a lifelong creative relationship, and the couple soon held a celebrated salon at the Liteinyi Prospekt in St. Petersburg, welcoming artists and intellectuals, all birds of different feathers. From the end of the 1890s, Merezhkovskii started publishing poetry, prose and critical essays on various subjects. He was a very active and prolific author: he left an impressive amount of lyrical, literary and journalistic texts which display many shifts in emphasis but simultaneously reveal a consistent thread of spirituality and the typical dualism of his thought. The two Russian ideologues Merezhkovskii admired most were Fëdor Dostoevskii and Vladimir Solov'ëv, both of whom he met in brief encounters which made a lasting impression on the young writer.[3]

In the 1890s, the Merezhkovskii's made several trips to Greece and Italy which aroused their interest in Greek pagan religion and early Christianity. The sights of the Greek temples and Italian churches inspired Dmitrii Merezhkovskii to indulge in the study of ancient Greek culture, early Roman Christianity and Italian renaissance art and values. The cultures of the antiquity and the renaissance offered him an aesthetic and religious salvation from the positivist and populist rigidity of present Russian culture. This was also the period that Nietzschean motives entered Merezhkovskii's poetry and works. Nietzsche's aestheticism and his study of the Dionysian and the Apollinian in *The Birth of Tragedy* (1872) reinforced Merezhkovskii's interest in Hellenic culture and religion. From 1900 on, Merezhkovskii became a central figure in the new religious seeking that pervaded the Russian Silver Age.

---

[3] Merezhkovskii met Dostoevskii at the age of fifteen and read him some of his poems. Dostoevskii's comment was harsh: "Weak, bad, not good at all [...] in order to write well, one should suffer, suffer" (Merezhkovskii [1914] 1972: 291).

After the failed revolution of 1905, Merezhkovskii, until then only on the sidelines engaged in politics, became a zealous revolutionary and steeped himself in political writing. He observed in the 1905 revolt a religious uprising, which he aimed to steer in the right direction by proclaiming himself the prophet of a new eschatology: he believed that the revolution was a necessary step towards the Apocalypse that would install a new religious society. However, the results of the revolution disappointed him and he started to change his apocalyptic anticipations with regard to the growing revolutionary wind. When the Bolsheviks seized power in October 1917, and installed a totalitarian regime, reigning with terror and executing thousands of people within the first months of its formation, Merezhkovskii identified Bolshevik rule as evil incarnate and engaged in active resistance. In December 1919, the Merezhkovskii's fled to Poland, then migrated in 1920 to France, where they continued their crusade against Bolshevism in political articles and pamphlets. In Paris, they held a salon which became a meeting point for Russian émigré writers and artists. Merezhkovskii died in 1941 in Paris and was buried there in the Russian cemetery.[4]

Dmitrii Merezhkovskii was one of the seminal figures of the Silver Age. His ideas, covering a wide range of disciplines, effected various shifts in several areas of Russian culture. He was one of the first instigators of a new and as it turned out, fruitful concept of art. By the 1880s, partly due to the loss of credibility in Populism, which had been dominating Russian culture from the 1870s onward, Russian literature had reached an ideological dead-end. The populist idea that art should be a bearer of idealistic moral principles, such as social justice and equality, and should contribute to the social upbringing of the people (hence, the term *narodnichestvo*), had lost its glitter for the younger intelligentsia. They could no longer side with an ideology that prioritized social well-being over individual aspirations. Instead, they aimed for new artistic values that would correspond to the demand for individual development and cultivation of creativity. As a critic, Merezhkovskii highly contributed to this new artistic wave and provided the young artists and intellectuals with a new aesthetics, partly based on French symbolism. He became one of the main

---

[4] For biographical information on Merezhkovskii, see Gippius' work, *Dmitrii Merezhkovskii* (1951). Merezhkovskii was nominated for the Nobel Prize in Literature in 1931. The prize was in 1933 awarded to Ivan Bunin.

ideologues of Russian symbolism and decadentism. The aesthetic phase in Merezhkovskii's intellectual career, in which he aspired to outline a new concept of art as a means to develop and transmit the artist's individual creativity, lasted from the end of the 1880s until about 1899. In 1893, he published his lectures *O Prichinakh Upadka i o novykh Techeniiakh sovremmenoi Literatury* (*On the Reasons for the Decline and on new Trends in contemporary Russian Literature*), the first manifesto of Russian symbolism. In this collection of essays, Merezhkovskii renounced prevailing aesthetic norms and argued that high culture did not exist yet in Russia; this would only come about when artists would grasp, through symbols, the mystical nature of art (Clowes 1988: 118). Symbolism entailed for the artists and critics involved more than a new aesthetic theory; rather, it held a whole new ideological view on life. They rejected "Philistine" mentality (so-called *meshchanstvo*) and sought a language that would grasp the transcendent reality beyond the one surrounding them. The symbolists Nikolai Minskii, Fëdor Sologub, Konstantin Bal'mont, and Merezhkovskii's wife, Zinnaida Gippius, frequently contributed critical articles and literary writings to the modernist journal *Severnyi Vestnik* (*The Northern Herald*), which had shifted ideologically from Populism to symbolism under the editorship of Akim Volynskii (pseudonym for Akim L'vovich Flekser). The symbolist poets and critics frequently attended Merezhkovskii's and Gippius' evenings in their home "Dom Muruzi" at Liteinyi Prospekt in St. Petersburg (Rosenthal 1975: 13ff; Pyman 1994: 19ff.). From 1898, the Merezhkovskii's eagerly participated in the new journal *Mir Iskusstva* (*The World of Art*, 1898-1904), founded by Sergei Diagilev and Aleksandr Benois; the magazine and the artistic movement it inspired, fostered an individualist and autonomous art.

   At the end of the 1890s, Merezhkovskii began to realize that an aesthetic worldview was insufficient to meet his demand for a spiritual and religious upheaval and he soon engaged in the search for a new faith. So he was not only a major contributor to the ongoing flux in aesthetics and art, but he was also a preeminent initiator of the new religious seeking around the turn of the century. He was the first to formulate and promulgate the "new religious consciousness" (*novoe religioznoe soznanie*). He phrased his new philosophy of religion in the two volume study *L. Tolstoi i Dostoevskii: Khristos i Antikhristos v russkoi literature* (*L. Tolstoi i Dostoevskii: Christ and Antichrist in*

Russian literature, 1900-1901). Together with Gippius and Filosofov, and with permission of the Procurator of the Holy Synod Pobedonostsev, Merezhkovskii founded in 1901 the St. Petersburg "Religious Philosophical Society" (*Religiozno-filosofskoe obshchestvo*) which organized debates between clergymen and lay intellectuals to reflect on the current state of the church and to reach a new delineation of Christianity, grounded both in official doctrines and non-denominational ideas. These "Religious-Philosophical Gatherings" (*Religiozno-filosofskie sobraniia*) featured discussions on actual and burning questions such as the rigid state control over the church (the church was organized as a state "Department of Orthodox Confession"), the poor education of the clergy, the church's excommunication of Lev Tolstoi, the church's severe rejection of sensuality etc. These meetings were attended by, among others, Berdiaev, Rozanov, Minskii, Blok and Belyi (Rosenthal 1975: 133-151; Novikov 1998: 221). The literary and philosophical journal of the new religious movement was the journal *Novyi Put'* (*The New Way*) (Berdiaev [1949] 2003: 385f.; Novikov 1998: 221).

In addition to the turning point he instigated in aesthetic and religious thought, Merezhkovskii initiated another shift in Russian consciousness. A concern with religious questions impelled him to reconsider one of the great icons of Russian literature, i.e. Fëdor Dostoevskii, in whom he discovered a previously overlooked motif. In literary criticism until then, Dostoevskii was above all assessed as an almost naturalistic chronicler of the social conditions and excrescences of civilization in contemporary Russia. In the mid-1840s Vissarion Belinskii and the representatives of the "Natural School" set the tone to focus primarily on the socio-realistic dimension of Dostoevskii's works, a trend that was continued by the radical critics of the 1860s and the populist commentators of the 1870s and 1880s. Around the turn of the century, Merezhkovskii broke with this tradition: he was one of the first to read Dostoevskii primarily as a religious writer and in that sense, contributed to the new, religiously inspired wave of Dostoevskii criticism that flourished in the beginning of the twentieth century (e.g. Volynskii's, Shestov's, Bulgakov's and Berdiaev's readings of Dostoevskii).

A landmark in the cultural and intellectual renaissance of the Silver Age, Merezhkovskii was also one of the first and most diligent intellectuals to introduce and disseminate Nietzsche's ideas in Russia.

At several moments in Merezhkovskii's intellectual development, Nietzsche's thoughts contributed to Merezhkovskii's critique on established standards in the various fields mentioned above and incited him to formulate an alternative for these deficient paradigms. In short, the German thinker was for Merezhkovskii a prolific source of inspiration to reconsider various aspects of Russian culture and consciousness.

3. The versatility of Nietzsche's thought in Merezhkovskii's intellectual development

Merezhkovskii learned about Nietzsche through different channels around 1890, this is almost a decade before the ban on the German thinker was officially abolished in Russia. Merezhkovskii was acquainted with Prince Aleksandr Urusov, a lawyer and respected intellectual in St. Petersburg circles, to whom Nietzsche, acting on Georg Brandes' suggestion sent a copy of *The Case of Wagner* at the end of 1888 (KSB 8: 450, 470, 514).[5] Another source was his friendship with the poet Nikolai Minskii, who had read Nietzsche while in Western Europe and in 1890 published *Pri Svete Sovesti* (*In the Light of Conscience*), with hindsight labeled the first 'Nietzschean-like' work in Russia. In 1891, Merezhkovskii traveled to Paris, where he learned about the French symbolists and became fascinated by Nietzsche who was a seminal source of inspiration for this movement. While in Paris, Merezhkovskii engaged in a thorough study of this thinker, whose works he probably read in the German original since at that time, there were neither French nor Russian translations available.[6] By his own account, he was "completely shaken" by Nietzsche's writings (Briusov 1927: 53). In the early 1890s, Merezhkovskii's Nietzscheanism was still restrained. In that period,

---

[5] During a literary evening, where both Merezhkovskii and his wife Zinaida Gippius were present, Urusov gave a lecture on Nietzsche (Gippius 1951: 63).

[6] In 1895 Henri Albert's translation *L'antéchrist: essai d'une critique du christianisme* appeared in *La société nouvelle*. He also translated *Ainsi parlait Zarathoustra: un livre pour tous et pour personne*, which was pulished in 1898. From 1901 on, the *Oeuvres complètes de Frédéric Nietzsche* began to be published (edited by Albert) (Jung and Simon-Ritz 2000 Bd.1: 235ff.). The first Russian translation of Nietzsche's works was published in 1898, i.e. *Tak Govoril Zaratustra* by M.Iu. Antonovskii.

he mainly concentrated on and assimilated Nietzsche's emphasis on aesthetic values and his interest in the Antique world. From 1891 onward, the Merezhkovskii's undertook several journeys to the Mediterranean; the sight of the ancient cities and monuments, as constructions of creative genius, intensified his interest in as well as his understanding of the German philosopher. He perceived of Nietzsche's thought as a return and tribute to ancient culture and the religiosity related to it. In the mid-1890s Merezhkovskii's indulgence in Nietzsche reached a climax (Rosenthal 1975: 57ff.). What initially attracted him, and for that matter the other symbolists, to Nietzsche was his aestheticism. In *The Birth of Tragedy*, Nietzsche glorified ancient Greek culture for its entrenchment in the aesthetic forces of the Dionysian and the Apollinian, and juxtaposed it to modern European culture which he saw as cut off from its aesthetic roots and subsiding into its own petty-bourgeois formalism. In order to revive contemporary culture, he promoted the re-installment of pagan Greek virtues, such as beauty, sensuality, and intuitive creativity. Nietzsche's cultural criticism appealed to Merezhkovskii because he also aimed to overcome the banality and mediocrity of Russian culture and strove to establish a higher culture which would no longer depreciate the sensuous pleasures of pagan art.[7] Furthermore, Nietzsche's duality (*Duplizität*) of the Dionysian and the Apollinian, as two entities fundamentally made up by the transactionality between them, suggested Merezhkovskii – in a later stage – the pattern for his new version of Christianity.

After having established a metaphysical aesthetics under the aegis of Nietzsche, Merezhkovskii turned by the end of the 1890s to Christianity in his search for an inclusive metaphysical system. Yet in its current form, the Christian model soon failed him in his ambition to construct a comprehensive metaphysics, and he set out to formulate a new philosophy of religion. And once again, he drew substantially on Nietzsche as he conceived his "new religious consciousness",.

Furthermore, Nietzsche had a considerable part in Merezhkovskii's re-evaluation of Dostoevskii: Nietzsche's idea of the *Übermensch* served as a catalyst to pinpoint and highlight the idea of the *chelovekobog*, a concept that had not been previously mentioned in the critical research on Dostoevskii. Merezhkovskii was the first to

---

[7] For a more detailed account of Nietzscheanism in Merezhkovskii's symbolist aesthetics, see Rosenthal (1975) and Lane (1976: 209-253).

introduce and analyze at length the concept of the *chelovekobog*,
which he already from the outset identified with Nietzsche's
Übermensch.[8] Moreover, the critic's focus on the idea of the
chelovekobog as one of the main themes in Dostoevskii's thought
contributed to his reading of Dostoevskii as a primarily religious
thinker.

Nietzsche's imprint in that matter was in fact dynamically
linked to his vital part in Merezhkovskii's reformulation of
Christianity. Merezhkovskii's reconsideration of Christianity was
prompted by both Dostoevskii and Nietzsche. However, the
relationship is reciprocal: Merezhkovskii's new interpretation of both
Dostoevskii and Nietzsche was also triggered by the reformulation of
Christianity. In fact, one cannot examine these aspects separately.
These shifts are all clustered together in Merezhkovskii's seminal
work *L. Tolstoi i Dostoevskii* (1900-1901).

4. Merezhkovskii's diagnosis: the vices of historical Christianity

In Merezhkovskii's view, the primary metaphysical problem is the
dualism of two antithetical entities that govern the cosmos and the
world and from which arise all conflicts and antagonisms in the
phenomenal world. These two opposite principles act upon the world
and manifest themselves in a variety of ways which all basically boil
down to what Merezhkovskii delineates as the antithesis between
"Christ and Antichrist." Under the "anti-Christian," Merezhkovskii
counts the worship of the "Flesh" (*Plot'*) as typically practiced in
pagan religions and ancient Greek culture. A religion of the Flesh
entails an intuitive devotion to the earth and exaltation of earthly
pleasures, such as beauty and sensuality. The gods are omniscient yet
not infallible and can be defeated by humanity. The "Christian" force,

---

[8] In critical literature, there is, to my knowledge, no specific information about the
person who introduced the *chelovekobog* in literary criticism on Dostoevskii.
Fridlender hints at Merezhkovskii and his symbolist companion Volynskii as the first
ones to see in the *chelovekobog* "a direct proof of congeniality between Nietzsche and
the author of *The Devils*" (1979: 218). Yet no mention is made of the identification of
chelovekobog and *Übermensch*. In recent literature on Dostoevskii and Nietzsche, in
which the perceived analogy between both is grounded on the identification of
chelovekobog and *Übermensch*, there is no reference whatsoever to any potential
initiators of this comparison (See e.g. Dudkin 1994; Ignatov 1993).

by contrast, covers the worship of the "Spirit" (*Dukh*) and posits the primacy of spirit over matter, of heaven over earth. There is but one Divinity, who is glorified as the prime and sole mover of the world and humanity. Anthropologically, the anti-Christian entity stands for the Promethean and individual self that strives to challenge the gods; the Christian entity, in contrast, foregrounds a collectivist and universalistic conception of the human. Merezhkovskii's thought constantly mediates between these poles.

In his trilogy of historical novels, entitled *Khristos i Antikhristos*, Merezhkovskii aims to describe the antithesis between the Christian and the anti-Christian by looking into specific historical cases. In *Smert' Bogov: Iulian Otstupnik* (*The Death of the Gods: Julian the Apostate*, 1895) and *Antichrist. Pëtr i Aleksei* (*The Antichrist. Peter and Aleksei*, 1904), emperor Julian's (fourth century A.D.) and Peter the Great's policies are explained in terms of their struggle to resist the Christian religion of the Spirit: Julian by making a return to paganism and Peter by reforming the Russian Church. The novel *Voskresshie Bogi: Leonardo da Vinchi* (*The Resurrected Gods: Leonardo da Vinci*, 1900) uses Leonardo as an example to show how the arts can be productive in efforts to dissolve the conflict of Christ and Antichrist (Bedford 1975: 60ff.). In spite of their perspicacity in addressing the problem, these three historical figures have eventually failed in their attempts to find a solution. Merezhkovskii finds fault with all historical efforts to resolve the bifurcation between Christ and Antichrist, or, "Spirit" and "Flesh," because they attempt to dissolve this antithesis into a monistic position. Since the relationship between Christ and Antichrist is essentially transactional, this opposition can only be settled by preserving both Christ and Antichrist as equal entities. Merezhkovskii, who is fundamentally rooted in the Christian sphere despite his preoccupation with the anti-Christian, insists that the problem should be resolved *within* the Christian framework.

However, as he diagnoses, Christianity is in its past and current condition inadequate to meet the metaphysical question of Christ and Antichrist. Traditional Christianity, or what Merezhkovskii labels "historical" Christianity, deliberately decries the pagan, pre-Christian worship of the Flesh and posits the preponderance of Spirit over Flesh, thereby exalting the spiritual realm and negating earthly life and its sensuous pleasures.[9] In this regard, Merezhkovskii adopts Nietzsche's critique that Christianity is a nihilistic religion which cultivates suffering and death and as a result, denies the Dionysian joys of earthly life. Historical Christianity brushes aside earthly sensuousness and takes refuge in an unworldly worldview that propagates asceticism and the suppression of physical desires. Rejecting the sexual drive in humanity, the historical Church also represses the exaltation or study of sensuality in the arts, psychology, philosophy and other areas of human intellectual activity. It is an unhealthy, static and narrow religion, because it cancels out the vital drive of the Flesh in humanity and the world and exclusively sublimates the Spirit. For Merezhkovskii, historical Christianity's exclusive devotion to the Spirit is epitomized in the historical representation of Christ in which Christ is glorified as pure Spirit, whereby his fleshly, earthly nature is labeled as inferior.

Nietzsche thus provides a criticism of Christianity that inspires Merezhkovskii to pinpoint the flaws of traditional Christianity. Still, unlike Nietzsche who abandons Christianity altogether, Merezhkovskii is persistent to retain the basic Christian message and to develop a more vital religion that includes and offers an answer to Nietzsche's challenge to Christianity. Merezhkovskii differentiates between historical Christianity and what he considers to be 'authentic' Christianity, as originally proclaimed by Christ but over the years corrupted by pragmatic dogmatists. Once again, Nietzsche's view on Christianity is highly appealing to Merezhkovskii; in *The Antichrist* (1888, not published until 1895), Nietzsche scorns the institute of the Church yet absolves the historical figure of Christ from any responsibility for the contents and program of this Church. Instead, he blames Paul for having perverted Christ's authentic teaching:

> The very word "Christianity" is a misunderstanding -, in fact, there was only one Christian, and he died on the cross. The "evangel" died on the cross. What has been called "evangel" from that moment on was actually the

---

[9] His intellectual companions ascribe the wording "historical Christianity" to Merezhkovskii (Koreneva 1991: 70). The critique on "historical Christianity" bears Nietzsche's watermark: "When Nietzsche maintains in his *Antichrist* that "Christianity is until now the most absolute form of mortal hate towards all that exists [...] he is of course not right in the religious, or mystical sense, but in the historical sense" (Merezhkovskii [1900-1901] 1995: 260).

opposite of that which he had lived: "ill tidings," a dysangel [...] On the heels of the "glad tidings" came the very worst: those of Paul. In Paul was embodied the opposite type to that of the "bringer of glad tidings": the genius in hatred, in the vision of hatred, in the inexorable logic of hatred. How much this dysangelist sacrificed to hatred! Above all, the Redeemer: he nailed him to his own cross. The life, the example, the doctrine, the death, the meaning and the right of the entire evangel, nothing remained once this hate-inspired counterfeiter realized what alone he could use. *Not* reality, *not* historical truth (KSA 6: 211ff.).

Inspired by Nietzsche's charges against Christianity, yet persistent to retain and reappraise the authentic word of Christ, Merezhkovskii formulates a new version of Christianity, or as he calls it, a "new religious consciousness" (*novoe religioznoe soznanie*). This "new religious consciousness" is not as much a well-defined religion as a search for a new interpretation of Christianity in which Merezhkovskii attempts to integrate both Spirit and Flesh, Christ and Antichrist. Having adopted Nietzsche's criticism on institutionalized Christianity, Merezhkovskii likewise relies on him to amend its vices.

5.   Merezhkovskii's cure: the identification of *Übermensch* and *chelovekobog*

Merezhkovskii, who was more a writer and critic than a learned theologian, developed his neo-Christian myth in a work of literary criticism, *L. Tolstoi i Dostoevskii: Khristos i Antikhristos v russkoi literature*, which appeared serially from 1900 onward in the decadent journal *Mir Iskusstva* and was published in book form in 1901. As his collection of essays, *O Prichinakh Upadka i o novykh Techeniiakh sovremmenoi Literatury* (1893) heralded the symbolist era in Russian culture, this work was a milestone in the Silver Age; it is the first expression of the new religious search that marks the philosophical renaissance at the beginning of the twentieth century. This two volume study is dedicated to Tolstoi and Dostoevskii, but Nietzsche is also very much present; they all function as a vehicle and catalyst to convey Merezhkovskii's own ideas concerning the history and future of Christianity. Merezhkovskii identifies Tolstoi and Dostoevskii as the proponents of Flesh and Spirit *within* Christianity. Within Russian Christianity, Tolstoi represents the "holiness of the Flesh" (*sviatost' Ploti*), whereas Dostoevskii reflects the "holiness of the Spirit" (*sviatost' Dukha*) (Merezhkovskii [1900-1901] 1995: 61). Although Tolstoi publicly carries on a controversy with the church, he represents paradoxically, for Merezehkovskii, the frame of mind of historical Christianity. Behind Tolstoi's ascetiscism and renunciation of sexuality Merezhkovskii observes a fixation with the "Flesh": the characters in his novels are described by means of their physical characteristics, whereby their psychological features are secondary. His merit as a writer is precisely in his "pagan" talent to portray the Flesh in all its manifestations and forms. Still, the dominant moralistic subtext in his works undermines his artistic competence to express the reality of the Flesh. Tolstoi refuses to describe the positive, healthy joys of the Flesh, but instead aims at abjuring the Flesh as a negative and corrupting factor in human existence. Instead of glorifying the Flesh, he stigmatizes it. His hatred of all fleshly matters is equal to historical Christianity's disgust at the Flesh. Moreover, Tolstoi's lifelong obsession with death withholds him from indulging in earthly life. Since his religion is fundamentally construed around his fear of death, it is – just like historical Christianity – a life-negating, even life-fearing religion. In Merezhkovskii's view, Tolstoi's new religious worldview is artificial and hypocritical because his activities do not correspond to his teaching. Nevertheless, his provocations against and polemics with the ecclesiastical authorities should be applauded.

Dostoevskii is the complete antipode of Tolstoi: he represents the holiness of the "Spirit", the "Spirit of the new Christianity." Dostoevskii does not portray his characters in physical, but in psychological and ideological terms. His artistic talent is in grasping and describing meticulously the characters' ideals and intellectual and spiritual ponderings that underlie their actions, so that what sticks in the reader's mind is not so much their physical appearance, but the ideals that consume and drive them. All of his heroes have an idea, or are in search of an idea, that guides them in life and enables them to overcome their present condition; through their idea they eventually accomplish the transfiguration of their current self. Dostoevskii's characters epitomize for Merezhkovskii that spiritual ideals can uplift humans from their fleshly, materialistic nature and raise them to a better self. Dostoevskii does not negate the Flesh, but attempts to temper it by infusing it with the "Spirit." In Dostoevskii's characters, "Flesh" and "Spirit", material and divine nature strive to come in balance.

Besides Tolstoi and Dostoevskii, Merezhkovskii needs another thinker that stands completely *outside* of the Christian framework to formulate his views on Christianity: the self-christened Antichrist Nietzsche, who is "of such an incredible cultural and religious power" (Merezhkovskii [1900-1901] 1995: 142).[10] In the preface to the study, composed in Merezhkovskii's typical dualistic style, Nietzsche is already emphatically in the foreground. Merezhkovskii reflects on modern Russian culture, which he diagnoses as torn between two opposing orientations: since Petrine reforms, Russian consciousness wavers between seeking an alliance with the West and safeguarding its national identity. Although Russia and Western Europe show many ideological differences, these are in Merezhkovskii's view only marginal, and he considers Europe to be the Russians' "second homeland" because he sees in the West a potential that can measure up to Russian culture. For Merezhkovskii, the most manifest substantiation of Europe's cultural and intellectual promise and its potential similarity with Russia is the philosophical import of Friedrich Nietzsche, who revived "in his youthful and spring like book *The Birth of Tragedy* (*Rozhdenie tragedii*)" the ancient gods Apollo and Dionysus (Merezhkovskii [1900-1901] 1995: 9). Furthermore,

> We were also present at the joining of these two opposing demons or gods in the even more exceptional and mysterious appearance of Zarathustra.[11] And how could we not recognize in him the One, Who haunted and tormented Dostoevskii his whole life, how could we not recognize the Chelovekobog in the *Übermensch*. And miraculous, almost unbelievable, for us was this coincidence of the most new, most extreme of extreme Europeans and the most Russian of the Russians (ibid.).

---

[10] For the purpose of this research, i.e. to explain the *God-seekers'* enthusiastic response to Nietzsche, as considerably determined by the horizon of expectations emerging from Dostoevskii, I restrict this study to Merezhkovskii's perception of Nietzsche and Dostoevskii. For a detailed account of his valuation of Tolstoi, see Rosenthal (1994b).

[11] Merezhkovskii's intuition that Zarathustra (in his discourse identical to the *Übermensch*) bears both Apollinian and Dionysian traits and is a further thinking through of the interactive duplicity of both complementary principles, is indeed correct. For the transactionality between Apollinian and Dionysian in the *Übermensch*, see Biebuyck and Grillaert (2003: 57f.).

At this point in the preface, Merezhkovskii introduces the idea of the *chelovekobog* and immediately relates it to Dostoevskii. The *chelovekobog* is presented as an ideology that is pivotal in Dostoevskii's oeuvre and that mesmerized the writer, not merely on a rational level. Note that in 1893, Merezhkovskii had already published three essays on the Russian writer: "Dostoevskii, kak khudozhnik" ("Dostoevskii as an artist"), "Raskol'nikov" and "Prestuplenie i Nakazanie" ("Crime and Punishment"), which reappeared in his collection of essays *Vechnye Sputniki* (*Eternal Companions*, 1897). In these articles, no reference whatsoever is made to the *chelovekobog*. And not unimportantly, neither Nietzsche nor the *Übermensch* are mentioned here. I stress the absence of references to Nietzsche in the previous essays on Dostoevskii because in the 1900 text, Merezhkovskii introduces the *chelovekobog* only in direct association with the very concept of the *Übermensch*. Nietzsche's *Übermensch*, at that time a pivotal religio-philosophical preoccupation for Merezhkovskii, reminds him of the *chelovekobog* and prompts him to highlight this idea in Dostoevskii's thought. At this point, the *chelovekobog* is not related to any of the actual discourses in which it appears in Dostoevskii's oeuvre but is described only as a major issue in Dostoevskii's thought, which Merezhkovskii claims to be identical to the *Übermensch*. In his perception, the connection is so accurate that Dostoevskii and Nietzsche, who are otherwise very divergent thinkers, come precisely together in these concepts, yet obviously from a different background and with different objectives. Unlike later interpretations by other critics, Merezhkovskii is certain that this case of convergence is not the result of influence or borrowing.[12] He believes that a similar cultural phenomenon, this is the moral decay in both European and Russian contemporary culture, drove them to "the same abyss" (ibid.). The *Übermensch* is Nietzsche's answer to the decomposition of European civilization and culture:

---

[12] The theory that Nietzsche was in the formation of his thought influenced by Dostoevskii had many followers and not only amongst Russian critics. The archpriest Smirnov claimed in a 1903 public speech that Dostoevskii had a direct influence on Nietzsche (Smirnov 1903: 13f.). Some forty years later Thomas Mann raised the idea that Nietzsche, in thinking out "the pale criminal" (*der bleiche Verbrecher*) might have had Dostoevskii in mind, in particular his nihilistic characters (Mann 1948: 78). This false idea was partly promoted by D. Vergun, who claimed in his 1901 article that Nietzsche became acquainted with Dostoevskii's works in 1873 (see chapter 2).

The *Übermensch* is the final point, the sharpest peak of the great mountain range of European philosophy with its century-long roots of the revolting, solitary and isolated personality. One cannot go further: the historical route has been walked till the end; further on, there is only precipice and abyss, fall or flight, or the supra-historical (*sverkhistoricheskii*) way, religion (ibid.).

For Merezhkovskii, the *Übermensch* is the logical outcome and inescapable upshot of the European spirit of the age, in which, over the course of centuries, the social dimension is superseded by the cultivation of the individual ego.[13] At face value, the *Übermensch* is a typically *European* phenomenon. Still, it seems to be manifestly epitomized in a Russian historical figure, i.e., Peter the Great. What Merezhkovskii identifies as *übermenschlich* in Peter the Great is that he, notwithstanding severe resistance in his time, radically transformed traditional Russian institutions and thereby disposed of the old morality and culture. Peter opened the window to the West and let in the individualist consciousness inherent to it. In that sense, Peter the Great, around whom floats the aura of the Antichrist, prefigures the *Übermensch* (ibid.).[14] The confrontation with and integration of Western values in Russian society and culture gradually led Russia to a state of being torn between East and West. In Merezhkovskii's view, contemporary Russian consciousness oscillates between, "to speak in Dostoevskii's language, the chelovekobog and the Bogochelovek, Christ and Antichrist" (id.: 10). Merezhkovskii distinguishes in contemporary Russian culture two categories: 1) the West, *chelovekobog*, and Antichrist on the one hand; 2) the East, *Bogochelovek*, and Christ on the other hand. He describes this bipolarity by a formula he borrows from Dostoevskii. In *The Diary of*

---

[13] In the article "Krizis Individualizma" ("The Crisis of Individualism", 1905), Viacheslav Ivanovich Ivanov advances a similar explanation of the *Übermensch*. He interprets the *Übermensch* as the end point of the Western European glorification of the emancipated individual. The *Übermensch* constitutes for Ivanov both the end and culmination of Western individualism. However longing for self-sufficiency, the *Übermensch* impersonates the Dionysian proclivity towards *sobornost'* (*collectivity*). Ivanov believes that "the taste for the *Übermensch* has killed in us the taste for the sovereign affirmation of the human in ourselves" (Ivanov 1971-1987 I: 836). See also Biebuyck and Grillaert (2003).

[14] Merezhkovskii alludes to the Old Believers and reactionary sects groups who perceived of Petrine reforms as the expression of the devil incarnate and viewed Peter as the Antichrist himself (Platt 2000: 93ff). He further elaborates on the representation of Peter as the Antichrist in his historical novel *Antichrist. Pëtr i Aleksei* (1904).

a Writer of August 1880, Dostoevskii identifies the Roman Catholic West with the *chelovekobog*, as being in opposition to the Orthodox East which he classifies as the *Bogochelovek*. Dostoevskii maintains that, due to its subordination to the Roman Caesar, the Catholic Church betrayed Christ's teaching that God's Kingdom is not of this world. When the Roman empire collided with the early Christian community, a confrontation occurred "between the two most completely opposite ideas that were ever to exist on earth: the *chelovekobog* encountered the *Bogochelovek*, Apollo Belvedere encountered Christ" (PSS 26: 169). In Dostoevskii's discourse, *chelovekobog* and *Bogochelovek* carry a multitude of connotations. *Bogochelovek* is the paradigm for the authentic Church, as preserved in the Eastern Church; *chelovekobog* implies Roman secularity, the subordination of divine truth to the state. In Merezhkovskii's analysis of Russian culture being swayed between East (Russian heritage) and West (Western European trends), he adopts Dostoevskii's explicit formula of *chelovekobog* and *Bogochelovek* in the *Diary* and blends it with his own antithetical discourse of Christ and Antichrist.

Western European culture suffers from a similar crisis: the age long bifurcation between Christ and Antichrist, Spirit and Flesh, has led European consciousness before the same abyss in front of which Russia is currently standing. In Merezhkovskii's view, both European and Russian consciousness cannot, within the limits of their present condition, overcome this abyss, he believes that "the historical way has reached its end" (Merezhkovskii [1900-1901] 1995: 10). Only religion can provide a solution to the present dualism. According to Merezhkovskii, the future of Russian and worldwide culture depends on one single, but primordial question: should humanity choose the path of religion or a worldview without God. Merezhkovskii renders this dilemma in a discursive constellation, appropriated from both Dostoevskii and Nietzsche with each being the exponent of a respective antithetical principle:

> Nietzsche, who struggled in the name of the Chelovekobog with the Bogochelovek, did he defeat Him? Dostoevskii, who struggled in the name of the Bogochelovek with the Chelovekobog, did he defeat him? (ibid.).

In Merezhkovskii's understanding, *Übermensch* and *chelovekobog* are identical to the point of interchangeability. The Dostoevskian model of *chelovekobog* and *Bogochelovek* is transposed to Nietzsche.

In his elaboration of the *chelovekobog* and the identification with the *Übermensch*, Merezhkovskii, for the most part, draws from Kirillov's argument, which he finds to be "one of the most striking cases of coincidence between Dostoevskii and Nietzsche [...] which is almost impossible to believe, like a miracle, had it not happened before our very eyes" (id.: 315). In his view,

> Kirillov anticipates the main ideas of Nietzsche, he expresses them with such a concentrated power, with which Nietzsche even never expressed them himself [...] what was secret in Kirillov, became clear in Nietzsche (ibid.).

Merezhkovskii links Kirillov to Nietzsche (the authors of respectively *chelovekobog* and *Übermensch*) on the basis of what he perceives as extraordinarily similar pronouncements on the current status of God and what they entail for the future condition of humanity.[15]

---

[15] Around the turn and the beginning of the 20th century, Merezhkovskii and the subsequent readers who sought to establish a match between Nietzsche's *Übermensch* and Kirillov's *chelovekobog*, had not yet the slightest idea that Nietzsche had actually read *The Devils* and jotted down some fragments from the novel and his commentaries on them. His notes on the novel were only published in 1970, in the new "Kritische Gesamtausgabe" (KGW) of Nietzsche's works, edited by Giorgio Colli and Mazzino Montinari (*Nietzsche. Werke. Kritische Gesamtausgabe*; the notes are included in the *Nachlass*, see KSA 13: 141-154). Enthused about Dostoevskii's "psychological genius" (KSB 8: 27 & 41), Nietzsche carefully read *The Devils* in an 1886 French translation by Victor Dérély and wrote down excerpts and own reflections, under the title "Bési" (subtitle of the French translation), in a notebook that dates from November 1887-March 1888. The excerpts reveal that Nietzsche – like the 'matchmakers' probably liked to envisage – took a special interest in the character Kirillov; it is interesting to see though, that Nietzsche was only concerned with the passages in which Kirillov explains his idea of the earthly paradise, or "eternal harmony" (KSA 13: 146; for the fragment in *The Devils*, PSS 10: 450) and the fragment in which Kirillov claims that the attribute of human divinity is one's "self-will" (KSA 13: 144f.; for the fragment in *The Devils*: PSS 10: 470f.). Both these fragments appear almost verbatim (in German translation) in the notebook. There is however no mention at all of Kirillov's specific terminology of the *chelovekobog* ("Menschgott"), nor is there any reference to Kirillov's conversation with Stavrogin, in which he launches the term, thereby embedding his anthropology in the Russian theological tradition by antagonizing it to the *Bogochelovek* (PSS 10: 189). Assuming that Nietzsche copied and marked out those fragments that somehow appealed to him, it is reasonable to conclude that Kirillov's anthropology of the *chelovekobog* aroused no specific interest in him, let alone struck him as an anthropology that showed any affinity or analogy with his own thought. Moreover, the glosses reveal that Nietzsche did not once observe any philosophical connection or similarity between the above mentioned fragments from Kirillov's theorizing and his own anthropology of the

Chelovekobog and *Übermensch* are for Merezhkovskii identical in the sense that both argue that the ancient need for God must be overcome. What binds them further, according to Merezhkovskii, is the requirement for physical transformation. When discussing the *chelovekobog*, Merezhkovskii also mentions the devil's speech to Ivan Karamazov: he highlights the formula that if God and the idea of human immortality are abandoned, then all is permitted for the human (PSS 15: 84). And once again, the link with Nietzsche is established: "This [the devil's formulation of the *chelovekobog*] is a drop of that poison, of which the creator of "Zarathustra" and "The Antichrist" served us a whole cup" (Merezhkovskii [1900-1901] 1995: 215). The ideas that Ivan's devil puts forward about the appearance of the *chelovekobog* are "Nietzschean, before Nietzsche, thoughts on the *Übermensch*" (id.: 301). For Merezhkovskii, the *chelovekobog* and *Übermensch* carry ethical implications: in a world devoid of God, one inevitably falls into immorality. By extension, he attaches the term *chelovekobog* to other nihilistic characters in Dostoevskii's oeuvre and hence rewrites the original discourse through his own ideological spectrum. He thus initiates the inaccurate thesis that all of Dostoevskii's nihilistic characters are *chelovekobogi* and thereby extends and reformulates the significance of the *chelovekobog* in Dostoevskii's actual writings. Furthermore, he pinpoints parallels between other nihilistic personages and Nietzsche's ideas. When Ivan Karamazov said that 'all is permitted' (*vsë pozvoleno*), he foretold

---

Übermensch (i.e. the *Übermensch* is not brought up at all in this context). What he found of significance in the figure of Kirillov is, most likely, consistent with his overall appraisal of Dostoevskii as "the only psychologist, from whom I had something to learn" (KSA 6: 147). In Kirillov, Dostoevskii explores the psychological ponderings and radical decisions of a character tormented by the "death of God," who finds no other alternative to the consequential void than suicide. Kirillov is, for Nietzsche, a refined example of the "psychology of the nihilist" (KSA 13: 142), of one who has overcome God and subsequently lives through the existential anxiety of post-God times, but who fails to provide a positive solution to the experience of nihilism. In Nietzschean terms, Kirillov cannot at all be qualified as an *Übermensch*, because he is stuck in an obsolete nihilistic consciousness. At the end of the day, history has thus played an odd trick with Nietzsche: where the philosopher himself paid no attention to the *chelovekobog*, nor observed in it any likeness with his own anthropology, Merezhkovskii and his successors saw in the *Übermensch* and Kirillov's *chelovekobog* a "most striking case of coincidence." For a thorough analysis of Nietzsche's notes on *The Devils*, see C.A. Miller (1975).

Nietzsche's formula "Alles ist erlaubt" (id.: 191).[16] Raskol'nikov's reasoning and behavior can be read as the manifestation of the inner struggle between *chelovekobog* and *Bogochelovek* (id.: 211). He also identifies Raskol'nikov's sublimation of the "extraordinary", of the "master" with Nietzsche's *Übermensch* (id.: 195-196). Furthermore, "the Nietzschean credo: all is permitted" is applied to Smerdiakov (id.: 301). Merezhkovskii perceives another analogy in the "metaphysical tedium," formulated both by the devil in his conversation with Ivan Karamazov and by the dwarf ("the spirit of gravity") in the dialogue with Zarathustra (KSA 4: 197ff.). The devil postulates that the earth might have repeated itself a million times (PSS 15: 79), an idea that Merezhkovskii compares with the dwarf's enigmatic reasoning on eternal recurrence (Merezhkovskii [1900-1901] 1995: 132). Yet, in spite of congruities with other Dostoevskian characters,

> the most deep connection of Nietzsche with Dostoevskii reveals itself in Kirillov, as if this character anticipates Nietzsche's basic religious thought of the *Übermensch* (id.: 307).

Merezhkovskii blends Dostoevskii's and Nietzsche's discourse in order to compose his own ideological forum, in which he can work on the contemporary crisis in Russian and Western consciousness. Both provide him with a language through which he can denominate the historical bifurcation between pagan and Christian principles. Nietzsche's thought epitomizes pagan ideology; through his concepts, Merezhkovskii is able to highlight the various phenomena occurring under the banner of the anti-Christian presence in the world. Dostoevskii provides him with the terminology to identify all phenomena that amount to the Christian drive. Both Dostoevskii and Nietzsche supply Merezhkovskii with an ideological and expressive arena in which he can assess the crisis of culture in all its levels and diagnose it as torn between two antithetical proclivities. And what is more, they inspire him to find a solution for the bifurcated culture. In Merezhkovskii's reading, the opposing voices of Dostoevskii and Nietzsche meet at some point, i.e. *chelovekobog* and *Übermensch*. This convergence incites him to dissolve the historical antitheses by joining them together.

---

[16] See chapter 2.

6. Merezhkovskii's new religious consciousness as a way out

Unlike the earlier critics (with the notable exception of Solov'ëv), who immediately brushed aside the *Übermensch* for its anti-Christian bias, Merezhkovskii believes that this concept should be seriously considered with regard to Christianity. *Übermensch* and *chelovekobog* (which are interchangeable in Merezhkovskii's discourse) raise a most fundamental problem in Christian consciousness and underscore the lacunae in historical Christianity. Both withstand the Christian horizon and provide an alternative to it; this is, for Merezhkovskii, the specific merit of both concepts.

Merezhkovskii finds fault with historical Christianity's one-sided glorification of the Spirit as absolutely fleshless. In its deliberate negation of the Flesh, historical Christianity failed to do justice to its pre-Christian legacy which cultivated sensuality and other earthly pleasures. Merezhkovskii discerns in history two stages of humanity, each related to a particular Divine revelation. God made the "First Revelation" in the Old Testament: His revelation is that the whole creation is a unity. The associated "First Humanity" is centered upon the Flesh; without consistent explanation, Merezhkovskii defines this as the predilection in both the Hellenistic and Old Testament world. The "Second Revelation" was made by Christ in the New Testament. He preached a purely spiritual love. This is the "Second Humanity," the Christian world of the "Spirit" in which the emphasis switched from earth to heaven (Rosenthal 1975: 93f.). Christ's message of the Spirit was by his successors (starting with Paul) transformed into a preaching of the primacy of Spirit over Flesh: in historical Christianity, the Flesh was outlawed.

Having pinpointed the deficiencies in historical Christianity and determined to retain the essence of authentic Christianity, Merezhkovskii proposes what he calls, a "supra-historical Christianity" (*sverkhistoricheskoe khristianstvo*) (Merezhkovskii [1900-1901] 1995: 147). This will be established in the "Third Revelation," to be announced by Christ's Second Coming, as prophesied in the Apocalypse. And related to this, a "Third Humanity" will come into being. The authentic Christian model is not grounded in the abnegation of either Flesh or Spirit but is only fully Christian in "the unity of both opposing poles of Christian holiness, the holiness of the Spirit and the holiness of the Flesh" (ibid.). In the new Christian consciousness, the age-old bifurcation of Spirit and Flesh, Christ and Antichrist is to be dissolved by assimilating these antithetical principles into a new synthesis. It is in this regard that Merezhkovskii is incited by Nietzsche who urges his readers to look *beyond* traditional dualistic classifications.

Übermensch and *chelovekobog* greatly contribute to Merezhkovskii's formulation of his neo-Christian model. Both anthropologies challenge the established Christian viewpoint and aspire to offer an alternative to it.[17] They search for meaning outside the Christian framework and in that capacity function for Merezhkovskii as the missing link in the previous Christian doctrine. *Übermensch* and *chelovekobog* epitomize the "new creature" (*novaia tvar'*), the one disregarded in historical Christianity:

> The human is for him [Nietzsche] not the end, not the last link, but merely one of the links in the chain of cosmic development: just like the human came into being out of the transmutation of the animal species, a new being will come out of the transmutation of the human, cultural-historical species. This new being, "the new creature" is the Übermensch; or, like the Russian nihilist expresses with naive cynicism: "from the gorilla till the human, and from the human till the annihilation of God", – until the Chelovekobog (Merezhkovskii [1900-1901] 1995.: 119).

This "new creature" is a reference to 2 Corinthians 5: 17: "So then, if anyone is in Christ, he is a new creation; what is old has passed away, what is new has come." Merezhkovskii maintains that historical Christianity failed to affirm the human as the new creature. *Übermensch* and *chelovekobog*, however, respond to this impulse to overcome the old and instigate the new. By considering the present

---

[17] Merezhkovskii's new version of Christianity is not only made up by the model of Nietzsche's *Übermensch* and Dostoevskii's *chelovekobog* but also by Tolstoi's intellectual legacy. Within Russian Christianity, Tolstoi represents the Flesh and Dostoevskii, the Spirit. As he aspires for the union of *chelovekobog/Übermensch* and *Bogochelovek* for the future of Christianity, he finds that both the philosophies of Tolstoi and Dostoevskii must be reconciled in order to reach a new Christian order: "Should we not look for this future, third and final, decisively beautiful, Russian and world-wide face exactly here, between both the greatest contemporary Russian faces, Tolstoi and Dostoevskii? Therefore we unite them, what we in mystery await: will there not flare up between them, as if between two opposing poles, a spark of that fire, of that lightning, out of which a great fire will burn, and which will be the appearance of the Chelovekobog for the Western World, the Bogochelovek for the Eastern World, and for the two united worlds there will be the One in the two" (Merezhkovskii [1900-1901] 1995: 69).

human to be still incomplete, Nietzsche's anthropology supports Merezhkovskii's idea that present humanity is still stuck in an obsolete consciousness and must be overcome in order to evolve into the "new creature." The *Übermensch* is both the symptom of and the solution for the abyss in front of which current Christian culture stands. He assimilates this irreligious anthropology into his prospective ideal of the new human, in whom the historical Christian conflict between Spirit and Flesh, Christ and Antichrist is overcome:

> "The human is something, that should be overcome", says Zarathustra. Only after having overcome, after having killed both in spirit and flesh the *"human all too human"* (*chelovecheskoe, slishkom chelovecheskoe*), only after having shed away the flesh of the "human of the Old Testament" (*vetkhii chelovek*) as an old and dead skin with the wisdom of animal and snake, the human can reach the divine essence, for whom there is "a new heaven and a new earth." Only after having been passed away, after having been returned to dust, he can resurrect in immortality (ibid.).

Nietzsche's anthropological imperative to overcome (*überwinden*) the "human, all too human" is fused with the Christian doctrine on the death and resurrection of Christ and the related apocalyptic idea of the resurrection of all humankind. In Merezhkovskii's discourse, both biblical and Nietzschean metaphors (the snake as Zarathustra's companion) are merged together.[18] In a mythopoetic process – in which the conflicting dialogue with Nietzsche is obvious – Merezhkovskii assimilates and rephrases two antithetical anthropological paradigms into his new Christian ideal of Third Humanity.

Besides fulfilling the criteria for a new Christian anthropology, *Übermensch* and *chelovekobog* take part in Merezhkovskii's reformulation of historical Christology to an even greater extent. In Merezhkovskii's opinion, Nietzsche and Kirillov touch upon one of the main failures in the historical view on Christ, specifically its approach to Christ's fleshly nature. In its preoccupation

---

[18] On his quest to the *Übermensch*, Zarathustra is accompanied by his animals, the eagle and the snake (KSA 4: 27). The whole book is populated by various snake images. In "The vision and the enigma," the shepherd is suffocating because a great black snake has crawled into his throat; this metaphor hints at the nauseating idea of the eternal recurrence (KSA 4: 197). In "The pale criminal," the snake is evil incarnate (KSA 4: 45). In "The ugliest man," Zarathustra enters a desert valley, devoid of any life, called "serpent-death" (KSA 4: 327).

to develop a doctrine that is exclusively centered upon the Spirit, whereby any earthly joy is labeled as sinful, historical Christianity has systematically made Christ's physical nature subordinate to his divine, spiritual nature. For Merezhkovskii, Nietzsche's and Kirillov's merit lies in the fact that they re-open the debate on Christ's material and hence mortal nature. In Kirillov's version of Christ's crucifixion, Christ's promise of resurrection turned out to be in vain.[19] In like manner, Nietzsche thinks of Christ as a mortal human whose all too common death could not be accepted by his followers; both challenge the dogma of Christ's resurrection (Merezhkovskii [1900-1901] 1995: 307).[20] What is more, *Übermensch* and *chelovekobog* reveal a very important aspect of Christ's personality which was excluded in historical Christianity, i.e. his Fleshly nature. Especially the *Übermensch* is a corrective to what Merezhkovskii experiences as the most pressing flaw in historical Christology. In his anthropology, Nietzsche attempted to revive the Dionysian emphasis on the joys and pleasures of earthly life. For Merezhkovskii, the *Übermensch* originated in the pagan sphere around Dionysus and hence reawakens the characteristic celebration of earthly life: the *Übermensch* incorporates the Dionysian life-affirmation (*Lebensbejahung*), orgiastic ecstasy, and cult of sensuality and beauty that is suppressed in historical Christianity. In Merezhkovskii's typical discourse, the *Übermensch*'s exaltation of the "Flesh" offers the required counterbalance to historical Christianity's exclusive devotion to the "Spirit." Revaluing the Dionysian craving for earthly pleasures, the *Übermensch* re-installs the pagan principle of the "Flesh." Merezhkovskii will draw from Nietzsche's Dionysian *Übermensch* to supplement the historical Christological representation of Christ as purely and exclusively spiritual. He also uses the *chelovekobog* – to a lesser degree – to formulate his amendments to historical Christology.

---

[19] "There was a day on earth, and in the middle of the earth stood three crosses. One at the cross already believed what he said to the other: "Today you will be with me in paradise." The day came to an end, they both died, departed and found neither paradise, nor resurrection. His words did not come true" (PSS 10: 471).

[20] Merezhkovskii quotes here from *The Antichrist*: "The catastrophe of the evangel was decided with death -, it was attached to the "cross" ... Only the death, this unexpected, disgraceful death, only the cross which was generally reserved for the rabble - only this horrible paradox confronted the disciples with the real riddle: "*Who was this? What was this?*" [...] And from now on an absurd problem emerged: "How *could* God permit this?" (KSA 6: 213f.).

The merit of both *Übermensch* and *chelovekobog* is in their role as inverted paradigms of traditional Christology. For Merezhkovskii, these anthropologies are essentially embedded in a worldview that overthrows any notion of a metaphysical godhead or transcendent reality, and aims to revalue earthly life at the core of its religious deliberations. *Übermensch* and *chelovekobog* dismiss the idea of spiritual resurrection, but instead champion physical transfiguration. In this capacity, both concepts reveal what is lacking in established Christology, i.e., the consideration of Christ's Flesh. Merezhkovskii claims that in historical Christianity this aspect of Christ's nature is consequently neglected for the sake of making the Spirit predominant. The historical negation of the Flesh reduced Christ to a mere "dead Jew" (Merezhkovskii [1900-1901] 1995: 307). By spotlighting the "Flesh," "Kirillov and Nietzsche were so close to Christ, like no one in history before" (id.: 321).

Merezhkovskii blends historical Christology and *Übermensch/chelovekobog* to formulate his Christology of the "new religious consciousness" that will come into being in the Third Revelation and will re-install and revalue the authentic personality of Christ. In the personality of Christ – which will be revealed by the Second Coming – Spirit and Flesh, Christianity and paganism will be reunited: He "will possess the new Flesh, that will not suffer, not die, imperishable" (id.: 317). Christ is equally divine and human, spiritual and material; His resurrection was a resurrection not merely of the soul, but also of the body. Historical Christianity's exclusive emphasis on the resurrection of the soul does not do justice to the genuine personality of Christ, who resurrected physically and overcame mortality and death, the most significant human limitations.[21] In Merezhkovskii's view, Nietzsche's *Übermensch* is a reanimation of this neglected aspect of Christ's total nature and in this capacity fills the gap in historical Christology. The *Übermensch* matches the physical or "fleshly" half of Christ and highlights its resurrection; the *Übermensch* celebrates the cult of the "Resurrected Flesh" (*Voskresshaia Plot'*):

---

[21] Solov'ëv had a similar appreciation of Christ as the One conquering death, but he did not carry it to Merezhkovskii's conclusion of the Resurrection of the Flesh.

The empire of the *Übermensch*, heralded by Zarathustra, is "the future Jerusalem", the empire of the Resurrected Flesh, as prophesied in the Apocalypse: *"they will reign on the earth"* (id.: 317).[22]

The Christ of the Second Coming will announce a Christianity of Resurrected Spirit (*Voskresshii Dukh*) *and* Resurrected Flesh (*Voskresshaia Plot'*). This is, according to Merezhkovskii, prophesied in 1 Corinthians 15: 51-52: "we will not all sleep, but we will all be changed. In a moment, in the twinkling of an eye, at the last trumpet. For the trumpet will sound, and the dead will be raised imperishable and we will be changed."

In Merezhkovskii's Christology, Flesh and Spirit are not two antagonizing or disparate truths but instead they become one single and coherent truth in a process of productive interaction. In the authentic personality of Christ, the oneness of Spirit and Flesh is affirmed. In giving humanity His Flesh to eat and His blood to drink, Christ proved that

> the sacrament of our God is not only the sacrament of the spirit and the word, but also of the flesh and the blood, because our Word became Flesh (*Slovo nashe stalo Plot'*). "Who does not eat My flesh and does not drink My blood, he does not have eternal life". Therefore, not without the flesh, but through the flesh to that which is beyond the flesh: here is the greatest symbol, the greatest joining (Merezhkovskii [1900-1901] 1995: 21).[23]

By combining two antithetical phenomena, Merezhkovskii arrives at an innovating religious syncretism. In his view, "the teaching of Kirillov and Nietzsche coincide with Christ's teaching" (id.: 316). He compares both seemingly opposing paradigms with two triangles, the one facing the top upwards, the other downwards. One of them should only be "turned upside down" in order to make them congruent, for the difference is not in their "interior essence" but only in their "exterior, temporary, historical condition" (ibid.). Merezhkovskii rotates one of the triangles so that they are both perfectly congruous:

> And thus [...] the seemingly anti-Christian teaching of Kirillov and Nietzsche concurs with the teaching of Christ [...] this is a geometric axiom (ibid.).

---

[22] Revelation 5: 10.

[23] This is an inverse of John 6: 54: "The one who eats my flesh and drinks my blood has eternal life."

The Christ of the Second Coming, or the authentic Christ, incorporates both the Christian principle of the Spirit/*Bogochelovek* and the anti-Christian principle of the Flesh/*Übermensch*/*chelovekobog*. The worth of each principle is not in their being *per se*, but in the transactionality between them: the two opposing forces only come into full being by the dialectical and ongoing countering of one another. The bifurcation is to be continually dissolved in a synthesis. Merezhkovskii's new religious consciousness wavers between Christianity and paganism: it proposes to combine the metaphysics of Christianity and the earthly values of paganism in a higher synthesis that is consistent with each of them but at the same time goes beyond them. He rejects the rigid Christology of historical Christianity but discovers the authentic Christ whom he views as a Christian successor of paganism.

The authentic Christ bears traits of the Dionysian *Übermensch*. Merezhkovskii believes that God would not have sent his Son to save a world that is completely sinful and evil and thus concludes that the pagan values of the Flesh are not as aberrant as historical Christianity used to label them. Instead of discarding the Flesh, Christ celebrates and exalts earthly life: in the personality of Christ the pagan values of sensuality and earthly beauty are sanctified and the Flesh becomes holy. Moreover, the authentic Christ rejects the moralistic rigidity of historical Christianity and embodies what Nietzsche glorifies as an individualistic morality "beyond good and evil":

> Yes, Christ is not a moral phenomenon, but a religious, supra-moral (*sverkhnravstvennoe*, in the sense of 'beyond the moral') phenomenon, *transgressing* all limits and barriers of the moral law, a phenomenon of the greatest freedom *"beyond good and evil"* (Merezhkovskii [1900-1901] 1995: 219).

Christ represents what Merezhkovskii calls "the final freedom" (*poslednaia svoboda*). Christ is the supreme individualist that Nietzsche aims at in his anthropology of the *Übermensch* and endorses the idea that "all is permitted" (*vsë pozvoleno*), in its most radical ramifications formulated by Ivan Karamazov, or in Merezhkovskii's wording, "the gift of the chelovekobog, the

Antichrist" (id.: 218).[24] And for Merezhkovskii, the concept of this final freedom as seemingly belonging to the anti-Christian proclivity is a basic feature of Christ's personality. Christ stands beyond established morality, and is therefore the authentic religious personality. He impersonates both the Christian and anti-Christian principle: Christ and Antichrist are one from the beginning, and are the offspring of the same God "from that moment on, when was said: "I and the Father are one" (id.: 302).[25] Historical Christianity, while mainly engaged in providing humanity with clear-cut definitions of 'good and evil,' ignored the initial oneness of them and imposed upon humanity an artificial ethical dualism.

Merezhkovskii needs the anti-Christian model of Nietzsche's *Übermensch* and Dostoevskii's *chelovekobog* to infuse Christianity with a Dionysian vigor. The Christianity of the Third Testament does not deny earthly life, but instead affirms and glorifies it. It does not teach a slave morality, but a morality beyond good and evil.

However useful, even indispensable, in his thinking out of the new religious consciousness and although identified as epitomizing the historically neglected half of Christ's authentic personality, in Merezhkovskii's final analysis *Übermensch* and *chelovekobog* eventually diverge from Christ's path. They connect with Christ in the sense that they represent the Flesh and thus complement Christ's spiritual nature. At this point, *chelovekobog/Übermensch* and *Bogochelovek* meet. Yet in the final outcome, both concepts lead to a path which is different from the Christian one because they rigidly cling on to their atheism and renounce any merit in the Christian worldview. Upon the path that *Übermensch* and *chelovekobog* have chosen, one can only perish because once one is so close to the Christian truth, but holds on to the assertion that there is no God, one is inevitably doomed to mental and spiritual loss. Kirillov and Nietzsche could have been saved if they had finally accepted the

---

[24] Merezhkovskii finds proof for his assertion that Christ possesses the final freedom in the bible. He refers to 2 Corinthians 3: 17 "Now the Lord is the Spirit, and where the Spirit of the Lord is present, there is freedom"; Romans 4: 15 "For the law brings wrath, because where there is no law there is no transgression either"; Galatians 2: 16 "yet we know that no one is justified by the works of the law but by the faithfulness of Jesus Christ. And we have come to believe in Christ Jesus, so that we may be justified by the faithfulness of Christ and not by the works of the law, because by the works of the law no one will be justified." (Merezhkovskii [1900-1901] 1995: 218).

[25] See John 10: 30: "The Father and I are one."

inescapable connection of their truth to Christ's teachings; yet they closed their eyes to it and consequently perished, Kirillov in suicide and Nietzsche, "this titan of Zarathustra and Antichrist," in madness (id.: 321). Madness or suicide is the only way out for one who senses the Christian truth yet does not accept it.[26] Christ affirmed his anti-Christian side and acknowledged it as an equal truth. Nietzsche and Kirillov, though, failed to comprehend the counterpart to their truth and scorned it. Merezhkosvkij offers two choices:

> We should either accept Him, but until the end, accept that He and the Father are one; and then we don't march onto that road, on which Kirillov and Nietzsche perished; then for us, the One who has come and the One who is coming (*Prishedshii i Griadushchii*), Bogochelovek and Chelovekobog are one; or we should reject Him, but once again reject until the end, and then it is inevitable that, returned to the basic principle of Kirillov and Nietzsche, we will walk upon that horrible road, upon which they only started: "if there is no God, then I am God" (ibid.).

7. Merezhkovskii's quotation of Nietzsche: reconstructing Nietzsche's tracks

In Merezhkovskii's reading, the *Übermensch* is above all identified with the *chelovekobog*. The link between *Übermensch* and *chelovekobog* is already established in the introduction to *L. Tolstoi i Dostoevskii*: "how could we not recognize the *Chelovekobog* in the *Übermensch*?" (Merezhkovskii [1900-1901] 1995: 9). The association is primarily made on the basis of what he perceives to be a similar discourse on the status of God and its ramifications for anthropological consciousness. In the course of his critical study, Merezhkovskii discusses, at length, the affiliation between Kirillov's representation of the *chelovekobog* and Nietzsche's argumentation on the *Übermensch*, and he also mentions similarities between the latter and the line of thought developed by Ivan's devil.

In this section, firstly, I document Merezhkovskii's quotes from and references to Nietzsche's texts, as deployed in his explanation of the *Übermensch*. Secondly, I describe the quotes from

---

[26] By explaining Nietzsche's madness and Kirillov's suicide as the inevitable outcome of their unwillingness to recognize God, Merezhkovskii returns to the Apocalyptic idea that all apostates will be punished in the end.

Kirillov's and the devil's discourse on the *chelovekobog* that Merezhkovskii uses to define this concept. By this approach, I aim to discover and explain which specific lines from Nietzsche's discourse on the *Übermensch* triggered Merezhkovskii to associate this idea with the *chelovekobog*. An analysis of these lines will reveal how Merezhkovskii at times modified Nietzsche's speech to make it correspond to the typical discourse on the *chelovekobog*, and ultimately fit both into his own ideological constellation of Christ and Antichrist.

For his understanding of Nietzsche's *Übermensch* and the identification with the *chelovekobog*, Merezhkovskii, for the most part, draws on quotes from *Thus spoke Zarathustra* (1883-1885; the fourth part was not published until 1892) and on aphorism 125 in *The Gay Science* (1882), i.e., "The madman" (*Der tolle Mensch*).[27]

One of the first correlations he observes is between Kirillov's and Nietzsche's pronouncements on the absence of God and its implications for the human condition. When Merezhkovskii reproduces primary quotes on *chelovekobog* and *Übermensch*, he seems to make no distinction between Kirillov's and Nietzsche's voice, as if both concepts are completely synonymous and as it were, formulated by the same author. This blending results in a confusing argumentation in which Nietzsche's sayings are presented as Kirillov's and *vice versa*: "Who says this? Again Kirillov? No, Friedrich Nietzsche" (Merezhkovskii [1900-1901] 1995: 119). Another area of confusion is that he does not distinguish between Zarathustra and the madman operating as narrative voices on the one hand and Nietzsche on the other hand. When quoting from Zarathustra and "the madman," these specific voices are presented as Nietzsche's.

For his identification of *chelovekobog* and *Übermensch* Merezhkovskii compares "quotes" from both Kirillov's and Nietzsche's speech. Firstly, he compares their alleged claims that God does not exist, and the ramifications of this for the future of human consciousness. More particularly, Kirillov's saying

> Сознать, что нет Бога, и не сознать в тот же раз, что сам Богом стал — есть нелепость, иначе непременно убьешь себя сам (To recognize that

---

[27] The quotes in Merezhkovskii's text are presented in Russian translation; some of the quotes are borrowed from Lev Shestov's study *Dobro v uchenii gr. L. Tolstogo i Fr. Nitsshe* (1899) (Merezhkovskii 1995 : 118).

there is no God, and not to recognize at the same time, that one has oneself become a God, is an absurdity, otherwise you will certainly kill yourself) [and] если нет бога, то я бог (if there is no god, then I am god) (PSS 10: 470f.)

is equated to "Nietzsche's" dictum

Если есть Бог, то как же вынесу я мысль, что этот Бог не я (If there is a God, how will I endure the thought, that this God is not me) (Merezhkovskii [1900-1901] 1995: 118).

This line is in fact a biased translation of Zarathustra's saying in "On the happy isles": "*wenn* es Götter gäbe, wie hielte ich's aus, kein Gott zu sein (*if* there were gods, how could I endure it, not to be a god)" (KSA 4: 110). The Russian translation obviously represents another rationale than the German original. For one thing, in the Russian phrase God is singular, whereas in Zarathustra's discourse, reference is made to gods in general, i.e., all gods as objects of worship in the history of humanity. In the Russian translation, Zarathustra's specific wording is modified in order to match Kirillov's pronouncement which is centered only upon the Christian God. Moreover, in the original text, this phrase is part of a syllogism:

Aber dass ich euch ganz mein Herz offenbare, ihr Freunde: *wenn* es Götter gäbe, wie hielte ich's aus, kein Gott zu sein! *Also* giebt es keine Götter (But that I reveal my heart entirely to you, my friends: *if* there were gods, how could I endure it, not to be a god! *Therefore*, there are no gods) (KSA 4: 110).

When reading the syllogism, one grows aware of a missing link in the line of thought. It is in fact an enthymeme. The reader is directed to conclude that the silent premise is that one *can* endure not to be a god, from which follows, via *modus tolens*, the logical conclusion that there are no gods. Why did the author omit this highly significant premise, i.e., 'I do endure it', from this aphorism? For one thing, he aimed to preclude that the words 'gods' (even in a negation) and 'I' should appear in the same text. Nietzsche felt that the human's emancipation from the gods was not a mere psychological process, but was also to occur equally in the experience of language because language is the sole instrument to communicate ideas. Present language is contaminated with metaphysical categories, yet since it is the sole mode of communication available, one must turn to rhetorical strategies to overthrow the traditional experience of language. If the word 'gods' and 'human' appear side by side in a text, then the category 'human' is affected because the human is paradigmatically and syntagmatically subordinated to the gods. Therefore, in this specific text which explicitly centers upon the gods, Nietzsche keeps silent about the human, as if to protect the human from a juxtaposition with the gods. The missing premise for the sake of the human is formally anticipated in the text during Zarathustra's democratic address to the audience ("But that I reveal my heart entirely to you, my friends"), in which the use of "heart" and "friends" especially points to an equalizing tendency. In the text, the human is obliterated yet reappears on a meta-level: the ellipse invites the reader to consider and fill in the missing link, and in this way to complete the syllogism. Through the intentional omission of the second premise, the author compels the reader to take an active part in this highly significant line of thought and to draw the ethical conclusion himself, instead of handing it over on a silver plate. This intended reader's function, i.e., the reader as an operating consciousness within the text, characterizes the text as a writerly text. As I see it, the author's handing over of ethical authority to the reader (who becomes an active co-thinker and co-author of the text) is a stylistic and ideological implementation of what Nietzsche intends with his anthropology. In the specific excerpt, the impulse for overthrowing the notion 'gods' emanates from the human. That the human can endure not to be a god should no longer occur in language and thought. The human is the primordial agent in the dismissal of the gods. Hence, the central status of the human in Nietzsche's anthropology, as the only one who can produce an overturn in anthropological and ethical consciousness, is reflected in the author's strategic enthymeme.

However, in Merezhkovskii's version of Zarathustra's saying, the conclusion "*therefore* there are no gods" is omitted. I take this to be a deliberate omission, or at least one that is consistent with Merezhkovskii's main religio-philosophical concerns. Whereas the missing premise in the original text directs the reader towards (and thereby stresses) the notion that there are no gods, the exclusion in Merezhkovskii's version clearly shifts the focus of attention towards the human's self-deification. As a matter of fact, Merezhkovskii almost turns the argument upside down. The original text deploys the allegedly unbearable thought that one is not a god to infer that there are none. By leaving out the conclusion, however, Merezhkovskii obscures a core postulation in Zarathustra's line of thought, i.e., that the human *can* endure not to be a god. In his version of Zarathustra's saying, one is led to infer from Zarathustra's conditional statement that it is unbearable not to be a god. After all, this need for self-deification is the central point of Kirillov's antinomy that it doesn't make sense to dismiss God without becoming oneself a god. So Merezhkovskii retains from Zarathustra's line of thought what he can match to Kirillov's argument on self-deification.

Merezhkovskii presents another excerpt from Nietzsche by which he aims to support his identification of Kirillov and Nietzsche:

> Бога нет, Бог умер. И мы его убили. — Не должны ли мы сами обратиться в богов? — Никогда не было совершено дела, более великого, и кто родится после нас, этим самым будет принадлежать к истории высшей, чем вся прежняя история (Merezhkovskii [1900-1901] 1995: 118-119).

These lines are adopted from the aphorism "The madman," in *The Gay Science*:

> Gott ist todt! Gott bleibt todt. Und wir haben ihn getödtet [...] Müssen wir nicht selber zu Göttern werden [...] Es gab nie ein grössere That, - und wer nur immer nach uns geboren wird, gehört um dieser That willen in eine höhere Geschichte, als alle Geschichte bisher war! (God is dead! God remains dead. And we have killed him [...] Must we ourselves not become gods? [...] There has never been a greater deed, - and whoever is born after us, he will, for the sake of this deed, belong to a higher history than all history hitherto) (KSA 3: 481).

There are some nuances in the Russian translation. The original "God is dead! God remains dead" is rendered as "There is no God, God has died." Furthermore, from the entire aphorism, Merezhkovskii selects only lines that can be matched to Kirillov's wording. In the original text, the madman confronts the people on the market with their active part in the killing of God (*"We have killed him* – you and I! All of us are his murderers") and with the ramifications of this murder for the future of humanity ("Whither we are moving? [...] Are we not plunging continually? And backward, sideward, forward, in all directions? [...] Are we not straying as through an infinite nothing?") (KSA 3: 480f.). He wonders whether humanity will be able to endure the burden of this act: "How shall we comfort ourselves, the murderers of all murderers? The holiest and mightiest of all that the world has yet owned, has bled to death under our knives, – who will wipe this blood off us?" How is humanity to acquiesce in the responsibility it bears for the murder of God and overcome the spiritual emptiness this will bring about? What sacred idols are to be erected to clear humanity's conscience and return it its spiritual rest? Can humanity live out the consequences of this act? ("Is not the greatness of this deed too great for us? "). And finally, "Must we ourselves not become gods, simply to appear worthy of this deed [i.e. the murder of God]?"

This specific phrase, as highlighted by Merezhkovskii as an incentive for self-deification, is in the original text embedded in a larger context than reported by Merezhkovskii. In his version, the second part of the original phrase ("to appear worthy of this deed") is left out. This omission renders an ambivalence to the rest of the quote because "the greater deed" can then simultaneously refer to the killing of God ("we have killed him") and to the idea that we ourselves should become gods. Note that, under the alternative interpretation, i.e., if "the greater deed" refers to the human's deification, the bottom line of the sentence changes ("There has never been a greater deed, – and whoever is born after us, he will, for the sake of this deed, belong to a higher history than all history hitherto"). The idea is that the event of the humans becoming gods, and not the act of deicide, will turn out to be a key moment in human history and lead humanity into a new era. Merezhkovskii apparently reads the madman's statement in that way, for he links this to Kirillov's claim that his deliberate suicide will bring about an overturn in human history:

> тогда — новый человек, тогда — все новое. Тогда историю будут делить на две части: от гориллы до уничтожения Бога и от уничтожения Бога до перемены земли и человека физически (Then there will be a new human, then everything will be new. Then they will divide history in two parts: from the gorilla to the annihilation of God, and from the annihilation of God [...] to the transformation of the earth and of the human physically, PSS 10: 94) (Merezhkovskii [1900-1901] 1995: 119).

Furthermore, Merezhkovskii equals the latter quote with "Nietzsche's" wording:

> сверхчеловек отделен от человека большею физическою пропастью, чем обезьяна от человека (the *Übermensch* is separated from the human by a larger physical abyss, than the ape from the human) (id.: 317).

This phrase, as presented in Merezhkovskii's text, is a biased and severely modified paraphrase of a fragment of Zarathustra's saying in the third preface, in which he delivers the first public speech on the *Übermensch* (KSA 4: 14f.). In this section, Zarathustra attempts to explain the anthropology of the *Übermensch* to the people assembled on the market place ("*I teach you the Übermensch*"). He presents to his audience neither a positive characterization nor a normative definition of what the concept of the *Übermensch* actually implies; instead, he explains the *Übermensch* in terms of what it should *not* be, i.e., in antinomy to the current human condition. The *Übermensch* is the one who exceeds the human, who goes *beyond* (*über*) the present human. The appearance of the *Übermensch* requires that the human is overcome: "Der Mensch ist Etwas, das überwunden werden soll (the human is something, that should be overcome)". To support and substantiate this thesis, Zarathustra proceeds in a rationale on the evolution of all living beings up to the present. He observes in the world and in all creatures a natural inclination towards progress: "Alle Wesen bisher schufen Etwas über sich hinaus (all beings hitherto have created something beyond themselves)." Evolution is not conceived of as a purely mechanical process that operates even without active participation of the living entities involved. Rather, living beings *create* (*schaffen*) beyond themselves, and are thus themselves the generators of evolution. Like other creatures in the evolutionary process, the human is a transition, a passageway towards another mode of being and should therefore create itself into something that is beyond itself. The human is distinct from all previous creatures because his creating is not an instinctive process, but a conscious one. Hence, the human can consciously decide whether to outgrow himself or to stagnate in his current status. Humankind has the potential to instigate the tide (*Fluth*) of this great wave towards the *Übermensch*, yet is by its nature more liable to oppose progress than to induce it. In that sense, humanity represents an ebb, a reversal to previous forms of life: "and you want to be the ebb of that great tide and rather return to the animals, than to overcome the human?" The hallmark of humanity is that the human does have the *will* to overcome himself; without this perpetual ability to overcome, i.e., to create *beyond* oneself, the human regresses to the animals, who lack the conscious motivation to overcome themselves.

At this point, Zarathustra confronts the audience with life forms preceding the human:

> Was ist der Affe für den Menschen? Ein Gelächter oder eine schmerzliche Scham. Und ebendas soll der Mensch für den Übermenschen sein: ein Gelächter oder eine schmerzliche Scham. Ihr habt den Weg vom Wurme zum Menschen gemacht, und Vieles ist in euch noch Wurm. Einst wart ihr Affen, und auch jetzt noch ist der Mensch mehr Affe, als irgend ein Affe.

> (What is the ape to the human? A laughing-stock or a painful shame. And just the same will be the human to the *Übermensch*: A laughing-stock or a painful shame. You have made your way from worm to human, and much within you is still worm. Once you were apes, and even now the human is more of an ape, than any ape) (KSA 4: 14).

When looking back to the evolutionary process, in which the simians represent an earlier life form than the human being, the human's reaction is ambivalent. On the one hand, the human cannot but laugh, for he observes how many human characteristics are already anticipated in these animals. Yet on the other hand, the sight of the simians confronts the human with how many ape-like traits are still in him and this fills him with painful shame. And as Zarathustra maintains, a similar ambivalent response, both laughter and shame, will come over the *Übermensch* when he beholds present humankind. The human already carries the potential for the *Übermensch*, i.e., the ability to continually overcome himself, and this will trigger a tender laugh in the *Übermensch*. Yet although the *Übermensch* has created himself beyond the human being, many human features will still be in the *Übermensch* and this will arouse shame in him.

For Zarathustra, the reconsideration of past evolution should be a form of self-criticism and a constant impulse to create and re-create oneself. He observes, however, that many humans have not yet made any progress in the overcoming of the apes or even worse, in outgrowing the worms.[28] If the present human has not yet created himself beyond the worms and the apes and is thus still in some way stuck in these previous life forms, at what point, as Zarathustra wonders, will the human create beyond himself towards the *Übermensch*?

---

[28] In one of the preliminary notes to *Thus spoke Zarathustra* (November 1882-February 1883), the human is defined as "Überaffe," implying that he is in fact something beyond the ape, yet just as much still too ape-like (KSA 10: 160).

In Zarathustra's account, the appearance of the *Übermensch* requires that the present human creates beyond himself. The *Übermensch* is in that sense a being that evolves from the human being, yet not in terms of mechanical evolution or natural selection. Evolution is a process of perpetual self-overcoming, which cannot occur without the active participation of the creatures involved. The succeeding line 'worm-ape-human-*Übermensch*' is not formulated in scientific or biological terms; instead, it is a progressive process of beings creating new modes of being beyond themselves.

In Merezhkovskii's reduced and biased paraphrase of this specific text from Zarathustra's discourse, i.e., "the *Übermensch* is separated from the human by a larger physical abyss, than the ape from the human," Nietzsche's anthropology is presented as a more perfected form in biological evolution. Whereas in Zarathustra's texst, no allusion is made to possible physical mutations, Merezhkovskii understands from these lines that the *Übermensch* is a being that is physically modified, and more importantly, that this corporeal change (or even improvement) is what makes up the hallmark of the *Übermensch*. The Russian author understands the succession of 'worm-ape-human-*Übermensch*' in a Darwinian context. He reads Zarathustra's line of thought as a biological evolutionary theory: the humans descend from the primates, and likewise will the *Übermensch* develop from present humankind. Yet as Merezhkovskii holds, the *Übermensch* is physically more distinct from the human than the human is from his ape-like ancestor; this establishes the emergence of the *Übermensch* in the evolutionary process as a more significant event than even the appearance of humanity.

This highly modified version of the original text attests once again to Merezhkovskii's reading of the *Übermensch* as being filtered through Kirillov's rationale of the *chelovekobog*. In Merezhkovskii's text, "Nietzsche's" alleged wording is explicitly associated with quotes from Kirillov's discourse on the requirement for physical transformation (see PSS 10: 94 & 450) and is, in particular, connected to Kirillov's pronouncement that the appearance of the *chelovekobog* will bring about a cosmic upheaval, after which human history will be split up in two parts: "from the gorilla to the annihilation of God, and from the annihilation of God [...] to the transformation of the earth and of man physically" (PSS 10: 94) (Merezhkovskii [1900-1901] 1995: 317). Kirillov believes that the appearance of the *chelovekobog* will bring about a radical overturn in the evolutionary process, and he therefore locates his idea in nineteenth- century scientific evolutionary discourse, which centers on the human's ape ancestry. With the obliteration of God, present human species cannot but disappear; the end of God entails the end of the evolutionary process from the primate to the human. From that point on, a new phase in evolution will dawn: this is the era of the *chelovekobog*, in which the human and the whole earth will be physically transformed.

So, Merezhkovskii's association of *Übermensch* and *chelovekobog* as anthropological paradigms that champion physical mutation, is in fact based on a kind of conceptual blend. He projects the physical transformation, which is postulated by Kirillov, onto Nietzsche's scheme, thereby embedding Nietzsche's anthropology in Darwinian evolutionist theory. The metaphorical deployment of the ape in Zarathustra's discourse (added to the link with Kirillov's evolutionary scheme) might have triggered Merezhkovskii to read the *Übermensch* from a Darwinian perspective.[29]

Merezhkovskii's identification of *chelovekobog* and *Übermensch* is, as far as the *chelovekobog* is concerned, primarily based on Kirillov's line of thought. Yet he also refers to the rationale formulated by Ivan's devil, and the supposed similarities this bears with Nietzsche's anthropology. In the first place, the link between Nietzsche and Ivan's devil is substantiated through Kirillov's basic imperative for self-deification, i.e., "if there is no god, then I am god." Merezhkovskii observes the same logic in the devil's saying that for an overturn in ethics and anthropological consciousness, "надо всего только разрушить в человечестве идею о боге" ("all that must be destroyed in humankind is the idea of God", PSS 15: 83) and in the madman's exclamation that "we have killed God" (Merezhkovskii [1900-1901] 1995: 314). So the keystone for Merezhkovskii's identification of *Übermensch* and *chelovekobog* is Kirillov's scheme,

---

[29] Nineteenth-century science and mentality were permeated with Darwinian and other evolutionist theories (Haeckel's and Spencer's among others). In fact, Nietzsche anticipated and opposed a Darwinist interpretation of the *Übermensch*. When in *Ecce Homo* speaking of the *Übermensch*, he refers to Darwinist readers as "learned cattle" (KSA 6: 300). In my opinion, the genealogical scheme 'Wurm-Affe-Mensch' in the specific text is rather meant to parody Darwin and to put the unobservant reader on the wrong track.

which is then implemented onto the devil's formulations on the *chelovekobog*.[30]

Furthermore, Merezhkovskii refers twice to Zarathustra's wording "the human is something, that should be overcome" (KSA 4: 14): "Человек есть то, что надо преодолеть" (Merezhkovskii [1900-1901] 1995: 119; 350). He reads this line as a prophecy about the end of humanity as foretold in the Apocalypse. The present human must be overcome in order for the new human to appear, who unites the new flesh and the new spirit (id.: 119). In that sense, it is a sign of our becoming Christ-like (id.: 350).

Merezhkovskii's references to and quotes from Nietzsche's original texts reveal that he reads the *Übermensch* primarily through the established link with the *chelovekobog*, in particular as outlined by Kirillov. He draws from Nietzsche what he can relate to Kirillov's discourse. He mainly focuses on fragments in which the main issues are the overcoming of God and the epochal significance of this act for humanity. In fact, he reduces Nietzsche's complex rationale on the *Übermensch* to Kirillov's basic formula: "if there is no god, then I am god." Moreover, obviously triggered by Kirillov's claim that the *chelovekobog* requires physical transformation, he reads in Nietzsche's *Übermensch* an equal incentive for physical modification. Merezhkovskii thus appropriates the *Übermensch* as a paradigm for self-deification, which is exactly at the core of Kirillov's idea of the *chelovekobog*.

8. The vicissitudes of Dostoevskii and Nietzsche

The established connection between *chelovekobog* and *Übermensch* provides Merezhkovskii with an ideological lexicon to describe the flaws of historical Christianity and to formulate an alternative to it. Moreover, the identification of *chelovekobog* and *Übermensch* serves as a catalyst for other reconsiderations and reformulations: in the

---

[30] Another correlation is observed between Nietzsche's idea of the "eternal recurrence" (*vechnoe vozvrashchenie*) and Ivan's devil's statement that the "present earth might have repeated itself a million times" (PSS 15: 79) (Merezhkovskii [1900-1901] 1995: 132). With regard to Nietzsche's doctrine, Merezhkovskii refers to Zarathustra's encounter with the dwarf, as related in the section "The Vision and the Enigma" in the third part of *Thus spoke Zarathustra* (KSA 4: 197f.).

introduction to this chapter, I pinpointed a cluster of explicit changes, in particular with regard to the prevailing responses to Dostoevskii and Nietzsche, which all occur around the turn of the last century. I will now argue that the shifts mentioned above are, at least partially, initiated by Merezhkovskii, and that they are inextricably linked to his identification of *chelovekobog* and *Übermensch*.[31]

8.1. Towards an affirmative assessment of Nietzsche

In Russian critical literature on Nietzsche before 1900, the main attitude towards the philosopher and his ideas was one of renouncement. Except for Preobrazhenskii's and Mikhailovskii's responses, the critics evaluated Nietzsche unfavorably for his alleged subversive views on morality and for his hostile approach to Christianity.[32] In the mid-1890s Vladimir Solov'ëv focused on Nietzsche's anthropology of the *Übermensch* and observed in it a faint religious desire to transcend present humanity and to realize a more perfected human condition. In that sense, he saw in the *Übermensch* an obscured reflection of his own religious anthropology. Yet Solov'ëv could not reconcile himself with the godless tenor of the *Übermensch* and opposed this concept to his Christian ideal of the *Bogochelovek*. In his later discourse, the *Übermensch* is, albeit implicitly, associated with the Antichrist.[33] In the first decade of the reception process, Nietzsche is received as a rigid counter-paradigm against which the critics antagonistically react. In none of these interpretations are the philosopher's ideas assimilated in the Russian intellectual context.

---

[31] Some other historical factors may have contributed to the shifts in the reading of Dostoevskii and Nietzsche. Nietzsche died in 1900, and this might have stimulated a more considerate approach to his works. The death of Solov'ëv in the same year likewise aroused a renewed interest in his works, and most probably in his response to Nietzsche (considering the temporal proximity of their deaths). As explained in chapter 4, Solov'ëv was the first to excavate religious aspirations in Nietzsche. His death might have triggered the new generation of religious thinkers to indulge in this religious motive in Nietzsche. Moreover, the shifts were probably in part determined by the *fin de siècle* climate, in which the intelligentsia sought to redefine established values. It is my viewpoint, however, that Merezhkovskii had a salient part in these shifts and I limit my research to his contribution.

[32] See chapter 2.

[33] See chapter 4.

Merezhkovskii's understanding of and response to Nietzsche marks a shift in the reception process. For one thing, his interpretation of the philosopher is definitely more favorable than the previous ones. And for another thing, his account of the philosopher's ideas is no longer confined to mere criticism. Nietzsche becomes an active mediator in the development of Merezhkovskii's thought, especially where Christianity is concerned. In contrast with the previous interpretations, Merezhkovskii finds Nietzsche to be a religious philosopher *pur sang*. In order to argue this, he does not obscure Nietzsche's discourse on the dismissal of God but instead makes it the hallmark of his religious assessment of him. In his incentive to overcome God (in Merezhkovskii's interpretation the Christian God), Nietzsche represents a voice that withstands and counters the age-old Christian supremacy in Western culture. Merezhkovskii recognizes in Nietzsche an anti-Christian leaning yet unlike in previous identifications of Nietzsche and Antichrist, he gives a favorable bias to "the Antichrist" Nietzsche. Nietzsche – as well as Kirillov – enables Merezhkovskii to put a face on the anti-Christian proclivity, which is obscured in historical Christianity but is actually a seminal element of the real personality of Christ.

Merezhkovskii's identification of *Übermensch* and Antichrist is highly different from Vladimir Solov'ëv's association of them. Both depart from an equal determination of the *Übermensch*. Although implicitly, Solov'ëv does relate the *Übermensch* to the Antichrist. And likewise, Merezhkovskii reads the *Übermensch* as an anti-Christian phenomenon. Yet the religious thinkers diverge in their final appropriation of Nietzsche's concept and in their approach to the constellation of the *Übermensch* as: (1) identified with Antichrist, and (2) opposed to the *Bogochelovek* Christ. In Solov'ëv's perspective, the identification of *Übermensch* and Antichrist is a necessary and sufficient condition to renounce the concept in the end. In his opinion both imperil Russian religious consciousness. Merezhkovskii, in contrast, assimilates *Übermensch* and Antichrist in his reconsideration of Christianity; in his reading, they are not opposing to, but rather complementary with, the *Bogochelovek* Jesus Christ.

Merezhkovskii finds fault with Solov'ëv's interpretation of Nietzsche's *Übermensch*. He criticizes Solov'ëv for his *a priori* hostility towards Nietzsche and finds that his unfavorable response to the German philosopher him a typical representative of historical Christianity:

> The fear of the Antichrist that Solov'ëv experienced not long before his death, emerged not only from personal experiences, but also from general phenomena both in Europe and Russia. His latest philosophical work, "The Justification of the Good" is directed against Nietzsche "the Antichrist". Solov'ëv did not only fail in overcoming Nietzsche, he did not even touch his genuine being. The absolutely non-paradoxical affirmation of demonical evil instead of human good, and the perfectly true, from Solov'ëv's own point of view, affirmation of the highest, "trans-human" (*sverkhchelovecheskoe*) or "divine human" (*bogochelovecheskoe*) - in Solov'ëv's words - religious values, which are "beyond" the human good and evil, that is the authentic being of Nietzsche. And this being brings him [Nietzsche] incredibly near to Solov'ëv, by the way through Dostoevskii, to which they were equally close, however from two opposite sides [...] Solov'ëv objects unsuccessfully to Nietzsche's new religion with the old morality [...] Nietzsche curses God, Solov'ëv blesses Him. Whence did this difference between both most deep mystical experiences, equally authentic, come from, that is the question that did not pop up in Solov'ëv's mind. He dealt with Nietzsche too lightly, and even thoughtlessly (Merezhkovskii [1908] 1914: 69-70).[34]

In Merezhkovskii's view, Solov'ëv does not do justice to the merits of Nietzsche's thought, i.e., that he revealed that the divine truth is beyond the established classifications of good and evil. Yet where Solov'ëv fails, Dostoevskii succeeds.

Merezhkovskii finds that Dostoevskii and Nietzsche offer an excellent diagnosis of the flaws in contemporary Christian culture. Both are highly perceptive to the untenable condition of current culture and humanity, torn between two opposing proclivities, i.e., Christ and Antichrist. In contrast with later interpretations, Merezhkovskii is certain that their perspicacity and pinpointing of an equal religious problem originated independently of each other.

> There is no doubt, that Nietzsche never copied from Dostoevskii, that he did not repeat his words; and still, however, there are some coincidences, repetitions, *that are almost verbatim*; these are not only the same thoughts, the most inner, the most secret, such that the one thinking them hardly dares to acknowledge them to oneself, but also almost the same words, almost the

---

[34] Merezhkovskii's criticism of Solov'ëv is partly rooted in Solov'ëv's polemics with the decadents in the late 1890s. Solov'ëv challenged the 'Russian Nietzscheans' in several articles. See chapter 4.

sound of one and the same voice. As if they overheard one another, or came to an agreement, after which the one desperately gives up the other. Miracles do not occur, but is this then not a miracle, a living miracle of history? Does the spirit of time not speak here of one and the same, in different ends of the world (Merezhkovskii [1900-1901] 1995: 306)?

The greatest "miracle" is the accordance between *chelovekobog* and *Übermensch*. In these identical anthropological thoughts, Dostoevskii and Nietzsche explore and capture the human's motivation to reject God and its implications for human consciousness. Both concepts anticipate the further development of humanity, if it were to pursue the Antichrist and completely cancel out Christ. When marking out *chelovekobog* and *Übermensch*, Dostoevskii and Nietzsche gaze into the anti-Christian abyss. For Merezhkovskii, this amounts to the Apocalyptic prophesy about the coming end. In *chelovekobog* and *Übermensch* Dostoevskii and Nietzsche explore the dead-end of historical Christianity. In its current condition, Christianity cannot come up with a solution to the imminent end. It aims to solve the problem of the anti-Christian presence by rigorously opposing it. Yet the anti-Christian tenor cannot be erased; it can only be countered by assimilating it into the Christian paradigm. Only a balance between Christ and Antichrist can save humanity from the abyss. Thus, by giving shape to the anti-Christian in its most explicit ramifications, Dostoevskii and Nietzsche put current Christianity face-to-face with a phenomenon that it can no longer brush aside. By bringing *chelovekobog* and *Übermensch* into the spotlight, they call for a re-evaluation of Christian consciousness. In that sense, they are in Merezhkovskii's mind the first instigators of the new religious consciousness.

Still, however closely they approach the anti-Christian proclivity, both fail to appreciate it in all its ramifications, i.e., that the Antichrist actually makes up the half of Christ's authentic personality and consequently must be explored in its reciprocal relationship with Christ. Merezhkovskii juxtaposes Dostoevskii and Nietzsche even in his analysis regarding their shortcoming. He finds that Nietzsche gazed deeper into the true nature of Christ than Dostoevskii dared. Dostoevskii looked away from "the final freedom" inherent in Christ and by averting his face from this essential aspect in Christ, he did not do justice to the real essence of the One he truly believed in. He could not endure the fearsome truth about Christ's real nature, which is that in His "final freedom" the two most striking poles, i.e. "the Chelovekobog and the Bogochelovek," are united in Christ (Merezhkovskii [1900-1901] 1995: 219). Dostoevskii sees the Antichrist as the one *"opposing Christ"* (ibid.). Nietzsche senses more deeply the fundamental nature of Christ as the One beyond good and evil yet ultimately there is also a flaw in his idea of Christ. Even though he does acknowledge the two faces of Christ, he could not imagine that the eventual solution to this bifurcation lies in "the symbolical joining of these opposites" (id.: 240). Nietzsche deliberately ignores that *Bogochelovek* and *Übermensch/chelovekobog* are "not two, but one" (id.: 302). It is exactly at this point that he fails in his attempt to counterbalance the Christian predominance by signaling the anti-Christian drive. In fact, Nietzsche failed to grasp the actual nature of the Antichrist. As one of the two faces of Christ, the Antichrist naturally emanates from God. Nietzsche rejected God, and in that sense, he overlooked the quintessence of the Antichrist. If one cancels out God as the prime origin and mover, one cannot comprehend neither the *Bogochelovek*/Christ nor the *chelovekobog*/Antichrist because "without God there is not Bogochelovek, nor Chelovekobog, just like without center there is no centripetal, nor centrifugal force" (ibid.). Merezhkovskii suspects that Nietzsche was actually aware of the likeness between Christ and the Antichrist and that this was his "most abysmal thought" and final cause of his madness.[35] Nietzsche returned to his contemporaries Dionysus yet failed to see that this pagan God in fact prefigured Christ. On the eve of his madness, he called himself "the crucified Dionysus."[36] This proves to Merezhkovskii that Nietzsche's exaltation of the Dionysian was in fact a lifelong latent recognition of Christ which drove him mad in the end. Nietzsche was a secret "disciple of Christ" (Merezhkovskii [1900-1901] 1995: 240). The explicit denier

---

[35] Merezhkovskii here uses Zarathustra's metaphor on the Eternal Recurrence as being his "most abysmal thought" (*abgründlicher Gedanke*) (KSA 4: 270).

[36] This self-characterization of Nietzsche is apocryphal. In January 1889 (only some days before his mental breakdown) Nietzsche signed some of his so-called "insanity letters" as either "Dionysus" or "the crucified" (See KSB 8: 571ff.). This gave way to the rumor that he signed as "the crucified Dionysus." Merezhkovskii obviously did not know that Nietzsche actually emphasized the disjunction between both, as indicated in the last lines of *Ecce Homo* (only posthumously published in 1908, thus a source not yet available to Merezhkovskii): "Have I been understood? - *Dionysus versus the crucified*" (KSA 6: 374).

of Christ gave humanity in the end Zarathustra, "the silent foreteller" of the Second Coming (id.: 263).

　　Merezhkovskii's juxtaposition of Nietzsche and Dostoevskii and his criticism of the Russian writer under a strong Nietzschean banner marks not only a shift in the Russian reading of Nietzsche, but also in the valuation of Dostoevskii.[37]

8.2. Towards a new reading of Dostoevskii

Nietzsche, who provided Merezhkovskii with a fresh perspective on aesthetics and religion, also infused his assessment of Dostoevskii. The German philosopher's undeniable role in Merezhkovskii's evaluation of Dostoevskii is most obvious in Merezhkovskii's launching and discussion of the *chelovekobog*. It was Nietzsche's idea of the *Übermensch* that drew Merezhkovskii's attention to this concept in Dostoevskii's broad oeuvre. The link between *Übermensch* and *chelovekobog* might have been prepared by the juxtaposing of Nietzsche's ideas and Dostoevskii's nihilistic characters (mostly Raskol'nikov and Ivan Karamazov) in the first critical articles on Nietzsche. However, in these associations, the *chelovekobog* is not yet mentioned.[38] This is also the case in the critical literature on Dostoevskii. To my knowledge, the concept of the *chelovekobog* is not referred to in critical literature on the Russian writer previous to Merezhkovskii's study *L. Tolstoi i Dostoevskii* (1900-1901).[39]

---

[37] This also applies to Merezhkovskii's reading of Tolstoi in which Tolstoi is criticized with Nietzsche in the background. Tolstoi represents for Merezhkovskii the asceticism of historical Christianity and is in this manner a typical representative of that altruistic and submissive attitude for which Nietzsche blames Christianity. Still, both coincide in their rejection of God and the preponderance of the Flesh over the Spirit (Merezhkovskii [1900-1901] 1995: 150 & 183-184).

[38] See chapter 2.

[39] The idea of the *chelovekobog* appears for the first time in Dostoevskii's oeuvre in 1870, in the novel *The Devils*. Still, I have opted to check the criticism on Dostoevskii from its very beginnings i.e. 1846 (the publication of his first novel *Poor Folk*) because in the first studies, which were already appearing during the writer's lifetime, there are frequent reminiscences to personal conversations with the writer. My point of departure was that this term might have cropped up in these biographical impressions. Here is an overview of the works on Dostoevskii that I read through and checked for the *chelovekobog*. V. G. Belinskii, 1846, *Peterburgskii Sbornik*, *Vzgliad na russkuiu literaturu 1846 goda* (otryvok)*, Vzgliad na russkuiu literaturu 1847 goda* (otryvok). N.A. Dobroliubov, 1861, "Zabitye Liudi". D.I. Pisarev, 1867, "Pogibshie i pogibaiushchie", "Bor'ba za zhizn'". G.I. Uspenskii, 1880, "Prazdnik Pushkina". K.

Merezhkovskii is thus the first to highlight, with Nietzsche's *Übermensch* in mind, the *chelovekobog*.

Moreover, in Merezhkovskii's text, Nietzsche and the *Übermensch* are related to other nihilistic characters, than the ones they are associated with in the first decade of the reception process. Whereas in the articles on Nietzsche before 1900, the main link is with Ivan Karamazov and Raskol'nikov, Merezhkovskii identifies Nietzsche and the *Übermensch* in the first place with Kirillov and Ivan's devil because these characters spell out the idea of the *chelovekobog*, which is at the core of Merezhkovskii's juxtaposition of Dostoevskii and Nietzsche.[40]

Furthermore, Merezhkovskii's 1900 text marks a shift in the assessment of Dostoevskii as an ideological voice. Note that the critics we are discussing do not distinguish between the voice of the narrator in the novel and that of Dostoevskii. They assume that the various fictional characters displayed in the novels represent, at least partially, Dostoevskii's views. In literary criticism at that time, characters' discursive speeches were used to argue for a specific interpretation of the author. Until 1900, Dostoevskii was traditionally read as a social critic. Such a naturalistic reading of Dostoevskii was initiated by the literary critic Belinskii, who embraced Dostoevskii's literary debut *Poor Folk* (1846) as a valuable model for his aesthetics of social realism and his program of the "natural school." The subsequent "radical" critics of the 1860s were also mainly preoccupied with Dostoevskii's attention for the more marginal figures in society, thereby deliberately eclipsing the religious subtext of his works. Consistent with their own ideological views, the literary critics contemporary with Dostoevskii granted a strong secular emphasis to

---

Leont'ev, 1880, "O vsemirnoi liubvi". M.A. Antonovich, 1881, "Mistiko-asketicheskii roman". V.S. Solov'ëv, 1881-1883, "Tri rechi v pamiat' Dostoevskogo". N.K. Mikhailovskii, 1882, "Zhestokii Talant". V.V. Rozanov, 1891, *O legende "Velikii Inkvizitor"*. In the works on Dostoevskii between 1892 and 1899 (i.e. the first phase in the reception process of Nietzsche) there are some rare references to Nietzsche, yet the *chelovekobog* is not spoken of. See Khrapovitskii ([1893] 1997: 159) and Mikhailovskii ([1894] 2000: 50).

[40] Nietzsche and his concept of the *Übermensch* are in Merezhkovskii's text also associated with other nihilistic characters, yet this connection only came into being after the primary identification of *chelovekobog* and *Übermensch* was made on the basis of the rationale of Kirillov and Ivan's devil.

Dostoevskii's works.[41] When attention was drawn to the religious motives in Dostoevskii's works, the writer was perceived as the spokesman of traditional Russian Orthodoxy: his religious meditations were scorned as conservative, reactionary, and antagonistic to real life Russian consciousness. These critics strongly objected to Dostoevskii's view of the Russian people as a "God-bearing" people, whom they instead saw as the bearers of their socialist ideas. In these perspectives, the nihilistic characters were perceived as formulating the radical opposite of Dostoevskii's own ideological point of view.[42]

In Merezhkovskii's understanding, by contrast, the nihilistic characters are not viewed as voices separate from the author's; they are instead considered to reflect the writer's own ideological deliberation process, at least as far as his view on religion is concerned. They represent a consciousness that is partly Dostoevskii's own consciousness. As a result, Merezhkovskii does not mark Dostoevskii as belonging to, let alone supporting or proclaiming ecclesiastical Orthodox ideology. Instead of classifying Dostoevskii as the voice of the Orthodox mainstream, Merezhkovskii views him as a Christian believer who went through serious religious doubts and crises that have determined the status of his religious thought. In his view, Dostoevskii is not a rigorous and normative Orthodox ideologue: his understanding of Christianity is a balanced one, in which he takes into account the anti-Christian drive inherent to human culture. He does not dispose of the problem in a light manner yet explores it – through his nihilistic characters – in its most extreme implications. In that sense, Dostoevskii is open to the actual problem of Christianity, this is that it fails to acknowledge the anti-Christian tenor in the world and humanity. Partly due to his personal struggle with religious questions, he pinpoints this and brings it to the fore in his fictional characters. Merezhkovskii identifies in Dostoevskii's discursive model what Bakhtin would later define as polyphonic discourse in Dostoevskii's novels. He perceives Dostoevskii's fictional setting of characters as an arena in which both the Christian

---

[41] For a more extensive overview of literary criticism on Dostoevskii, see Seduro (1981).

[42] Exemplary of this is Mikhailovskii's article "Zhestokii Talant" ("A cruel talent, 1882). The populist ideologue claimed that Dostoevskii's overly negative description of the nihilistic characters revealed the reactionary standpoint of the author (Seduro 1981: 28ff.)

and anti-Christian drives are given a voice. These voices, each characterized by a typical idiom, are in constant dialogue. The ongoing confrontation with the other's arguments invites them to reconsider and reformulate their own standpoint. The continuous interaction between the opposing ideological voices is an ongoing process of deconstructing and reconstructing the self's and the other's thesis. Merezhkovskii's approach to Dostoevskii's nihilistic characters as giving voice to the author's own problematical attitude to Christianity brings about a change in the perception of Dostoevskii's religiosity.

Merezhkovskii was not the first to touch upon religious motives in Dostoevskii's works and to question whether the religious subtext in his writings echoes or endorses the traditional Christian viewpoint. In the essay "O vsemirnoi liubvi" ("On universal love," 1880), Konstantin Leont'ev claims that Dostoevskii's view of Christianity is a too optimistic one ("rozy nuance") that transcends the essence of Orthodox theology (Leont'ev [1880] 1997: 89). Commenting on Dostoevskii's portrayal of monastic life in *The Brothers Karamazov*, Leont'ev (who was himself a monk at Optina Pustyn', the monastery that served Dostoevskii as a historical model for his novel) argues that "in the *Brothers Karamazov* the monks talk not quite, or, more precisely, not at all like very good monks talk in reality [...] this, we think, is not the way how one should have written about all this" (id.: 87). In his *Tri Rechi v pamiat' Dostoevskogo* (*Three Speeches in memory of Dostoevskii*, 1881-1883), Vladimir Solov'ëv, who was a personal friend of Dostoevskii, also emphasizes the religious dynamics of his works. He hails Dostoevskii as the forerunner of "the new religious art," which is required to re-establish the religious ideal in society and culture (SS III: 190). He finds in Dostoevskii's works "the religious ideal that is based on the belief in Christ" (SS III: 196). Solov'ëv distinguishes Dostoevskii's Christianity from "temple" (*khramovoe*) and "domestic" (*domashnee*) Christianity, but instead embraces it as a universal form of Christianity (*vselenskoe khristianstvo*). Dostoevskii transcends the formalistic and limited official Russian church: he is the prophet of a trans-national Christian brotherhood that includes the whole of humanity (SS III: 199).

Merezhkovskii is partly indebted to these religious interpretations of the Russian writer yet his religious appropriation of

Dostoevskii is in the end fundamentally different from theirs because he does not base his reading of Dostoevskii as a religious thinker on the multitude of devout characters in his novels, such as Sonia Marmeladova, Prince Myshkin, *starets* Zosima, Alësha Karamazov etc. Instead, he substantiates Dostoevskii's views of religion by bringing into prominence the *chelovekobog* and in addition, the nihilistic characters. This is in sharp contrast with the previous critical literature in which these nihilistic characters were mainly given an unfavorable bias and were brushed aside as voicing the opposite of Dostoevskii's Christian outlook. Merezhkovskii, however, partly observes Dostoevskii's own views of religion in these characters. In his new Christian paradigm, Merezhkovskii is mesmerized by the anti-Christian tenor, which he claims to be at the core of the religious question. Consistent with this, his evaluation of Dostoevskii as primarily a religious thinker is mainly grounded in the characters that advocate the anti-Christian proclivity. For Merezhkovskii, these characters express the dilemma in current Christianity, i.e., the dialectics of two opposing proclivities. He observes in these particular characters an inner dualism which stems from their detachment from God. Having renounced God, they lose all sense of morality and compassion for the other. Using arguments which renounce God to different degrees, each character trespasses against the established notion of the moral good and operates in an ideological space beyond common ethical categories. Yet, at the same time, they all show a tendency towards the good.[43] They move on the interface between good and evil, and explore the borders of this. In Merezhkovskii's perception, their alleged immorality boils down to the forsaking of God. They give voice to the psychological and social ramifications of a worldview devoid of God, and operate in an ideological frame where all previous metaphysical motivation is absent. Applying his typical discursive model on these characters, Merezhkovskii sees them as the

---

[43] While contemplating his crime, Raskol'nikov is torn between his elitist theory that the extraordinary may rightfully overstep the moral law and the altruist idea that the pawnbroker's money will enable him to help his family and society. He gives the Marmeladovs money. Ivan Karamazov formulates the idea that, if there is no God and no immortality, all is permitted yet his conscience prevents him from putting this theory into practice. Kirillov cancels out God and the related categories of good and evil. In real life, he loves children and helps Shatov's wife during labor. And Stavrogin, who ruined other people's life (the rape of Matrësha, the murder on Lebiadkina), is tormented by his conscience in the end.

exponents of the Antichrist, the Flesh, the *chelovekobog*. The constant and dynamic conflict between the two antithetical drives in these personages provides Merezhkovskii with an arena to sort out the religious problem of the Christian and anti-Christian and to come up with a solution for it. By embodying the anti-Christian drive, these characters are for Merezhkovskii of more importance for the problem of religion than the pious ones are because they express a religious phenomenon that was kept in the margins of Russian culture until this point. Merezhkovskii credits Dostoevskii's nihilistic characters because they defy the dogmatic discourse of historical Christianity and embody the anti-Christian drive in humanity which has been traditionally suppressed. In a broad range of theories, these 'anti-heroes' all represent a voice that withstands and challenges established Christian ethics. Dostoevskii is able to demonstrate through these characters the most explicit ramifications of a worldview without God. And exactly herein is also the merit of Nietzsche's anthropology of the *Übermensch*.

9.   The vicissitudes of Merezhkovskii's paradigm

From the date of its publication, Merezhkovskii's study *L. Tolstoi and Dostoevskii* was widely read and highly determined further readings of Nietzsche and by extension, the reconsideration of Dostoevskii in the beginning of the twentieth century. Already in 1901, while this work was still being published serially in *Mir Iskusstva*, Merezhkovskii's typical discursive approach to Dostoevskii's nihilistic characters (as all representing the principle of the *chelovekobog*) and the link with Nietzsche's *Übermensch* was adopted by affiliated intellectuals and critics. From 1902 on, there was a boom of critical literature on Dostoevskii and Nietzsche in which *chelovekobog* and *Übermensch* were almost invariably the main point of focus.

9.1.   Akim Volynskii: *Tsarstvo Karamazovykh*

From 1901 on, Akim Volynskii (pseudonym for Akim L'vovich Flekser, 1861-1926) published his study of Dostoevskii's *Brothers Karamazov* in a series in *Sankt-Peterburgskie Vedomosti* (*The St.*

Petersburg Newspaper) under the title *Tsarstvo Karamazovykh* (*The Karamazov Empire*). The literary critic and leading theoretician of *Severnyi Vestnik* - the literary journal of the symbolists - was a close friend of Merezhkovskii.[44] Aleksei Remizov later remarked that Volynskii "always wrote on the same subjects as Merezhkovskii" (quoted in Pyman 1994: 22). This applies in particular to their critical appraisal of Dostoevskii. In 1895, the year that the Merezhkovskiis and Volynskii traveled together through Italy, Merezhkovskii started working on his critical study *L. Tolstoi i Dostoevskii* (Merezhkovskii 1995: 618). It is thus highly probable that Merezhkovskii infused Volynskii with his new ideas on Dostoevskii and in particular, with his focus on the *chelovekobog*. At any rate, the publication of Merezhkovskii's study coincided with Volynskii's preparation of his monograph *Tsarstvo Karamazovykh*.

As a literary critic seeking to overthrow the populist tradition of literary criticism and to establish a new concept of art in which the individual artist would be reappraised, Volynskii responded favorably to Nietzsche's aesthetics. He became acquainted with Nietzsche's works in the beginning of the 1890s, most probably through his close association with Merezhkovskii and Minskii.[45] In 1895 he had a meeting with Lou Andreas-Salomè, whose study *Nietzsche in his works* (1894) was to be published serially in Russian translation in *Severnyi Vestnik* (1896) (Gurevich [1914] 1972: 255). In 1896

---

[44] Volynskii met Merezhkovskii in 1888, and the critic soon became a regular guest of Merezhkovskii's literary evenings (Merezhkovskii [1900-1901] 1995: 618). The friendship between Merezhkovskii and Volynskii grew so close that Volynskii accompanied the Merezhkovskiis in 1895 on a journey to Italy. Merezhkovskii had plans to write a sequel to his first historical novel *Smert' Bogov: Iulian Otstupnik*, which was published in *Severnyi Vestnik* under the title *Otverzhennyi* (*The Outcast*) through the agency of Volynskii. During the trip to Italy, Merezhkovskii took an interest in Leonardo Da Vinci and suggested that Volynskii should study a related subject, i.e., the works of Machiavelli. Yet Volynskii left the couple and continued the trip through Italy on his own. He published his life of *Leonardo da Vinci* in 1900 which was the same year that Merezhkovskii's own study *Voskresshie bogi: Leonardo da Vinchi* (*The Resurrected Gods: Leonardo da Vinci*) appeared. This caused a split between Merezhkovskii and Volynskii (Gippius 1951: 70-73 & Pyman 1994: 22-23).

[45] In an overview of the reception of Nietzsche in Russia that appeared in 1900, Merezhkovskii, Minskii, and Volynskii are grouped and all identified as the first Nietzscheans in Russia: "Yes, Volynskii, Minskii, Merezhkovskii, Gippius! For a long time already they had been searching for a formula that would give them some answer to their own cloudy and vague searchings. Nietzsche gave them this formula, and they kneeled before him" ("Nittsshe v Rossii", 1900: 102).

Volynskii published the article "Literaturnye zametki: Apollon i Dionis" ("Literary notes: Apollo and Dionysus"), in which he analyzed Nietzsche's explication of the Dionysian and the Apollinian as the driving forces of art. He opposed the radical criticism of Nietzsche as expressed by the older generation of idealists and defended the philosopher's aesthetic ideas in *The Birth of Tragedy*, which would prove to be useful for the regeneration of Russian culture. In Volynskii's study, there are obvious motifs of religious mysticism, and he perceives in Nietzsche's aesthetic principles a metaphysical dimensionality.[46] Volynskii introduced to the later decadents and symbolists the motive of the correlation between philosophy and art and the idea that art is a means to see beyond the phenomenal world. He advocated a new form of idealism in the arts which was to be permeated with spiritual and religious values.

Volynskii's Nietzscheanism, however, was not as enduring and profound as Merezhkovskii's. Whereas Merezhkovskii looked for a synthesis between Nietzsche and Christianity, i.e. between the Flesh and the Spirit, Volynskii identified idealism purely with Christianity. He did not accept the Nietzschean exaltation of Antiquity and the Renaissance. Instead, he affirmed that Christianity did not represent the ending but rather the culmination of the Antique spirit (Strada 1987: 29).

Dostoevskii was a fruitful source for literary criticism for Volynskii. From 1897 on, Volynskii published several articles on Dostoevskii in which he discussed the writer's biography, journalistic and polemical activity, and literary production. Important in his research was his study of original and first-hand sources, such as authentic letters, articles in the original newspapers and journals (Iakubovich 2000: 72). In his first articles on Dostoevskii, Volynskii writes in a dialogical style, whereby two or more opponents discuss

---

[46] "Being the expression of the mystical secret of life in abstract concepts, philosophy gives the light by means of which elements can be studied in their most different relations and are subject to a deep analysis. Philosophy unites the concrete world of illusory visions and hallucinations with this truth that forms its living breath, its immortal sense [...] That is why the real artist with talent is in the same manner an enormous intellectual source. Nietzsche often returned to this theme [...] The Kingdom of Apollo, he writes, submits to the Kingdom of Dionysus. This means, that the whole individual submits to the universal, that the phenomena of life are in an unbreakable bound with metaphysical forces" (Volynskii [1896] 2001: 201).

Dostoevskii's heroes.[47] There is no mention of the *chelovekobog* in these essays. In the 1897 sketch "Raskol'nikov" there is a reference to Nietzsche. In a discussion on Raskol'nikov, one of the interlocutors claims that this character is a "hero, in the newest sense of this word. Here, so many years in advance, Nietzsche's theories are in the air" ([Volynskii 1897: 11] quoted in Iakubovich 2000: 73).

In his 1901 monograph on *The Brothers Karamazov*, Volynskii highlights the religious motive in Dostoevskii. He attempts to reveal in the fictional characters "what was invisible to the eyes." He explains their inner and outer conflicts not in terms of natural or social laws but by representing these conflicts as the inevitable result of the characters' abandonment of God (Skuridina 1990: 155). Volynskii perceives in Dostoevskii's characters a universal battle between what he calls '*bogofil'stvo*' (love for God) and '*bogoborchestvo*' (struggle with God, theomachy). *Bogofil'stvo* means the active and deliberate love for God and the related attitude to life and humanity, as opposed to *bogoborchestvo*, which is the voluntary choice to struggle against God. The ideal exponent of *bogofil'stvo* is the *Bogochelovek* Christ in whom the authentic love for God the Father is incarnated. In Dostoevskii, Volynskii finds the re-affirmation of his own idea that the figure of Christ, as portrayed in the Italian Renaissance by Michelangelo, Rafael, and Leonardo da Vinci does not correspond to the real *Bogochelovek* but is instead an image that inclines towards the Antichrist (Iakubovich 2000: 78). In Volynskii's opinion, Catholicism is a perversion of the authentic Christian ideal. Only in Orthodox faith is this ideal preserved in its perfection. Note that the idea that the West represents the anti-Christian and the East the Christian principle is also argued by Merezhkovskii who seeks to reconcile these antithetical elements in his new Christian ideal and strives to unify the Eastern and Western Church. Volynskii, in contrast, attempts to discredit Catholicism by highlighting its anti-Christian tenor and to affirm Russian Orthodox values.

In each chapter of *Tsarstvo Karamazovykh*, one of the novel's characters is analyzed in his/her moments of religious despair and attitude to God, and is thereby tested against the ideal of *bogofil'stvo*. In the chapter with the revealing title "Chelovekobog i

---

[47] All articles were published in *Severnyi Vestnik* and are, among others, "V Kupe" ("In the compartment", 1897), "Raskol'nikov" (1897), "Velikii bezumets" ("The great madman", 1899).

Bogochelovek," Volynskii focuses on and analyzes the character of Ivan Karamazov by means of these inverse terms. In this context the idea of the *chelovekobog* is used to analyze Ivan Karamazov's approach to God. Volynskii interprets Ivan's anger and anguish during the third conversation with Smerdiakov (in which Smerdiakov suggests that he might have killed their father under the impulse of Ivan's theory that 'all is permitted') as follows:

> Ivan is at that moment more than ever in complete dissension with himself: the divine principle (*bozheskoe nachalo*) in him was so weakened and the chelovekobog had raised his voice, the one who is in al his pretensions always weak, terribly weak. This is the dissension between the bogochelovek and the chelovekobog, this tragic discord (Volynskii [1901] 1906: 248-249).

The *chelovekobog* is introduced as an anthropomorphized principle ("raised his voice") that operates within the human being as some irrepressible force that is equally powerful as its complete opposite, the *Bogochelovek*, and is able to suppress and overcome this divine principle in the human. From the outset, the *chelovekobog* is opposed to the *Bogochelovek*. This inner battle and balancing between the *chelovekobog* (evil principle) and *Bogochelovek* (good principle) is what, in Volynskii's opinion, haunts Ivan Karamazov. The *chelovekobog*, "this living in him [Ivan Karamazov] young Apollo" urges Ivan to advocate and aspire to "unconditional personal freedom," while the *Bogochelovek*, i.e., "what is timid, but holy in the human, cries inside him" (Volynskii [1901] 1906: 253). This inner conflict is "a terrible tragedy in the soul" (id.: 253-254). Volynskii uses the wording of *chelovekobog* and *Bogochelovek* to describe the inner conflict between good and evil, to illustrate the psychological ramifications of Ivan's "demonical" conviction that humankind, confronted with the evil and suffering in this world, should renounce the idea of God and recognize that "all is permitted." During the conversation with Smerdiakov, who derives cruel pleasure in burdening Ivan's consciousness with the allusion that he might have murdered their father under the influence of Ivan's theories, but leaves the question of whether he truly did commit the murder unanswered, Ivan gradually faces the real implications of his theorizing and is in his *psyche* torn between the *chelovekobog* and the *Bogochelovek*, almost to the point of madness. In this mental state of complete disharmony and instability, Ivan's *alter ego*, the personification of his own 'evil' side, the devil appears to him as if in a nightmare. The devil is a mere hallucination, the embodiment of what is "base and foul" in Ivan's nature, the exteriorization of the *chelovekobog* which Ivan must face. Volynskii transposes the idea of the *chelovekobog*, as put forward by the devil, to the character of Ivan. This principle is a phantasm:

> In his mind, the human renounces his divine principle and it seems to him that he in actual fact flies up, in thunder and brilliance, up to a new, unwitnessed heaven. He says to himself, that there is no God, and he perceives this proud, but hollow vision as a new reality. And in his mind he becomes chelovekobog (id.: 259).

What is false and misleading in the idea of the *chelovekobog* is that it presupposes God to be merely a philosophical conception, which can be lightly exchanged with another concept. The *chelovekobog* deliberately overlooks God's actual immanence in the nature of all things. The human cannot ignore or detach himself from this divine element which is rooted in the ontological status of his whole being, he cannot free himself from this condition of being affiliated with "the impersonal and eternal metaphysical basis of the world, he cannot become a chelovekobog. He can only be a bogochelovek" (ibid.). In order to realize the metamorphosis into the *Bogochelovek*, i.e., an existential condition of absolute fusion with God, the human should entrust his individuality to God. The *chelovekobog*, by contrast, aims in his "titanic pride" (the devil's wording, PSS: 15: 83) to guarantee and consolidate his specificity towards the world surrounding him.[48] He assumes a self-permissiveness in all his actions, and is not hindered by any moral obstacles.

In his elaboration of the *chelovekobog*, Volynskii at some point uses the term *Übermensch*, apparently as a synonym for the *chelovekobog*: "The dreaming of the chelovekobog, the sverkhchelovek (*Übermensch*), arises out of the tears of a true religious despair" (Volynskii [1901] 1906: 260). Like in Merezhkovskii's discourse, *chelovekobog* and *Übermensch* are

---

[48] In Solov'ëv's opinion, the Antichrist's rejection of God is likewise grounded in his personal pride. See his article "Lermontov" (1899) and "Kratkaia Povest' ob Antikhriste" (1900).

identical. In this text, Volynskii does not refer to Nietzsche.[49] In
Volynskii's reading, the *Übermensch* is an anthropological category
that subsumes individuals who cling on to the illusionary prospect that
they can detach themselves from God and affirm their own
individuality and personal freedom: the actual purport of the
Übermensch is reduced to the *chelovekobog*. Further on in the essay,
chelovekobog and *Übermensch* are used interchangeably.

The human being, inclining towards the *chelovekobog*, is yet
to some extent still restrained by the *Divine Human*
(*bogochelovecheskii*) element, which resides in him, together with its
evil opposite. The human being balances between two poles: on the
one side the divine (*Bogochelovek*), on the other side a "chimera"
(*chelovekobog*). This chimera or "satanic fantasy" is by nature not
Russian because the Russian man lives for the most part following his
heart, which touches upon and grasps the essence of the *Bogochelovek*
(ibid.). In defining the *chelovekobog* as a typically and intrinsically
non-Russian concept that threatens and destabilizes the specific
Russian principle of the *Bogochelovek*, Volynskii follows
Dostoevskii's discourse on the *chelovekobog* in *The Diary of a Writer*
of August 1880 in which he defines the *chelovekobog* as a typical
manifestation of Western Christianity while the true *Bogochelovek* is
to be found in Eastern Christianity. In highlighting the *chelovekobog*
as a non-Russian principle, the identification with the *Übermensch* is
anticipated. Volynskii equates "chelovekobog, sverkhchelovek
(*Übermensch*) and Apollo Belvedere" (Volynskii [1901] 1906: 260).
This is a reformulation of Dostoevskii's statement in the *Diary* (PSS
26: 169) whereby the *Übermensch* is integrated in this line of
concepts. The lining up of the West, *chelovekobog* and *Übermensch*
on the one hand, and the East and the *Bogochelovek* on the other hand,
is adopted from Merezhkovskii.

In spite of Ivan's inclination towards the *chelovekobog*, the
divine principle or *Bogochelovek* is still present in him and is
eventually able to overcome the *chelovekobog*: "The whole history of
Ivan is as it were the history of the struggle of the bogochelovek with
the chelovekobog and the victory of the bogochelovek" (Volynskii
[1901] 1906: 261). Volynskii concludes that the figure of Ivan, and his

---

[49] In a later work on Dostoevskii's *Devils*, *Kniga velikogo gneva* (*A book of great anger*, 1903), Volynskii expounds Kirillov's theory on the *chelovekobog* and claims that Dostoevskii introduced this idea "even before Nietzsche" (Iakubovich 2000: 84).

inner conflict between *chelovekobog* and *Bogochelovek*, is typical for contemporary consciousness. Once again, this conviction coincides with Merezhkovskii's, who perceives both contemporary Russian and European culture to be standing at an abyss, vacillating between *chelovekobog/Übermensch* and *Bogochelovek* (Merezhkovskii [1900-1901] 1995: 9f.).

In his study of Ivan Karamazov as a person who at least partially embodies the principle of the *chelovekobog*, Volynskii identifies the *chelovekobog* with the *Übermensch* yet he does not mention Nietzsche in his discourse. This shows that the term *Übermensch* is by that time a well-known concept, at least among Russian intellectuals, and more importantly, it suggests that the connection between *chelovekobog* and *Übermensch*, as established by Merezhkovskii, was rapidly assimilated in Russian intellectual discourse.

9.2. Sergei Bulgakov: "Ivan Karamazov kak filosofskii tip"

In the paper "Ivan Karamazov kak filosofskii tip" ("Ivan Karamazov as a philosophical type"), delivered as a public lecture on 21 November 1901 and published in 1902, another seminal intellectual of the Russian religious renaissance, the philosopher and theologian Sergei Nikolaevich Bulgakov (1871-1944) elaborates further on the character Ivan Karamazov as a typical exponent of the *chelovekobog*. As he sees it, in this character, Dostoevskii pursues the fundamental problem in ethics from Socrates onwards, i.e., the question for criteria of good and evil. Dostoevskii exposes the ramifications of atheism, stating that in an outlook devoid of any religious or metaphysical touchstone, there are no standards for good and evil, and hence no normative morality (Bulgakov [1901] 1991: 200). For Bulgakov, this "atheistic amoralism" (*ateisticheskii amoralizm*), as outlined by Dostoevskii in Ivan Karamazov, is also found in "the similar seeking of a restless mind, who was, to the whims of fashion, predestined to become the idol of the current moment, Fr. Nietzsche" (ibid.). The Russian literary character and the German philosopher share their questioning of the necessity and tenability of morality. As a substitute for universal morality, Nietzsche puts forward the *Übermensch* and Ivan Karamazov advances the *chelovekobog*, both standing "beyond good and evil" (*po tu storonu dobra i zla*) and to whom "all is permitted" (*vsë pozvoleno*) (id.: 201). Still, in spite of his definite religious outlook, Bulgakov considers Nietzsche's "atheistic amoralism" and his questioning of morality of great value. The greatness of Nietzsche is that he sincerely experienced and lived through this rejection of God and an overall morality. This "drama of the soul," this attempt to survive in a world devoid of God, was bound to result in madness, but this tragic outcome does not reduce the sincerity and authenticity of Nietzsche's raising of the question (ibid.).

For Bulgakov, living in a transition period in which socialist and Marxist theories pervade Russian reality, Ivan Karamazov and Nietzsche are typical phenomena of socialism and the related anthropology of "a new, free, individual, scientifically controlling nature, in Dostoevskii's expression, the chelovekobog" (id.: 206). The "religion of humanity" has temporarily replaced the religion of God; the belief in the *chelovekobog* has superseded the belief in the *Bogochelovek*. Yet Bulgakov does not completely disapprove of this new outlook because he observes a religious quest at the heart of every ideology, even an atheist one. What is genuine and valuable in this contemporary worship of the human – appearing in the various forms of atheism, socialism and Nietzscheanism – is that it raises humanity to a yet unprecedented height: "to realize the hope for a bright and beautiful future humanity [...] one should believe in humanity; should believe that the human is indeed capable of being a chelovekobog" (ibid.). Although deeply religious, Bulgakov does not *a priori* reject what he perceives as the religion of the *chelovekobog*, i.e., any atheist ideology that puts the human individual first, in his day most manifest in Nietzsche's anthropology of the *Übermensch*. This worship of the human, this "religion of humanity," is not so different from the religion of the *Bogochelovek*; both promote an equal objective of elevating the human type. Yet the way to realize this anthropological ideal is completely divergent in both ideologies. In the religion of the *Bogochelovek*, the human merges with God and realizes his divine potential. In the religion of the *chelovekobog*, or *Übermensch*, the human type has taken the place of God and becomes a god himself. This kind of atheist anthropology might be perceived as an incentive to re-appreciate the Christian ideal of *Bogochelovechestvo*.

Bulgakov adopts Merezhkovskii's paradigm of *chelovekobog* and *Übermensch* to proceed in a similar appreciation of both. Like

Merezhkovskii, he claims that these pose the religious problem in all its ramifications and should therefore be taken into account where Christianity is concerned.

9.3. The Nietzsche boom in Dostoevskii criticism

The Nietzschean "change of horizon" towards Dostoevskii, initiated by Merezhkovskii, generated a whole new approach to the Russian writer in the beginning of the twentieth century. Volynskii's and Bulgakov's studies were still centered upon Dostoevskii's nihilistic characters, but Nietzsche was very much present. From 1902 on, a whole flood of new studies appeared, in which Dostoevskii and Nietzsche were explicitly juxtaposed and read in comparison with each other.

In 1902, N.D. Tikhomirov published his public lecture "Nitsshe i Dostoevskii. Cherty iz nravstvennago mirovozzreniia togo i drugogo" ("Nietzsche and Dostoevskii. Features of the moral ideology of the one and the other") in *Bogoslovskii Vestnik* (*The Theological Herald*). Focusing on Nietzsche's idea of the *Übermensch*, the religious author presents this anthropology as freed from all "moral chains," as living and acting by the principle that "all is permitted" (Tikhomirov 1902: 512). He observes in Dostoevskii's works "a striking anticipation of Nietzschean ideas," which can be explained by the fact that both were confronted with the symptoms of a morally sick age (id.: 517). Nietzschean-like ideas are especially found in *Crime and Punishment* and *The Brothers Karamazov*. In Tikhomirov's perception, some of the features in Raskol'nikov's character and reasoning are highly reminiscent of the *Übermensch*. In particular Raskol'nikov's anthropological category of the extraordinary is an "almost literal" account of Nietzsche's classification of the "master morality." Furthermore, for both Raskol'nikov and Nietzsche, the only purpose and *raison d'être* for the common masses lies in the procreation of "great people," for the sake of which it is permitted to transgress moral laws and commit crimes. In his discourse, Tikhomirov uses Raskol'nikov's and Nietzsche's sayings interchangeably and thus presents them as identical (id.: 519-521). Another parallel is obvious between Nietzsche and Ivan Karamazov, "Raskol'nikov's direct successor" (id.: 525). Ivan's reasoning always leads to the same question: does

God, and consequently immortality, exist or not? He contends that humankind has until now loved one another not on the basis of some natural law but on the false premise of God and immortality. Once this delusional belief is annihilated, there is no more ground for the existing moral laws, and consequently, "all is permitted." Tikhomirov charges that

> in these words of Ivan Karamazov we hear exactly the same that Nietzsche advocated, recognizing egoism to be the best human power and legitimating the principle: everything is untrue, all is permitted (id.: 526).

The devil presents Ivan's theories in their most radical form, that the *chelovekobog* is "the twin brother of the Nietzschean *Übermensch*" (id.: 527). Both Ivan and Nietzsche rebel against God (id.: 529). In their rigid rejection of God and advocacy of "amoralism," both suffer from a "tragedy in the soul" (*dushevnaia tragediia*). Yet Nietzsche mourned for this loss of God and attempted his whole life to find Him again, until in the end he paid for this rejection with madness and an early death (id.: 533).

In 1903, A.V. Smirnov, archpriest and professor of Theology at Kazan University, delivered and published the lecture "Dostoevskii i Nitsshe." Peculiarly, he contends that before Tikhomirov, no one came up with the idea of comparing Nietzsche and Dostoevskii (Smirnov 1903: 4). Another crucial and misleading bit of information in his lecture is that Nietzsche already knew Dostoevskii's works from 1873, a claim drawn from Vergun's article. This results in the tendentious and incorrect claim that "Nietzsche's ideas are genetically dependent of Dostoevskii" and that one "should not ignore the direct influence of Dostoevskii on Nietzsche" (id.: 13-14). For Smirnov, the parallels between Nietzsche's ideas and Dostoevskii's nihilistic figures are evidence to Dostoevskii's prophetic insight. Dostoevskii anticipated Nietzsche in 'the man from the underground,' Raskol'nikov, Ivan Karamazov, and Kirillov (id.: 27ff.). Throughout the article, *chelovekobog* and *Übermensch* are used synonymously and transposed to all the mentioned Dostoevskian personages.

Also in 1903, the article "Dostoevskii i Nittsshe" by M. Kheisin appeared in *Mir Bozhii* (*The World of God*). Kheisin expresses right from the start that the comparison of both authors is not new, but the question is not completely settled. Both moral philosophers are complete opposites ("where Nietzsche cries 'halt,'

Dostoevskii exclaims 'take off'"), but "Dostoevskii penetrated deeply into the *Nietzschean* side of the human soul" (Kheisin 1903: 119). Both sought answers to the same questions. Dostoevskii was highly preoccupied with the problem of crime and in this matter he approaches Nietzsche.

> All of Dostoevskii's main heroes, i.e. Raskol'nikov, Versilov, Ivan and Dmitrii Karamazov, Stavrogin and others [...] are criminals, in the sense that they committed a crime or are capable of committing one [...] In uniting all these "criminal" thoughts one receives a single whole figure ... the *Übermensch*, who went through the hands of the Public Prosecutor Dostoevskii (id.: 123).

These characters rebel against God, against established morality. This kind of rebellion is, according to Kheisin, akin to Nietzsche's "will to power" (*volia k vlasti*) (id.: 126). Dostoevskii and Nietzsche completely converge on the notion of *chelovekobog* and *Übermensch* respectively.

> The idea of the *Übermensch* was completely reasoned out by Dostoevskii's criminals, and if this word is not used, then its synonym is: cheloveko-bog, that is repeatedly mentioned by Dostoevskii (id.: 128).

Chelovekobog and *Übermensch* are used interchangeably. In this specific discourse, the idea of the *Übermensch* is, as it were, coined by Dostoevskii. This contributes to the confusion between Nietzsche's anthropology and the *chelovekobog*. The fragment also testifies how in the Dostoevskii research from 1900 on, the idea of the *chelovekobog* is granted more significance and given a wider connotation than the notion in reality has in Dostoevskii's oeuvre. Dostoevskii did not "repeatedly mention" the *chelovekobog*: he only referred to it three times. The term *chelovekobog* is transposed to other Dostoevskian nihilists, *in casu* Ivan Karamazov and Raskol'nikov (id.: 129). However diverse in their reasoning, Kirillov, Ivan Karamazov, and Raskol'nikov are all called *chelovekobog*.

Still in 1903, I. Verner published his study "Tip Kirillova u Dostoevskogo" in *Novyi Put'* (*The New Way*). He draws up an analysis of what he calls "Kirillov's type," which he sees as a recurring motif in all of Dostoevskii's nihilistic characters. In his reading, the various theories put forward by the different characters can all be reduced to Kirillov's formula that if there is no god, the human becomes himself a god, with all the psychological and ethical ramifications related to it. Nietzsche, treated as an identical ideological voice as Kirillov and the other nihilists is explicitly in the foreground in this text. Nietzsche is allied with the nihilistic characters (all advocating the *chelovekobog*) and opposed to Dostoevskii: "[Dostoevskii] believed in the Bogochelovek and refuted the "chelovekobog," [Nietzsche] believed in the sverkhchelovek (*Übermensch*) and denied the Bogochelovek" (Verner 1903, 10: 54).

In 1903, Lev Shestov published his legendary study of Dostoevskii and Nietzsche: *Dostoevskii i Nitshe. Filosofiia Tragedii (Dostoevskii and Nietzsche. The philosophy of tragedy)*. He had already published a seminal work on Tolstoi and Nietzsche: *Dobro v uchenii gr. Tolstogo i F. Nitshe: filosofiia i propoved' (The good in the teaching of count Tolstoi and F. Nietzsche: philosophy and sermon*, 1899). In his interpretation of Dostoevskii and Nietzsche, he focuses for the most part on biographical facts to explain his idea that both represent the philosophy of tragedy. He analyzes turning points in their life as the source of a radical change in their reasoning. At some point in their lives, both Dostoevskii and Nietzsche went through a spiritual crisis, ensuing in, in Dostoevskii's case "the regeneration of his convictions" (*pererozhdenie svoikh ubezhdenii*), and, in Nietzsche's condition "the revaluation of all values" (*pereotsenka vsekh tsennostei*) (Shestov [1903] 1909: 23). Dostoevskii's turning point is his penal servitude in the beginning of the 1850s, Nietzsche's is his physical weakness, forcing him to resign from the Basel professorate in 1879. Shestov believes that these personal experiences initiated an intellectual shift in both authors. Whereas in their previous works, there was a proclivity towards idealism, after their 'regeneration' they opposed the Kantian rational system and proceeded in irrationalism. Dostoevskii and Nietzsche rebel against idealist and positivist morality and expose the egoism in humanity. Theirs is a "morality of tragedy" (*moral' tragedii*), as distinct from a "morality of commonplaceness" (*moral' obydennosti*) (id.: 217). Dostoevskii's regeneration is apparent in his work from *Notes from Underground* onwards (1864); Nietzsche's rebellion starts with *Human, All Too Human* (1878-1879). The kinship between their biography and its psychological and intellectual outcome reveals that Dostoevskii and Nietzsche are "kindred spirits." For Shestov,

"Nietzsche and Dostoevskii can be called brothers, even twin brothers" (id.: 23).[50]

It is uncertain whether Merezhkovskii had such a significant impact on Shestov's juxtaposition of Dostoevskii and Nietzsche because Shestov's opinion of Nietzsche was already profoundly shaped during his work on the study of Tolstoi and Nietzsche (1899). Furthermore, he does not use Merezhkovskii's constellation of *chelovekobog* and *Übermensch* in his comparison of the Russian writer and the German philosopher.[51] His focus is instead on the authors' biography and psychological development in the elaboration of their ideas. Still, his work on Dostoevskii and Nietzsche clearly fits in the new wave of studies on both writers as affiliated thinkers.

9.4. The further functioning of *chelovekobog* and *Übermensch*

In critical literature from that moment on, Merezhkovskii's identification of *chelovekobog* and *Übermensch* is an established discursive paradigm. And in addition, the connection between *Übermensch* and Dostoevskii's nihilistic characters is a recurring constellation.

In an essay on the religious motives in Dostoevskii's works ("Religioznaia-nravstvennaia problema u Dostoevskogo", 1905), Volzhkii (pseudonym for Aleksandr Sergeevich Glinka) highlights the *chelovekobog* as a major religious theme in Dostoevskii's thought. The concept is used interchangeably with the *Übermensch*. He speaks of "the Nietzschean individualist cult of the chelovekobog" (Volzhskii [1905] 1997: 183). Dostoevskii anticipated the "Nietzschean chelovekobog" in Raskol'nikov, Kirillov, and Ivan Karamzazov (id.: 201). The idea that *chelovekobog* and *Übermensch* are a fundamental religious problem is also indicated by Dmitrii Filosofov (Filosofov 1903: 170). In "Legenda o velikom inkviztore," in which Semën Frank deals with Dostoevskii's dialectics of freedom, he refers more frequently to Dostoevskii's nihilistic characters by the term

---

[50] For a detailed analysis of Shestov's reading of Nietzsche, see Lane (1976: 418-486).

[51] Where Merezhkovskii centers for the most part on Kirillov, Shestov highlights Raskol'nikov as advocating Nietzschean-like ideas: "Raskol'nikov stands "beyond good and evil", and this was 35 years ago, when Nietzsche was still a student and was dreaming of lofty ideals [...] the idea is most original and belongs entirely to Dostoevskii" (Shestov [1903] 1971: 106).

sverkhchelovek (*Übermensch*) than by the *chelovekobog*: "Raskol'nikov, Stavrogin and Kirillov, and also Ivan Karamazov are conceived to testify to this dialectics. A bare, baseless interpretation of the notion of freedom inevitably grows into a consciousness that one is an *Übermensch*" (Frank [1932] 1991: 248). Following Merezhkovskii's mythopoem of Christ as incorporating the *Übermensch*, Andrei Belyi compares the message in the Gospel with Zarathustra's teachings and concludes eventually that "one can compare Christ with Nietzsche" (Belyi [1908] 2001: 886). As I will demonstrate in the next chapter, Merezhkovskii's constellation of *Übermensch* and *chelovekobog* is functionally productive in Berdiaev's assessment of Nietzsche and Dostoevskii.

At the end of the day, Merezhkovskii's introduction of the *chelovekobog*, and his identification of this concept with Nietzsche's *Übermensch*, initiated a shift in the further readings of both Dostoevskii and Nietzsche. His study *L. Tolstoi and Dostoevskii* was widely read amongst the Russian intelligentsia and aroused a lively discussion in the intellectual journals. Lev Shestov pinpointed the Nietzschean tenor in Merezhkovskii's line of thought (Shestov, [1903] 2001: 114, 115, 127). Andrei Belyi observed Nietzsche's influence on Merezhkovskii's reconsideration of Christianity (1911: 419f.). Berdiaev found that the study "had a great significance" because Merezhkovskii "tried to discover the religious meaning in the works of the great Russian writers [...] He awakened the religious concern and seeking in literature." And he boldly called Merezhkovskii's new version of Christianity, "a Nietzscheanized Christianity" ([1949] 2003: 387, 393). Furthermore, he finds that of all critics "Merezhkovskii wrote the best of all on Dostoevskii in his book *L. Tolstoi i Dostoevskii* (Berdiaev [1923] 1991: 29).

Merezhkovskii's study also gained fame outside Russia. Georg Brandes commented that "Merezhkovskii took a particular pleasure in the opportunity to bring his two favorite names into association, Nietzsche and Dostoevskii" (Brandes [1913] 2001: 320). Merezhkovskii decisively shaped the German reception of Dostoevskii. His study on Tolstoi and Dostoevskii appeared in 1903 in German translation; no other critic of Russian literature was known by the German public as he was (Heftrich 1995: 76). In 1908, he edited a new German translation of *Crime and Punishment*, entitled *Rodion Raskolnikoff*. Already on the first page of his preface to the work,

Merezhkovskii characterizes Dostoevskii as the creator of the *chelovekobog* ("Menschgott") (Dostojewski 1908: XX). Thomas Mann, e.g., who almost half of a century later called Dostoevskii and Nietzsche "spiritual brothers" (Mann 1948: 78), eulogized Merezhkovskii's study and some other of his critical works: "Dmitrii Merezhkovskii! The most brilliant critic and world psychologist since Nietzsche! He, whose book on Tolstoi and Dostoevskii made such an indelible impression on me" (Mann [1921] 1953: 470). André Gide, who claims in his 1923 study of Dostoevskii that all his nihilistic characters are preoccupied with typical Nietzschean questions (Gide 1923: 230f.), was also considerably influenced by Merezhkovskii in his reading of Dostoevskii and the association with Nietzsche (Gesemann 1961: 129f.).[52]

10. Conclusion

Dissatisfied with historical Christianity for ignoring the Flesh and the Antichrist, Merezhkovskii discovered in Nietzsche what he found lacking in the established Christian paradigm. On the one hand, Nietzsche provided him with a discourse by means of which he was able to pinpoint the lacuna in historical Christianity. On the other hand, Nietzsche supplied him with a life-affirming, Dionysian model required to reinvigorate Christian culture. Enwrapped in his own cultural reality, highly constructed around Orthodox Christianity, Merezhkovskii needed Nietzsche's anti-Christian paradigm to formulate his critique on traditional Christianity which he considered to be subsiding into its own preponderance of the Spirit, and to provide an alternative to it.

The religious thinker drew in particular on Nietzsche's *Übermensch*, which was in the previous critical responses rigorously renounced for its supposed immoral character. For Merezhkovskii, however, this concept made up the keystone of what was missing in

---

[52] "[Shestov] und vor allem Merezhkovskii wirkten [...] auf Westeuropa ein. [...] Auf M. [Merezhkovskii] fussten u.a. Thomas Mann und André Gide, wie überhaupt die westeuropäische D [Dostoevskii] – Renaissance kurz vor und nach dem ersten Weltkrieg ohne die Popularisierung der Anschauungen M.s in der vorliegenden Form undenkbar gewesen wäre. Die so oder ähnlich verstandene D.N. – Relation [Dostoevskii and Nietzsche] gilt bis in die jüngste Zeit" (Gesemann 1961: 129f.).

normative Christianity: an awareness of Christ's second, anti-Christian nature. He appropriated Nietzsche's *Übermensch* as the missing link in Christian anthropology and Christology and assimilated this concept in his new Christian model. Equally important for his new version of Christianity, was the idea of the *chelovekobog* which was typically ascribed to Dostoevskii and only launched after a substantial amount of Nietzsche-appropriation.

The horizon of expectations emerging from Nietzsche's discourse also stirred up Merezhkovskii's assessment of Dostoevskii. His approach to Dostoevskii, as partially mediated by Nietzsche, marks a seminal shift in literary criticism on the Russian writer. The mainspring of Merezhkovskii's reconsideration of Dostoevskii was the idea of the *chelovekobog*, which he unambiguously identified with the *Übermensch*. The *chelovekobog* embodied for Merezhkovskii the anti-Christian drive in humanity and the world and served therefore, together with Nietzsche's *Übermensch*, as the ideal prototype for his delineation of phenomena that counter the Christian dominance.

Mesmerized by *chelovekobog* and *Übermensch* as touching upon the failure of current Christianity, Merezhkovskii found in Dostoevskii and Nietzsche the religious inspiration for his neo-Christian myth. At this point, he brought together, on an equal basis, the icon of nineteenth century Russian literature and the dubbed atheist philosopher.

Merezhkovskii was not an epigone of Nietzsche's ideas; rather, he engaged in an agonal dialogue with the philosopher in a process of both assimilation and overcoming. He turned to Nietzsche for an ideological and discursive ground to phrase his analysis of the crisis in current Christianity, and to spell out his alternative Christian version of the new religious consciousness. Nietzsche moved the *God-Seeker* to re-Christianize Christianity. In turn, Merezhkovskii applied his Christian paradigm onto Nietzsche and by that diminished the philosopher's reputation as the rigid Antichrist. One can say, that in Merezhkovskii's ideal of the new religious consciousness, Christianity was Nietzscheanized and Nietzsche was Christianized. Or to use Berdiaev's phrase, Merezhkovskii' advanced "a Nietzscheanized Christianity" (*nitssheanizirovannoe khristianstvo*) (Berdiaev [1949] 2003: 393).

In the end, we may conclude that Merezhkovskii's connection of Kirillov and Nietzsche functioned as a prolific paradigm to reconsider the philosopher and integrate his ideas, in particular the *Übermensch*, into the Russian, highly religious, cultural context. Merezhkovskii's reading and religious appropriation of Nietzsche was a seminal landmark in the reception process of the German philosopher, and by extension, in the literary criticism on Dostoevskii. His identification of *chelovekobog* and *Übermensch* became an established and habitual paradigm in later critical literature on both Dostoevskii and Nietzsche. In fact, the constellation of *chelovekobog* and *Übermensch* eventually outgrew its author and became self-standing. Whereas Merezhkovskii, at least on Western European soil, remained in the wings of cultural and philosophical history, the association of *Übermensch* and *chelovekobog* became a popular motif in both critical and vulgarized studies on Dostoevskii and Nietzsche. This proves how ideas can evolve independently from the author, into a self-operating canon, which is time and again adapted for others' ideological purposes.

Chapter 7

Free from God, free within God:
Nikolai Berdiaev's use of Nietzsche's *Übermensch*

> *World culture must freely and immanently come to a new religious life. We cannot hold back from Nietzsche, we must experience him and overcome him from within (Berdiaev, Smysl Tvorchestva, 1916).*

> *Not without reason someone called me a Christian-Nietzschean (Berdiaev, "Avtobiografiia," 1917).*

1. Introduction

The concept of the *chelovekobog*, launched in critical literature by Merezhkovskii and soon grown into a frequently used paradigm in Russian ideological and cultural discourse, did not only bring about a shift in Russian history of ideas in general, but also in the intellectual development of individual thinkers. This is the case for Nikolai Berdiaev, in whose line of thought the idea of the *chelovekobog* marks an ideological change, at least as far as his assessment of Nietzsche is concerned.

Like Solov'ëv and Merezhkovskii, Berdiaev constitutes a landmark in the Russian reception of Nietzsche. For one thing, his reading of Nietzsche, and in particular of the *Übermensch*, is decisively shaped by the field of expectations established by Solov'ëv and Merezhkovskii. For another, he adds up to their interpretation of the *Übermensch* and makes up the culmination of the religious appropriation of Nietzsche on Russian soil.

2. Berdiaev's background

Nikolai Aleksandrovich Berdiaev (1874-1948) was born in Kiev into a family of military aristocrats and received his primary education in a military school. At an early age he was already fascinated by philosophical problems and steeped himself in various philosophical works, ranging from the native ideologues such as Dostoevskii, Leont'ev, Tolstoi and Solov'ëv to the German idealists. He started studying law at the University of Kiev, where he became interested in Marxist thought. In 1894 he joined the Social Democratic Party and in 1898 he was arrested for his participation in Marxist circles and was forced to interrupt his academic studies. In 1901 he was banished to Vologda until 1902. His expulsion from university and temporary exile, however, did not stop his intellectual activity.[1]

At the end of the 1890s, Berdiaev and his fellow Marxist intellectuals, Pëtr Struve (1870-1944), Sergei Bulgakov (1871-1944) and Semën Frank (1877-1950), grew dissatisfied with Marxism for its monistic materialist and positivist tenets. They found that an empirical worldview of law and necessity was insufficient to grasp the reality that exists beyond the phenomenal world. Idealism offered them a way out: they moved "from Marxism to Idealism."[2] These self-proclaimed "neo-idealists" attempted to dissolve the dichotomy between the positivist creed of a strictly empirical reality and the idealist belief in a spiritual world. Faulting Marxist anthropology for its predominant preoccupation with the collective well-being, they aimed to restore individual consciousness as the central value of philosophy. Inspired both by the revival of metaphysics in German idealism and Nietzsche's incentive for a revaluation of all values, they renounced the Marxist determinist doctrine of collective happiness and instead sought to explore the individual's moral motivation in the realm of metaphysics. They proposed an ethics of individual self-realization based on the belief that the human is the prime producer of

---

[1] For Berdiaev's course of life, see his intellectual autobiography *Samopoznanie. Opyt filosofskoi Avtobiografii* (*Dream and Reality. An Essay in Autobiography*, 1949) and Lowrie's comprehensive biography *Rebellious Prophet. A life of Nicolai Berdyaev* (1974).

[2] The phrase is borrowed from Bulgakov's work on this ideological change, *Ot Marksizma k Idealizmu* (1903).

values and naturally strives to realize his metaphysical craving for the absolute good.

In 1901 Berdiaev published his first book *Sub'ektivizm i Individualizm v obshchestvennoi Filosofii* (*Subjectivism and Individualism in social Philosophy*) in which he criticized Nikolai Mikhailovskii's positivist ethics. According to Berdiaev, Mikhailovskii's attempt to construe a moral system that centered upon free will and the individual's right to self-realization was *a priori* undermined by his resoluteness to recognize only empirical reality. In a long preface to the book, Pëtr Struve honors Nietzsche for posing "the most tormenting problem of the age," i.e., how to combine the human's innate yearning for individual perfection with the social striving for the collective well-being (quoted in Kelly 1998: 159f.).

In 1902 the neo-idealist views found expression in the collection of essays *Problemy Idealizma* (*Problems of Idealism*), to which the four former Marxists contributed together with eight other intellectuals (historians, philosophers and jurists alike).[3] Covering the fields of ethics, anthropology, sociology, and law, the volume's connecting thread was an attempt to sketch out an idealist system that posited the individual as the prime source of values. To quote the editor, the new categorical imperative "gives primary importance to the principle of the absolute significance of the personality" (Novgorodtsev 1902, quoted in Poole 2003: 83).[4] For the neo-idealists, philosophical idealism was not to be explored in abstract isolation from other, even rival, ideological currents. They drew on conflicting ideas to promote their new idealist positions. Interestingly, Friedrich Nietzsche, the self-characterized opponent of idealist thought, played a productive role in the formation of the neo-idealist creed. Especially Berdiaev and Frank relied manifestly on Nietzsche in spelling out their version of neo-idealism. In his "Eticheskaia problema v svete filosofskogo idealizma" ("The ethical problem in the light of philosophical idealism"), Berdiaev aimed to supplement

---

[3] The other contributors were, amongst others, Lev Lopatin, the princes Sergei and Evgenii Trubetskoi, Sergei Askol'dov and Pavel Novgorodtsev, who edited the volume. For a detailed overview of the book's goal and content, see Randall Poole's introduction to his translation of *Problems of Idealism* (2003: 1-78).

[4] In the 1909 collection *Vekhi* (*Signposts*) and *Iz Glubiny* (*Out of the Depths*, 1918), some of the contributors returned to the questions posed in *Problemy Idealizma* and drew conclusions on the contemporary state of the intelligentsia. For the *Vekhi* debate see Kelly, "Which Signposts?" in her *Toward Another Shore*, 1998: 155-200.

Kantian ethics with Nietzsche's views on the problem of morality and thereby attempted to qualify Nietzsche's alleged immoralism. In "Fr. Nitsshe i 'etika liubvi k dal'nemu'" ("Fr. Nietzsche and the ethics of 'love of the distant'"), Frank gave an idealist bias to Nietzsche's distinction between "love of one's neighbor" and "love of the distant."[5] Whereas the first formula indicates the utilitarian moral ideal of compassion and collective welfare, the second implies, in Frank's interpretation, an imperative to autonomous and individual values. Both moral principles display only gradual differences, for they both emerge from the metaphysical need for social happiness (Frank 1902: 137-195).[6]

Like Bulgakov and Frank, Berdiaev was not occupied with neo-idealism for a long time, and he soon moved on to the issue of Christianity (Berdiaev [1946] 1997: 193; [1949] 2003: 415ff.). From then on, his philosophical activity was mainly centered on the problem of religion, specifically on the status of the human being in relation to the Godhead. Berdiaev became, according to his own account, a seminal spokesman of the new religious seeking that marked the Russian intelligentsia in the beginning of the twentieth century, and was "one of the initiators of the religious philosophy arising in Russia" (Berdiaev [1946] 1997: 208). From the turn of the century on, he was actively involved in the St. Petersburg literary, religious and philosophical circles that flourished in the rich ferment of the Russian cultural renaissance. He attended Viacheslav Ivanov's Wednesday sessions in the famous "Tower" and Merezhkovskii's "Religious-Philosophical Gatherings." In these years, Berdiaev, who later described himself as being "penetrated not only by the breath of the Spirit, but also by that of Dionysus," eagerly joined in Merezhkovskii's search for a new religious consciousness (Berdiaev [1949] 2003: 372). Recalling this period of cultural and philosophical awakening, Berdiaev points to Nietzsche as a seminal source of inspiration:

> We found ourselves in an era unusually gifted in creativity. Nietzsche was highly experienced, although not by everybody in the same way. The influence of Nietzsche was fundamental in the Russian renaissance at the beginning of the century [...] He was the greatest Western influence on the

---

[5] See KSA 4: 77f. ("From the Neighbour-Love").

[6] Sergei Trubetskoi, however, was not so pleased with the Nietzschean undercurrent of *Problemy Idealizma* (Berdiaev [1949] 2003: 378).

Russian renaissance. But in Nietzsche was not sensed, what was mostly written about him in the West, i.e. not his closeness to biological philosophy, not the struggle for an aristocratic race and culture, but rather the religious theme. Nietzsche was perceived as a mystic and a prophet (Berdiaev [1946] 1997: 194 & 199).

Along with Merezhkovskii and the other *God-seekers*, Berdiaev welcomed the 1905 revolution as the beginning of the anticipated Apocalypse that would herald the new religious consciousness. But the political and social outcome of the revolution smashed his hopes for the expected religious and cultural transformation, and he turned against the radical left revolutionaries. In 1908 Berdiaev moved to Moscow, and through Sergei Bulgakov, he became acquainted with other religious philosophers who had returned to the Orthodox Church. These religious thinkers and a handful of clergymen founded a new Moscow branch of the "Religious Philosophical Society," which had been set up by Merezhkovskii in 1901 but was shut down in 1903 by the Procurator of the Holy Synod Pobedonostsev for its supposedly heretical lectures and debates. Still, the ecclesiastical authorities could not stop the fresh breeze of religious renewal that pervaded intellectual circles and in 1905 the Society revived, on Sergei Bulgakov's initiative, in Moscow as the "Religious-Philosophical Vladimir Solov'ëv Society" (Scherrer 1973: 202-226). Berdiaev became actively engaged in the Society's meetings whose objective was to renew Russia's spiritual and religious self-consciousness. Due to his numerous publications and lectures and his editing activities, Berdiaev was a leading figure in the religious and philosophical renaissance of his time. In 1913 he published his notorious article "Gasiteli Dukha" ("Quenchers of the Spirit") in which he strongly criticized the Holy Synod and the official Church; as a result he was brought to trial for blasphemy and risked exile to Siberia, but the start of World War I and the upcoming revolution intervened his banishment. After the revolution of 1917, he was able to maintain his intellectual status during the first years of communist rule. In 1918 Berdiaev founded the "Free Academy of Spiritual Culture" (*Vol'naia Akedemiia Dukhovnoi Kultury*) and in 1920 he received an appointment to the Chair of Philosophy at Moscow University. His academic activities were however strongly censured, and in 1922 he was expelled from Russia. He settled first in Berlin where he founded the "Russian Academy of Philosophy and

Religion." In 1924 he joined the Russian émigrés in Paris where he organized and lectured at a similar "Russian Academy," like the one he founded in Berlin. He also established and edited the religious-philosophical journal *Put'* (*The Way*) and the YMCA-Press, the publication outlet for the Russian émigré philosophers. Until his death in 1848, he lived in Clamart, a suburb of Paris.

3. The fruitful Nietzsche

According to his own account, Berdiaev was already highly familiar with Nietzsche's thought, "when he [Nietzsche] was not yet popular in Russian cultural circles" (Berdiaev [1939] 1995: 8). Berdiaev became acquainted with Nietzsche's works during the 1890s, probably through fellow Russian intellectuals, in particular Lev Shestov with whom he had a cordial relationship and who devoted two major works to Nietzsche, dealing with Tolstoi (1899) and Dostoevskii (1903) respectively.[7] Berdiaev studied Nietzsche exhaustively in an original, eight-volume German edition which at his request was sent from Berlin by his friend V.V. Vodovozov (Vadimov 1993: 51).[8] In 1898 he translated Ludwig Stein's *Friedrich Nietzsche's Worldview and its dangers: a critical essay* (*Friedrich Nietzsches Weltanschauung und ihre Gefahren: Ein kritischer Essay*, 1893) into Russian.[9] At the end of the 1890s, Berdiaev outgrew his earlier socialist and Marxist convictions and experienced a prolific period of renewed spiritual and intellectual creativity, in which he, as he recounts, "returned to my own spiritual homeland, to philosophy, religion and art." In this process of philosophical, artistic and religious rebirth, Nietzsche was

---

[7] See Lev Shestov, *Dobro v uchenii gr. Tolstogo i F. Nitsshe (Filosofiia i propoved')* and *Dostoevskii i Nitsshe (Filosofiia Tragedii)*. See Berdiaev in *Samopoznanie*: "I was particularly interested in his [Shestov's] book on Dostoevskii and Nietzsche" ([1949] 2003: 371).

[8] This is most probably the first complete edition of Nietzsche's works, published in eight volumes, i.e. *Nietzsche's Werke*, edited by Peter Gast, Leipzig: Naumann, 1893-1894 (known as the *Gast'sche Ausgabe*). This edition contains *Untimely Meditations, Human, All Too Human, Thus spoke Zarathustra* (including the fourth part, only published in a private edition by Nietzsche himself), *Beyond Good and Evil* and *On the Genealogy of Morals* (Jung & Simon-Ritz 2000, Vol.1: 3).

[9] *Fridrikh Nitsshe i ego filosofiia: kritiko-biograficheskii ocherk*, published in series in *Mir Bozhii* (1898, 9: 61-79, 10: 51-69, 11: 63-79 (Sineokaia 2001b: 1006).

"highly significant" (letter to Erikh F. Gollerbakh, October 1918).[10] From 1900 on, Berdiaev's familiarity with Nietzsche intensified further due to his regular contact with Merezhkovskii, whose Religious-Philosophical Gatherings he frequently attended and with whom he edited the journal *Novyi Put'* until 1905 (Berdiaev [1949] 2003: 385).[11] During this time, Nietzsche's works and thoughts served as a prolific source of inspiration in Berdiaev's philosophical reflection. In "Moe filosofskoe mirosozertsanie" ("My philosophical worldview," written in 1937 but not published until 1952), Berdiaev sketched out the main principles of his philosophy and testified that Nietzsche – side by side with Dostoevskii and Tolstoi – played a prominent role in the development of his thought (Berdiaev [1937] 1991: 19).

Except for the article "Nitsshe i sovremennaia Germaniia" ("Nietzsche and contemporary Germany", 1915) in *Birzhevye vedomosti*, Berdiaev never published a special monograph or scholarly paper on Nietzsche. He rather discussed his thought in several writings, as it were engaging in a conversation with him on the most diverse topics. Nietzsche acted on Berdiaev's thought in a dynamic process of both assimilation and overcoming:

> The Nietzschean revaluation of values (*pereotsenka tsennostei*), the aversion to rationalism and moralism, had a profound impact on my spiritual struggle and became as it were a subconsciously operating force. But in the search for truth, there was also much conflict with Nietzsche (Berdiaev [1939] 1995: 8).

Nietzsche and his 'untimely meditations' frequently crop up in Berdiaev's texts from 1900 onwards. In his first book *Sub'ektivizm i Individualizm v obshchestvennoi Filosofii*, Nietzsche is discussed briefly and labeled an advocate of "artistic-aristocratic individualism"

---

[10] "Pis'ma N.A. Berdiaeva k E. F. Gollerbakhu". See Internet Source http://www.krotov.info/library/02_b/berdyaev/1993goll.html. See also Berdiaev [1949] 2003: "In that period I read Nietzsche, whom I highly experienced."
[11] An anecdote in a bookshop, described by Vadimov, is evidence of Berdiaev's thorough knowledge of Nietzsche. He starts a conversation with someone who is looking for a Russian translation of Nietzsche's works. Berdiaev overwhelms him with information on all the Russian translations, which one is good, which one is insufficient, and so on. He even lectures on the available literature on Nietzsche (1993: 197-199).

(quoted in Lane 1976: 307).[12] In the article "Bor'ba za idealizm" ("The Struggle for Idealism", 1901) Berdiaev claims that Nietzsche makes a great impression because of the "living good in him" and that his ethical individualism is highly significant for the "new culture" (Berdiaev [1901] 1907: 21 & 32). However, it is not until 1902, in "Eticheskaia problema v svete filosofskogo idealizma," that Berdiaev proceeds in a detailed analysis of and commentary on Nietzsche's thoughts and tries to fit them into his own ideological creed.

Consistent with his self-characterization as the "philosopher of freedom," Berdiaev time and again insisted on his philosophical independence. Nevertheless, entrenched in the intellectual and cultural flux of his time, he indulged in various philosophical sources and retained bits and pieces from each of them in the formulation of his own thought.[13] He acknowledged that, among others, Kant, Marx, Jacob Böhme, Dostoevskii, and Vladimir Solov'ëv had an impact on the development of his thought (Berdiaev [1949] 2003: 336 ff.; [1946] 1997: 209). He also credited Nietzsche (Berdiaev [1949] 2003: 311). Nietzsche's provocative thought was a productive source for Berdiaev as he challenged traditional paradigms and pinpointed their flaws. What is more, the German philosopher not only provided Berdiaev with a diagnosis of the decline in contemporary philosophical patterns, but he also supplied him with a cure for it. As Berdiaev pointed out, "old medicines do not help against new diseases" (Berdiaev [1907] 1991: 237). Berdiaev did not copy from Nietzsche; rather, he engaged in a vacillating and fruitful dialogue with him and transformed his ideas in such a way that they could answer the needs of Russian consciousness. Exemplary for this is his statement in "Nitsshe i sovremennaia Germaniia" that Nietzsche was closer to Russian culture

---

[12] Berdiaev might have borrowed this characterization from Georg Brandes' 1888 study of Nietzsche, *Friedrich Nietzsche. An Essay on Aristocratic Radicalism*. This work appeared in Russian in 1900 in the journal *Russkaia Mysl'*: "Fridrikh Nitsshe: aristokraticheskii radikalizm." In his autobiography, Berdiaev wrote much later: "I have always defined my position with the words Brandes used with reference to Nietzsche: aristocratic radicalism" (Berdiaev [1949] 2003: 382).

[13] "I always received my thought as being originally born in freedom [...] That is not to say, that I did not want to learn from others, from all the great teachers of thought, and that I did not undergo any influence, or that I am obliged to no-one. I continuously fed myself with world thought, received intellectual stimuli, I owe much to thinkers and writers, whom I read all my life [...] Yet, it all went through my freedom, went in the depths of myself. I could only take every intellectual influence with the approval of my freedom" (Berdiaev [1949] 2003: 302).

and mentality than to the German state of mind (quoted in Dmitrieva & Nethercott 1996: 338-339). In the 1907 article "Bunt i pokornost' v psikhologii mass" ("Rebellion and submissiveness in the psychology of the masses"), Berdiaev defended Nietzsche against the fashionable vulgarizations of his thought, especially against what he calls "the democratization" (*demokratizatsiia*) of the *Übermensch*.[14] In his view, "the herd of '*Übermenschen*'"(*stado 'sverkhchelovekov*), – which is not so different from "a flock of sheep" –, were swarming over the Russian soil in these days: they bring Nietzsche the final "posthumous wound." The only right way to do justice to "the unfortunate Nietzsche, who went mad on the religious idea of the *Übermensch*, who sought God in this idea," is to restore his religiosity (Berdiaev [1907] 1910: 77-78). And this is the task Berdiaev undertakes.

4. "Idealizing" Nietzsche: the immoralist rethought

In "Eticheskaia problema v svete filosofskogo idealizma," Berdiaev's contribution to the neo-idealist manifesto, he draws from Nietzsche, the dubbed immoralist and challenger of metaphysics - guises the German philosopher at times liked to cloak himself in - to promote his new idealist ethics. He finds in Nietzsche, who incited his readers to smash the old value tablets, an impulse to overthrow established definitions of ideas such as good, evil, truth and beauty and to identify values and ideals as emanations of the individual human being. In his quest to uncover the origin and essence of values, Nietzsche was "first of all an idealist" (Berdiaev 1902: 120).

Nietzsche's ideas mediate Berdiaev's overcoming of the Marxist morality of the collective well-being, in the sense that he urges casting off altruistic motives and establishing the individual at the core of the moral question. For Berdiaev, Nietzsche's so-called immorality is in fact a "passionate protest against historical morality, against the morals of altruism and social utilitarianism [...] a protest

---

[14] Around 1905 the *God-builders (Bogostroiteli)* appropriated Nietzsche's *Übermensch* for their political and social agenda: they proclaimed a self-overcoming, strong humanity that would replace God and install Marxist society. Another "democratic" adaptation of the *Übermensch* was its use in mass literature. In Mikhail Artsybashev's novel *Sanin* (1907), for example, the protagonist models his life motto of sexual hedonism on the *Übermensch*.

in the name of the sovereign 'I'" which paves the way for a new and more correct understanding of the moral problem (ibid.). Having touched the sore spot of Marxist ethics, Nietzsche further contributes to the formation of Berdiaev's idealist ethics by offering him a context to evaluate and supplement Kantian morality. Kant established the independence and self-sufficiency of ethics from empirical knowledge, and he put moral duty at the core of his ethical system. In that sense, he "offers the philosophical foundations for ethical individualism, for the acknowledgment of the human as a goal in itself and an unconditional value" (id.: 126). Yet in his notion of the categorical imperative (act as if the maxim of your action was to become through your will a universal law of nature), Kant eventually missed the quintessence of morality. He assumed the preponderance of a universal moral law over the individual's moral freedom and hence failed to do justice to the human's autonomous moral nature. In its most radical ramifications, Kant's moral formula is tantamount to slavery in Berdiaev's view. Borrowing from Nietzsche's discourse, Berdiaev criticizes Kant for grounding his ethics on the "far too traditional idea" that human nature is determined by original sin and is naturally depraved, whereby he totally denied "the *Dionysian* roots of life" (id.: 130). At this point, Nietzsche, who "raised in all his works such a beautiful monument to the god Dionysus," corrects and surmounts Kant: "Nietzsche overcomes the Philistine (*meshchanskie*) elements in Kantian practical morality and prepares the free morality of the future, the morality of a strong human individuality" (id.: 126). Berdiaev hails Nietzsche as the first one to reveal that the altruist imperative of moral duty is incompatible with the individual's craving for the affirmation and realization of the self. Nietzsche dares to question traditional normative morals because these lower the sovereignty of the self. He exposes the ethics of altruism as a "police morality" (*politseiskaia moral'*) or "Philistine morality" (*meshchanskaia moral'*) and strives instead for moral sanctioning that is not enforced by laws external to the human but is fully rooted in the individual's personal motivation (Berdiaev 1902: 120). Unlike the moralists of altruism, whose ethics is one of negation and curtailment of the individual self, Nietzsche aspires to a "*positive* morality" that affirms the self as the sole basis of values (id.: 121).

Endorsing the Dionysian creed of the human's intensive craving for life, Berdiaev claims that the moral task is not to restrict this passion for life but to affirm it by positing the primacy of the "spiritual self" (*dukhovnyi ia*) and to warrant the ongoing development of it (id.: 131). Inspired by Nietzsche, Berdiaev proposes an ethics of moral autonomy: each individual can and should determine his own moral standards, without interference from an externally imposed moral system. All moral systems based on altruism – labeled by Berdiaev as "morals of external drill, police and hygienic moralities of life comfort" – disregard the variety of individualities and level out the individual's human powers (id.: 122). For Berdiaev, morality is not an external problem but an interior and personal matter. The human should free himself from the compelling bond with the other and aim for the realization and perfection of his individual qualities: "The human self must not bend its proud head before anything but its own ideal of perfection, its own God to which it alone answers" (id.: 123). In Berdiaev's neo-idealist perspective, an ethics of moral individualism in which the individual rebels against any externally imposed law and public opinion is the sole authentic moral imperative: it fulfils the autonomous moral law and legitimizes the absolute being of every individual personality. Nietzsche's so-called "immoral demonism" contains the seeds of the "higher morality" (id.: 124).[15] Therefore, Nietzsche is for Berdiaev one of "the greatest of moral prophets, the prophets of a new, positive and free morality" (id.: 120).

5. The Antichrist remodelled: proselytizing a new Christianity

Neo-idealism soon proves to be insufficient to answer Berdiaev's questions concerning the human being and his metaphysical status. Inspired by the new religious seeking that stirred up the intelligentsia around the turn of the century – instigated by Dmitrii Merezhkovskii's writings on the "new religious consciousness" and his well-attended "Religious-Philosophical Gatherings" – Berdiaev immersed himself into the issue of religion in the beginning of the twentieth century. He experienced a genuine conversion to Christianity that was marked by

---

[15] With the formula "immoral demonism" Berdiav refers to Vladimir Solov'ëv's illustrious delineation of Nietzsche's *Übermensch* as a very fashionable "demonology" (SS IX: 266).

his search for a new interpretation of it: his purpose was to formulate a "neo-Christianity" (*neo-khristianstvo*) (Berdiaev 1907: 4).

Like Merezhkovskii, Berdiaev rejects "historical Christianity" and believes in the coming era of a religious upheaval, or the epoch of "the new religious consciousness" (Berdiaev 1905: 151). His interpretation of the new religious consciousness soon outgrows Merezhkovskii's delineation of it and in his 1905 article "O novom religioznom soznanii" ("On the new religious consciousness"), Berdiaev formulates his neo-Christian creed with a more detailed philosophical basis than Merezhkovskii did. In Berdiaev's view, Merezhkovskii neglected to put the finger on the essence of "Spirit" and "Flesh," and thus failed to grasp the metaphysical reality of the religious problem.[16] Hence, Berdiaev – who calls himself in his autobiography *Samopoznanie* "a spokesman of the new religious consciousness" – attempts to substantiate a new religious paradigm that encompasses the metaphysics fundamentally related to it (Berdiaev [1949] 2003: 390). The chief principles of his philosophy of religion are for the first time coherently explained in *Smysl Tvorchestva* (*The Meaning of the Creative Act*), which he wrote between 1912 and 1914 but was not published until 1916: it turned out to be his last work published in Russia.[17]

Like Merezhkovskii, Berdiaev finds in his quest to reanimate Christianity an ally in Nietzsche, in whose God-fighting or Bogoborchestvo he suspects a true religious striving. He values Nietzsche for pinpointing the chief deficiency in historical Christianity, i.e., that it imposes upon humanity an external law and morality and in that way restrains the individual's creative capacity for self-realization. In traditional Christian morality, the human is deprived of his spiritual freedom and of any claim to self-authority: he is thus bound to live by ethical standards that are not his own. Although Berdiaev is at the core a defender of the Christian idea, he does agree with Nietzsche that historical Christian morality has brushed aside the human's freedom and creativity and instead lowered

---

[16] For Merezhkovskii's and Berdiaev's debate on the "new religious consciousness", see Scanlan (1970).

[17] "I consider this book [...] the most inspired of my writings, and it is herein that my original philosophical thought found expression for the first time. In this book is put my basic theme, my first intuition about the human being" (Berdiaev [1949] 2003: 460).

the human to a slave of its normative valuation. Christian morality is based on obedience and fear and has canceled out the human's free will and creative capacity to determine his own moral criteria. It has glorified what Berdiaev labels as the negative virtues of humility and self-denial and was, in fact, "hostile to all heroism, to all elevation of life, to the heroic upsurge, to the heroic sacrifice" (Berdiaev [1916] 2002: 222). Traditional Christian ethics is an opportunist and legalistic moralism, obtaining virtue from humanity by sanctioning punishment in the afterlife. Berdiaev subscribes to Nietzsche's delineation of Christian morality as a slave morality in the sense that it ignores the creative powers in humanity:

> Nietzsche considered Christian morality slavish, plebeian, a morality of weakness and so he hated it. He contrasted it with a lordly morality, an aristocratic and noble morality of power. Nietzsche said much about Christianity that is remarkable, exciting and valuable for the moral resurrection of the human being (Berdiaev [1916] 2002: 228).

Although highly motivated by Nietzsche's charges against established Christianity, Berdiaev does not renounce Christianity entirely, as did Nietzsche. Instead, he draws on Nietzsche's critical commentaries to formulate a new version of Christianity, or in his discourse, a "new religious consciousness." He retains the Christian idea by distinguishing between authentic and historical Christianity, the latter being a seriously distorted account of Christ's original teachings. And once again, like for Merezhkovskii, this is were Nietzsche's view on Christ is highly attractive to Berdiaev: in *The Antichrist*, Nietzsche reproaches the Church, and in particular Paul, for corrupting Christ's original message.[18] Having adopted Nietzsche's criticism of the institutionalized Church, Berdiaev aspires to restore the authentic word of Christ and to reestablish authentic Christianity. Interestingly, he finds a way to regenerate Christ's original message in Nietzsche.

Christ proclaimed that the human was made in the image and likeness of God and by that, he implied, according to Berdiaev, that the human is by nature an autonomous and absolute being. Christ declared morality to be a purely individual issue: each individual determines for himself his relationship to God and to the other human beings. For Berdiaev, there is no fundamental difference between Nietzsche's immorality and authentic Christian morality because both

---

[18] See KSA 6: 211ff, already quoted in chapter 6.

assume the primacy of moral individualism: "Christian spiritualism gives eternal approval to this ethical individualism, to which we aspire, and which was dear to the 'immoralist' Nietzsche" (Berdiaev 1902: 126). Reading Christ's Word as an imperative for moral individualism, Berdiaev rejects historical Christianity for its normative ethics and aims to revive the authentic Christian message of an individualist ethics:

> Christianity, as an ideal (not the historical) religious doctrine, never lowers itself to a police understanding of morality (*politseiskoe ponimanie nravstvennosti*), and its respect for the dignity of the human and for his inner freedom – which constitutes the unfading moral essence of Christianity – cannot be taken away from it by modern-day hypocrites (ibid.).

Nietzsche is for the "God-seeker" an inexhaustible inspiration to reconsider historical Christianity and to compose a neo-Christian philosophy that redefines the relationship between humanity and the Deity and that affirms the human's craving for self-realization. Borrowing from Nietzsche's discourse, Berdiaev claims that ideal Christianity is not "slavish or plebeian, but aristocratic and noble [...] a religion for the strong spirits, and not for the weak." Authentic Christian morality gives the human "the free responsibility for his own destination and the destination of the world" (Berdiaev [1916] 2002: 228). Berdiaev integrates Nietzsche's urge for self-valuation in his Christian ideal and withstands the traditional Christian ethics of the collective welfare. Echoing Zarathustra's metaphorical speech, he states that

> [Ideal] Christian morality is always something of the heights, something that uplifts, rather than a thing of the valley, something that flattens out. Christian morality is a morality of values, of the creative elevation of life, rather than a morality of well-being for the people; it is not an altruistic and distributive morality. Christianity does not allow for a lowering of quality for the sake of quantity, it is whole in quality, i.e. in aristocratic value (id.: 229).

The new Christianity is for Berdiaev primarily "a religion of freedom" (*religiia svobody*), in contrast to the historical "religion of fear" (*religiia strakha*) (id.: 142). With the new religious consciousness, Berdiaev hopes to overcome historical Christianity which is a religion of moralism and replace it by the neo-Christian "religion of creativity": "The new religious consciousness posits the question of the creative experience as a religious experience, self-justifying, rather than demanding justification" (id.: 145). Like Merezhkovskii, who distinguishes between the Old Testament emphasis on the Flesh and the New Testament preoccupation with the Spirit and believes in the coming of a Third Testament in which both Flesh and Spirit are reconciled, Berdiaev discerns three eras in the history of Christianity. The Old Testament world is governed by an ethics of law, subjecting humanity to an abstract law and external normative morality. The New Testament era is marked by a morality of redemption and already gives more attention to the individual, who nevertheless still submits to the sanctioning idea of salvation in the hereafter. In both these periods the vocation for creativity is completely ignored. In the third and final era of Christianity, which in Berdiaev's view will necessarily and naturally follow from historical Christianity, the human will no longer be subject to a law that is not his own. This shift in anthropological consciousness will be established in the religion of creativity.

6. Re-Christianizing the *Übermensch*

Once again spurred by Nietzsche, Berdiaev passes judgment on established anthropological theories to arrive at a new religious delineation of humankind. Nietzsche condemns Christianity for loading humanity with an external set of values, thereby reducing the human to a mere submissive and docile being. Nietzsche's critique, for Berdiaev, diagnoses the chief flaws of traditional Christianity. In historical Christian consciousness, shaped by the doctrines of the Church Fathers and earliest theologians, the human is envisioned as a passive and weak being who is absolutely determined by original sin. In Berdiaev's view, the doctrine of original sin is a detrimental flaw in Christian anthropology because it represents the human as a captive of this world and deprives humanity of any hope for spiritual regeneration. Each individual human bears responsibility for the Fall, a spiritual burden one is to accept obediently. This earthly world is defined as evil and considered inferior to the heavenly world. The human, sinful and weak by nature, is not able to elevate himself spiritually from this world and is dependent on God's grace for his spiritual redemption (Berdiaev [1916] 2002: 17ff.). Berdiaev finds fault with this deterministic conception of humanity which portrays it as enslaved by its sinful nature and forced to rely on the Deity to escape from its current condition. He claims that this idea of the human is a fundamental denial of the human's essence as a being that is created in the image and likeness of God. What is more, by ignoring the quintessence of human nature, historical Christianity likewise falls short in its understanding of the paradigm for which Christ stands. Dogmatic Church thinkers failed to think through the logical ramifications of the dogma of Christ's human nature: if Christ is both God and human, the human is in an equal manner both human and divine. Historical Christian anthropology recoiled from articulating *"what one must dare to call a Christology of the human, i.e. the secret of the human's divine nature, a dogma of the human, similar to the dogma of Christ"* (Berdiaev [1916] 2002: 75-76). Being made in the image of God, or the primal Creator, the human is by his very nature self-creative. This most essential element in human nature, its divinity and capacity for creation, is what the human is deprived of in normative Christian ethics and anthropology. In this anthropological system, the human is bound to live by a law and ethics that is externally imposed and thus not intrinsically willed. The failure to exhibit the truth about human nature led, according to Berdiaev, to the emergence of humanistic anthropology, marking a shift towards an affirmative portrayal of humankind. The merit of humanism is that it established the human as a creative being and made him the highest and final goal of the world process. In the humanistic anthropocentric perspective, the human is returned his authentic status as a being made in the image and likeness of God. Yet in the end, humanism also fails to measure up to the human's essence because it basically abandons the notion of God: by canceling out God, it fails to appreciate that the human's essence is made up by his divine nature. Humanism deprives the human of his spiritual, divine nature and reduces him to a mere material object who is subjected only to physical and natural necessities. It disregards the human as a "trans-natural subject" (*sverkhprirodnyi sub'ekt*) (Berdiaev [1916] 2002: 81). Although humanistic anthropology is a necessary and worthwhile experience in the history of humankind, it lost all consciousness of God and hence does not do justice to the human who is by nature inevitably bound to the Deity.

For Berdiaev, historical Christianity and the humanistic creed both exhibit shortcomings and as a result neither can fulfill his need for an inclusive religious model that covers the absolute truth about humanity: "if patristic consciousness, while having a Christology, lacks a corresponding anthropology, humanistic consciousness has no Christology to correspond with its anthropology" (ibid.). He aspires to find a solution for the anthropological problem within the Christian framework and not in an ideology that excludes the Deity as the prime mover of the universe and humanity. The new religious consciousness requires a shift from an exclusively theocentric to a more anthropocentric point of view. Consistent with his hopes for a third era in the history of Christianity, Berdiaev awaits a third anthropological revelation in which the human can fully develop and draw on his creativity. He sees this revelation initiated by Nietzsche, "the most significant phenomenon of modern history" and "the sin-offering for the sins of modern times" (id.: 83). With his concept of the *Übermensch*, Nietzsche exposes the contemporary anthropological deadlock and offers a way out of it. He pinpoints the flaw in the established Christian representation of the human which is its negation of the human's capacity for self-valuation and self-realization. He likewise exposes the humanist overemphasis on "the human, all too human" and insists that the human's goal should not be the current happiness of the "last people" (KSA 4: 19f.), but a willed fate of creativity. The *Übermensch* epitomizes for Berdiaev – like for Merezhkovskii – the logical dead-end of the humanistic imperative of the collective well-being and summons to overcome this petty moralism by positing the primacy of the individual's autonomy.

> After Nietzsche, after his works and his fate, humanism is already impossible, it is for ever overcome. "Zarathustra" is the greatest human book without grace [...] In its final form the crisis of humanism had to lead to the idea of the *Übermensch*, to the overcoming of the human. For Nietzsche, the final value is not the human, but the *Übermensch*, since he has overcome humanism. The human is for him shame and pain, the human should be overcome, the human should go to what is higher than the human, to what is already the *Übermensch*. In Nietzsche, humanism is overcome not from above, through grace, but from below through the human's own powers, and herein is the great achievement of Nietzsche (Berdiaev [1916] 2002: 84).

Zarathustra – who in Berdiaev's reading represents Nietzsche's voice – urges humanity to overcome the present human. And it is highly significant for Berdiaev's anthropological concerns that this upheaval in anthropological consciousness is to be established from within the human, by his own powers. Zarathustra is a paragon of "the human abandoned to himself" (ibid.). He stands for the bare and essential human who has shed away all external burdens that hinder him in the development of the individual self. Having thrown off the age-old value patterns and left only with himself, Zarathustra is reborn into a higher self solely by his own powers. Berdiaev finds that "never did a man left to himself and to his own powers, rise higher" (ibid.). Zarathustra personifies what Berdiaev seeks in anthropological consciousness: a drawing upon the human's individual creative potential.

Nietzsche's *Übermensch* embodies the particular qualities Berdiaev finds missing in traditional Christian anthropology, specifically a focus upon and faith in the human's creative powers which for him is where the religious dimension of Nietzsche's thought lies:

> *Nietzsche is the forerunner of a new religious anthropology.* Through Nietzsche a new humanity moves from godless humanism to divine humanism, to a Christian anthropology. Nietzsche is the prophet of the religious Renaissance of the West [...] As no one else in the course of whole history, Nietzsche sensed the creative calling of the human, which neither patristic nor humanistic anthropology was aware of [...] We must share Nietzsche's torment, it is through and through religious (Berdiaev [1916] 2002: 84).

Although the *Übermensch* was spelled out by Nietzsche to overcome the Christian paradigm, it makes up, in Berdiaev's appropriation, the basis of his neo-Christian anthropology. Finding fault with the historical Christian life-negating anthropology, Berdiaev aspires to an anthropological paradigm that does justice to the ontological status of humanity as beings created in the image and likeness of God. He is in search of a new conception of humanity in which the old theocentric hope for salvation – the idea that the human can only be spiritually regenerated by God's grace – is replaced by an anthropocentric view on the human's elevation into a higher self. He identifies this ideal of individual self-realization in the *Übermensch*. Unlike traditional Christian anthropology, Nietzsche's *Übermensch* measures up to the creative potential of the human. Berdiaev finds in the *Übermensch* the core of his new Christian anthropology which is that the human is completely free in the realization of the self. He observes in Nietzsche the required shift in anthropological consciousness: "Through Nietzsche begins a new anthropological revelation in the world, which in its final realization, in its Logos, should become the Christology of the human" (*Khristologiia cheloveka*) (ibid.).

Because Berdiaev is mainly concerned with the status of the human in his formulation of the new religious consciousness, he seeks a third "anthropological revelation of creativity" (id.: 90). The neo-Christian anthropology is distinct not only from the Old Testament image, in which the human submits to external law (ethics of law), but also from New Testament anthropology, in which the human is subject to redemption (ethics of redemption). In contrast with the Old and New Testament representation of the human, in which revelation comes "from above," this third revelation is to occur from within humanity. In that sense, it is a truly anthropological and not a theological revelation. Interpreting Nietzsche's *Übermensch* as an urge to generate oneself, Berdiaev claims that the anticipated anthropological revelation will not be initiated by God but will be realized within and by humanity. Being by nature self-determining and free, the human should live up to his divine potential and accomplish the "Christology of the human" (id.: 98). Because the human is created in the image of God, he is endowed with a divine and creative nature: "God the Creator (*Bog-Tvorets*) created the human through an act of his All-mighty and Omniscient will, to his image and likeness as a free being, possessing the creative power and called to rule over Creation" (id.: 92). The focus is on the human as an active and dynamic being, fully and freely developing his divine potential, i.e. his creativity.

> Creativity is a matter of the human's Godlike freedom, the revelation of the Creator's image within him [...] In creativity the divine in the human is revealed from below, by the human's free, own initiative, and not from above. In creativity the human himself reveals the image and likeness of God, discovers the divine power within himself (id.: 90-91).

God's calling for the human to reveal the spiritual freedom and creative power within himself is, as Berdiaev asserts, substantiated in the appearance of Christ: there would have been no incarnation if human nature were merely passive, obedient, and lacking free will. For Berdiaev, the coming of the *Bogochelovek* or *God-Man* Christ was not only a revelation of Divinity but also a revelation of "the human greatness" and holds the affirmation of both faith in God and in humanity (id.: 91). The relationship between God and human is mutual and of equal standing and hence requires a belief in both God and humanity. The new religious anthropology that Berdiaev aims for, i.e. the free union of Divinity and humanity, or *Bogochelovechestvo* (*Divine Humanity*), is initiated by the *Bogochelovek* Christ, the first to have incorporated both divine and human nature:

> The initial phenomenon of religious life is the encounter and interaction (*vzaimodeistvie*) between God and human, the movement from God to human and from human to God [...] In Christianity is the humanity of God (*chelovechnost' Boga*) revealed. The humanization of God (*ochelovechenie Boga*) is the fundamental process in the religious consciousness of humanity [...] The origin of the consciousness that the human is the likeness of God is the other side of the consciousness that God is the likeness of the human [...] The appearance of Christ the Bogochelovek is exactly the complete joining of both movements, from God to the human and from the human to God, the final birth of God in the human and of the human in God, the realization of the mystery of the two-unity (*dvuedinstvo*), the mystery of Divine Humanity (*Bogochelovechestvo*) (Berdiaev [1927] 1994: 129).

In a theogonic process "the Creator comes into being together with creation, God comes into being together with the human" (ibid.: 132). In Berdiaev's anthropology of *Bogochelovechestvo*, the human is thus mutually related to God and is the co-creator of the universe. Humanity is approaching a "cosmic anthropological turning point, a great religious revolution in the human self-consciousness" (Berdiaev [1916] 2002: 95). In this new Christian anthropology the human is not restrained by any normative morality; "the creative mystery" of humanity lies in its "final freedom" (*poslednaia svoboda*), this is inner freedom in its most radical form.[19] In Berdiaev's new Christianity, each individual is granted the ultimate freedom to establish for himself the criteria to live by and engage in a free and equal relationship with the Deity on a self-willed basis: "the human is completely free in the revelation of his creativity" (Berdiaev [1916] 2002: 97). He claims that the human's emancipation from any external law adds a new, more profound dimension to his religiosity and experience of God.

---

[19] Merezhkovskii applies this formula in his Christology: in a Nietzschean phraseology, he characterizes Christ as representing "the greatest freedom *beyond good and evil*" (Merezhkovskii [1900-1901] 1995: 219).

Berdiaev finds in Nietzsche's *Übermensch* a new way to relate to God. Dissatisfied with historical Christian anthropology because it negates the human's ontological status as a self-creative being, he finds in Nietzsche's *Übermensch* what is missing in Christian consciousness: the apotheosis of human creativity. Nietzsche's anthropology of the self-determining individual is appropriated by Berdiaev as an incentive towards a new religious experience in which the human engages in a reciprocal relationship with the Deity on a self-willed basis and is no longer under compulsion of an external law:[20]

> The human does not only have the right, but even the duty to become an "Übermensch", since the "Übermensch" is the way from the human to God [...] the idea of the "Übermensch" is a religious-metaphysical idea, Zarathustra is a religious prophet and idealist (Berdiaev 1902: 124).

For Berdiaev, Nietzsche stands "on the world threshold to a religious epoch of creativity" (Berdiaev [1916] 2002: 97).[21]

7. What Dostoevskii knew: moral freedom *versus* moral freedom

Berdiaev finds in Nietzsche's *Übermensch* the stimulus for individual self-realization which is required to establish the neo-Christian anthropological creed of the morally free and self-creative individual.

---

[20] Ludolf Müller explains Berdiaev's positive assessment of Nietzsche only in terms of the latter's reflections on humanist consciousness, a position that negates Nietzsche's fruitful role in Berdiaev's proposed solution for the crisis in Christian and humanist consciousness (Müller 1952).

[21] Soon after the publication of *Smysl Tvorchestva*, Shestov reviews this work as follows: "Nietzsche completely possessed Berdiaev's soul [...] Even Berdiaev's style of writing reminds of Nietzsche, and, what is especially curious, the Nietzsche of the very last period, when he wrote the "Antichrist". Like Nietzsche's "Antichrist", Berdiaev's book is written at the highest pitch of his voice. [...] The resemblance is so striking, that it leaves the impression that the content of Berdiaev's book is completely covered by the content of Nietzsche's "Antichrist". [...] When Berdiaev, with a despairing break in his voice, speaks about the "justification of the human being", I clearly hear the word *Übermensch*. [...] When, finally, Berdiaev rises passionately against the family, science, and the arts with all the energy he is capable of, and places an anathema on modern culture, which is, according to his own account, no more than "a great failure", I begin to feel, that I am not reading Berdiaev's "Smysl Tvorchestva", but Nietzsche's 'Antichrist'" (Shestov 1916: 91-92).

In this perspective, the *Übermensch* comes close to his understanding of the *Bogochelovek* Christ. Eventually, though, after a substantial amount of Nietzsche-appraisal, the *Übermensch* fails to serve the religious philosopher in the formulation of his new religious consciousness. In order to pinpoint the flaws in Nietzsche's anthropology, Berdiaev turns to Dostoevskii. More specifically, he brings in the *chelovekobog* to give a precise account of where Nietzsche's *Übermensch* falls short. The identification of *chelovekobog* and *Übermensch* enables Berdiaev not only to indicate at what point Nietzsche eventually proves insufficient for the final delineation of the new Christian anthropology but also to demonstrate that Dostoevskii succeeds where Nietzsche fails.

In *Smysl Tvorchestva* Berdiaev claims that as far as the anthropological question is concerned, only one thinker can compete with Nietzsche, and this is Dostoevskii "who is at once so different from and so alike" Nietzsche (Berdiaev [1916] 2002: 84). In *Mirosozertsanie Dostoevskogo* (*Dostoevskii's Worldview*, 1923), the monograph in which Berdiaev draws on Dostoevskii and his well-known characters to explain his own philosophical views, he also elaborates on the *perceived* affiliation between both Dostoevskii and Nietzsche to arrive eventually at a moral deliberation of them. For Berdiaev, the value that Dostoevskii and Nietzsche share is that they pinpoint the flaws of contemporary anthropological consciousness and offer a way out of the deadlock. Both argue the case of the human's individual autonomy, and in doing so, do not close their eyes to the ramifications of this absolute freedom. They bring the complex dialectic of human freedom to light and describe its moral implications. They expose the ambiguity and irrationality of freedom – covered up for centuries in historical Christianity – which is that freedom necessarily entails the individual choice between good and evil. The ontological status of the human as a free and self-determining being has ethical implications, specifically that an overall normative morality can no longer exist. Yet the absence of any sanctioning moral system brings the danger of immorality. For Berdiaev, Dostoevskii and Nietzsche are allies because they both stand for the "final freedom" (*poslednaia svoboda*) and grasp its ethical corollaries (Berdiaev [1923] 1991: 57). Dostoevskii and Nietzsche recognize "that the human is terribly free and that this freedom is tragic, for it lays on burden and suffering" (id.: 54). With regard to the new anthropological consciousness of the morally autonomous individual, Dostoevskii "knew everything that Nietzsche knew", yet in the end, "Dostoevskii knew, what Nietzsche did not know" (ibid.).

For Berdiaev, what both Dostoevskii and Nietzsche knew is clustered around and united in *chelovekobog* and *Übermensch*. He adopts Merezhkovskii's identification to document and explain the congruent motive in Dostoevskii's and Nietzsche's thought. And like Merezhkovskii, he finds in *chelovekobog* and *Übermensch* the most explicit demonstration of what historical Christianity has systematically ignored: the anthropological problem of the final freedom. Berdiaev considers the authors of these ideas to be "great anthropologists": with the concepts of *Übermensch* and *chelovekobog* respectively, they touch upon the final points of anthropological consciousness. In his words, "what Dostoevskii says about the *chelovekobog* and Nietzsche about the *Übermensch*, is an apocalyptic thought about the human being" (Berdiaev 1918).[22]

In Berdiaev's understanding, "the revelation of the idea of the *chelovekobog* belongs entirely to Dostoevskii." He sees the idea most explicitly personified in Kirillov, in whom "the last problem of human fate" is brought up (Berdiaev [1923] 1991: 132). In his desire to become a god himself, Kirillov posits the ultimate challenge to God. In that perspective, the *chelovekobog* is the ultimate icon of the human's emancipation from any external restraint and thus fulfills, at least partially, Berdiaev's criteria of the absolutely free individual. The association with Nietzsche's *Übermensch* is anticipated. Whereas Merezhkovskii centers his explanation of the *chelovekobog* for the most part on Kirillov, Berdiaev does not pin this idea exclusively down on this one character. When he speaks of the *chelovekobog*, he has several of Dostoevskii's nihilistic characters in mind, in particular Raskol'nikov, Stavrogin, Kirillov and Ivan Karamazov (Berdiaev [1923] 1991: 54; 61). In progressively differing arguments, they all stand for the human urge to final freedom, the freedom beyond the established ethics of good and evil. They represent "revolting freedom" (*buntuiushchaia svoboda*) in its final ramifications.

---

[22] The paper "Otkrovenie o cheloveke v tvorchestve Dostoevskogo" ("The revelation of the human in Dostoevskii's works" appeared in the 1918 issue of *Russkaia Mysl'* (March-April). See the internet source http://www.krotov.org/berdyaev/1918/19180301.html

Berdiaev appropriates the *chelovekobog*, which he observes in several of Dostoevskii's characters, as a most manifest and salient personification of the moral freedom he aspires to in his new Christian paradigm. These nihilistic characters mark "the end of a whole period of universal history." With them, "the search for human freedom enters a new phase" (id.: 61). "Their tragedy is a hymn to freedom" (id.: 62). The nihilistic characters embody the revolt against the age-long normative morality of historical Christianity and break loose from any externally imposed restraints. They all strive to establish their individual freedom against external laws. In this respect, they pave the way for humanity's emancipation from dogmatic laws and stand up for the new Christian anthropology of the free and self-realizing individual.

Berdiaev believes that the only authentic way to God is through ultimate freedom. The only worthy relationship with the Deity is the one that is freely and deliberately willed. Being a pioneer of moral freedom, the *chelovekobog* fulfills the criteria for the authentic free religious experience. The idea of absolute moral autonomy is also at the core of Berdiaev's religious and favorable assessment of Nietzsche's *Übermensch*. In Berdiaev's reading, *chelovekobog* and *Übermensch* are identical in the sense that they promote the human's ethical freedom. However, in the final outcome, *chelovekobog* and *Übermensch* do not measure up to the authentic Christian paradigm of the self-realizing individual because at the basis of these anthropological theories is the aspiration to overcome God, the primal source from Whom emanates the whole world and humanity. By denying the Deity, *chelovekobog* and *Übermensch* fail to appreciate the human's essential nature as a being made in the image and likeness of God, and in the end, they fall short in their understanding of the final freedom.

As Berdiaev claims, this is what Nietzsche failed to understand but what Dostoevskii "knew" (id.: 54). Both constitute a landmark in anthropological consciousness. They find contemporary Christian anthropology problematical and, offer a similar alternative to it: an anthropology of individual self-realization. Yet in the final analysis, Dostoevskii and Nietzsche take diverging paths. Whereas Dostoevskii opts for the way to the *Bogochelovek*, Nietzsche chooses the path of the *Übermensch* or the *chelovekobog*, terms which are interchangeable in Berdiaev's discourse (id.: 55). At this crossroad,

Nietzsche fails to see the truth about humanity and eventually goes in the wrong direction. In his desire to overcome God, Nietzsche eventually also overcomes the human:

Nietzsche wants to overcome the human, like a shame and disgrace, and goes to the *Übermensch*. The last limits of humanist self-will and self-assertion are the death of the human in the *Übermensch*. In the *Übermensch* the human is not preserved, he is overcome, like a shame and disgrace, like a weakness and *non-entity*. The human is only a means for the appearance of the *Übermensch*. The *Übermensch* is an idol, for whom the human kisses the ground, who devours the human and all humanlike (ibid).

With the conception of the *chelovekobog*, Dostoevskii already anticipated this ruination of the human; he knew "the tempting and alluring ways of *chelovekobozhestvo* (man-godhood)" and exhibited them in Raskol'nikov, Stavrogin, Kirillov, and Ivan Karamazov (id.: 54). However, what distinguishes him from Nietzsche is that he also "knew another thing, he saw the light of Christ, in which the darkness of *chelovekobozhestvo* is unmasked" (id.: 55). Whereas Nietzsche remained mesmerized by *Übermensch* or *chelovekobog*, anthropological concepts in which the human is actually worn out, Dostoevskii found salvation in the *Bogochelovek* Christ. Berdiaev asserts that Dostoevskii's turn to Christ enabled him to uphold his anthropology of the morally free and self-determining individual without falling into the trap of obliterating what is essential in the makeup of humanity: its divine nature. By retaining the idea that God and Christ constitute the core of humanity, Dostoevskii preserves and does justice to the human as a being made in the image and likeness of God.

Berdiaev finds the dialectics of final freedom in Dostoevskii. On the one hand, Dostoevskii refrains from any deterministic anthropology and affirms the human's moral freedom to be the highest anthropological good. On the other hand, he understands that final freedom can be turned into a license for moral lawlessness and indulgence in one's egotistical desires. He feels that "the way to Christ runs through infinite freedom (*bespredel'naia svoboda*)," and knows at the same time that the temptation of the *chelovekobog* or *Übermensch* lies "on the same way of infinite freedom" (id.: 54f.). In *chelovekobog* and *Übermensch*, final freedom turns into "self-will" (*svoevolie*), into "rebellious self-assertion (*buntuiushchee samoutverzhdenie*)" (id.: 61). This kind of freedom is empty and purposeless and eventually destroys the human. This is saliently and most diversely represented in the fate of Raskol'nikov who murders to prove his theory right, Kirillov who commits suicide to realize his idea, and Ivan Karamazov who is ruined by his own theory that "all is permitted." When one draws on his final freedom in this manner, freedom paradoxically changes into slavery, ruining the authentic image of the human. The human is made in the image and likeness of God and only fully becomes who he really is by unfolding his immanent divinity. If freedom is not directed towards this higher nature, towards God, then this is not authentic freedom but enslavement.

In Berdiaev's Christology, Dostoevskii's representation of Christ, especially in the 'legend' of the "Grand Inquisitor," is more authoritative than the Gospel image of Christ: "The 'Legend of the Grand Inquisitor' made such an impression on my young mind that when I turned to Christ for the first time, I turned to the appearance he bears in the Legend" (id.: 26).[23] Berdiaev finds the ultimate legitimization of his anthropological ideal of the self-realizing individual in Dostoevskii's Christ, who withstood the devil's temptations. Instead of offering humanity a set of normative rules to live by, Christ brought humanity the message of moral freedom. Dostoevskii's Christ is for Berdiaev the paragon of the final freedom. By refusing the devil's temptations, which can be reduced to a religion based on authority and compulsion, he demonstrates that humanity is free to choose between good and evil, and more importantly, to choose deliberately for God. This is consistent with Berdiaev's view on the self-willed reunion with the Deity which is realized "through an inner experience of freedom" (id.: 62). In the legend, "Dostoevskii wrathfully exposes all inclinations towards a religion of compulsion and religion" (ibid.).

Through the failure of the *chelovekobog* via suicide or murder, Dostoevskii suggests that true moral freedom, or "the highest freedom," lies in the deliberate acceptance of the *Bogochelovek* as the moral paradigm to which humanity must aspire (ibid.). He exposes the falseness of moral freedom, if this is realized in a worldview devoid of God.

---

[23] See also Berdiaev [1939] 1995: 9.

Berdiaev finds in Dostoevskii's conception of the human the same Dionysian drive that Nietzsche aims for in his anthropology of the *Übermensch*. In his anthropology, Nietzsche sets out with the ambition to overcome God and the related theocentric anthropological and ethical framework. He deliberately ignores that the human is a being made in the image and likeness of God and consequently, his Dionysianism fails to measure up to the human's potentiality. Dostoevskii's Dionysianism, however, is constructed around God, which enables him to retain and confirm the divine essence of humanity (Berdiaev 1918).

In the end, Berdiaev overcomes Nietzsche through Dostoevskii. The Russian writer provides him with an ideologically rich concept, i.e. the *chelovekobog*, which enables him to delineate as precisely as possible what he finds problematic in Nietzsche's *Übermensch*. Dostoevskii also offers him a positive alternative to Nietzsche: the image of the *Bogochelovek* Christ in the 'legend' of the "Grand Inquisitor," which fundamentally legitimizes Berdiaev's Christian anthropology of free self-realization.

8. What Solov'ëv and Merezhkovskii failed to know: the other *Übermensch*

Berdiaev marks a shift in the Russian reading of Nietzsche, specifically with regard to the religious appropriation of the *Übermensch*. Firstly, his delineation of the *Übermensch* is partly shaped by Solov'ëv's and Merezhkovskii's discourse on Nietzsche's concept. Secondly, his specific appreciation of the *Übermensch* clearly goes beyond and substantially adds to their responses.

8.1. The antidote to Solov'ëv's "Antichrist"

Vladimir Solov'ëv was the first Russian critic to observe religious aspirations in the *Übermensch* and hence cleared the way for the *God-seekers'* further religious interpretations of it. In his neo-Christian adaptation of the *Übermensch*, Berdiaev is to some degree indebted to Solov'ëv. Furthermore, in his final appreciation of Nietzsche's anthropology – i.e. under the identification with the *chelovekobog* – Berdiaev takes up Solov'ëv's formula, which is that the only authentic delineation of the *Übermensch* is the Christian one: "the idea of God is the only trans-human idea (*sverkhchelovecheskaia ideia*) that doesn't ruin the human" (Berdiaev [1923] 1991: 74). Nonetheless, he opposes to Solov'ëv's eventual determination of the *Übermensch* as personifying the Antichrist. Referring to Solov'ëv's illustrious statement that Nietzsche's idea of the *Übermensch* is nowadays a fashionable "demonology" (SS IX: 267), Berdiaev claims that

> Nietzsche's demonism is an enormous phenomenon, truly new and infinitely important for our religious consciousness [...] all the complexity and depth of the problem of Nietzsche is that he is a pious demonist (Berdiaev [1907] 1991: 237).

He disagrees with Solov'ëv's final unfavorable interpretation of the *Übermensch* because he believes that this concept should be taken into account when dealing with the issue of Christianity: "one cannot do away with Nietzsche that easily, like Solov'ëv thought" (ibid.). Unlike Solov'ëv, Berdiaev believes that Nietzsche's theomachy (*bogoborchestvo*) contains a positive element for the religious experience. He considers the struggle with God a necessary stage in the process of freely and deliberately opting for Him. As described in the Book of Job and analyzed in depth by Dostoevskii in the character of Ivan Karamazov, a crisis in faith is "infinitely important for the fullness of religious consciousness" (ibid.). Struggling with God is not "a metaphysical loathing of God" nor a choosing for evil but is rather a psychological and religious process of seeking God. In line with Merezhkovskii, who sees the world as a dialectical struggle between polar opposites (Flesh and Spirit, West and East, *chelovekobog* and *Bogochelovek*, Antichrist and Christ), and believes that this bifurcation will be finally dissolved in a religious union, Berdiaev postulates that "demonism is an aspect of Divinity, a pole of the Good" and claims that this truth will only be fully acknowledged when "the mystical dialectics of being" come to a religious synthesis (id.: 238). Good cannot exist without evil, true religion cannot exist without a certain extent of theomachy; the path to God runs through a religious crisis. Berdiaev appreciates Nietzsche because he had the courage to question God and in this manner, pioneered the new religious experience, in which one opts for God deliberately rather then under the pressure of an externally imposed normative morality.

In opposition to Solov'ëv, who sees the *Übermensch* as the absolute antagonist of the authentic *sverkhchelovek*, or *Bogochelovek* Christ, Berdiaev sees the *Übermensch* as approaching the *Bogochelovek*. In his evaluation, Nietzsche's anthropology epitomizes the ideal of free self-realization, which is also at the core of his interpretation of the *Bogochelovek* Christ. Although it was designed as a concept to overcome the notion of God, the *Übermensch* aspires to establish an anthropology of autonomous self-determination similar to what Berdiaev finds in Christ's message to humanity. In this perspective, Nietzsche stands "close to Christ" (Berdiaev [1907] 1991: 238). In his "proud freedom," Zarathustra is familiar to Christ (Berdiaev [1923] 1991: 133).

Solov'ëv implicitly associates the *Übermensch* with the Antichrist. For Berdiaev, although the *Übermensch* eventually fails to meet up to the Christian ideal, it does not bear traits of the Antichrist. Rather, he finds the Antichrist embodied in Dostoevskii's representation of the Grand Inquisitor. The Inquisitor's arguments against Christ boil down to a "metaphysical loathing" of and a direct "hostility" towards Christ and God (Berdiaev [1907] 1991: 238). Berdiaev uncovers the Antichrist in the Grand Inquisitor because he consciously deprives humanity of the message that Christ left them: moral autonomy. Moral freedom implies existential suffering, wrestling with good and evil, and thus excludes instant happiness. Posing as a philanthropist, the Grand Inquisitor, who is convinced that the majority of humanity cannot bear the existential burden of the final freedom, decided to falsify Christ's teaching. Instead of freedom, he provides humanity with bread and happiness. For Berdiaev, the Inquisitor's betrayal of Christ amounts to a betrayal of humanity: he ignores the human's "highest spiritual nature," his divine makeup (Berdiaev [1923] 1991: 125). If one does not acknowledge God, one does not fully grasp the essence of humanity. The new Christianity "requires not only belief in God, but also belief in the human" (ibid.). The Grand Inquisitor, as Berdiaev asserts, rejects both. Berdiaev holds the same view that Solov'ëv outlined in his "Kratkaia Povest' ob Antikhriste": the chief danger in the Antichrist is that he appears in the image and name of Christ, pretending to be full of compassion for humankind and bringing happiness and collective welfare. In actuality the Antichrist is evil incarnate but comes to the people in the disguise of Christian good; "such is the tempting anti-Christian nature" (id.:

132). Nietzsche shares with the Grand Inquisitor the fundamental dismissal of God. In that sense, he likewise ignores the ontological status of the human as a being made in the image and likeness of God. Yet in Berdiaev's interpretation, Nietzsche cannot be identified with the Antichrist because he puts moral freedom at the core of his anthropology, which also constitutes the principal fundament of Berdiaev's own neo-Christian anthropology. Like Merezhkovskii, Berdiaev will instead connect the *Übermensch* to Dostoevskii's image of the *chelovekobog*.

8.2. Re-modelling Merezhkovskii's paradigm

Merezhkovskii also contributes to Berdiaev's appreciation of the *Übermensch*. His study *L. Tolstoi i Dostoevskii* is a landmark in the Russian reception of Nietzsche and in particular in the religious assimilation of his philosophy. He incorporates Nietzsche's *Übermensch* in his neo-Christological mythopoem of Christ being equally made up of the Antichrist. His religious appropriation of Nietzsche paves the way for a new approach to the German philosopher, in which he is primarily read a religious thinker. Berdiaev's interpretation of Nietzsche is partly entrenched in Merezhkovskii's assessment of him. However, consistent with his critique on Solov'ëv, Berdiaev counters Merezhkovskii's idea that the *Übermensch* is a phenomenon of the anti-Christian proclivity. Merezhkovskii lines up Christ/*Bogochelovek* and Spirit on the one hand, and Antichrist, *chelovekobog*, *Übermensch*, and Flesh on the other hand. Berdiaev partly grounds his interpretation of Nietzsche in this discursive constellation yet at the same time goes beyond it to arrive at a new conceptual configuration. Rejecting the association between *Übermensch* and Antichrist, he borrows the identification of *Übermensch* and *chelovekobog* from Merezhkovskii's discourse.

There are, however, some gradual differences in Merezhkovskii's and Berdiaev's associations of *Übermensch* and *chelovekobog*. In Merezhkovskii's perception, *chelovekobog* and *Übermensch* are identical in that they aspire to overcome the Christian God, in order to become a god oneself. They stand for the ultimate counterpoint to the Christian paradigm and thus give voice to the anti-Christian proclivity. In this capacity, they add to historical Christology. In Merezhkovskii's understanding of the new religious consciousness, *chelovekobog* and *Übermensch* are opposite to, yet simultaneously compatible with the *Bogochelovek*. In his constellation, the identification with the *chelovekobog* makes up the core of his favorable assessment of the *Übermensch*. In Berdiaev's valuation of the *Übermensch*, by contrast, the association with the *chelovekobog* only comes into being after a substantial amount of Nietzsche-appropriation and marks an altered understanding of the *Übermensch*. The *chelovekobog* is brought into prominence to indicate the flaws of the *Übermensch*, i.e., it deploys its moral freedom to assert the ego independently from the Deity.

Berdiaev credits Merezhkovskii for pinpointing the duality in religious consciousness and for discovering a religious synthesis of the Christian and anti-Christian (Berdiaev 1905: 153). Yet he faults Merezhkovskii's new version of Christianity for its predominant focus on Christ and Antichrist as transcendent entities. In Berdiaev's opinion, Merezhkovskii fails to understand the quintessence of Christ and Antichrist, i.e., that they are immanent in humanity and that the ongoing dialectics between them constitute the religious problem within the human (Berdiaev [1916] 2001: 336f.). Berdiaev believes that each human is torn between his Christian, spiritual, and his anti-Christian, material nature. This explains the personal struggle between good and evil, between *Bogochelovek* and *chelovekobog*. Berdiaev finds that Merezhkovskii's all too transcendent worldview is also responsible for his misunderstanding of the *Übermensch*. For Berdiaev, the *Übermensch* represents more than an anti-Christian current in the world. It stands instead for a proclivity inherent in the human: the urge to break loose from the Godhead and to find a way to substantiate one's autonomous status.

9. Berdiaev's quotation of Nietzsche: reconstructing Nietzsche's tracks

In his writings on Nietzsche, Berdiaev occasionally includes some literal citations from or approximate allusions to the philosopher's original texts. His selection of exactly these passages (and hence the omission of others), his characteristic way of rendering them (as different from, e.g. Merezhkovskii's), are indicative of his particular appropriation of Nietzsche's thought. To appreciate in full Berdiaev's dynamic understanding of Nietzsche and to attest to its originality in relation to the other *God-seekers'* interpretation, his quotation of Nietzsche deserves ample scrutiny.

Like in the case of Merezhkovskii, Berdiaev's assessment of Nietzsche draws for the most part on *Thus spoke Zarathustra* and on aphorism 125 in *The Gay Science*, i.e. "the Madman." In "Eticheskaia problema v svete filosofskogo idealizma," in which he claims that the godless philosopher is in fact "longing for the lost Divinity," Berdiaev renders some lines (in Russian) from the madman's speech, to prove his thesis that Nietzsche – whose voice is in his interpretation identical to the madman's – is basically seeking God and mourning for his death:

> Разве вы ничего не слышите? [...] разве уже не шумят могильщики, которые Бога погребают? Вы не чувствуете запаха разлагающегося Божества? - и Боги ведь разлагаются! Бог умер! Останется мертвым! И убили его мы! Убийцы из убийц, в чем найдем мы себе утешение? Самое святое и могущественное что было доселе у мира, истекло кровью под нашим ножом! (Berdiaev 1902 : 120)

The original text is as follows:

> Hören wir noch Nichts von dem Lärm der Todtengräber, welche Gott begraben? Riechen wir noch Nichts von der göttlichen Verwesung? – auch Götter verwesen! Gott ist todt! Gott bleibt todt! Und wir haben ihn getödtet! Wie trösten wir uns, die Mörder aller Mörder? Das Heiligste und Mächtigste, was die Welt bisher besass, es ist unter unseren Messen verblutet. (Do we still not hear anything of the noise of the gravediggers, who are burying God? Do we smell nothing yet of the divine decomposition? – Gods too decompose! God is dead! God remains dead! And we have killed him! How shall we comfort ourselves, the murderers of all murderers? What was holiest and mightiest of all that the world has yet owned, has bled to death under our knives.) (KSA 3: 481).

As documented in the preceding chapter, Merezhkovskii puts forward the same aphorism in his explanation of Nietzsche's *Übermensch*. Yet whereas Merezhkovskii highlights the lines that he interprets as an urge to self-deification from this aphorism ("Must we ourselves not become gods?" [1900-1901] 1995: 118), Berdiaev reports the sentences that express the sorrow and grieving inevitably emerging from the death of God. This fragment is, in his reading, testimony to Nietzsche's latent mourning for his refutation of God and shows that the German philosopher has, in fact, not yet completely dealt with the issue of God and is still, in his account, "longing for the lost Divinity."

For Berdiaev, the religious dimension of Nietzsche's thought is most emphatically exhibited in the concept of the *Übermensch*. He perceives in the *Übermensch* an incentive to transcend the present human condition and to attain a higher, more perfected form of the human being. In his view, Nietzsche's anthropology of the self-creating and self-determining individual corresponds to the authentic Christian anthropological paradigm of the human being made in the image and likeness of God. The human is established as potentially godlike and is hence by his nature challenged to participate in God's creation. This process of co-creating begins with the free creating of oneself. For Berdiaev, Nietzsche's concept of the self-valuing being, though basically designed to overcome the gods, turns out to be a catalyst towards the original Christian ideal of the human as the one who creates himself and in that sense re-attains the original oneness with God. Rendered in this neo-Christian perspective, the *Übermensch* is "the way from the human to God" (Berdiaev 1902: 124). To support his religious understanding of the *Übermensch*, Berdiaev quotes from Zarathustra's teaching of this new anthropology to the people on the marketplace, as presented in the third preface to *Thus spoke Zarathustra* (KSA 4: 14f.). Some slight modifications in the Russian translation reveal Berdiaev's tendency to perceive the *Übermensch* as a pre-eminently religious anthropology.

Original German text	Berdiaev's version
Ich lehre euch den Übermenschen.	*Я пришел проповедывать вам сверхчеловека.*
Der Mensch ist Etwas, das überwunden werden soll. Was habt ihr gethan, ihn zu überwinden?	Человек есть нечто такое, что должно быть превзойдено. Что вы сделали, чтобы превзойти его?
Alle Wesen bisher schufen Etwas über sich hinaus:	Все существа, какие были доселе, давали рождение чему-нибудь более, чем они, высокому;
und ihr wollt die Ebbe dieser grossen Fluth sein und lieber noch zum Thiere zurückgehn, als den Menschen überwinden?	и вы хотите явиться отливом этого великого прилива, и, пожалуй, предпочтете вернуться к состоянию зверя, лишь бы не превзойти человека?
Was ist der Affe für den Menschen? Ein Gelächter oder eine schmerzliche Scham.	Что такое для человека обезьяна? Посмешище или стыд и боль.
Und ebendass soll der Mensch für den Übermenschen sein: ein Gelächter oder eine schmerzliche Scham. Ihr habt den Weg vom Wurme zum Menschen gemacht, und Vieles ist in euch noch Wurm. Einst wart ihr Affen, und auch jetzt noch ist der Mensch mehr Affe, als irgend ein Affe. Wer aber der Weiseste von euch ist, der ist auch nur ein Zwiespalt und Zwitter von	И тем же самым должен стать для сверхчеловека человек: посмешищем или стыдом и болью...

Pflanze und von Gespenst. Aber heisse ich euch zu Gespenstern oder Pflanzen werden?	
Seht, ich lehre euch den Übermenschen!	Внимайте, я проповедую вам сверхчеловека!
Der Übermensch ist der Sinn der Erde. Euer Wille sage: der Übermensch *sei* der Sinn der Erde! (KSA 4: 14).[24]	Сверхчеловек это смысль земли. Пусть же и воля ваша скажет: *да будет* сверхчеловек смыслом земли! (Berdiaev 1902: 124).

Zarathustra's first phrase "*I teach you the Übermensch*" is rendered as "I have come to preach you the *Übermensch*." This version calls forth associations with the canonical representation of Christ as the one who appeared on earth to bring God's word to the people. By this translation, Zarathustra is made identical to Christ; so the message he brings, i.e. the *Übermensch*, is in Berdiaev's account equally significant for humanity as Christ's revelation. The German "überwinden" ("to overcome") is translated as "превзойти." As shown above, the same verb is rendered as "преодолеть" in Merezhkovskii's text ([1900-1901] 1995: 119, 350). Both these verbs indicate an overcoming, but there is a significant semantic difference between them. "Превзойти" entails 'becoming better or more' and thus holds the meaning of a qualitative elevation. "Преодолеть" implies that there was some sort of obstacle that is successfully

---

[24] "*I teach you the Übermensch*. The human is something, that should be overcome. What have you done to overcome him? All beings hitherto have created something beyond themselves: and you want to be the ebb of that great tide, and would rather go back to the animals, than to overcome the human? What is the ape to the human? A laughing-stock or a painful shame. And just the same will be the human to the *Übermensch*: a laughing-stock or a painful shame. You have made your way from worm to human, and much within you is still worm. Once you were apes, and even now the human is more of an ape, than any ape. Even the wisest among you, is only a disharmony and hybrid of plant and phantom. But do I bid you to become phantoms or plants? Lo, I teach you the *Übermensch*. The *Übermensch* is the meaning of the earth. Let your will say: the *Übermensch shall be* the meaning of the earth!"

overcome. In Russian, these verbs are not synonyms. Berdiaev's preference to translate "überwinden" as "превзойти" reveals that he observes in the *Übermensch* an aspect of human transcendence and perfection of the current self. Furthermore, Zarathustra's view of evolution as a process in which all creatures thus far have created something beyond themselves ("Alle Wesen bisher schufen Etwas über sich hinaus") is in Berdiaev's translation modified into "all beings, that existed up to now, gave birth to something more, something higher, than they are." This translation shows, firstly, that Berdiaev – like Merezhkovskii – understood Zarathustra's account in terms of biological evolution, as a process in which one species naturally generates another. In Zarathustra's rationale, however, the procreative dimension is not that the *Übermensch* is born out of an ancestor; rather, the *Übermensch* is the one giving birth to and being born out of oneself. Secondly, Zarathustra's saying that beings create *beyond* (*über*) themselves is misrepresented; in Berdiaev's version, this is translated in terms of elevation of the species (более, чем они, высокому); in this context, evolution is the natural and mechanical reproduction of beings becoming gradually perfected. The religious appropriation of the *Übermensch* is prepared in the translation of this indicative phrase. Furthermore, Berdiaev's version leaves out Zarathustra's observation that the present human has not yet fully outlived his worm- and apelike self and that even the wisest among humans is still yet "a conflict and hybrid of plant and phantom" because these lines, however articulated to stimulate the human to overcome his conditioned self, initially strike the reader as a harsh critique on humanity. Berdiaev retains from Zarathustra's discourse only these phrases that fit into and do not conflict with his interpretation of the *Übermensch*. The omitted lines threaten what is at the core of Berdiaev's religious philosophy: the human being. The religious thinker assimilates the *Übermensch* as a prospective paradigm of human transfiguration and therefore cannot allow any degradation of what he considers to be the fundament of the *Übermensch* in his explanation of this anthropology. The quote is concluded with: "The *Übermensch* is the meaning of the earth. Let your will say: the *Übermensch shall be* the meaning of the earth!" This formula is the apotheosis of Nietzsche's anthropology in Berdiaev's reading. In the *Übermensch*, the religious thinker finds an answer to his anthropological search. His philosophy of religion is primarily concerned with the human, and he aspires to a new Christian anthropological paradigm that guarantees the essence of the human as a creative being. He wants to turn the historical Christian preoccupation with the otherworld – in his view a life-negating attitude – into a renewed interest in this current life as a potentiality for self-generated elevation. The human will not be saved from above, by God's grace, yet is himself the prime and sole mover of transfiguration. The required upheaval in Christian anthropological consciousness, the transition from theocentric hopes for salvation to a purely anthropocentric formulation of humanity's regeneration and realization of a higher self, is what Berdiaev finds at the core of Nietzsche's anthropology of the self-realizing and self-creating human. He reads in Zarathustra's dictum that the *Übermensch* is 'the meaning (*Sinn*) of the earth' the imperative dogma of human self-determination and self-creation in this life. Moreover, this quote is all the more appealing to Berdiaev because it centers upon the will as the fundamental starting point to realize the condition of the *Übermensch*. In Berdiaev's anthropological model, the human is an essentially free and self-determining being. The realization of oneself into a higher self is for each individual a deliberate choice to make.

Berdiaev maintains that both historical Christian and humanistic anthropological consciousness fail to do justice to the human's essence as a being created in the image and likeness of God. The historical Church distorts Christ's message and relates to the human as a passive and determined being, who is dependent on God's grace to restore his original godlike status, and thereby neglects to acknowledge the human's creative capacity to uplift himself and reunite with the Deity. In historical Christian consciousness, the emphasis is on God. Humanistic anthropology, on the other hand, notwithstanding its primary preoccupation with the human, falsifies and even obliterates the human because it is only focused on the human's material nature and denies the human's higher essence. Observing the merits and deficiencies in both anthropological ideologies, Berdiaev aspires to a new anthropological revelation in which both God and the creative human are guaranteed and brought to reconciliation. In Nietzsche's anthropology of the *Übermensch*, the religious thinker finds the prerequisite for the new Christian anthropological consciousness. Nietzsche, the defeater of the gods, is hailed as "*the forerunner of a new religious anthropology*" (Berdiaev [1916] 2002: 84).

This is for Berdiaev most saliently expressed by the character Zarathustra, whom he identifies completely with Nietzsche. In *Smysl Tvorchestva*, he credits Zarathustra's aphorisms as "the most powerful human book without grace" (id.: 83). Zarathustra gives voice to the crisis in anthropological consciousness and formulates a solution for it. He dares to pronounce the ramifications of the humanistic denial of God, this is that the human is essentially left to his own devices. Zarathustra's unique merit is that he turns this unfavorable condition into an advantage because he makes it the starting point for overcoming the anthropological predicament. Having cast aside the ancient theocentric model, Zarathustra retains only the self as the prime and sole basis of existence. And through this self, through his own individual strength, he is able to elevate himself and rise higher than his former, externally determined self. Zarathustra embodies for Berdiaev the inner motivation to transcend oneself by one's own will. Hence, in Nietzsche's anthropology, as presented through Zarathustra's quest of becoming, the human relies on the creative self to transfigure and redeem himself.

Berdiaev's religious appropriation of the *Übermensch*, this as is an anthropology that incites the human to transcend his present state and to reach a higher, more perfected stage in the human status, is primarily founded on his interpretation of Zarathustra's phrase "the human is something, that should be overcome" (*Der Mensch ist Etwas, das überwunden werden soll*).[25] In this context, the religious thinker understands the verb *überwinden*, and in particular the prefix *über*, as a transition into a higher condition, an act of going *above* the present state. In Berdiaev's view, the motto that the human is something that should be overcome is an imperative to rise above the present human who is in his current condition held back by an external ethics in the development of the self and, an incentive to elevate oneself from within oneself. He recalls especially this formula from Zarathustra's whole discourse on the *Übermensch* and employs it most frequently where it concerns Nietzsche's anthropology (Berdiaev

---

[25] In *Thus spoke Zarathustra*, this line appears for the first time in the third preface (KSA 4: 14), and is a recurrent motive in Zarathustra's quest for the *Übermensch*. Sometimes it appears as "Der Mensch ist Etwas, das überwunden werden muss"(Cfr. KSA 4: 44, 60, 72, 248).

1902: 91, 124; [1916] 2002: 306). In this perspective, the *Übermensch* is a paradigm for both retaining the human and transcending the 'human, all too human.' Having shaken off any external restraint, the *Übermensch* is an innocent new-born. Only the personal self is preserved. It is precisely on the basis of this personal self that the new human will realize and transfigure himself.

Although it was initially assimilated as the maxim for the neo-Christian anthropological consciousness, this same phrase will facilitate a decisive shift in the interpretation of the *Übermensch* in a later phase of Berdiaev's Nietzsche-reading. In *Mirosozertsanie Dostoevskogo* a quite different understanding of the *Übermensch* is rendered:

> Ницше хочет преодолеть человека, как стыд и позор, и идет к сверхчеловеку. Последние пределы гуманистического своеволия и самоутверждения — гибель человека в сверхчеловеке. В сверхчеловеке не сохраняется человек, он преодолевается, как стыд и позор, как бессилие и ничтожества. Человек есть лишь средство для явления сверхчеловека. Сверхчеловек есть кумир, идол, перед которым падает ниц человек, который пожирает человека и все человеческое (Berdiaev [1923] 1991: 55).

> (Nietzsche wants to overcome the human, like a shame and disgrace, and goes to the *Übermensch*. The last limits of the humanist self-will and self-assertion are the death of the human in the *Übermensch*. In the *Übermensch* the human is not preserved, he is overcome, like a shame and disgrace, like a weakness and nonentity. The human is only a means for the appearance of the *Übermensch*. The *Übermensch* is an idol, for whom the human kisses the ground, who devours the human and all humanlike.)

Nietzsche's anthropology is again explained by alluding to the same metaphors as the ones deployed to support the sympathetic reading of the *Übermensch*. In this context, however, the figure of speech in question – the human as object of shame and hence as something to be overcome – has grown into the counter program of Berdiaev's own anthropological expectations. Note that in the rivaling interpretation *überwinden* is translated as "преодолеть", whereas in the more favorable reading, the verb is rendered as "превзойти" (Berdiaev 1902: 124). This translation reveals that Berdiaev no longer reads the *Übermensch* as an anthropological ideal of self-transfiguration ("превзойти"), yet has begun to see it as a concept that has overcome the 'obstacle' of the human ("преодолеть"). Another point of difference is in the way Berdiaev communicates the idea that the human is the object of laughter or painful shame ("ein Gelächter oder eine Schmerzliche Scham") for the *Übermensch*. In the favorable interpretation, both *Gelächter* and *Scham* are rendered; however, in this text, *Gelächter* is left out and *Scham* is emphasized by presenting it twice, by "стыд" and "позор," both words having a slightly differentiating connotation. The omission of the word laughter, combined with the shifted accent on the idea that the human is a shame, presents the human in a more detrimental and inferior perspective than outlined in the original phrase.

Since Berdiaev's interpretation of Nietzsche's anthropology is primarily based on Zarathustra's line "the human is something, that should be overcome," a change in the representation of this line obviously indicates a shift in Berdiaev's delineation of the *Übermensch*. In this text, the *Übermensch* is no longer presented as an anthropology that incites the human to transcend into a higher level, and in that sense, corresponds to the ontological status of the human as a godlike being. The *Übermensch* is instead explained in complete opposite terms, i.e. as a being, whose appearance requires the annihilation of the human. In Berdiaev's altered reading, the human is not retained in the *Übermensch* yet is completely and utterly overcome. When juxtaposed to the *Übermensch*, the human is trivialized and reduced to a mere prerequisite for the *Übermensch* to emerge.

Berdiaev's occasionally biased rendering of Nietzsche's original wordings reveals his eagerness to bring in and use the *Übermensch* effectively in his philosophical and religious search, even when his judgment is no longer unambiguously favorable. His shifting account of Zarathustra's urge to overcome the human displays how his assessment of the *Übermensch* changes in relation to his philosophical position and marks different stages in his intellectual development. Whereas this phrase activates his initial affirmative interpretation of the *Übermensch*, i.e., as an anthropological ideal that borders on the divine truth incarnated in the *Bogochelovek*, in a later phase, the same line is at the core of his less favorable reading of the *Übermensch* in the context of its identification with the *chelovekobog*.

10. Conclusion

At first, Nietzsche's anthropology of the *Übermensch* strikes Berdiaev for its potential likeness with what he believes to be the authentic Christian anthropology. Berdiaev finds in the *Übermensch* what he misses in contemporary Christian consciousness, this is a conception of the human that does justice to the human's ontological make-up of being like the image and likeness of God. Nietzsche's anthropology of the self-realizing human constitutes the hallmark of the "Christology of the human" that Berdiaev aspires to in his new version of Christian anthropology (Berdiaev [1916] 2002: 84). In this perspective, Berdiaev finds at the core of the *Übermensch* the equal anthropological paradigm that the *Bogochelovek* Christ stands for, this is the human as a morally free and self-realizing being.

In his final assessment, though, Berdiaev faults the *Übermensch* for its negation of God, and consequential denial of the human's ontological status as the co-creator. In the concluding interpretation of the *Übermensch*, Berdiaev reads Nietzsche through Dostoevskii. In order to document his reservations concerning Nietzsche's anthropology, the link is established with the *chelovekobog*. So, Berdiaev's eventual understanding of the *Übermensch* is, at least partially, mediated by Merezhkovskii, who launched the identification of *Übermensch* and *chelovekobog* in Russian religio-philosophical discourse. However, whereas for Merezhkovskii the identification with the *chelovekobog* makes up for a constructive reading of the *Übermensch*, for Berdiaev this same match triggers off a less favorable understanding of the *Übermensch*. Under the association with the *chelovekobog*, the *Übermensch* represents in Berdiaev's discourse no longer the aspired for Christian anthropology of the self-realizing personality, yet stands for the detrimental ramifications of this moral autonomy, if deployed in a worldview devoid of God. Berdiaev brings in the *chelovekobog* to prove what "Dostoevskii knew, what Nietzsche did not know" (Berdiaev [1923] 1991: 54).

So, like Merezhkovskii, Berdiaev reads Nietzsche, at least in the final appreciation, through the "horizon of expectations" emerging from Dostoevskii's discourse. Yet, his juxtaposition of Dostoevskii and Nietzsche is different from Merezhkovskii's. In Merezhkovskii's interpretation, Nietzsche serves as a catalyst to reconsider

Dostoevskii, and, in turn, Dostoevskii triggers him to discover in Nietzsche a religious motive, which was hitherto unnoticed. There is an obvious reciprocity in his appreciation of both. Berdiaev, in the initial phase of his Nietzsche-reading not influenced by Dostoevskii, observes from the onset in Nietzsche a religious aspiration. And the association with Dostoevskii moves him in the end to modify his former appraisal of Nietzsche as the harbinger of a new religious anthropology. In Berdiaev's final evaluation of Dostoevskii and Nietzsche, Dostoevskii succeeds exactly at the point where Nietzsche fails.

Although Berdiaev eventually distanced himself from Nietzsche's thought, he kept   acknowledging Nietzsche's significance for culture and religion until the end of his life.[26] In *Ekzistentsial'naia dialektika bozhestvennogo i chelovecheskogo* (*The existential dialectics of the divine and the human*), which he wrote in 1945, he brings Nietzsche once again into the spotlight:

> Three problems govern Nietzsche's oeuvre: the relationship of the human and the divine, which is for him the trans-human (*sverkhchelovecheskoe*), the creativity of the human, who ought to create new values, and suffering, the heroic power of resistance against suffering [...] he preaches the *Übermensch*, which is for him a pseudonym for the divine [...] Nietzsche wants God to return. Like Dostoevskii's heroes, he is tormented by God [...] He struggled with Christ, but struggled like one, for whom Christ is dear in the depths of his being [...] The essence of Nietzsche is highly linked up with the dialectics of the divine and the human (Berdiaev 1952: 50-55).

Nietzsche's provocative thought was for Berdiaev an intensive interlude that functioned to define his subsequent philosophical and religious creed. In that respect, selected aspects of Nietzsche's thought left a subtle, yet permanent, imprint on Berdiaev's philosophy.

---

[26] In 1947 he still delivered lectures on Nietzsche and he kept until his death a portrait of Nietzsche – amongst pictures of Dostoevskii, Tolstoi and Gogol' – and Nietzsche's works in his study in the house at Clamart (Lowrie 1974: 180f. & 276).

Chapter 8

Conclusion

> The Russian man becomes so easily an atheist, more
> easily than any other people in the world! And our
> people do not simply become atheists, but they
> decisively believe in atheism, as in a new religion
> (Dostoevskii, The Idiot. PSS 8: 452).

One should always be careful when identifying landmarks and turning points in the history of ideas. The very least one can do in that respect is to recognize that there is always an irreducible degree of arbitrariness to any such claims. Nevertheless, my identification of Merezhkovskii as a landmark and of 1900 as a turning point in the religious reading of Nietzsche can be legitimated, given my overall approach. I have tried to do justice to the dynamics of the reception of Nietzsche by focusing on the changes in the "constellations," which encompass not only Nietzsche's *Übermensch*, but also Dostoevskii's so-called nihilistic characters. Even if one refrains from digging into the microstructure of these characters, one can hardly escape noticing that there had been a change around 1900 with regard to the specific characters linked up with Nietzsche's *Übermensch*. In this study, I have advanced the thesis that this change and the related ones described in chapter 1 can be traced back, to a significant extent, to a constellation advanced by Dmitrii Merezhkovskii. I have suggested specifically that Merezhkovskii's identification of the *Übermensch* with an idea in Dostoevskii's oeuvre that had been previously unnoticed in critical literature, i.e. the *chelovekobog*, at least partially explains the fundamental changes in the understanding and appreciation of the *Übermensch* and by extension, of Nietzsche.

Let me first sketch out the results of this research as far Merezhkovskii's own line of thought is concerned: the identification with the *chelovekobog* clearly brought about a change in Merezhkovskii's assessment of the *Übermensch*. Initially, Merezhkovskii primarily related this idea to pagan phenomena in cultural history. In the association with the *chelovekobog*, he started to read the *Übermensch* within a typically Christian framework.

In his substantiation of what the *chelovekobog* implies, Merezhkovskii mainly focuses on Kirillov's rationale. Subsequently, the connection with the *Übermensch* is established on the basis of what he reads as an affiliated motive in Nietzsche's discourse. Merezhkovskii's understanding of the *Übermensch* is refracted through Kirillov's speech on the *chelovekobog*. He integrates the concepts of *chelovekobog* and *Übermensch* into the general framework of his religious philosophy. They even play a crucial role in his line of thought, in particular where Christianity is concerned: they enable him to concretize and give voice to the anti-Christian paradigm which he perceives to be co-existing with the Christian current. Moreover, they offer him a discursive lexicon through which he can pinpoint the lacunae in present Christian consciousness, specifically its monolithic approach to Christ.

Merezhkovskii observes a bifurcation between a Christian and an anti-Christian impulse in all phenomena. His entire thought is construed around an antithetical worldview in which he lines up the pagan legacy of Antichrist and Flesh on the one hand and the Christian preoccupation with Christ and Spirit on the other. During different phases of his intellectual development, he searches for a way to dissolve this antithesis, which he sees inherent in all layers of human culture. Around 1900, Merezhkovskii moves to the issue of Christianity, which he finds is failing to measure up to the anti-Christian drive, at least in the historical conditions in his own time. The main vice in historical Christianity is that it has deliberately and systematically ignored Christ's dualist makeup. In historical Christology, Christ and the moral paragon for which he stands, is exalted as pure Spirit and ultimate good. Yet as Merezhkovskii asserts, Christ stands beyond the artificial moral categories of good and evil and equally incarnates Spirit and Flesh, Christ and Antichrist.

Accordingly, he searches for an upheaval in traditional Christian consciousness.

It is in this upheaval that the concepts of *chelovekobog* and *Übermensch* prove their merit. Merezhkovskii identifies in them the counter paradigm of the historical Christian model. Basically, both concepts aspire to overcome God and establish a new anthropological paradigm of self-deification. Or, in Kirillov's formula – which constitutes the quintessence of Merezhkovskii's interpretation of both *chelovekobog* and *Übermensch* – "if there is no God, then I am god". The act of deicide results in an overthrowing of the age-long theocentric anthropological and moral consciousness. *Chelovekobog* and *Übermensch* represent the drive to emancipate the human ego from the age-long bond to God.

Merezhkovskii blends Kirillov's and Nietzsche's discourses and he comes up with a syncretistic paradigm through which he can document the anti-Christian element, appearing in the world as various phenomena and which enables him to formulate a solution to the eternal metaphysical bifurcation between Christ and Antichrist, Spirit and Flesh. The worth of each entity is not in its individual quality *per se*, but rather in the transactionality between them: the two opposing forces only come into full being by the dialectical and ongoing countering of one another.

The influence of Merezhkovskii's philosophy of religion can hardly be overestimated. However, in my study of the reception of Nietzsche's *Übermensch* the main point is that Merezhkovskii has put the *Übermensch* on par with the *chelovekobog* and by doing so, has initiated crucial changes not only in the religious reading of Nietzsche, but also in that of Dostoevskii. One could even suggest that Merezhkovskii's constellation was the starting point of a genuine "change of horizon" in the reception because it triggers attempts to give meaning to Nietzsche's *Übermensch* and to situate it into a religious frame of reference rather than to dismiss the whole idea from the outset. However, such a suggestion would not do full justice to the earlier seminal contribution by Vladimir Solov'ëv.

Solov'ëv's understanding of Nietzsche displays a gradually changing attitude towards his ideas. Moreover, each phase of Solov'ëv's appropriation is marked by a response that recurs in Merezhkovskii's and Berdiaev's constellations even though their arguments differ.

Unlike the other Nietzsche-critics of his time, who focused mainly on his arguments against established moral valuation, Solov'ëv reads Nietzsche primarily from a religious point of view. Moreover, he is the first critic to ground his interpretation of the philosopher in his anthropology of the *Übermensch*, which is also the hallmark of Merezhkovskii's and Berdiaev's enthusiastic response to Nietzsche.

At the core of Nietzsche's anthropology, Solov'ëv finds an authentic religious truth, this is the striving towards infinite human perfection. Read from this perspective, the *Übermensch* lives up to the human's natural or divine (in Solov'ëv's religious view) urge to transcend the present self and to realize a higher, more perfect condition. He reads in the *Übermensch* a latent ideal of human elevation, an objective that is consistent with his own prospective anthropology of *Bogochelovechestvo*. For Solov'ëv, the *Übermensch* clearly holds an appealing motive.

However, in spite of the initial anthropological truth contained in the *Übermensch*, Solov'ëv cannot compromise with it. In fact, he observes in Nietzsche's idea a potential menace to his own anthropological paradigm, which is all the more intensified by the term in which Nietzsche couched his idea. For in Solov'ëv's Russian Orthodox lexicon the term *sverkhchelovek* refers to the *Bogochelovek* Christ, an identification entrenched in the tradition of early Christian mysticism and Greek patristic thought. Nietzsche's anthropology, created to overcome the ancient need for a deity yet all the while bearing the same name of Christ, is a great cause of anxiety.

For Solov'ëv, an anthropology embedded in and construed around a worldview devoid of God is necessarily detrimental for moral consciousness. There is but one legitimate moral outlook and that is the one that is framed in Christianity and concerned with the collective well-being.

In Solov'ëv's discourse on Nietzsche, the *Übermensch* is explicitly opposed to the *Bogochelovek* Christ, and implicitly allied with the Antichrist. Both constellations are constitutive of the *God-seekers'* reading of the *Übermensch*. The antithetical configuration of *Bogochelovek* and *Übermensch* prepares Merezhkovskii's identification of *chelovekobog* and *Übermensch*. Furthermore, the myth of the *Übermensch*/Antichrist turns out to be functionally productive for the further reading of Nietzsche. In a way, Merezhkovskii makes an explicitly formulated paradigm of what

Solov'ёv kept silent about. It is precisely through construing a constellation in which *Übermensch*, *chelovekobog* and Antichrist are identified that Merezhkovskii is able to phrase his new philosophy of religion.

The religious appropriation of Nietzsche, initiated by Solov'ёv and fully established by Merezhkovskii, reaches its culmination in Nikolai Berdiaev's assimilation of the German philosopher. Berdiaev finds in Nietzsche, and especially in his idea of the *Übermensch*, a solution to the flaws in Christian anthropology. He faults historical Christian doctrine for its negation of what he believes to be the essence of the human as a being essentially created in the image and likeness of God. Because the human is made like the primal Creator, he is self-creative and self-realizing, which is a fundamental anthropological principle systematically ignored in the traditional doctrine of the passive and weak human as fully determined by original sin.

Nietzsche's anthropology of the *Übermensch* is for Berdiaev a re-evaluation of the human's initial Godlike status. Like Solov'ёv, he reads in the *Übermensch* an incentive to transcend present humanity and attain a higher state of religious consciousness. Yet, while Solov'ёv immediately set out to discredit the *Übermensch* for its godless tenor and rigorously held on to his own anthropological paradigm of *Bogochelovechestvo*, Berdiaev finds in the *Übermensch* the fundament for a neo-Christian anthropology. The *Übermensch* makes up the hallmark of the human's creative potentiality and stands for the initial Christian ideal of free self-realization. Nietzsche's concept contains the qualities required to overturn the ancient theocentric hopes for salvation and re-establish the human's potential for self-generated transfiguration. For Berdiaev, the *Übermensch* lives up to the ontological status of the human as a morally free and self-creative being and in that sense, it paves the way for a new anthropological revelation, for "the Christology of the human" (Berdiaev [1916] 2002: 84).

Berdiaev's appropriation of the *Übermensch* is partly shaped by the horizon of expectations emerging from Solov'ёv's and Merezhkovskii's interpretation. However, at the same time his assessment of this concept marks yet another shift in the religious reading of Nietzsche. Solov'ёv and Merezhkovskii, though in a different ideological framework, identify in the *Übermensch* the radical counter paradigm of the *Bogochelovek* Christ. Whereas Solov'ëv contrasts the *Übermensch* with the *Bogochelovek* and merely alludes to the anti-Christian quality of Nietzsche's idea, Merezhkovskii explicitly identifies the *Übermensch* with the Antichrist. Berdiaev, however, does not place the *Übermensch* in opposition to the *Bogochelovek*. Rather, he reads in the *Übermensch* an anthropological truth, similar to the one contained in the ideal of Christ, i.e., a paradigm for free self-realization. From this perspective he finds that the *Übermensch* approaches the *Bogochelovek*. As a consequence, for Berdiaev, the *Übermensch* does not stand for the Antichrist. Instead, he finds the real Antichrist in Dostoevskii's image of the Grand Inquisitor. Because Berdiaev models his affirmative interpretation of Christ (as the one who teaches an anthropology of free self-determination) on the figure of Christ in Dostoevskii's "legend" of the Grand Inquisitor, he evidently sees the Antichrist in Christ's opponent in the legend. By correcting Christ's promise of moral freedom, the Grand Inquisitor deprives humanity of its ontological makeup as a co-creating being, and he is therefore the real antagonist of the *Bogochelovek*. Dostoevskii's Grand Inquisitor saves Nietzsche from the canonical identification with the Antichrist.

Although Nietzsche's *Übermensch* restores the human's creativity in anthropological consciousness, it eventually fails Berdiaev in his formulation of a new Christian anthropology. And here Berdiaev once again reverts to Dostoevskii, this time to pinpoint the vices of Nietzsche. More specifically, he brings in the *chelovekobog* to indicate exactly where the *Übermensch* falls short with regard to the authentic Christian paradigm of free self-realization.

Dostoevskii is a productive mediator in Merezhkovskii's and Berdiaev's understanding of Nietzsche. However, the *God-seekers* are not the only Russian readers who engage in a dialogue with Dostoevskii while reading Nietzsche. From the very start of Nietzsche's debut in Russian intellectual circles on, Nietzsche and his ideas are refracted through the prism of Dostoevskii's prominent discourse.

In the first decade of the reception process, Dostoevskii and especially his fictional nihilists Raskol'nikov and Ivan Karamazov, are in the spotlight and are used to expose the perceived immoral tenor of Nietzsche's philosophy. In this reading, Nietzsche's thought is reductively boiled down to these characters' ethical formula that "all is permitted" (*vsë pozvoleno*). Nietzsche's subtle concept is translated into Raskol'nikov's and Ivan Karamazov's ideological language in a straightforward way. These characters' arguments are supposed to rival with and even be antagonistic to Dostoevskii's Christian standpoint. Consequently, in this interpretation, Nietzsche and the nihilistic characters are discredited for their alleged immoral rationale, which is considered to contain a concrete peril to Russian moral consciousness. Thus we can conclude that in this phase Nietzsche is read through the Russian ideological "horizon of expectations," which is, in turn, substantially generated by Dostoevskii.

Merezhkovskii's and Berdiaev's juxtaposition of Dostoevskii and Nietzsche is in part a corollary of this tradition, yet at the same time significantly adds to it. The main shift lies in the interplay between Dostoevskii's and Nietzsche's ideological legacies. Whereas the critics of the 1890s monolithically explained Nietzsche in terms of Dostoevskii, the *God-seekers* establish a reciprocity between them.

This is manifest in Merezhkovskii's assessment of Dostoevskii, which is, as I suggest, largely determined by "the horizon of expectations" emerging from Nietzsche's discourse. And in turn, Dostoevskii clearly participates in Merezhkovskii's understanding of Nietzsche. The most concrete substantiation of the mutual operation of both in Merezkhovskii's reasoning is the extent to which Merezhkovskii is fascinated by *chelovekobog* and *Übermensch*: it is exactly Nietzsche's idea of the *Übermensch* that triggers Merezhkovskii to signal the previously overlooked concept of the *chelovekobog* in Dostoevskii's oeuvre. And as I already indicated, the identification with the *chelovekobog* brings about a gradual modification in Merezhkovskii's appreciation of the *Übermensch*: whereas in an earlier stage this idea mainly operated in Merezhkovskii's discourse on philosophy of culture and was applied to delineate pagan motives in the course of history, it is, under the association with the *chelovekobog*, primarily interpreted as a religious concept. In Merezhkovskii's constellation, which is equally permeated with Dostoevskii's and Nietzsche's lexicon, *chelovekobog* and *Übermensch* fathom the core of the religious problem: the undeniable presence of an anti-Christian drive. These concepts pose an authentic religious question.

The highlighting and connecting of Dostoevskii's *chelovekobog* and Nietzsche's *Übermensch* clearly brings about a shift in the appraisal of both. Whereas Dostoevskii was thus far interpreted mainly as a socio-realistic writer, Merezhkovskii tends to read him from a religious point of view. Characteristically, he finds the religious dimension of Dostoevskii's discourse primarily in the "anti-Christian" characters, which are all subsumed under the principle of the *chelovekobog*. Instead of approaching these characters as voices which are antagonistic to Dostoevskii's ideological consciousness, Merezhkovskii takes them to embody the writer's own deliberation process, at least as far as his view on religion is concerned. Their struggle with God and the Christian imperative of altruistic love is in part also Dostoevskii's struggle. In Merezhkovskii's assessment, Dostoevskii is no longer the conservative advocate of the traditional Christian framework. Rather, he exposes the shortcomings of historical Christian consciousness, specifically its systematic negation of the anti-Christian proclivity. Through the fictional voices, whose arguments go further than any existing Russian atheist theory, Dostoevskii shows the ultimate ramifications of the anti-Christian tenor and urges the reconsideration of Christian consciousness. Dostoevskii demonstrates that the anti-Christian principle can only be countered by integrating it into the Christian paradigm, whereby the one constantly tempers the other.

Merezhkovskii's appraisal of Dostoevskii's nihilistic characters, all of which he identifies as *chelovekobog*, also applies to his appraisal of Nietzsche. In contrast with the earlier readings, in which Nietzsche is primarily refuted for antagonizing the Christian paradigm, this countering of the Christian model is the root of Merezhkovskii's favorable assessment of Nietzsche. For Merezhkovskii, what is most attractive in Nietzsche is that he dared to pronounce what historical Christianity has obscured.

In Merezhkovskii's assessment, Dostoevskii's eminent position as the icon of traditional Russian Christianity and Nietzsche's reputation as the rigorous anti-religious thinker are intertwined, qualified, and mediated, in order to connect them and to blend both into his neo-Christian model. A transsubjective horizon is established in which Christianity, Dostoevskii's heritage, and Nietzsche's philosophy dynamically operate on each other and modify the others' meaning.

For Merezhkovskii, the identification of *chelovekobog* and *Übermensch* makes up the hallmark of his assessment of both

Dostoevskii and Nietzsche. *Chelovekobog* and *Übermensch* function as a conceptual frame of reference on the basis of which Merezhkovskii delineates his appreciation of both authors. In Merezhkovskii's reception model, both Dostoevskii and Nietzsche bring in a concept that is functionally productive in his assessment of each. Whereas in Merezhkovskii's reading, both authors equally contribute to and operate in his appreciation of both, Berdiaev's eventual appreciation of Dostoevskii and Nietzsche is marked by a hierarchic constellation. In his initial reading of the *Übermensch*, as an anthropology that reanimates the human's original Godlike status as a self-creative and self-realizing being, Berdiaev does not yet connect the *Übermensch* to the *chelovekobog*, or in other words, Nietzsche is read and approved without associating him with Dostoevskii (as occurred in Merezhkovskii's favorable assessment). At this point, the *Übermensch* is instead brought into a constellation with the *Bogochelovek*: the *Übermensch* and the *Bogochelovek* Christ fundamentally contain an equal truth about humanity. It is only after a fair amount of Nietzsche-reading that Berdiaev makes the link with Dostoevskii. More specifically, he identifies the *Übermensch* with the *chelovekobog* to pinpoint and phrase exactly the vices of Nietzsche's anthropology. Merezhkovskii's ideological constellation is turned upside down. Whereas the connection between *chelovekobog* and *Übermensch* is at the core of Merezhkovskii's affirmative assessment of Nietzsche, this same connection marks Berdiaev's less favorable reading of Nietzsche. Where Merezhkovskii needs the specific frame of reference supplied by Dostoevskii to value Nietzsche, Berdiaev turns to Dostoevskii to distance himself from and overcome Nietzsche. In Merezhkovskii's reciprocal reading, Dostoevskii knew what Nietzsche knew, and vice versa. For Berdiaev, however, "Dostoevskii knew, what Nietzsche did not know" (Berdiaev [1923] 1991: 54).

   Although my methodological framework involved a specific combination of history of ideas and reception aesthetics, I will now conclude this study by recapping the main results in terms of these methodologies taken separately. As far as history of ideas is concerned, one could be tempted to subscribe to Lovejoy's "unit-ideas" and take the *Übermensch* and the *chelovekobog* as one such idea expressed by two authors. However, from the outset, I have made it clear that treating concepts as units would merely serve the heuristic function of finding out what "aggregates" or "constellations" particular thinkers have in mind. In that respect, I have: (1) described the place and function of the *Übermensch* in Solov'ëv's, Merezhkovskii's, and Berdiaev's constellations; (2) studied its respective relations to Dostoevskii's nihilistic characters and his idea of the *chelovekobog*; (3) identified 1900 as a turning point in the reception of Nietzsche's *Übermensch* and Dostoevskii's nihilistic characters, and as a consequence, of the authors, too; (4) traced back this cluster of shifts in the valuation of Nietzsche and Dostoevskii to Merezhkovskii's identification of *Übermensch* and *chelovekobog*.

In terms of reception aesthetics, the most important changes in the reception process can be described as follows. Initially, Nietzsche is mainly read from the "horizon of expectations" shaped by Dostoevskii. Without a doubt, his concept of the *Übermensch* worked provocatively at this early stage, but with the notable exception of Solov'ëv, one can hardly say that it really stimulated philosophers to think carefully through its ramifications and grant it a place in their lines of thought.   Instead, Nietzsche and his *Übermensch* were conceived of in such a way that allowed for a comparison with some of Dostoevskii's nihilistic characters and as a consequence, for a rather frank rejection on roughly the same basis as the value-judgments attached to these characters. From 1900 onwards, there is not only a genuine "change of horizon" in the intersubjective sense but also in the intrasubjective sense as my accounts of Merezhkovskii and Berdiaev testify. The meaning of Nietzsche's *Übermensch*, as well as of some *other* nihilistic characters of Dostoevskii, clearly changes as the reading and associated interpretative reasoning of these *God-seekers* proceed. Nietzsche's *Übermensch* is now provocative in a different sense: through the juxtaposition with Dostoevskii's characters, the concept starts to *appeal* genuinely to the *God-seekers*, directing them to construe seminal interpretations that not only shed new light on Dostoevskii, but also guide them in their search for a new religious consciousness.

Ultimately, there is nothing anomalous in the fact that the *God-seekers* did not straightforwardly dismiss Nietzsche's candidly anti-religious thought but instead wrestled with it to try to accommodate it within their own frame of reference. As my analyses of Solov'ëv, Merezhkovskii, and Berdiaev show, Nietzsche's *Übermensch*, or rather their amended version of it, showed each of them the way out of what they experienced as a religious predicament. And there is nothing anomalous in the connection between Nietzsche's *Übermensch* and Dostoevskii's nihilistic characters either: Dostoevskii's nihilists and his idea of the *chelovekobog* enabled the *God-seekers*, firstly, to make a diagnosis, that is to pinpoint the crisis in Christianity, and secondly, to re-conceptualize the *Übermensch* in such a way that it hinted at the proper cure. To answer the question underlying this study: what exactly did these *God-seekers* find in Nietzsche? They found in him "an idea," the *Übermensch*, which they, each in a different chain of associations or "constellations," situated *within* the Russian frame of reference which was in turn largely determined by Dostoevskii's "ideas." And precisely in the dynamics of Dostoevskii and Nietzsche, the *God-seekers* found a new way to relate to God.

Bibliography

Andler, Charles. 1930. 'Nietzsche et Dostoievsky' in *Mélanges offerts á Fernand Baldensperger*. Paris: 1-14.

Antonovich, Maksim Alekseevich. [1881] 1956. 'Mistiko-asketicheskii roman'. Reprint in *F.M. Dostoevskii v russkoi kritike*. Moskva: Gosudarstvennoe Izdatel'stvo Khudozhestvennoi Literatury: 255-305.

Aschheim, Steven E. 1992. *The Nietzsche Legacy in Germany (1890-1900)*. Berkeley: University of California Press.

Astaf'ev, Pëtr Evgen'evich. [1893] 2001. 'Genezis nravstvennogo ideala dekadenta' in *Voprosy Filosofii i Psikhologii* 16: 56-75. Reprint in *Nitsshe: Pro et Contra*. Antologiia. Iuliia.V. Sineokaia (ed.). Sankt-Peterburg: Izdatel'stvo Russkogo Khristianskogo Gumanitarnogo Instituta: 95-112.

Azadovskii, Konstantin Markovich. 1999. 'Russkie v arkhive Nitsshe' in *Fridrikh Nitsshe i filosofiia v Rossii*. Sbornik statei. Nelli V. Motroshilova and Iuliia.V. Sineokaia (eds.). Sankt-Peterburg: Izdatel'stvo Russkogo Khristianskogo Gumanitarnogo Instituta: 109-129.

Bakhtin, Mikhail. 1984. *Problems of Dostoevsky's poetics*. Ed. and translated by Caryl Emerson; introd. By Wayne C. Booth. Manchester: Manchester University Press.

Bedford, Charles Harold. 1975. *The Seeker D.S. Merezhkovsky*. Lawrence, Manhattan and Wichita: The University Press of Kansas.

Belinskii, Vissarion Grigor'evich. [1846-1847] 1956. Peterburgskii Sbornik, Vzgliad na russkuiu literaturu 1846 goda (otryvok). Vzgliad na russkuiu literaturu 1847 goda (otryvok). Reprint in F.M. Dostoevskii v russkoi kritike. Moskva: Gosudarstvennoe Izdatel'stvo Khudozhestvennoi Literatury: 3-35.

Belov, S.V. 2001. F.M. Dostoevskii i ego okruzhenie. Entsiklopedicheskii slovar'. 2 Vols. Sankt-peterburg: Aleteiia.

Belyi, Andrei. [1907] 1991. 'Vladimir Solov'ëv. Iz Vospominanii' in *Kniga o Vl. Solov'ëve*. Moskva: Sovetskii Pisatel: 277-282.

—. [1908] 2001. 'Fridrikh Nitsshe'. Reprint in *Nitsshe: Pro et Contra*. Antologiia. Iuliia. V. Sineokaia (ed.). Sankt-Peterburg: Izdatel'stvo Russkogo Khristianskogo Gumanitarnogo Instituta: 878-903.

—. 1911. 'Merezhkovskii' in *Arabeski. Kniga statei*. Moskva: Musaget.

—. [1928] 1982. Pochemu ia stal simvolistom i pochemu ia ne perestal im byt' vo vsekh fazakh moego ideinogo i khudozhestvennogo razvitiia. Michigan: Ardis/Ann Arbor.

Benders, Raymond J., Oettermann, Stephan et al. (eds.). 2000. *Friedrich Nietzsche: Chronik in Bildern und Texten*. München: Stiftung Weimarer Klassik bei Hanser Deutscher Taschenbuch Verlag.

Benz, Ernst. 1961. 'Das Bild des Übermenschen in der europäischen Geistesgeschichte' in *Der Übermensch: eine Diskussion*. Zürich: Rhein-Verlag: 23-161.

Berdiaev, Nikolai Aleksandrovich. [1901] 1907. 'Bor'ba za idealizm' in *Mir Bozhii*, June: 1-26. Reprint in *Sub Specie Aeternitatis. Opyty filosofskie, sotsial'nie i literaturnye (1900-1906)*. Sankt-Peterburg: Izdanie M.V. Pirozhkova: 5-34.

—. 1902. 'Eticheskaia Problema v Svete Filosofskogo Idealizma' in *Problemy Idealizma*. Pod redaktsiei P.I. Novgorodtseva. Moskva: Izdanie Moskovskogo Psikhologicheskago Obshchestva: 91-136.

—. 1905. 'O novom religioznom soznanii' in *Voprosy Zhizni* 9: 147-188.

—. 1907. Sub Specie Aeternitatis. Opyty filosofskie, sotsial'nie i literaturnye (1900-1906). Sankt-Peterburg: Izdanie M.V. Pirozhkova.

—. [1907] 1910. 'Bunt i pokornost' v psikhologii mass' in Dukhovnyi krizis intelligentsii: stat'i po obshchestvennoi i religioznoi psikhologii (1907-1909). Sankt-Peterburg: 73-83.

—. [1907]1991. 'Velikii Inkvizitor'. Reprint in *O velikom inkvizitore. Dostoevskii i posleduiushchie*. Moskva: Molodaia Gvardia: 219-241.

—. [1916] 2001. 'Novoe Khristianstvo (D.S. Merezhkovskii)'. Reprint in *Merezhkovskii: Pro et Contra. Lichnost' i tvorchestvo Dmitriia Merezhkovskogo v otsenke sovremennikov.* A.N. Nikoliukin (ed.). Sankt-Peterburg: Izdatel'stvo Russkogo Khristianskogo Gumanitarnogo Instituta: 331-353.

—. [1916] 2002. *Smysl Tvorchestva. Opyt opravdaniia cheloveka.* Khar'kov: 'Folio'/Moskva: 'ACT'.

—. [1917] 1988. 'Avtobiografiia' in *Vestnik Russkogo Khristianskogo Dvizheniia* 177: 122-134.

—. 1918. 'Otkrovenie o cheloveke v tvorchestve Dostoevskogo' in *Russkaia Mysl'*, March-April. See http://www.krotov.org/berdyaev/1918/19180301.html

—. [1923] 1991. *Mirosozertsanie Dostoevskogo.* Reprint in *N. Berdiaev o russkoi filosofii.* B.V. Emel'ianov and A.I.Novikov (eds.), Vol. 1, Sverdlovsk: Izdatel'stvo Ural'skogo Universiteta: 26-148.

—. [1927] 1994. Filosofiia svobodnogo dukha. Problematika i apologiia khristianstva. Moskva: Respublika.

—. [1937] 1991. 'Moe filosofskoe mirosozertsanie'. Reprint in *N. Berdiaev o russkoi filosofii.* B.V. Emel'ianov and A.I.Novikov (eds.), Vol. 1, Sverdlovsk: Izdatel'stvo Ural'skogo Universiteta: 19-25.

—. [1939] 1995. O rabstve i svobode cheloveka. Opyt personalisticheskoi filosofii in Tsarstvo dukha i tsarstvo kesaria. Moskva: Respublika.

—. [1946] 1997. Russkaia Ideia. Osnovnye problemy russkoi mysli XIX veka i nachala XX veka. Moskva: Svarog i K.

—. [1949] 2003. *Samopoznanie. Opyt filosofskoi avtobiografii.* Moskva and Kharkov: Eksmo/Folio.

—. 1952. Ekzistentsial'naia dialektika bozhestvennogo i chelovecheskogo. Paris: YMCA-Press.

—. 1993. 'Pis'ma N.A. Berdiaeva k E. F. Gollerbakhu'. See the Internet source http://www.krotov.info/library/02_b/berdyaev/1993goll.html.

Bevir, Mark. 1999. *The Logic of the History of Ideas.* Cambridge: Cambridge University Press.

Biebuyck, Benjamin and Grillaert, Nel. 2003. 'Between God and *Übermensch*: Viacheslav Ivanovich Ivanov and his Vacillating Struggle with Nietzsche' in *Germano-Slavica* XIV: 55-73.

Blumenkrantz, Mikhail. 1996. 'From Nimrod to the Grand Inquisitor: the problem of the demonisation of freedom in the work of Dostoevskii' in *Studies in East European Thought* 48: 231-254.

Boborykin, Pëtr. 1900. 'O nitssheanstve. (Pamiati V.P. Preobrazhenskogo)' in *Voprosy Filosofii i Psikhologii* 54: 539-547.

Brandes, Georg. [1888] 1895. 'Friedrich Nietzsche. Eine Abhandlung ueber aristokratischen Radicalismus' in *Menschen und Werke. Essays von Georg Brandes*. Frankfurt am Main: Rütten and Loening: 137-224.

—. [1913] 2001. 'Merezhkovskii'. Reprint in *Merezhkovskii: Pro et Contra. Lichnost' i tvorchestvo Dmitrija Merezhkovskogo v otsenke sovremennikov*. Sankt-Peterburg: Izdatel'stvo Russkogo Khristianskog Gumanitarnogo Instituta: 313-321.

Briusov, Valerii. 1927. *Dnevniki, 1890-1910*. Moskva: Sabashnikov.

Bulgakov, F.I. 1893. 'Uchenie Nitsshe o zhelanii vlasti i t.d.' in *Vestnik Inostrannoi Literatury* 5: 206-216.

Bulgakov, Sergei Nikolaevich. [1901] 1991. 'Ivan Karamazov kak filosofskii tip'. Reprint in *O velikom inkvizitore. Dostoevskii i posleduiushchie*. Moskva: Molodaia Gvardiia: 193-217.

Chadwick, Henry. 1993. *The Early Church*. London: Penguin Books.

Chuiko, V.V. [1893] 2001. 'Obshchestvennye Idealy Fridrikha Nitsshe' in *Nabliudatel'* 2: 231-247. Reprint in *Nitsshe: Pro et Contra*. Antologiia. Iuliia.V. Sineokaia (ed.). Sankt-Peterburg: Izdatel'stvo Russkogo Khristianskogo Gumanitarnogo Instituta: 113-132.

Clowes, Edith W. 1983. 'Friedrich Nietzsche and Russian censorship' in *Germano-Slavica* 4(3): 135-142.

—. 1988. The Revolution of Moral Consciousness. Nietzsche in Russian Literature, 1890-1914. DeKalb, Illinois: Northern Illinois University Press.

Craig, Edward. 1998. 'Ontology' in *Routledge Encyclopedia of Philosophy*. Edward Craig (ed.). 10 Vols. London and New York: Routledge, Vol.7: 117-118.

Dahl, Per and Mott, John. 1980. 'Georg Brandes: A bio-bibliographical survey' in *Orbis Litterarum, International Review of literary studies*, supplement 5: 303-360.

Davies, Richard D. 1986. 'Nietzsche in Russia, 1892-1919: a chronological checklist' in *Nietzsche in Russia*. Bernice Glatzer Rosenthal (ed.). Princeton: Princeton University Press: 355-392.

Davydov, Iurii. 1981. 'Dva ponimaniia nigilizma (Dostoevskii i Nitsshe)' in *Voprosy Literatury* 9: 115-160.

Deppermann, Maria. 1998. 'Nietzsche in der Sowjetunion. Den begrabenen Nietzsche ausgraben' in *Nietzsche-Studien*, Bd. 27: 481-514.

Dmitrieva, Katia and Nethercott, Frances. 1996. 'De Nietzsche à Bergson: la nouvelle conscience philosophique en Russie au début du XXe siècle' in *Transferts culturels triangulaires France - Allemagne - Russie*, Paris: 337-366.

Dobroliubov, Nikolai Aleksandrovich. [1861] 1956. 'Zabitye Liudi'. Reprint in *F.M. Dostoevskii v russkoi kritike*. Moskva: Gosudarstvennoe Izdatel'stvo Khudozhestvennoi Literatury: 39-95.

Dolinin, A. [1914] 1972.'Dmitrii Merezhkovskii' in *Russkaia Literatura XX Veka*. S.A.Vengerov (ed.). 3 Vols. Moskva. Reprint in München: Wilhelm Fink Verlag. Vol. 1: 295-356.

Dostoevskii, Fëdor Mikhailovich. 1972-1990. *Polnoe Sobranie Sochinenii v tridtsati tomakh (PSS)*. Akademiia Nauk SSSR. Institut russkoi literatury (Pushkinskii Dom). Leningrad: Nauka.

Dostoevsky, Fyodor. 1968. *The Notebooks for The Possessed*. Edited and with an introduction by Edward Wasiolek. Translated by Victor Terras. Chicago and London: The University of Chicago Press.

Dostojewski, F.M. 1908. *Rodion Raskolnikoff*. München.

Dudkin, Viktor Viktorovich. 1994. *Dostoevskii-Nitsshe (Problema cheloveka)*. Petrozavodsk: KGPI.

Filosofov, Dmitrii. 1903. 'Literaturnaia khronika' in *Novyi Put'* 2: 167-170.

Foucault, Michel. 1696. *L'Archéologie du Savoir*. Paris: Galimard.

Frank, Joseph. 1976. *Dostoevsky. The Seeds of Revolt, 1821-1849*. Princeton and Oxford: Princeton University Press.

—. 2002. *Dostoevsky. The Mantle of the Prophet 1871-1881*. Princeton and Oxford: Princeton University Press.

Frank, Semën Liudvigovich. [1902] 2001. 'Fr. Nitsshe i etika liubvi k dal'nemu'. Reprint in *Nitsshe: Pro et Contra. Antologiia.* Iuliia V. Sineokaia (ed.). Sankt-Peterburg: Izdatel'stvo Russkogo Khristianskogo Gumanitarnogo Instituta: 586-635.

—. [1932] 1991. 'Legenda o velikom inkvizitore'. Reprint in *O velikom inkvizitore. Dostoevskii i posleduiushchie.* Moskva: Molodaia Gvardiia: 193-217.

—. [1950] 2002. 'Dukhovnoe nasledie Vladimira Solov'ëva'. Reprint in *Vladimir Solov'ëv: Pro et Contra. Lichnost' i tvorchestvo Vladimira Solov'ëva v otsenke russkikh myslitelei i issledovatelei.* Sankt-Peterburg: Izdatel'stvo Russkogo Khristianskogo Gumanitarnogo Instituta, 2 Vols. Vol. 2: 953-961.

—. 1956. *Biografiia P.B. Struve.* New York: Izdatel'stvo imeni Chekhova.

Fridlender, Georg. 1979. 'Dostoevskii i F. Nitsshe' in *Dostoevskii i mirovaia literatura.* Georg Fridlender (ed.). Moskva: 214-254.

Galaktionov, A.A. and Nikandrov, P.F. 1970. *Russkaia filosofiia XI-XIX vekov.* Leningrad: Nauka.

Gesemann, Wolfgang. 1961. 'Nietzsches Verhältnis zu Dostoevskii auf dem europäischen Hintergrund der 80er Jahre' in *Welt der Slaven* VI: 129-156.

Ghuys, Walter. 1962. 'Dostoievski et Nietzsche. Le tragique de l'homme souterrain' in *La Lampe Verte* 11: 11-16.

Gide, André. 1923. *Dostoïevsky.* Paris : Librairie Plon.

Grillaert, Nel. 1998. Normloosheid als ethisch principe. Een comparatieve analyse van Raskol'nikov's 'buitengewone' mens en Nietzsche's Übermensch. MA-Thesis, Ghent University.

—. 2003. 'A Short Story about the *Übermensch*: Vladimir Solov'ëv's Interpretation
of and Response to Nietzsche's *Übermensch*' in *Studies in East European Thought* 55(2): 157-184.

—. 2004. 'Re-Christianizing Christianity: Nikolai Berdiaev's mythopoetic   response
to Friedrich Nietzsche' in *Slavica Gandensia* 31: 65-75.

—. 2005. 'Only the Word Order has Changed: the Man-God in Dostoevsky's Works' in *Dostoevsky Studies* IX: 80-105.

—. 2007. 'Orthodoxy regained: the theological subtext in Dostoevskij's 'Dream of a Ridiculous Man'' in *Russian Literature* 62(2): 155-173.

Grillmeier, Alois. 1983. 'Gottmensch' in *Reallexikon für Antike und Christentum*. Theodor Klauser, Carsten Colpe et all. (eds.) Stuttgart: Anton Hiersemann (1950...), 19 Vols. Vol. 12: 155-366.

Grossman, Leonid Petrovich. 1996. 'Speshnev i Stavrogin' in *'Besy': Antologiia russkoi kritiki*. Ed. L. I Saraskina. Moskva: Soglasie: 614-618.

Grot, Nikolai Iakovlevich. [1893] 2001. 'Nravstvennye idealy nashego vremeni: Fridrikh Nitsshe i Lev Tolstoi' in *Voprosy Filosofii i Psikhologii* 16: 129-154. Reprint in *Nitsshe: Pro et Contra*. Antologiia. Iuliia V. Sineokaia (ed.). Sankt-Peterburg: Izdatel'stvo Russkogo Khristianskogo Gumanitarnogo Instituta: 75-94.

Gurevich, L. [1914] 1972. 'Istoriia Severnago Vestnika' in *Russkaia Literatura XX Veka*. S.A.Vengerov (ed.). 3 Vols. Moskva. Reprint in München: Wilhelm Fink Verlag, Vol. 1: 235-264.

Heftrich, Urs. 1995. 'Thomas Manns Weg zur slavischen Dämonie. Überlegungen zur Wirkung Dmitri Mereschkowski' in *Thomas Mann Jahrbuch* 8: 71-91.

Gippius-Merezhkovskaia, Zinaida. 1951. *Dmitrii Merezhkovskii*. Paris: YMCA-Press.

Iakubovich, I.D. 2000. 'Dostoevskii v religiozno-filosofskikh i esteticheskikh vozzreniiakh A. Volysnkogo' in *Dostoevskii. Materialy i issledovaniia*: 67-89.

'Idei Fridrikha Nitshe'. 1895. In *Vestnik Inostrannoi literatury*: 192-206.

Ignatov, Assen. 1993. 'Chërt i sverkhchelovek. Predchuvstvie totalitarizma Dostoevskim i Nitsshe' in *Voprosy Filosofii* 4: 25-46.

Ivanov, Viacheslav Ivanovich. 1971-1987. *Sobranie Sochinenii I-IV (SS)*. Brussels: Foyer Oriental Chrétien.

Jaspers, Karl. [1935] 1981. Nietzsche. Einführung in das Verstandnis seines Philosophierens. Berlin and New York: de Gruyter.

Jauss, Hans Robert. [1967] 1970. *Literaturgeschichte als Provokation*. Frankfurt am Main: Suhrkamp.

Jones, Malcolm V. 1976. *Dostoyevsky. The Novel of Discord*. London: Paul Elek.

—. 1990. Dostoyevsky after Bakhtin. Readings in Dostoyevsky's Fantastic Realism. Cambridge: Cambridge University Press.

—. 2005. Dostoevsky and the Dynamics of Religious Experience. London: Anthem Press.

Jung, Susanne, Simon-Ritz, Frank et al. (eds.). 2000-2002. *Weimarer Nietzsche-Bibliographie (WNB)*. 5 Vols. Stuttgart/Weimar: J.B. Metzler.

Kantor, V.K. 2002. 'Antikhrist, ili ozhidavshiisia konets evropeiskoi istorii (Solov'ëv contra Nitsshe)' in *Voprosy Filosofii* 2: 14-27.

Karutov, N. 1900. 'Dve smerti (Vladimir Solov'ëv i Fridrikh Nitsshe)' in *Novyi Vek* 10: 507-510.

Kaufmann, Walter. 1988. *Nietzsche. Philosoph, Psychologe, Antichrist*. Darmstadt: Wissenschaftliche Buchgesellschaft.

Kelly, Aileen M. 1998. *Toward Another Shore: Russian Thinkers between Necessity and Chance*. New Haven and London: Yale University Press.

Kheisin, M. 1903. 'Dostoevskii i Nittsshe' in *Mir Bozhii* 6: 119-141.

Khrapovitskii, Antonii. [1893] 1997. 'Pastyrskoe izuchenie liudei i zhizni po sochineniiam F.M.Dostoevskogo'. Reprint in *Vlastitel' Dum: F.M. Dostoevskii v russkoi kritike kontsa XIX-nachala XX veka*. N. Ashimbaevaia (ed.). Sankt-Peterburg: Khudozhestvennaia Literatura: 137-171.

Kirillova, Irina. 2001. 'Dostoevsky's markings in the Gospel according to St John' in *Dostoevsky and the Christian Tradition*. Georges Pattison and Diane Oenning Thompson (eds.). Cambridge: Cambridge University Press: 41-50.

Kline, George L. 1968. 'Nietzschean Marxism in Russia' in *Boston College Studies in Philosophy* 2: 166-183.

Kochetkova, Tatjana J. 2001. *Vladimir Solov'jov's Theory of Divine Humanity*. PhD thesis. Radboud Universiteit Nijmegen.

Kogan, Galina. 1996. 'Vechnoe i tekushchee (Evangelie Dostoevskogo i ego znachenie v zhizni i tvorchestve pisatelia)' in *Dostoevskii v kontse XX veka*. Karen Stepanian (ed.). Moskva: Klassika Plius: 147-166.

Koreneva, M.Iu. 1991. 'D.S. Merezhkovskii i nemetskaia literatura (Nitsshe i Gete. Pritiazhenie i ottalkivanie) in *Na Rubezhe XIX i XX vekov: iz istorii mezhdunarodnykh sviazei russkoi literatury*. Iu.D. Levin (ed.). Leningrad: Nauka: 44-76.

Kostalevsky, Marina. 1997. *Dostoevsky and Soloviev. The Art of Integral Vision*. New Haven and London: Yale University Press.

Lane, Ann Marie. 1976. *Nietzsche in Russian Thought 1890-1917*. PhD thesis. University of Wisconsin.

—. 1986. 'Nietzsche comes to Russia: Popularization and Protest in the 1890s' in *Nietzsche in Russia*. Bernice Glatzer Rosenthal (ed.). Princeton: Princeton University Press: 51-68.

Leatherbarrow, William J. 1992. *Fyodor Dostoevsky: The Brothers Karamazov*. Cambridge: Cambridge University Press.

Leont'ev, Konstantin Nikolaevich. [1880] 1997. 'O vsemirnoi liubvi'. Reprint in *Vlastitel' Dum. F.M. Dostoevskii v russkoi kritike kontsa XIX- nachala XX veka*. Sankt-Peterburg: Khudozhestvennaia Literatura: 68-102.

Leporskii, P. 1903. 'Bogochelovek' in *Pravoslavnaia bogoslovskaia entsiklopediia*. Petrograd: 863-878.

Levitskii, S. 1901. 'Sverkhchelovek Nitsshe i chelovek Khrista' in *Bogoslovskii Vestnik* 7-9.

Lopatin, Lev Mikhailovich. [1893] 2001. 'Bol'naia iskrennost'' (Zametka po povodu stat'i V. Preobrazhenskogo 'Fridrikh Nitsshe: Kritika Morali Al'truizma')' in *Voprosy Filosofii i Psikhologii* 16: 109-114. Reprint in *Nitsshe: Pro et Contra. Antologiia*. Iuliia.V. Sineokaia (ed.). Sankt-Peterburg: Izdatel'stvo Russkogo Khristianskogo Gumanitarnogo Instituta: 70-74.

—. [1901] 2002. 'Filosofskoe mirosozertsanie V.S. Solov'ëva'. Reprint in *Vladimir Solov'ëv: Pro et Contra. Lichnost' i tvorchestvo Vladimira Solov'ëva v otsenke russkikh myslitelei i issledovatelei*. Sankt-Peterburg: Izdatel'stvo Russkogo Khristianskogo Gumanitarnogo Instituta, 2 Vols. Vol. 2: 787-822.

Losev, Aleksei Fëdorovich. 1990. *Vladimir Solov'ëv i ego vremia*. Moskva: Progress.

Lossky, Vladimir. [1944] 1991. *The Mystical Theology of the Eastern Church*. Cambridge: James Clarke and Co.

Lovejoy, Arthur O. 1933. *The Great Chain of Being. A Study of the History of an Idea.* Cambridge, Massuchesetts: Harvard University Press.

Lowrie, Donald A. 1974. *Rebellious Prophet. A life of Nicolai Berdyaev.* Westport, Connecticut: Greenwood Press.

Lunacharskii, Anatolii V. 1902. 'Russkii Faust' in *Voprosy Filosofii i Psikhologii*, Vol. 63: 783-795.

Macksey, Richard . 1994. 'History of Ideas' in *The Johns Hopkins Guide to Literary Theory and Criticism.* Micheal Groden and Martin Kreiswirth (eds.). Baltimore and London: Johns Hopkins University Press: 388-392.

Makovskii, Sergei Konstantinovich. [1955] 2000. 'Vladimir Solov'ëv i Georg Brandes' in *Vl. Solov'ëv: Pro et Contra.* Antologiia. V. F. Boikov (ed.). Sankt-Peterburg: Izdatel'stvo Russkogo Khristianskogo Gumanitarnogo Instituta. 2 Vols. Vol.1: 514-527.

Mandelbaum, Maurice. 1965. 'The History of Ideas, Intellectual History and the History of Philosophy' in *History and Theory* 5.

Mann, Thomas. [1921] 1953. 'Russische Anthologie' in *Stockholmer Gesamtausgabe der Werke von Thomas Mann. Altes und Neues: Kleine Prosa aus fünf Jahrzehnten.* Frankfurt am Main: S. Fischer: 464-477.

—. 1948. 'Dostojewski – mit Maassen' in *Neue Studien.* Stockholm: Bermann-Fischer Verlag: 73-102.

Marti, Urs. 1989. 'Der Plebejer in der Revolte – ein Beitrag zur Genealogie des 'höheren Menschen'' in *Nietzsche-Studien* 18: 550-572.

Merezhkovskii, Dmitrii Sergeevich. 1893. 'Dostoevskii, kak khudozhnik' in *O Prichinakh Upadka i o novykh Techeniiakh sovremennoi russkoi literatury.* Sankt-Peterburg: 163-171.

—. 1893. 'Raskol'nikov' in O Prichinakh Upadka i o novykh Techeniiakh sovremennoi russkoi Literatury. Sankt-Peterburg: 172-181.

—. 1893. 'Prestuplenie i Nakazanie' in *O Prichinakh Upadka i o novykh Techeniiakh sovremennoi russkoi Literatury.* Sankt-Peterburg: 182-192.

—. [1900-1901] 1995. L. Tolstoi i Dostoevskii. Khristos i Antikhristos v russkoi literature. Reprint in L. Tolstoi i Dostoevskii. Vechnye Sputniki. Moskva: Respublika.

—. [1908] 1914. 'Revoliutsiia i religiia' in *Polnoe Sobranie Sochinenii Dmitriia Sergeevicha Merezhkovskago*. Moskva, Tom XIII: 36-97.

—. 1911. 'Lermontov. Poet sverkhchelovechestva'. Sankt-Peterburg: Prosveshchenie.

—. [1914] 1972. 'Avtobiograficheskaia zametka' in *Russkaia Literatura XX Veka*. S.A.Vengerov (ed.). 3 Vols. Moskva. Reprint in München: Wilhelm Fink Verlag. Vol. 1: 288-294.

Mikhailovskii, Nikolai Konstantinovich. [1882] 1956. 'Zhestokii Talant'. Reprint in *F.M. Dostoevskii v russkoi kritike*. Moskva: Gosudarstvennoe Izdatel'stvo Khudozhestvennoi Literatury: 306-385.

—. 1894a. 'Literatura i Zhizn'' in *Russkoe Bogatstvo* 7: 76-102.

—. 1894b. 'Literatura i Zhizn': Eshche o F. Nitsshe' in *Russkoe Bogatstvo* 11, otdel 2: 111-131.

—. 1894c. 'Literatura i Zhizn': Eshche o F. Nitsshe' in *Russkoe Bogatstvo* 12, otdel 2: 84-110.

Miller, C.A. 1973. 'Nietzsche's 'discovery' of Dostoevsky'' in *Nietzsche-Studien* 2: 202-257.

—. 1975. 'The nihilist as tempter-redeemer: Dostoevsky's 'man-god' in Nietzsche's notebooks' in *Nietzsche-Studien* 4: 165-226.

Mink, Louis O. 1968. 'Change and Causality in the History of Ideas' in *Eighteenth-Century Studies* 2.

Mochulsky, Konstantin. 1951. *Vladimir Solov'ëv: Zhizn' i Uchenie*. Paris: YMCA-Press.

—. 1973. *Dostoevsky: His Life and Work*. Translated by Michael A. Minihan. Princeton University Press.

Motroshilova, Nelli Vasil'evna and Sineokaia, Iuliia Vadimovna (eds.). 1999. *Fridrikh Nitsshe i filosofiia v Rossii*. Sbornik statei. Sankt-Peterburg: Izdatel'stvo Russkogo Khristianskogo Gumanitarnogo Instituta.

Müller, Ludolf. 1947. 'Nietzsche und Solovjev' in *Zeitschrift für philosophische Forschung*, Bd. I, Heft 4: 499-520.

—. 1952. 'Berdjajev und Nietzsche' in *Oekumenische Einheit*, München: 125-134.

Müller-Lauter, Wolfgang. 1971. Nietzsche. Seine Philosophie der Gegensätze und die Gegensätze seiner Philosophie. Berlin and New York: dtv/De Gruyter.

Nietzsche, Friedrich. 1975-1984. *Nietzsche Briefwechsel. Kritische Gesamtausgabe (KGB)*. Giorgi Colli and Mazzino Montinari (eds.). Berlin and New York: dtv/De Gruyter.

—. 1986. *Sämtliche Briefe. Kritische Studienausgabe sämtlicher Briefe Nietzsches (KSB) in 8 Bänden*. Giorgio Colli and Mazzino Montinari (eds.). Berlin and New York: dtv/De Gruyter.

—. 1988²/Neuausgabe 1999. *Sämtliche Werke. Kritische Studienausgabe (KSA) in 15 Einzelbänden*. Giorgio Colli and Mazzino Montinari (eds.). Berlin and New York: dtv/De Gruyter.

Nikol'skii, N. 1891-1903. 'Bogochelovek' in *Entsiklopedicheskii Slovar' Granat*: 118-119.

'Nittsshe v Rossii'. 1900. In *Novyi Zhurnal Inostrannoi Literatury* 1: 100-103.

'Nitsshe. Nekrolog'. 1900. In *Mir Iskusstva* 17-18: 1.

Novgorodtsev, Pavel Ivanovich. 1902. 'Predislovie' to *Problemy Idealizma*. Moskva: Izdanie Moskovskogo Psikhologicheskago Obshchestva.

Novikov, A.I. 1998. *Istoriia russkoi filosofii*. Sankt-Peterburg: Lan'.

Offord, Derek. 1998. *'Lichnost'*: Notions of Individual Identity' in *Constructing Russian Culture in the Age of Revolution: 1881-1940*. Catriona Kelly and David Shepherd (eds.). Oxford: Oxford University Press: 13-25.

Pelikan, Jaroslav. 1977. *The Christian Tradition*. Vol. 2, *The Spirit of Eastern Christendom (600-1700)*. Chicago and London: The University of Chicago Press.

Pfeiffer, Ernst. 1970. Friedrich Nietzsche, Paul Ree, Lou von Salomé. Die Dokumente ihrer Begegnung. Frankfurt am Main: Insel Verlag.

Pisarev, Dmitrij Ivanovich. [1867] 1956.: 'Pogibshie i pogibaiushchie', 'Bor'ba za zhizn''. Reprint in *F.M. Dostoevskii v russkoi kritike*. Moskva: Gosudarstvennoe Izdatel'stvo Khudozhestvennoi Literatury: 96-228.

Platt, Kevin. 2000. 'Antichrist Enthroned: Demonic Visions of Russian Rulers' in *Russian Literature and its Demons*. Pamela

Davidson (ed.). *Studies in Slavic Literature, Culture and Society* 6. New York and Oxford: Berghahn Books: 87-124.

Pokrovskaia, E. [1922] 1970. 'Dostoevskii i Petrashevtsy' in *F.M. Dostoevskii. Stat'i i materialy*. Pod redaktsiei A.S.Dolinina. Sankt-Peterburg.

Polnyi pravoslavnyi bogoslovskii enciklopedicheskii slovar'. s.d. Sankt-Peterburg.

Poole, Randall A. (ed. and transl.). [1902] 2003. *Problems of Idealism. Essays in Russian Social Philosophy*. New Haven and London: Yale University Press.

—. 2002. 'Moscow Psychological Society' in *Routledge Encyclopedia of Philosophy*. E. Craig (ed.). London: Routledge. Retrieved September 12, 2007, from http://www.rep.routledge.com/article/E077.

Preobrazhenskii, Vasilii Petrovich. [1892] 2001. 'Fridrikh Nitsshe. Kritika Morali Al'truizma' in *Voprosy Filosofii i Psikhologii* 15: Reprint in *Nitsshe: Pro et Contra*. Antologiia. Iuliia.V. Sineokaia (ed.). Sankt-Peterburg: Izdatel'stvo Russkogo Khristianskogo Gumanitarnogo Instituta: 35-69.

Pyman, Avril. 1994. *A History of Russian Symbolism*. Cambridge: Cambridge University Press.

Read, Christopher. 1979. Religion, Revolution and the Russian Intelligentsia 1900-1912. London: The Macmillan Press.

Rosenthal, Bernice Glatzer. 1975. Dmitri Sergeevich Merezhkovsky and the Silver Age: The Development of a revolutionary Mentality. The Hague: Martinus Nijhoff.

—. (ed.) 1986. *Nietzsche in Russia*. Princeton: Princeton University Press.

—. 1986. 'Stages of Nietzscheanism: Merezhkovsky's Intellectual Evolution' in *Nietzsche in Russia*. Bernice Glatzer Rosenthal (ed.). Princeton: Princeton University Press: 69-94.

—. (ed.) 1994a. *Nietzsche and Soviet Culture. Ally and adversary*. Cambridge: Cambridge University Press.

—. 1994b. 'Merezhkovskii's Readings of Tolstoi: Their Contemporary Relevance' in *Russian Thought after Communism. The Recovery of a Philosophical Heritage*. James P. Scanlan (ed.). New York and London: M.E. Sharpe: 121-146.

—. 2002. *New Myth, New World. From Nietzsche to Stalinism.* Pennsylvania: The Pennsylvania State University Press.

Rozanov, Vasilii Vasil'evich. [1891] 1991. *O legende 'Velikii Inkvizitor'.* Reprint in *O velikom inkvizitore. Dostoevskii i posleduiushchie.* Moskva: Molodaia Gvardiia: 73-191.

Saraskina, Liudmila. 2000. *Nikolai Speshnev. Nesbyvshaiasia sud'ba.* Moskva: Nash Dom.

Scanlan, James P. 1970. 'The New Religious Consciousness: Merezhkovskii and Berdiaev' in *Canadian Slavic Studies,* Vol. 4(1): 17-35.

—. 1999. 'The Case against Rational Egoism in Dostoevsky's *Notes from Underground*' in *Journal of the History of Ideas,* Vol. 60(3): 549-567.

—. 2002. *Dostoevsky the Thinker.* Ithaca and London: Cornell University Press.

Scherrer, Jutta. 1973. Die Petersburger religiös-philosophischen Vereinigungen. Die Entwicklung des religiösen Selbstverständnisses ihrer Intelligencija-Mitglieder (1901-1917). Forschungen zur osteuropäischen Geschichte, Bd. 19, Berlin.

Schloezer de, Boris. 1964. 'Nietzsche et Dostoievski' in *Cahiers de Royaumont Philosophie.* Paris: 168-176.

Seduro, Vladimir. 1981. Dostoyevski in Russian Literary Criticism 1846-1956. New York: Octagon Books.

Shcheglov, V.G. 1898. Graf Lev Nikolaevich Tolstoi i Fridrikh Nitsshe. Ocherk filosofsko-nravstvennogo ikh mirovozzreniia. Jaroslavl'.

Shestov, Lev. [1899] 2001. *Dobro v uchenii gr. Tolstogo i F. Nitsshe: Filosofiia i Propoved'.* Reprint in *Nitsshe: Pro et Contra. Antologiia.* Iuliia.V. Sineokaia (ed.). Sankt-Peterburg: Izdatel'stvo Russkogo Khristianskogo Gumanitarnogo Instituta: 329-437.

—. [1903] 1909. Dostoevskii i Nitshe. Filosofiia Tragediia. Sankt-Peterburg.

—. [1903] 2001. 'Vlast' Idei (D.S. Merezhkovskii. L. Tolstoi i Dostoevskii)' in *D.S. Merezhkovskii: Pro et Contra. Lichnost' i tvorchestvo Dmitriia Merezhkovskogo v otsenke sovremennikov.* Sankt-Peterburg: Izdatel'stvo Russkogo Khristianskogo Gumanitarnogo Instituta: 109-134.

—. 1916. 'Viacheslav velikolepnyi' in *Russkaia Mysl'* 10: 80-110.

Sineokaia, Iuliia Vadimovna. 1999. 'Vospriiatie idei Nitsshe v Rossii: osnovnye etapy, tendentsii, znachenie' in *Fridrikh Nitsshe i filosofiia v Rossii*. Sbornik statei. Nelli V. Motroshilova and Iuliia V. Sineokaia (eds.). Sankt-Peterburg: Izdatel'stvo Russkogo Khristianskogo Gumanitarnogo Instituta: 7-37.

—. (ed) 2001a. *Nitsshe: Pro et Contra*. Antologiia. Sankt-Peterburg: Izdatel'stvo Russkogo Khristianskogo Gumanitarnogo Instituta.

—. 2001b. 'Bibliografiia (rasshirennaia) rabot po filosofii F. Nitsshe, vyshedshikh v Rossii s 1892 po 2000 gg' in *Nitsshe: Pro et Contra*. Antologiia. Iuliia V. Sineokaia (ed.), Sankt-Peterburg: Izdatel'stvo Russkogo Khristianskogo Gumanitarnogo Instituta : 971-1007.

—. 2002. 'Problema sverkhcheloveka u Solov'ëva i Nitsshe' in *Voprosy Filosofii* 2: 69-80.

Skuridina, I.I. 1990. 'Volynskii A.' In *Russkie Pisateli. Biobibliograficheskii slovar'*. P.A. Nikolaeva (ed.). Moskva: Prosveshchenie, Vol.1: 153-156.

'Smert' Nitsshe'. 1900. In *Istoricheskii Vestnik* 9: 1127-1130.

Smirnov, Aleksandr Vasil'evich. 1903. 'Dostoevskii i Nitsshe'. Kazan.

Solov'ëv, Sergei Mikhailovich 1977. *Zhizn' i tvorcheskaia Evoliutsiia Vladimira Solov'ëva*. Brussels: Zhizn' s Bogom.

Solov'ëv, Vladimir Sergeevich. [1911-1914] 1966-1970. *Sobranie Sochinenii Vladimira Sergeevicha Solov'ëva (SS)*. Sergei M. Solov'ëv and Ernst L. Radlov (eds.). Sankt-Peterburg: Prosveshchenie. Reprint Brussels: Zhizn' s Bogom. 12 Vols.

—. 1958. *Übermensch und Antichrist: über das Ende der Weltgeschichte*. Ludolf Müller (ed. and transl.). Freiburg: Herder.

—. 1977. Deutsche Gesamtausgabe der Werke von Wladimir Solowjew. Ergänzungsband: Solowjews Leben in Briefen und Gedichten. Ludolf Müller and Irmgard Wille (eds. and transl.). München: Erich Wewel.

—. 2000. *Politics, Law, and Morality. Essays by V.S. Soloviev*. Vladimir Wozniuk (ed. and transl.) New Haven and London: Yale University Press.

—. 2000-2001. Polnoe Sobranie Sochinenii i Pisem v dvatsati tomakh. Vol. 3. Moskva: Nauka.

Speshnev, Nikolai Aleksandrovich. [1847] 1953. 'Pis'ma k K.E. Khoetskomu' in *Filosofskie i obchshestvenno-politicheskie proizvedeniia Petrashevtsev*. V.E. Evgrafov (ed.). Moskva: Gospolitizdat: 477-502.

Spitzer, Leo. 1944. '*Geistesgeschichte* vs. History of Ideas as applied to Hitlerism' in *Journal of the History of Ideas* 5.

Strada, Vittorio. 1987.'La littérature de la fin du XIX siècle' in *Histoire de la littérature Russe. Le XX siècle, L'Age d'argent*. Librairie Arthème Fayard: 13-50.

Strakosch, H.E. 1963. 'Nietzsche and Dostoevsky' in *Archiv für Rechts- und Sozialphilosophie* 49: 551-564.

Sutton, Jonathan. 1988. The Religious Philosophy of Vladimir Solovyov. Towards a Reassessment. New York: St.Martin's Press.

Terras, Victor. 1981. A Karamazov Companion. Commentary on the Genesis, Language, and Style of Dostoevsky's Novel. Wisconsin: The University of Wisconsin Press.

Thompson, Martyn P. 1993. 'Reception Theory and the interpretation of historical meaning' in *History and Theory*, Vol. 32(3): 248-272.

Tikhomirov, Boris Nikolaevich. 1994. 'O Khristologii Dostoevskogo' in *Dostoevskii. Materialy i issledovaniia* 11:102-121.

Tikhomirov, N.D. 1902. 'Nitsshe i Dostoevskii. Cherty iz nravstvennago mirovozzreniia togo i drugogo' in *Bogoslovskii Vestnik* 7-8: 505-532.

Tolstoi, Lev Nikolaevich [1897] 1983. *Chto takoe iskusstvo?* in *Lev Nikolaevich Tolstoi. Sobranie Sochinenii v dvadtsati dvukh tomakh*, Vol. 15, Moskva: Khudozhestvennaia Literatura: 41-221.

—. [1900] 1985. Dnevniki 1895-1910 in Lev Nikolaevich Tolstoi. Sobranie Sochinenii v dvadtsati dvukh tomakh, Vol. 22, Moskva: Khudozhestvennaia Literatura.

Trubetskoi, Evgenii Nikolaevich. [1903] 2001. *Filosofiia Nitsshe. Kriticheskii Ocherk*. Reprint in *Nitsshe: Pro et Contra. Antologiia*. Iuliia V. Sineokaia (ed.). Sankt-Peterburg: Izdatel'stvo Russkogo Khristianskogo Gumanitarnogo Instituta: 672-793.

—. [1913] 1995. *Mirosozertsanie V.S. Solov'ëva*. Moskva: Moskovskii filosofskii fond/izdatel'stvo 'Medium', 2 Vols.

Tsertelev, Dmitrii Nikolaevich. [1897] 2001. 'Kritika vyrozhdeniia i vyrozhdenie kritiki'. Reprint in *Nitsshe: Pro et Contra. Antologiia*. Iuliia V. Sineokaia (ed.). Sankt-Peterburg: Izdatel'stvo Russkogo Khristianskogo Gumanitarnogo Instituta: 205-289.

Uhl, Anton. 1981. 'Leiden an Gott und Mensch: Nietzsche und Dostojewski' in *Concilium. Internationale Zeitschrift für Theologie* 17: 382-389.

Uspenskii, Gleb Ivanovich. [1880] 1953. 'Prazdnik Pushkina' in *Polnoe Sobranie Sochinenii*. Moskva. Vol. 6: 409-430.

Vadimov, Aleksandr. 1993. *Zhizn' Berdiaeva. Rossiia*. Oakland, California: Berkeley Slavic Specialties.

Valliere, Paul. 2000. *Modern Russian Theology: Bukharev, Soloviev, Bulgakov. Orthodox Theology in a New Key*. Grand Rapids, Michigan: William B. Eerdmans Publishing Company.

Verner, I. 1903. 'Tip Kirillova u Dostoevskago' in *Novyi Put'*, 10: 48-80, 11: 52-80, 12: 128-182.

Volynskii, Akim L'vovich. [1896] 2001. 'Literaturnye zametki: Apollon i Dionis'. Reprint in *Nitsshe: Pro et Contra. Antologiia*. Iuliia V. Sineokaia (ed.). Sankt-Peterburg: Izdatel'stvo Russkogo Khristianskogo Gumanitarnogo Instituta: 180-204.

—. [1901] 1906. *Tsarstvo Karamazovykh*. Reprint in A.L. Volynskii: *Dostoevskii*. Sankt-Peterburg: Energiia.

Volzhskii, Aleksandr Sergeevich. [1905] 1997. 'Religioznaia-nravstvennaia problema u Dostoevskogo'. Reprint in *Vlastitel' Dum. F. M. Dostoevskii v russkoi kritike kontsa XIX- nachala XX veka*. Sankt-Peterburg: Khudozhestvennaia Literatura: 172-241.

Ward, Bruce K. 1986. Dostoevsky's Critique of the West. The Quest for the Earthly Paradise. Waterloo: Wilfrid Laurier University Press.

Wesling, Molly W. 2001. *Napoleon in Russian Cultural Mythology*. New York: Peter Lang.

Woolfolk, Alan. 1989. 'The two switchmen of nihilism: Dostoevsky and Nietzsche' in *Mosaic – a journal for the interdisciplinary study of literature* 22(1): 71-86.

Zakydalsky, Taras D. 1986. 'Fëdorov's Critique of Nietzsche, the 'Eternal Tragedian'' in *Nietzsche in Russia*. Bernice Glatzer Rosenthal (ed.). Princeton: Princeton University Press: 113-125.

Zen'kovskii, Vasilii Vasil'evich. [1948] 1991. *Istoriia russkoi filosofii*. Leningrad. 2 Vols.

Ziolkowski, Margaret. 2001. 'Dostoevsky and the kenotic tradition' in *Dostoevsky and the Christian Tradition*. Georges Pattison and Diane Oenning Thompson (eds.). Cambridge: Cambridge University Press: 31-40.

Znamenskii, S.P. [1909] 2001. 'Sverkhchelovek Nitsshe'. Reprint in *Nitsshe: Pro et Contra*. Antologiia. Iuliia.V. Sineokaia (ed.). Sankt-Peterburg: Izdatel'stvo Russkogo Khristianskogo Gumanitarnogo Instituta: 904-94.

Index

A

Antichrist/anti-Christian, 3, 5, 13, 15,
    61, 84, 92, 97, 99-103, 105, 135,
    136, 139, 143, 147-150, 152, 154,
    155, 160, 161, 166-168, 178-181,
    188, 191, 193, 203, 204, 227, 233-
    237, 250-252, 254
Astaf'ev, P., 29, 41, 261

B

Bakhtin, M., 65, 124, 125, 185, 261
Bal'mont, K., 36, 143
Belyi, A., 6, 7, 15, 36, 81, 82, 103,
    104, 144, 202, 262
Berdiaev, N., 1-3, 6, 8, 12, 13, 15-18,
    36, 51, 79, 81, 105, 107, 109, 144,
    202, 204, 207-248, 251-255, 257,
    258, 262
    Dostoevskii's Worldview, 228, 245
    *Dream and Reality. An Essay in
        Autobiography*, 208, 212, 218
    'Nietzsche and contemporary
        Germany', 213, 214
    'On the new religious
        consciousness', 218
    'Quenchers of the Spirit', 211
    *Subjectivism and Individualism in
        social Philosophy*, 209
    'The ethical problem in the light of
        philosophical idealism', 16,
        209, 214, 215, 238
    The Meaning of the Creative Act,
        207, 218, 227, 228, 244
Blok, A., 36, 81, 82, 144

Boborykin, P., 22, 34, 41, 264
Bogdanov, A., 37
*Bogochelovechestvo/Divine
    Humanity*, 86-89, 96, 100, 103,
    104, 196, 226, 252, 253
Bogochelovek, 13, 18, 55, 77, 87-89,
    91, 92, 95, 105, 107, 108, 112,
    120, 122, 132, 136, 154-156, 158,
    160, 165-167, 178, 179, 182, 191-
    194, 196, 200, 225, 226, 228, 230-
    237, 246, 247, 252, 254, 257
Bogostroitel'stvo, 2, 37
Brandes, G., 20, 21, 23, 40, 145, 202,
    214, 264
Briusov, V., 36, 145, 264
Bulgakov, F., 30, 42
Bulgakov, S., 15, 17, 125, 139, 144,
    195-197, 208, 210, 211, 264

C

Chelovekobog, 5, 13, 18, 74, 107,
    109-137, 139, 146, 147, 150, 153-
    156, 158-161, 163, 165-168, 175-
    177, 181-184, 187-189, 191-196,
    198-205, 207, 228-234, 236, 237,
    246, 247, 249-252, 254-257, 259
Christ, 6, 7, 15, 36, 38, 46, 54, 55, 66,
    68, 69, 73, 76, 77, 85-92, 95, 97,
    99, 100, 105, 108, 112, 113, 117,
    120, 122, 126, 128, 130-136, 139,
    147-150, 154, 155, 159-161, 163-
    166, 168, 179-181, 186, 191, 202,
    204, 219, 222, 225, 226, 228, 231-
    237, 241, 243, 247, 248, 250-252,
    254, 257
Chuiko, V., 29, 42, 264

D

Dostoevskii, F., 1, 3, 4, 5, 7, 8, 12-15, 17, 37, 39-41, 44-47, 49, 51-77, 79, 80, 87, 96, 97, 107, 109, 112-115, 121, 122, 124, 128-132, 134-136, 139-141, 143, 144, 146, 147, 150-158, 160, 166, 177, 178, 180, 181, 183-191, 194-205, 208, 212, 214, 227-235, 247-249, 251, 254-259, 265
  'Apollo Belvedere', 132, 155, 194
  chelovekobog, see *Chelovekobog*
  Crime and Punishment, 44, 153, 197, 202
  Notes from the House of the Dead, 38, 39
  Notes from Underground, 37, 45, 200
  Poor Folk, 183, 184
  Pushkin speech, 129
  The Brothers Karamazov, 186
  The Devils, 52, 54, 65, 113-115, 147, 156, 183
  The Diary of a Writer, 54, 67, 70, 113, 124, 129, 136, 155, 194
  The Gambler, 45
  The Idiot, 38, 249
  The Landlady, 38
  Fictional Characters
    Alësha Karamazov, 187
    Christ (in Ivan's 'Grand Inquisitor'), 56, 58, 60, 62, 64, 134, 136, 232
    Devil (Ivan's devil), 61, 124, 126-128, 136, 140, 157, 167, 176, 184, 193, 198
    Devil (Satan in 'Grand Inquisitor'), 61, 135, 232
    Dmitrii Karamazov, 57, 199
    Grand Inquisitor, 46, 55-58, 60-65, 97, 120, 126, 131, 134-136, 232, 233, 235, 254
    Ivan Karamazov, 4, 5, 40, 41, 46, 48, 49, 56, 70, 73, 80, 124, 125, 133, 136, 139, 140, 157, 165, 183, 184, 187, 192, 195-199, 202, 229, 231, 232, 234, 254
    Kirillov, 5, 52, 114-123, 126-128, 136, 140, 156, 158, 161, 163, 164, 166-169, 171, 172, 175-177, 179, 184, 187, 194, 198, 199, 201, 204, 229, 231, 232, 250, 251
    Myshkin, 135, 187
    Raskol'nikov, 4, 8, 42-45, 47-49, 140, 153, 158, 183, 184, 187, 191, 197-199, 201, 229, 231, 232, 254
    Shatov, 54, 116, 187
    Smerdiakov, 124, 125, 158, 192
    Sonia Marmeladova, 187
    Stavrogin, 54, 114, 115, 118, 120, 122, 156, 187, 199, 202, 229, 231
    Underground man, the, 45
    Zosima, 56, 57, 66, 75, 133, 187

F

Fëdorov, N., 16, 95, 102
Feuerbach, L., 109, 111, 112, 116
Filosofov, D., 15, 144, 201, 265
Frank, S., 6, 15, 16, 81, 114, 201, 208-210, 266, 268

G

Gide, A., 203, 266
Gippius, Z., 15, 36, 141-145, 189, 267
Gorkii, M., 37
Grot, N., 28, 40, 41, 267

I

Ivanov, V., 3, 6, 7, 15, 22, 36, 81, 82, 154, 210, 267

K

Kheisin, M., 42, 140, 198, 199, 268

Khrapovitskii, A., 48, 184, 268

L

Leont'ev, K., 24, 83, 184, 186, 208, 269
Lermontov, M., 96, 97, 100, 193
Lopatin, L., 16, 28, 81, 209, 269
Lunacharskii, A., 37, 125, 270

M

Mann, T., 153, 203, 270
Marxism/Marxist, 2, 14, 15, 17, 37, 47, 102, 196, 208, 209, 212, 215
Merezhkovskii, D., 8, 12, 13, 15, 17, 18, 22, 36, 75, 79, 81, 83, 96, 98, 109, 139-187, 188-191, 193-197, 201-204, 207, 210, 211, 213, 217-219, 221, 223, 226, 229, 233, 234, 236-238, 241, 247, 249-256, 258, 270
  'Flesh', 147, 148, 150, 151, 155, 159-166, 183, 188, 190, 203, 218, 221, 234, 236, 250, 251
  'Spirit', 20, 62, 89, 148, 150, 151, 155, 159-166, 183, 190, 203, 210, 218, 221, 234, 236, 250, 251
  Eternal Companions, 153
  L. Tolstoi and Dostoevskii - Christ and Antichrist in Russian Literature, 15, 143, 147, 150, 167, 183, 189, 202, 236
  On the Reasons for the Decline and on new Trends in contemporary Russian Literature, 84, 143
Mikhailovskii, N., 21, 31, 32, 42, 44, 45, 48, 49, 84, 178, 184, 185, 209, 271
Minskii, N., 22, 33, 36, 83, 143-145, 189

N

'new religious consciousness', 7, 15, 17, 143, 146, 150, 159, 163, 165, 166, 181, 204, 210, 211, 217-220, 223, 225, 228, 237, 258
Nietzsche, F.
  'Apollinian/Apollo', 33, 132, 141, 146, 152, 190, 192
  'Dionysian/Dionysus', 2, 3, 6, 7, 21, 33, 35-37, 141, 146, 149, 152, 154, 162, 165, 166, 182, 190, 203, 210, 216, 233
  Übermensch, see *Übermensch*
  Beyond Good and Evil, 22, 27, 212
  Human, All Too Human, 83, 200, 212
  Nietzsche Contra Wagner, 22
  On the Genealogy of Morals, 27, 41, 212
  Richard Wagner in Bayreuth, 21
  The Antichrist, 5, 21, 38, 83, 100, 101, 148, 149, 157, 162, 217, 219
  The Birth of Tragedy, 2, 20, 22, 35, 83, 141, 146, 152, 190
  The Case of Wagner, 21, 23, 38, 145
  The Dawn, 22, 39
  The Gay Science, 168, 171, 238
  Thus spoke Zarathustra, 8, 27, 30, 34, 40, 43, 83, 85, 92, 168, 174, 177, 212, 238, 239, 244
  Twilight of the Idols, 22, 38, 39, 44
  Untimely Meditations, 86, 212
Novgorodtsev, P., 17, 209, 272

P

Preobrazhenskii, V., 24-29, 31, 33, 38, 44, 49, 84, 178, 273
Pushkin, A., 47, 81, 129

R

Rozanov, V., 15, 56, 83, 144, 184, 274

S

Salomé, L., 21, 23
Shestov, L., 14, 28, 140, 144, 168, 200-203, 212, 227, 274
Smirnov, A., 140, 153, 198, 275
Sologub, F., 36, 143
Solov'ëv, V., 5, 8, 12-14, 16, 18, 24, 32, 47, 79-105, 107, 141, 159, 163, 178-180, 184, 186, 193, 207, 208, 211, 214, 217, 233-236, 251-253, 258, 275
Bogochelovechestvo/Divine Humanity,   see *Bogochelovechestvo*
sverkhchelovek, 4, 18, 85, 90-92, 95, 99-101, 105, 193, 194, 200, 202, 235, 252
'A first Step towards a positive Aesthetics', 32, 83
'A short Story about the Antichrist', 90, 97, 98, 101-103, 105, 193, 235
'Faith, Reason and Experience', 86
Lectures on Divine Humanity, 86
'Literature or Truth', 90
The History and Future of Theocracy, 87
'The Idea of the Trans-human', 90, 92, 102
The Justification of the Good, 82, 180
Three Conversations on War, Progress and the End of History, 97
Three Speeches in memory of Dostoevskii, 80, 184, 186

Speshnev, N., 109-115, 276
Struve, Pëtr, 15, 208, 209
Symbolism/symbolist, 2, 22, 30, 35-37, 81, 82, 84, 85, 98, 143, 145-147, 150, 189, 190

T

Tikhomirov, N., 140, 197, 198, 276
Tolstoi, L., 14, 15, 28, 33, 40, 44, 47, 93, 98, 101, 102, 143, 150-152, 160, 183, 188, 200-202, 208, 212, 248, 276
Trubetskoi, E., 6, 15, 103, 209, 210, 276
Trubetskoi, S., 15, 101, 209, 210
Tsertelev, D., 42, 45, 46, 277
Turgenev, I., 22

U

Übermensch, 2-8, 10-13, 18, 27, 32, 34, 35, 37, 40-43, 45, 47, 49, 85, 90-96, 101-105, 107, 139, 140, 146, 147, 150, 152-156, 158-161, 163-168, 172-179, 181-184, 188, 193-205, 207, 215, 217, 221, 223-225, 227, 229-231, 233-239, 241, 243-258

V

Vergun, D., 39, 153, 198
Verner, I., 199, 277
Volynskii, A., 33, 36, 48, 139, 143, 144, 147, 188-195, 197, 277
Volzhkii, A., 201